Introduction to Music

HARPERCOLLINS COLLEGE OUTLINE

Introduction to Music

3rd Edition

Hugh M. Miller

Paul Taylor
The Catholic University of America

Edgar W. Williams, Ph.D.
College of William and Mary

HarperPerennial
A Division of HarperCollins*Publishers*

An American BookWorks Corporation Production
Project Manager: Mary Mooney

Library of Congress Cataloging-in-Publication Data

Miller, Hugh Milton, 1908—
  Introduction to music / by Hugh M. Miller, Paul Taylor, and Edgar Williams
—1st HarperPerennial ed.
      p.   cm. — (HarperCollins college outline series)
  Includes bibliographical references and index.
  ISBN 0-06-467108-9 (pbk.)
    1. Music appreciation.   I. Taylor, Paul, 1945–   II. Williams,
Edgar, 1947–   III. Title.   IV. Series
MT6,M45815   1991
781.1'7—dc20   90-56020

91 92 93 94 95 ABW/RRD 10 9 8 7 6 5 4 3 2 1

Contents

Preface

The late Hugh M. Miller's *Introduction to Music* first appeared in 1958 as part of the Barnes & Noble College Outline Series, with a second edition in 1978. Like those earlier editions, the present edition attempts to summarize the subject material found in the leading music appreciation texts in a concise and appealing manner for the student and general reader.

There are many excellent music appreciation texts available today. Several of these come in extremely attractive and complete packages, which contain not only the text itself, but also a workbook, listening guides, and recordings. The intent of this outline is not to replace those texts, but to supplement them. It is directed primarily toward the college or university student, with no prior formal training in music, who is enrolled in a music appreciation course. It is assumed that the student will have, as a required text, one of the leading books in the field. It is hoped that this outline, used in conjunction with the required text, can help focus the student's attention on the most essential topics and clarify problem areas. Material is presented as concisely as possible, with clear definitions and explanations and with much use of musical examples, tables, and other non-narrative types of organization.

This outline may also serve as a brief introduction to the subject of music in its own right, preparing the general reader for the more detailed treatments to be found in full-fledged music appreciation texts or in the books and other sources recommended at the end of each chapter.

In order to make this outline as useful as possible as a supplement to the leading music appreciation texts, we have followed the organization used by the majority of these books: an opening section on the fundamentals of music (chapters 1–10), followed by a chronological survey of Western art music (chapters 11–26), and an introduction to American popular music and jazz (chapters 27–28). Since earlier editions were not organized in this manner, this has necessitated extensive rewriting and reordering of material. We have tried to retain as much of Dr. Miller's prose as possible, however, incorporating it at appropriate places within the present format.

In addition to the discussions in the text, each chapter contains recommendations for additional study, which include audiovisual materials as well as books. Most chapters also contain recommended listening and, in Parts Two and Three, time lines to help clarify the historical context of the material discussed.

We owe a great debt of gratitude to our editor, Judith A.V. Harlan, whose expert technical advice, generosity, and unfailing support and encouragement were an inspiration to us throughout this project. We also wish to thank Fred N. Grayson of American BookWorks Corporation, the coordinator of the project; our publisher, HarperCollins; our copyeditor, Susan McClosky; Robert A. Weinstein, who read chapters 27 and 28; and those who reviewed the manuscript. All offered excellent suggestions, which we have tried to incorporate. We hasten to add, though, that errors and shortcomings that remain are our responsibility, not theirs. Finally, and above all, we wish to thank Sharon Taylor and Gary Taylor for their work in preparing the manuscript and the musical examples. This outline is as much theirs as it is ours, and it could not have been completed without them.

Abbreviations

The title of a composition is often followed by cataloging information (e.g., Op. 8 or K. 467) added by the composer, the publisher, or a later writer to identify the composition chronologically within the composer's output. Higher opus or other cataloging numbers usually reflect a composer's later works although exceptions do occur, as when an opus number reflects the order of publication rather than the order of composition. Cataloging abbreviations used in this outline are explained below.

BWV *Bach Werke Verzeichnis* (Bach Works Catalog), a method of cataloging Johann Sebastian Bach's compositions. Established by the *Thematisch-systematisches Verzeichnis der musikalischen Werke von Johann Sebastian Bach*, ed. Wolfgang Schmieder (Leipzig, 1950; 6th ed., Wiesbaden: Breitkopf & Härtel, 1977). Sometimes, though not in this outline, the abbreviation S. (for Schmieder) is used instead of BWV to identify Bach's works.

D. In relation to the works of Franz Schubert: *Deutsch*, a numbering system used in the thematic catalogue of Schubert's works prepared by Otto Erich Deutsch.

H. In relation to Franz Joseph Haydn's works: *Hoboken*, a cataloging system used in Anthony van Hoboken's *Thematisch-bibliographisches Werkverzeichnis* (Mainz: B. Schott's Söhne, 1957–1978). In relation to C. P. E. Bach's works, refers to a cataloging system established by E. Helm.

K. In relation to the works of Wolfgang Amadeus Mozart: *Köchel*, a cataloging system used in Ludwig Köchel's *Chronologisch-thematisches Verzeichnis* (6th ed., Wiesbaden: Breitkopf & Härtel, 1964). In relation to the sonatas of Domenico Scarlatti, refers to a cataloging system devised by Ralph Kirkpatrick.

L. *Longo*, a system for identifying Domenico Scarlatti's sonatas used in Alessandro Longo's collected edition of Scarlatti's sonatas (Milan: 1906–1908; New York: Ricordi, 1947–1951).

Op.   *Opus* (Latin, *work*), the most common cataloging symbol. Several compositions of the same type sometimes share the same opus number (e.g., Op. 8, No. 1; Op. 8, No. 2; and so on).

Opp.   Plural of *opus*.

W.   *Wotquenne*, a system for identifying C. P. E. Bach's sonatas used in Alfred Wotquenne's *Verzeichnis der Werke Ph. E. Bachs* (Leipzig and New York: Breitkopf & Härtel, 1905; reprint, Wiesbaden, 1964).

Part One

Fundamentals of Western Art Music

1

Introduction

Reflect a moment on the idea that your life is made up of many kinds of experiences. Some experiences are agreeable, others unpleasant; some are profound, others leave little imprint; some are valuable while others contribute no enrichment. Human experiences are, of course, infinitely diversified, and no two people have exactly the same ones. Yet there are many kinds of experiences that people have in common. Music is one of these. The fact that musical experience is inevitable and immediately accessible suggests the possibility that music confers numerous benefits on human beings.

If you realize the potential significance of music in your life, you will be eager to make that experience more meaningful. This chapter explores ways to accomplish this by considering implications of the phrase "appreciation of music," types of listening, ways of developing perception in listening, and obstacles to musical appreciation.

APPRECIATION OF MUSIC

The appreciation of music may be defined as *the acquired ability to listen to music intelligently*. Although people have different aptitudes in their musical perceptiveness, no one is born with this ability; it is acquired. We will be concerned, therefore, with the means by which you can acquire the ability to listen intelligently.

Enjoyment and appreciation are related terms, but they are not synonymous. It is quite possible to enjoy music—that is, to receive pleasure from it—without understanding it or appreciating it in the sense described above. It is also possible to understand the technicalities of a musical composition without enjoying it fully. However, remember that to obtain the greatest enjoyment from music you must have some understanding of it, and that no matter how sublime an experience a musical performance proves to be for you, any additional understanding that you can bring to the music will probably enhance your ultimate pleasure.

TYPES OF LISTENING

The extent to which you can attain true appreciation of music depends largely on your attitudes as a listener. Four types of listening can be distinguished in musical experience: (1) passive listening, (2) sensuous listening, (3) emotional listening, and (4) perceptive listening.

Passive Listening   In certain situations music is not intended to claim the full attention of the listener. Unlike concert music, dinner music functions as "background music" intended to enhance the pleasures of dining and conversation. A good share of the music on a movie sound track is intended merely to reinforce the moods of the visual scene. The marching band on the football field provides more of a show than a concert. In such situations, the listener's relationship to music is a passive one. He or she hears the music but does not actually listen closely to it and therefore does not really appreciate it. But when music is being performed for its own sake, the listener should realize that something more than a passive attitude is essential to its enjoyment.

Sensuous Listening   A greater degree of attention is required for sensuous listening. Here the listener obtains pleasure from an awareness of the sheer beauty of the sound. The clear tones of a flute or of distant bells, the sonority of a cathedral organ or of a large choir, the richness of a symphony orchestra—all these are sounds that the listener can enjoy whether or not he or she has an extensive understanding of music. But while the pleasurable sensations of musical tone have some value to the appreciator, they do not constitute the sum total of what is meant by true appreciation.

Emotional Listening   The listener with this attitude toward music is concerned mainly with his or her own reactions to the music, with the emotions and moods that the music arouses. This is by no means an undesirable attitude. Music is capable of producing sublime emotions. Emotional listening, however, is an inherent attitude toward music, and therefore it does not require intense concentration or training.

Perceptive Listening

Perceptive listening—as opposed to passive, sensuous, and emotional listening—requires concentration on the music itself and a sharp awareness of what is going on musically. It is this type of listening, more than any other, that brings true appreciation. Music appreciation in this sense means knowing what to listen for, understanding what is heard, and thereby having an objective basis for experiencing musical art.

Attitudes Combined

It is probably true that no one of these four attitudes toward music exists in a pure form in any individual. Certainly no one's total musical experience is exclusively passive, sensuous, emotional or perceptive. It is likely that in hearing a long composition the listener's attitude will shift from one to another type of listening. Of the four attitudes, however, it is perceptive listening that requires the most effort on the part of the listener, and it is through the development of this attitude that one's capacity to appreciate music grows most fully.

HOW TO DEVELOP PERCEPTION IN LISTENING

The following paragraphs summarize certain prerequisites to the development of perceptive listening.

Attention

It is imperative that you learn to concentrate on the music. Previously acquired attitudes may make it difficult to develop this habit. The sedative character of music, its emotional "pull," and the natural inclination of the listener to let the mind wander are barriers to be overcome on the road to appreciation. Above all, avoid talking or letting yourself be distracted by extraneous sounds while music you want to listen to is being played.

Repetition

No one can hope to grasp in one hearing all that goes on in a piece of music. Most people do not retain auditory impressions as readily as they do visual impressions. Therefore, it is necessary to listen again and again to a piece of music that you wish to understand. (This is obviously easier to accomplish with recorded music.) There is virtually no limit to the benefits to be gained by repeated listening; there is always something new to be heard in any composition.

Familiarity

One is naturally attracted to old friends and familiar faces. So it is with music. You naturally prefer, and perhaps get more out of, music with which you have become familiar through repeated listening. But you should not base musical appreciation entirely on familiar compositions, for that would deprive you of the satisfaction of broadening your musical horizons by exploring new compositions.

Background Knowledge

To achieve an appreciation of music one must acquire a musical background. By musical background is meant not only a general acquaintance with a quantity of musical literature but also knowledge about that music. In this sense musical background can be divided into two types: (1) general background and (2) specific background.

The sum total of your musical experience constitutes your *general background* in music. This includes such musical activities as going to concerts, listening to live broadcasts and recordings, singing in choral groups, and playing in orchestras or bands. It also includes any formal study such as music lessons and reading musical biography and history, as well as books about music theory (the mechanics of musical construction: harmony, counterpoint, form, orchestration).

One also builds musical appreciation by the study of individual works. What one is able to learn about a particular composition creates a *specific background* for that composition, and that background, in turn, enhances the appreciation of the music itself. Specific background includes information about the form of the composition, its outstanding characteristics (style), its composer, and its history (when, why, and under what circumstances it was written). Some of this background is acquired through astute listening to the music, and some of it is acquired through reading.

Participation

Although active participation in the production or creation of music undoubtedly contributes to appreciation, it is not essential. You do not have to play in a symphony, sing in an opera, or conduct a chorus to appreciate symphonic, operatic, and choral music. Furthermore, amateur performers are usually so preoccupied with the mechanics and technical difficulties of reading the score that they are hardly in a position to listen to the music as a whole.

Auditory and Visual Approaches

Two additional approaches contribute to the development of an appreciation of music: (1) the auditory approach and (2) the visual approach.

The *auditory approach* simply means studying music by listening to it. Because music is essentially an auditory art, i.e., one that exists through the medium of sound, the auditory approach is much more important in acquiring an appreciation of music.

You can also greatly increase your musical perceptiveness by developing the ability to follow a score while the music is being played. The listener who can follow a score can "see" things in the music that the ear does not catch. This constitutes the *visual approach*.

A more common aspect of the visual approach—the natural inclination to watch the performer when possible—is of less value. The solo performer does not convey by his or her appearance and mannerisms much of the essence of the music. People enjoy watching the conductor of a symphony orchestra and the various actions of the musicians under his or her direction. But these actions too provide few clues about the real content of the composition. In fact, watching the performer actually distracts from the sound of the music.

OBSTACLES TO APPRECIATION

Facility in a discipline and mastery of a technique—and musical appreciation depends upon both of these—are not acquired easily. Although the difficulties encountered on the road to music appreciation are often overemphasized, it is wise to be fully aware of them in advance.

Auditory Difficulties

As previously pointed out, most people's auditory sense is less perceptive than their visual sense. Hence, perception of an art that is based on sound requires a special effort. Habits of passive listening must be overcome.

Even the simplest music presents to the ear a complex auditory stimulus. Intelligent, perceptive listening enables you to unravel the complex arrangements of the musical elements, to evaluate them in terms of context, and thus to understand the whole.

Time Element

Another aspect of auditory difficulty results because music moves in time rather than in space. Any moment in music must be grasped "as it goes by" and must be related to what has gone before and what is yet to come. When the performance of a piece is finished, one must see the whole composition in retrospect. In examining a picture, a piece of sculpture or a building, you can stop to examine any detail, and you can see whole sections of the creation at a time. This is not possible in music. Thus, the development of musical memory is essential to musical appreciation.

Preferences and Prejudices

Perhaps the most serious obstacles to true musical appreciation are preferences and prejudices. We are all too prone to let our likes and dislikes determine or affect our musical experiences. We may like this composer and not that one; we may like piano music but not voice, symphonic music but not opera; we may prefer popular music to "classical" music. If preferences and prejudices dominate our musical choices, or if prejudices against certain kinds of music are allowed to affect our listening, then our appreciation of music will be an exceedingly narrow one. True musical appreciation is not based on likes and dislikes. Its solid foundation is the intellectual acumen that can be brought to bear on a piece of music. And so, if you can approach new types of music with an open mind, you will be amazed at how much more music you can enjoy.

Because of space considerations, the following introduction to music is limited to Western (i.e., European and American) art music and to developments in American popular music. (Art music, commonly referred to as "classical" music, is music that is intended to be listened to carefully, judged as a work of art, and appreciated as an end in itself for its beautiful sound, elegant construction, and expressive qualities.) This limitation is not intended to imply that Western music is in any way "better" than that of non-Western cultures; it only means that an examination of the often vastly different premises from which non-Western musics arise is beyond the scope of this study. Excellent detailed treatments of these musics are available to the interested reader. (A few are listed at the end of chapter 11.)

Chapters 2 through 10 present, by way of background, information concerning basic fundamentals of Western music, particularly Western art music. Chapters 11 through 28 survey developments in Western art music and American popular music.

2

Sound

*A*rt appreciation depends in part upon familiarity with the artist's materials. The architect needs structural materials such as stone, wood, steel,
glass, and concrete; the painter employs water color, oil, and pastel; the
composer, sound. For musical purposes, sound may be divided into two
categories: tone and noise.

TONE VS. NOISE

We perceive sound when sound waves are transmitted from a vibrating
object to our ears. Regular vibrations produce *tone*, whereas irregular
vibrations produce *noise*. Sounds produced by whistling, humming, singing,
plucking a taut string, blowing into a woodwind or brass instrument, and
pressing the keys of a keyboard instrument are tones because the vibrations
are regular. Sounds made by wind, traffic, clapping hands, and breaking
glass are noise because their vibrations are irregular.

Of these two properties, tone—because it is fundamental to melody and
harmony—is the more important in music, but noise also has a place. Many
types of percussion instruments, for example, produce noiselike sounds. In
the twentieth century, musicians have introduced still other methods of
producing noise effects. In rock music, noise produced by synthesizers and
by distortion devices on the electric guitar as well as by sirens, explosions,
and other means are common. In art music, composers have explored the
use of electronically generated sounds and novel sound effects produced by
traditional instruments, some going so far as to attempt to include all the
sounds of everyday life as source material for musical expression. John
Cage's famous *4' 33"* is an extreme example of this. In this work, the

performer simply sits at the piano for four minutes and thirty-three seconds, and the random sounds of the audience during this time constitute the music.

Thus, composers use noise as well as tone for expressive purposes. Since the manipulation of tones has commanded their greatest attention, however, we turn now to this category of sound.

PROPERTIES OF TONE

Musical tone consists of four properties: (1) pitch, (2) duration, (3) intensity, and (4) timbre.

Pitch

Pitch refers to the relative highness or lowness of a tone. It is a physical principle that the faster the vibrations are, the higher the pitch seems; the slower the vibrations, the lower the pitch. Although the human ear can detect pitches ranging from about 20 to 20,000 vibrations per second, most of the music we hear normally employs a much narrower range, from about 30 to 4,200 vibrations per second.

The distance in pitch between two tones is called an *interval*. Large intervals tend to produce a feeling of expansiveness, of opening up musical "space," while small intervals convey a sense of gradual motion.

Duration

Duration refers to the relative length of time that a tone is sustained. Musical notation indicates precisely when a tone is to begin and when it is to end. Duration is one of the bases of musical rhythm (see chapter 4).

Intensity

Intensity refers to the relative loudness or softness of a tone. Symbols in musical notation that indicate relative levels of intensity are known as *dynamic marks*. We refer to the effect these symbols have as the *dynamics* of the music. It is traditional to use Italian terms to indicate dynamics. Common examples and their abbreviations appear in Fig 2.1.

```
┌─────────────────────────────────────────────────────────────┐
│              COMMON DYNAMIC INDICATIONS                       │
│                                                               │
│       Term              Abbreviation          Meaning         │
│                                                               │
│   pianissimo                pp            very soft           │
│   piano                     p             soft                │
│   mezzo piano               mp            moderately soft     │
│   mezzo forte               mf            moderately loud     │
│   forte                     f             loud                │
│   fortissimo                ff            very loud           │
│   forte-piano               fp            loud followed suddenly by soft │
│   sforzando, sforzato       sf, sfz       sudden accent on a single      │
│                                             tone or chord     │
│                                                               │
│   crescendo (◄═══════ )    cresc.         gradually louder    │
│   decrescendo or            decresc.,     gradually softer    │
│     diminuendo                dim.                            │
│     (═══════► )                                               │
└─────────────────────────────────────────────────────────────┘
```

Fig 2.1

Dynamics play an important role in musical expression because, generally, the louder music is, the more exciting or tense it becomes, and conversely, the softer the music, the calmer it becomes. A *crescendo*, therefore, causes increasing tension and excitement, whereas a *diminuendo* relaxes tension and conveys a sense of calm.

Timbre

Timbre (also referred to as *tone color* or *tone quality*) refers to the property of sound that enables us to distinguish one instrument or voice from another. Timbre is affected by such things as the material from which an instrument is made, its size and shape, and the manner in which the sound is produced (i.e., by blowing, plucking, and so on).

Among instruments and voices, there are several levels of difference in tone color: (1) the fairly obvious differences that distinguish one family from another, such as men singers from women singers or string instruments from wind, brass, and percussion instruments; (2) the more subtle differences among members of the same family; and (3) the contrasts of tone color that can be produced on a single instrument or within a single voice type.

An almost unlimited variety of tone colors is available to the composer today, not only from traditional instruments but also from electronically generated sounds and other sound sources. A skilled composer uses these to create colorful and moving effects.

Timbre is also basic to musical mediums and genres.

Medium

A *medium* in music is the intermediary between the composer's ideas on the printed page and their realization in musical sound. Individual voice types and instruments are mediums, as are groups of instruments such as the string quartet, the concert band, the chorus, and the orchestra. As listeners, we distinguish among the various mediums on the basis of timbre.

Genre

Genre refers to works composed for a certain medium. These works are characterized by a particular style, form, or content. The symphony, the piano sonata, and the Mass are examples of genres.

In summary, musical tones may range from high to low, from long to short, and from loud to soft and may possess different timbres. Each of the four properties of tone, in turn, contributes in a fundamental way to one or more of the primary elements of music: pitch contributes to melody, harmony, and texture; duration is one of the bases of rhythm; intensity is the source of dynamics; and tone color is basic to the study of musical mediums and genres. These elements of music are the subject of the remainder of Part One.

For Additional Study

Cogan, Robert. *New Images of Musical Sound*. Cambridge, MA: Harvard University Press. 1984.

Gordon, Roderick D. *The World of Musical Sound*. Dubuque, IA: Kendall/Hunt. 1979.

Musical Notes. From *The Light and Sound Series*. Produced by United World Films. Distributed by Universal Educational and Visual Arts. 12 min. Sound film.

The Science of Sound. Produced by the Bell Telephone Laboratories. Folkways FX 6007 (abridged version, 6136). Phonograph recording.

Recommended Listening

While listening to the tones in the following compositions, identify the different properties separately. Notice that some tones are higher than others (pitch), that some are longer than others (duration), that some are louder than others (intensity), and that some differ from others in quality, especially in the orchestral pieces.

Berlioz, Hector. *Symphonie fantastique*: V ("Dream of a Witches' Sabbath") (exciting use of tone colors for descriptive effects)

Britten, Benjamin. *The Young Person's Guide to the Orchestra* (excellent demonstration of the tone colors and range of pitches available to the orchestra)

Cowell, Henry. *The Banshee* (piano) (novel tone color effects for piano)

Debussy, Claude. *Nocturnes* (3 pieces for orchestra): "Fêtes" (Festivals) (varied tone colors and extended orchestral crescendo and diminuendo used for descriptive effects)

Haydn, Franz Joseph. *The Creation* (oratorio): "In the Beginning" (use of dynamics, particularly the startling fortissimo on "light")

Mendelssohn, Felix. *A Midsummer Night's Dream* (orchestra): "Scherzo" (use of soft dynamics, fast notes, and light tone colors to create an elfin atmosphere)

Penderecki, Krzysztof. *Threnody to the Victims of Hiroshima* (strings) (classic 20th-century exploration of new approaches to duration and string tone color)

Ravel, Maurice. *Bolero* (orchestra) (gradual orchestral crescendo from beginning to end)

Schoenberg, Arnold. *Five Orchestral Pieces*, Op. 16: No. 3, "Summer Morning by the Lake (Colors)" (famous experiment in tone color melody [Klangfarbenmelodie])

Schumann, Robert. *Fantasiestücke* (Fantasy Pieces), Op. 12 (piano): No. 2, "Aufschwung" (Soaring) (contrast and gradations of dynamic level)

Stockhausen, Karlheinz. *Gesang der Jünglinge* (Song of the Youths) (electronic sound and manipulation of voices)

Stravinsky, Igor. *Le sacre du printemps* (ballet): "Danses des adolescentes" (striking use of repeated notes, percussive accents, and tone color to create the impression of a primitive ritual dance)

Tchaikovsky, Pyotr. *Symphony No. 4 in F Minor*, Op. 36: III (variety in tone color through alternation of instrumental families)

Varèse, Edgard. *Ionisation* (use of nonpitch percussion sounds)

Webern, Anton. *Symphonie*, Op. 21: I ("pointillistic" effects in tone color and durations)

3

The Notation of Pitch

*M*odern musical notation is the result of centuries of development, a development that is still continuing. It provides a means of communication between composers and performers and a way of preserving music.

The ability to read music is not essential to the appreciation of music, but an understanding of the basic principles of musical notation can enable the listener to compare music that is heard with its visual representation, and this can often give a clearer idea of the music's flow, which, in turn, can help focus the ear. Musical notation also makes possible the inclusion in the text of simple musical examples as a type of shorthand, to show things rather than explain them in words.

Musical notation serves mainly to indicate pitches and silences and their durations. The first of these is the subject of this chapter; the latter two are explored in chapter 4.

THE PIANO KEYBOARD

The piano keyboard is a convenient tool for introducing pitch notation because it encompasses virtually every pitch normally used in music and because the visual arrangement of its keys is easy to understand.

Orientation

Figure 3.1 illustrates the piano keyboard and shows the names of the white keys. The complete keyboard contains eighty-eight keys (fifty-two white, thirty-six black). Except for a single black key at the far left end, the black keys occur in alternating groups of two and three, with two white keys between each group. The beginner can use this consistent pattern of black and white keys as a means of orientation.

Each key on the piano corresponds to a specific pitch, motion to the right producing successively higher pitches, motion to the left, successively lower ones.

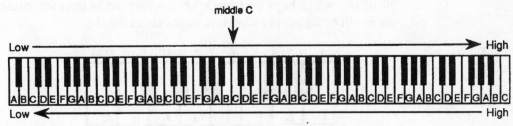

Fig 3.1

The Names of Pitches

Pitches are named, from low to high, using the seven letters A B C D E F G, this sequence being repeated over and over as pitches continue to ascend. These letters correspond to the white keys on the piano (as in figure 3.1) and are considered "natural." The C located approximately in the middle of the keyboard, directly below the maker's name, is called *middle C*.

Octave and Octave Duplication

The interval formed by any pitch and the next higher or lower pitch having the same letter name is called an *octave* because of the eight letter names encompassed by the two pitches:

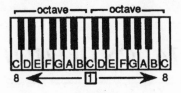

Fig 3.2

When any pitch and its higher and lower octaves are played, each pitch sounds like a higher or lower duplicate of the others. This phenomenon is referred to as *octave duplication* (or *octave equivalence*). It is in recognition of this similarity of sound that pitches an octave apart are given the same letter name, thereby breaking down the total pitch spectrum into a series of octave segments and pitch classes, each labeled by one of the seven letters.

Division of the Octave

In Western music, the space *within* an octave is normally divided in one of two ways: into seven pitches or into twelve pitches. The **seven-pitch division of the octave** is exemplified by the white keys on the piano and the seven-letter system for naming pitches. This method of dividing the octave is absolutely fundamental to Western music. From it derive our diatonic scales and such basic concepts as "conjunct/disjunct" and "major/minor." (These topics are discussed in chapters 5 and 6.)

A **twelve-pitch division of the octave** results, on the other hand, when all of the white keys *and* black keys within an octave are counted (the thirteenth being simply an octave duplicate of the first):

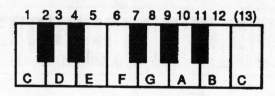

Fig 3.3

A consecutive arrangement of all twelve pitches within the octave, ascending or descending, is called a *chromatic scale*. The distance between any two successive tones of the chromatic scale is referred to as a *half step* or *semitone*, the smallest interval normally used in Western music. On the piano, a half step is the interval between closest adjacent keys.

THE NOTATION OF PITCH

Note, Staff

To indicate a pitch, a symbol called a *note* is placed on a *staff* consisting of five horizontal lines and four intervening spaces. A note may be placed either on a line or in a space. The higher a note is placed on the staff, the higher its corresponding pitch:

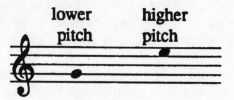

Fig 3.4

The Treble Clef   A *clef* is a sign that is placed at the beginning of a staff to show the exact pitches represented by each line and space. The G clef or *treble clef* (𝄞) is used for higher pitches and identifies the second line of the staff as the pitch G above middle C.

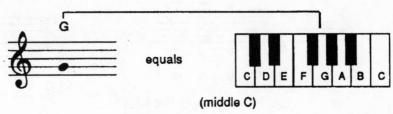

Fig 3.5

The progression from any line to the next higher space, or from any space to the next higher line, implies an alphabetical succession. Therefore, once G is established as the second line of the staff, the remaining pitches on the staff may be determined:

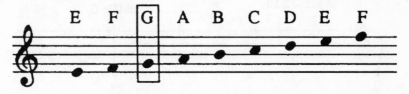

Fig 3.6

The Bass Clef   The F clef or *bass clef* (𝄢) is used for lower pitches and identifies the fourth line as the pitch F below middle C. Other pitches on the staff, in turn, are derived from F:

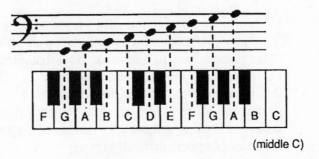

Fig 3.7

Ledger Lines

Pitches lying above or below the range of the staff may be indicated by short staff extensions called *ledger lines* (sometimes spelled *leger lines*). The alphabetical succession of notes continues as on the staff.

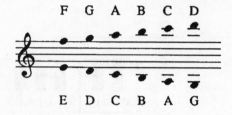

Fig 3.8

The Grand Staff

The *grand staff* (or *great staff*) is a two-staff combination formed by placing the treble staff above the bass staff, joined by a vertical line and a brace at the left. Middle C appears on a ledger line between the two staves (*staves* is the plural for *staff*), making it possible to continue consecutively from one staff to the other.

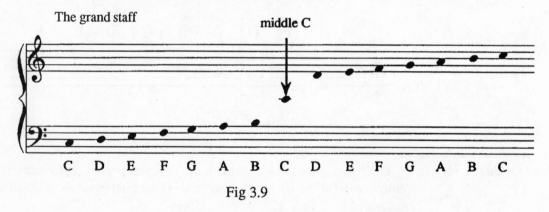

Fig 3.9

Music for piano is normally written on the grand staff.

Figure 3.10 illustrates a grand staff with the notation for each white key of the piano keyboard indicated. Note that pitches in the octave above and below middle C may be notated in either the treble or bass clef. Note also that, in the extreme high register, the symbol 8va is used, which indicates that pitches are to be played an octave higher than written. This symbol is necessary because without it the number of ledger lines required would make the notes extremely difficult to read.

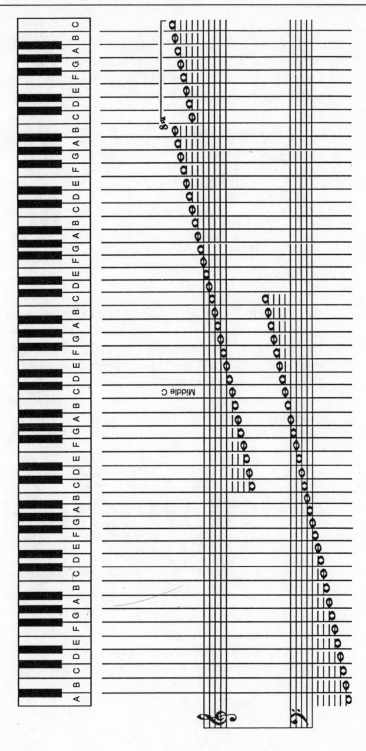

Fig. 3.10

Sharps and Flats

The black keys on the piano are identified by sharp and flat signs. A *sharp* sign (♯) preceding a note raises a natural (i.e., white-key) pitch a half step—one key to the right on the piano. A *flat* sign (♭) preceding a note lowers a natural pitch a half step—one key to the left on the piano.

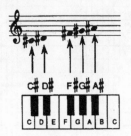 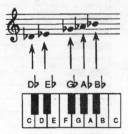

Fig 3.11

As figure 3.11 illustrates, each black key may represent either a sharp of the white-key pitch below it (i.e., to the left) or a flat of the white-key pitch above it (i.e., to the right). Thus, C-sharp, for example, is the same sounding pitch (or *tone*) as D-flat, even though C-sharp and D-flat are different "notes." (Remember: a tone is the actual sound of a pitch. A note is a symbol used to indicate a tone.) Because there are no black keys between E and F or between B and C, the pitches E-sharp, B-sharp, F-flat, and C-flat all fall on white keys (E-sharp = F, B-sharp = C, F-flat = E, C-flat = B).

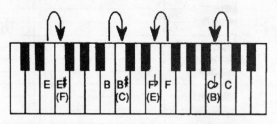

Fig 3.12

Other Signs for Raising and Lowering Pitches

A *double sharp* (✖) raises a pitch two half steps. A *double flat* (♭♭) lowers a pitch two half steps. A *natural* (♮) cancels a previous sharp, flat, double sharp or double flat, restoring the original letter-name ("white-key") pitch.

Vertical vs. Horizontal Placement of Notes

Notes placed vertically on the staff are played simultaneously. Notes placed horizontally are played consecutively.

Played simultaneously   **Played consecutively**

Fig 3.13

Combination of Elements

As a final example, figure 3.14 illustrates various combinations of the elements of pitch notation discussed in this chapter.

Fig 3.14

*T*his chapter has introduced basic elements and principles of pitch notation. Using this information and figure 3.10, the reader should be able to identify—and locate on the piano, if desired—pitches encountered in most musical sources. At the very least, the reader should be able to follow the general rise and fall of pitches in a musical score and gain some idea of the music's direction.

For Additional Study

Cooper, Helen. *The Basic Guide to How to Read Music.* A Perigee Book. New York: The Putnam Publishing Group [copyright 1982 by Omnibus Press]. 1982.

Harder, Paul O. *Basic Materials in Music Theory: A Programed Course.* 6th ed. Boston: Allyn and Bacon. 1986.

Lilienfeld, Robert. *Learning to Read Music.* New York: Barnes & Noble. 1976.

Manoff, Tom. *The Music Kit.* 3d ed. New York: Norton. 1988.

4

Rhythm and Its Notation

Rhythm is that aspect of music that encompasses all elements relating to the forward flow of music through time. It includes the speed at which music is performed, the various types of note lengths used, and the ways in which notes of varying lengths are grouped. To understand rhythm, the listener needs to know how musical time is organized.

ELEMENTS OF RHYTHM

Beat
The most basic unit of musical time is the *beat*, a regular underlying pulsation that divides music into equal units of time. Like the steady ticking of a clock, beats form the stable background against which tones of varying length occur. When we listen to music, we often respond to these pulsations by tapping our feet in time with the beats. Beats are so basic to musical time, in fact, that a musical sound is described in terms of how many beats, rather than seconds, it lasts.

Tempo
Tempo, Italian for "time," refers in music to relative speed, specifically the rate at which beats recur. The faster the beat, the faster the tempo; the slower the beat, the slower the tempo.

Tempo may be indicated precisely by metronome designations, which specify the number of beats per minute, or less precisely through the use of descriptive terms. In art music, the terms describing tempo are traditionally written in Italian. Common tempo indications are as follows:

Largo	very slow, broad	Allegretto	"little allegro,"
Grave	very slow, solemn		moderately fast
Lento	slow	Allegro	fast, brisk
Adagio	slow, leisurely	Vivace	lively, quick
Andante	moderately slow, Presto	Presto	very fast
	"walking tempo	Prestissimo	extremely fast
Moderato	moderate speed		

These terms can be qualified by the addition of other words, such as *molto* (much, very), *meno* (less), and *non troppo* (not too much). Gradual changes in tempo may be indicated by such words as *accelerando* (becoming faster) or *ritardando* (becoming slower). Often, too, tempo designations are coupled with terms that convey the general style in which the music is to be performed, such as *cantabile*, singing (as in *Andante cantabile*), or *con brio*, with spirit (as in *Allegro con brio*).

Meter

The organization of beats into recurring groups (e.g., into groups of two, three or four beats) is known as *meter*. Each individual group of beats, in turn, is called a *measure*. The grouping of beats necessary for meter is usually created by emphasizing certain beats. For example:

"STRONG - weak, STRONG - weak" creates a two-beat pattern;

"STRONG - weak -weak, STRONG - weak - weak" creates a three-beat pattern.

The most common types of meter are duple meter, triple meter, and quadruple meter.

DUPLE METER

Duple meter is a grouping of two beats per measure in which a strong (i.e., emphasized) beat alternates with a weaker beat:

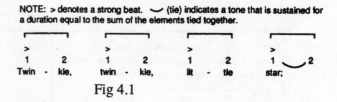

Fig 4.1

Nursery songs and marches are usually in duple meter.

TRIPLE METER

Triple meter is a grouping of three beats per measure, with one strong beat followed by two weaker beats:

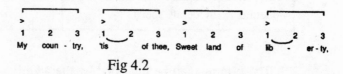

Fig 4.2

Waltzes, minuets, mazurkas, and certain other dance forms are typically in triple meter. Triple meter may be used also for other types of music, particularly where a "lilting" quality is desired.

QUADRUPLE METER

Quadruple meter is a grouping of four beats per measure. The primary accent falls on beat one, with a secondary accent on beat three; beats two and four are weaker.

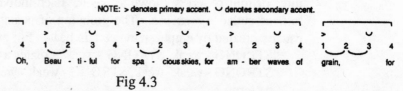

Fig 4.3

As figure 4.3 illustrates, music does not always begin on the first beat of a measure. Sometimes it begins one or more beats before the arrival of the first complete measure.

Quadruple meter is the most common meter of all. Much art music is written in this meter, as are most folk, gospel, country, popular, jazz, and rock songs.

Simple Time and Compound Time

In order to accommodate tones that are faster than the prevailing beat in a given piece of music, principles for dividing and subdividing the beat have been established.

The most common ways of dividing the beat are into two parts or three parts, giving rise to simple time and compound time.

SIMPLE TIME

In *simple time*, each beat is divided into two equal parts; the divisions of the beats are, thus, exactly twice as fast as the beats themselves:

Some musicians keep track of these divisions by mentally "counting" the beats in each measure while thinking "and" on the second half of each beat. Figure 4.4 illustrates this process in duple meter.

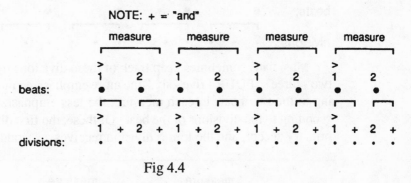

Fig 4.4

A familiar example of simple time is "Yankee Doodle":

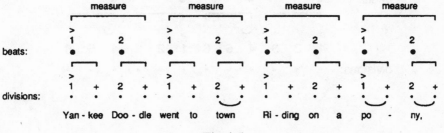

Fig 4.5

COMPOUND TIME

In *compound time*, each beat is divided into *three* equal parts; the divisions of the beats are, thus, exactly three times as fast as the beats themselves:

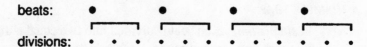

The most common use of compound time is in connection with *sextuple* meter. Most often, sextuple meter is performed as a kind of duple meter, in which there are *two* beats per measure, each one divided into three parts:

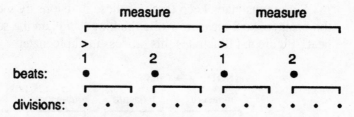

Musicians sometimes keep track of these divisions by counting "ONE - two - three - FOUR - five - six," the more emphasized numbers corresponding to the two beats in each measure, the less emphasized numbers corresponding to the divisions of the beat. Of these, the first division receives the primary accent, and the fourth division receives a secondary accent:

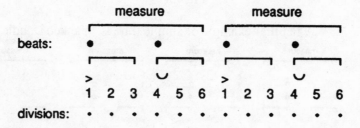

An example of compound time is "For He's a Jolly Good Fellow":

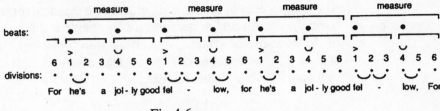

Fig 4.6

Beats may also be subdivided further. Simple time may be subdivided further into four or eight parts per beat, while compound time may be subdivided further into six or twelve parts per beat.

Syncopation

As noted earlier, the first beat of a measure normally receives the most emphasis (called *accent* in music). Sometimes, however, composers or performers place accents in unexpected places—on another beat of the measure or on offbeats (i.e., between the beats). The shifting of the accent to a weak beat or to an offbeat is known as *syncopation*. Syncopation occurs when a tone introduced on a weak beat is held over into a stronger beat or when a tone beginning on an offbeat is carried over into the next beat. Syncopation is one of the most characteristic features of ragtime, jazz, and rock music.

Irregular Metric Schemes

Composers sometimes use irregular metric schemes with five, seven, ten or other unusual numbers of beats per measure. In the twentieth century, composers have also experimented with metric effects in which the meter signature changes every few measures (e.g., Stravinsky's *L'Histoire du soldat*) and have even combined several different meters simultaneously. These devices result in complex time factors that produce intriguing effects.

Nonmetric Music

Some music is nonmetric, meaning that it has no fixed grouping of beats, no meter signature, and no bar lines. Gregorian chant (see chapter 12) is traditionally performed in a free, nonmetric fashion (although some recent scholarship suggests that originally it may have been metric). Composers of the twentieth century have also written nonmetric music, some even going so far as to replace traditional rhythmic notation with *proportional* notation, in which the duration of musical events is indicated in seconds of "clock" time or by the proportion of horizontal space events occupy on the staff in relation to other events.

Rhythmic Character

The particular combination of rhythmic and metrical elements in a piece of music gives the piece its individual rhythmic character. It may be regular when its patterns of accent and duration are repeated, or it may be irregular when the accents and/or duration are constantly changing. Through the use of rhythmic-metric patterns associated with a particular musical or dance style (e.g., Charleston or cha-cha), it may assume a conventional character, or it may be highly individualistic.

THE NOTATION OF RHYTHM

Note Values

Whereas the pitch of a tone is shown by the position of a note on the staff, the duration of a tone is indicated by the note's *shape*—more specifically, by symbols known as *note values*. The main note values are the whole note (○), half note (♩), quarter note (♩), eighth note (♪), and sixteenth note (♪), each of which lasts twice as long as the next:

Fig 4.7

(NOTE: As shown above, eighth and sixteenth notes may be written either as separate notes with flags [♪♪. ♪♪♪♪] or grouped together with beams [♫ . ♬♬].)

A single note is thus able to show simultaneously both the pitch *and* the duration of a tone:

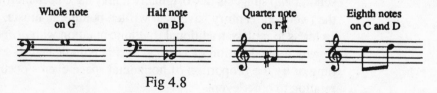

| Whole note on G | Half note on B♭ | Quarter note on F♯ | Eighth notes on C and D |

Fig 4.8

Tie, Dot

The length of a note can be extended by a tie or dot. When two or more notes of the same pitch are connected by a *tie* (‿ or ⌢), the pitch is sustained for a duration equal to the sum of the tied notes:

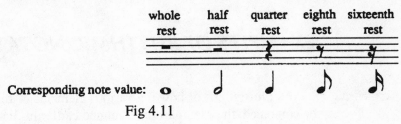

Fig 4.9

A *dot* placed to the right of a note extends the length of the note by half of its original length:

Fig 4.10

Rest

The duration of silence is indicated by a symbol called a *rest*. The various types of rests are equal in duration to their corresponding note values.

whole rest	half rest	quarter rest	eighth rest	sixteenth rest

Corresponding note value:

Fig 4.11

Fermata

Another symbol, the fermata (⌢), placed above a note or rest, extends the note or rest longer than its normal time value; the exact length is left to the discretion of the performer.

Notation of Meter

Two notational devices are used to indicate meter: the meter signature and the bar line.

METER SIGNATURE

The *meter signature* consists of two numbers, one above the other. The top number indicates the number of beats per measure; the bottom number indicates the type of note value that gets one beat (1=whole note, 2=half note, 4=quarter note, 8=eighth note, 16= sixteenth note).

For example: **3** - - - - - - - - - - -   3 beats per measure
                    4 - - - - - - - - - -   quarter note gets one beat

Two abbreviated meter signatures are also seen frequently:

𝄴 (common time)   means $\frac{4}{4}$

𝄵 (cut time, or *alla breve*)   means $\frac{2}{2}$

BAR LINE

The *bar line* is a vertical line drawn through the staff; it separates one measure from the next. The beat before the bar line is called an *upbeat*; the beat immediately after the bar line (the first beat of the measure) is called the *downbeat*.

EXAMPLES OF RHYTHMIC NOTATION

As illustrations of how the various elements of rhythmic notation may be combined, the examples diagrammed earlier in figures 4.1, 4.2, 4.3, and 4.5 are rewritten below using pitch and rhythmic notation. To assist in reading, the "counting" of beats and divisions of beats is shown, but this is not included in regular musical notation.

Fig 4.12

The final example below, in 6/8 meter, was used earlier (in figure 4.6) as an example of compound time. Thus, although the meter signature indicates six beats per measure, with the eighth note getting one beat, 6/8 meter is most often performed in *two* beats per measure, each beat being divided into three equal parts.

Fig 4.13

*T*he elements of rhythm and principles of rhythmic notation introduced in this chapter have been presented to give the reader a general understanding of how musical time is organized, not with the expectation that a beginner will be able to perform rhythms from written notation. That is a complex skill that can require years to master. Nevertheless, even at this beginning level, the reader should now be able to glean certain information about musical time from notated musical scores: tempo (from Italian tempo indications), meter (from the meter signature), and the relative speed of the notes (from note values).

For Additional Study

Harder, Paul O. *Basic Materials in Music Theory: A Programed Course.* 6th ed. Boston: Allyn and Bacon. 1986.

Sadie, Stanley, ed. The New Grove Dictionary of Music and Musicians. New York: Macmillan. 1980. S.v. "Rhythm," by Walther Dürr, Walter Gerstenberg, and Jonathan Harvey.

Recommended Listening

COMPARISON OF TEMPOS:

Largo Dvořák, Antonin. *Symphony No. 9 in E Minor*, Op. 95 ("From the New World"): II

Lento Chopin, Frédéric. *Mazurka in A Minor*, Op. 17, No. 4 (piano)

Adagio Barber, Samuel. *Adagio for Strings*

Andante Mozart, W. A. *Piano Concerto in C Major*, K. 467: II

Allegro Vivaldi, Antonio. *Concerto Grosso in A Minor*, Op. 3, No. 8: I (strings and continuo)

Vivace Haydn, Franz Joseph. *String Quartet in D Major*, Op. 64, No. 5 ("The Lark"): IV

Presto Mendelssohn, Felix. *Symphony No. 4 in A Major*, Op. 90 ("Italian"): IV

DUPLE AND QUADRUPLE METERS:

Handel, George Frideric. *Messiah*: "Hallelujah" Chorus

Sousa, John Philip. *The Stars and Stripes Forever* (march, band)

Tchaikovsky, Pyotr. *Nutcracker Suite* (orchestra): "Chinese Dance," "Dance of the Reed Flutes," "Dance of the Sugar Plum Fairy," "March," "Overture," "Russian Dance"

TRIPLE METER:

Haydn, Franz Joseph. *Symphony No. 100 in G Major* ("Military"): III
Strauss, Johann. *Blue Danube Waltz* (orchestra)
Tchaikovsky, Pyotr. *Nutcracker Suite* (orchestra): "Arabian Dance," "Waltz of the
     Flowers"
Traditional. *Amazing Grace*

COMPOUND TIME:

Dukas, Paul. *The Sorcerer's Apprentice* (orchestra)
Mendelssohn, Felix. *Symphony No. 4 in A Major*, Op. 90 ("Italian"): I
Sousa, John Philip. *Semper Fidelis* (march, band)

SYNCOPATION:

Bernstein, Leonard. Symphonic Dances from *West Side Story* (orchestra)
Ellington, Duke. *Satin Doll*
Gershwin, George. *I Got Rhythm*
___. *Preludes* (3, for piano)
Joel, Billy. *Just the Way You Are*
Joplin, Scott. *Maple Leaf Rag*

IRREGULAR OR CHANGING METER AND COMPLEX RHYTHMIC CHARACTER:

Boulez, Pierre. *Le marteau sans maître* (voice and chamber ensemble)
Brubeck, Dave. *Take Five*, *Unsquare Dance*
Crumb, George. *Ancient Voices of Children* (2 voices, instruments)
Stravinsky, Igor. *L'Histoire du soldat* (The Soldier's Tale; ballet for narrator and
     7 instruments)
___. *Le sacre du printemps* (The Rite of Spring, a ballet)
Tchaikovsky, Pytor. *Symphony No. 6 in B Minor* ("Pathétique"): II (5/4 meter)

NONMETRIC AND PROPORTIONAL NOTATION:

Any example of Gregorian Chant
Berio, Luciano. *Circles*
Penderecki, Krzysztof. *Threnody to the Victims of Hiroshima* (strings)

5

Melody

With a few exceptions, all music has melody. It is the element that we are often drawn to first, follow with greatest interest, and remember the longest. In this chapter, the properties of melody, characteristics of melodic structure, and melodic types are considered.

PROPERTIES OF MELODY

A *melody* is a series of tones, usually varying in pitch and duration, that form a satisfying musical idea. Just as random words do not form a meaningful sentence, random sounds do not constitute a melody. A convincing melody has a definite beginning and ending and conveys a sense of direction, shape, and continuity.

Melody has a number of properties that give it infinite variety. An understanding of these properties helps one listen perceptively.

Progression

Melodic progression refers to the intervals (pitch distance) between tones as a melody moves from one tone to the next. A melody may move mostly stepwise; that is, it may progress to adjacent letter-name pitches or adjacent keys of the piano (as in "America"). This is called *conjunct progression*. On the other hand, a melody may contain numerous prominent skips (as in "The Star-Spangled Banner"), in which case it is said to have *disjunct progression*. A melody usually contains both conjunct and disjunct motion.

Range

The range of a melody is the pitch distance from its lowest to its highest tone. A melody may have a wide range, a narrow range, or a moderate range.

Register

Register is the relative highness or lowness of the melody as a whole. A melody may occupy a high, medium, or low register. In a given composition, the same melody may shift from one register to another. Regardless, register affects the quality of a melody.

Length

Melodies may be short, long, or moderate in length.

Tempo and Rhythm

Rhythm is an indispensable element of melody. Whereas rhythm can exist without melody (as in beating a drum, tapping a pencil on a desk, or clapping the hands), melody cannot exist without rhythm. Most melodies have distinctive rhythmic and tempo features that affect their characters, and melody is subject to all the properties discussed in chapter 4.

Contour

The upward and downward motion of pitches in a melody creates its characteristic shape, or contour. Some melodies move predominantly upward, some move predominantly downward, and others show motion around a central pitch. Most melodies, however, exhibit a wavelike contour of rising and falling pitches. Usually a melodic line moves toward a high point, called a *climax*, which gives direction to the line and serves as its musical and emotional focal point. A melodic climax may appear near the beginning, in the middle, or at the end of the line. Observation of these contours will greatly increase the listener's perception and enjoyment of melodies.

Character

The character of a given melody is the result of the combination of all the properties discussed earlier. To see how these work in a given melody, let us examine the theme of Johann Sebastian Bach's (1685–1750) *Passacaglia in C Minor*.

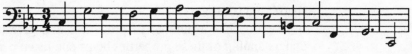

Fig 5.1

The progression of the melody is basically disjunct because of its numerous prominent skips, yet conjunct motion is also present (e.g., the third through sixth notes). The range from the lowest tone (last note of the melody) to the highest tone (A-flat, the sixth note of the melody) is a distance of an octave and a sixth, a wide range. The register of the melody is low. (But if you listen to the Passacaglia all the way through, you will hear the theme appearing in an upper register.) The length of the melody is eight measures, a moderate length. The rhythm consists of a regular alternation between short and long notes. As for the melody's contour, motion is basically upward to the high note that is the climax of the melody in the third full measure; then the melody descends gradually to its lowest tone at the end.

MELODIC STRUCTURE

Phrase and Cadence

A melody is often divided into smaller units called *phrases*. Like a clause in language or a line of poetry, a phrase in music usually forms at least a partially complete idea and is normally set off from other phrases by punctuation of some sort. This punctuation may convey varying degrees of incompleteness (similar to a comma, semicolon or colon in language), or it may convey a definite close (like a period in language). In music the punctuation at the end of a phrase is called a *cadence*.

For the present, we may define a melodic cadence as a conclusive or non-conclusive pause or punctuation in a melody, during which the melody usually comes to rest on a longer note placed on a more or less final degree of the scale. (Cadences are discussed in more detail in chapter 6.) A phrase, in turn, may be defined as a musical unit, comparable to a clause in language, that conveys at least a partially complete musical idea and ends with a cadence. The most common phrase length is four measures, although some phrases are shorter (particularly in very slow tempos) or longer (particularly in very fast tempos).

Relationships between Phrases

The phrases that make up a melody generally show a balance of repeated musical ideas (to convey a sense of unity) and contrasting ideas (to create variety). They may also balance each other in other ways; for example, a phrase containing mostly ascending tones may be balanced by another containing mostly descending tones, or long phrases may be balanced by shorter ones.

Phrases may relate to each other in virtually unlimited ways; a few of the more conventional ways will be discussed in chapter 8. *All* the phrases that make up an effective melody, however, contribute in a significant way to the melody's overall direction, shape, and continuity, so that the melody as a whole emerges as a convincing entity.

MELODIC TYPES

There are many melodic types. Three of the most common are introduced below.

Motive

The smallest recognizable structural unit in music is the *motive*. A motive is a short melodic, rhythmic or melodic-rhythmic figure, generally consisting of from two to eight notes, that receives structural importance in a musical composition through recurrence and development. Like a prepositional phrase or other short syntactical unit in language, a motive is a fragmentary idea, incapable of standing alone; yet it can often serve as the "cell" out of which a whole composition evolves.

A motive may be used as the building block of a phrase, tune, theme, or longer musical segment. The composer establishes the significance of a motive (1) by restating it literally, (2) by restating it at a higher or lower pitch level (known as *sequential repetition* or more simply as a *sequence*), (3) by restating it with modifications of its characteristic rhythmic and/or melodic features, (4) by combining it with other motives, (5) by imitating it in other voices or instruments or by other techniques. These motivic recurrences, in turn, contribute greatly to the overall unity of the composition.

An example of how a motive (in this case, a rhythmic motive) may serve as the building block of a melody may be seen in the familiar song "America" (figure 5.2). This example also illustrates the use of a sequence.

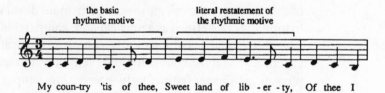

My coun-try 'tis of thee, Sweet land of lib - er - ty, Of thee I

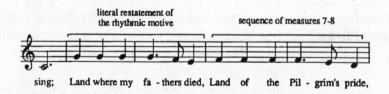

sing; Land where my fa - thers died, Land of the Pil - grim's pride,

From ev - 'ry   moun- tain side Let   free - dom ring.

Fig 5.2

Probably the most familiar motive in music is the short-short-short-long motive that opens Beethoven's *Symphony No. 5 in C Minor*:

Fig 5.3

This rhythmic motive underlies virtually the entire first movement of the symphony and, in fact, figures prominently in the other movements as well—truly a device that unifies the whole symphony.

Tune

The *tune* is perhaps the most common type of melody. A tune is a simple melody that is easy to sing and remember and seems complete in itself. "America" is an example of a tune, as are many folk songs, dance melodies, popular songs, and some melodies from symphonies, operas, and other forms of art music.

Theme

An extended musical work, such as a movement of a symphony, often contains a number of melodies and melodic fragments, some of which generally serve a more central purpose within the piece than others. Melodies that contain the main ideas of a musical composition—the ideas that the composer builds upon and develops—are called *themes*. Just as the main themes of a novel serve as the basis for the story's action and plot twists, so the themes of a musical work serve as the basis of the musical development. In a general sense, an extended musical composition represents an exploration of the "life" of its main themes—their origins, interactions, growth, change, and ultimate fate. During the course of the work, the themes will be brought back, often altered or even fragmented to suit different circumstances, as the composer probes the different sides of their characters.

A musical theme may be as short as a single phrase or as long as a full tune or other self-contained unit. It may be cast in a conventional form (such as one of the forms discussed in chapter 8), or it may take the shape of a looser, freer motivic melody. Its character will vary, depending upon the type of composition in which it appears and its specific role within the composition. In keeping with its function as a main musical idea, a theme usually has melodic, harmonic, rhythmic, or other features that make it easy to recognize when it reappears.

*M*elody, with its consecutively sounding pitches, represents the horizontal aspect of music, the line that we follow as a composition unfolds in time. Whether a melody assumes the shape of a motive, tune, or theme, its general character is determined by its phrase and cadence structure and by the specific way in which the various properties of melody are combined. Although there is no absolute basis for judging a melody "good" or "bad," the same general criteria that apply to all the arts apply to melody, such as the need for intelligibility, coherence, satisfying proportions and formal shape, and a balance between unity and variety.

For Additional Study

Copland, Aaron. *What to Listen for in Music*. New York: Mentor. 1964.
Edwards, Arthur C. *The Art of Melody*. New York: Philosophical Library. 1956.
Holst, Imogene. *Tune*. New York: October House. 1966.
Toch, Ernst. *The Shaping Forces in Music* (especially the second part, "Melody"). New York: Criterion, 1948; reprint, New York: Dover, 1977.
The University of Delaware Videodisc Music Series. Distributed by the University of Delaware (Newark, DE). Interactive videodiscs (particularly the Mozart *Quintet for Clarinet and Strings*, the Brahms *Schaffe in Mir, Gott,* and the Beethoven *"Pathétique" Sonata*).

Recommended Listening

The following music has been selected for diversity of melodic styles and for the prominence of one or more melodic traits. In each case listen to the melody several times and focus your attention on the different melodic properties separately.

LENGTH

Bach, J. S. *Suite No. 3 in D Major for Orchestra*, BWV 1068: "Air" (long line)
___. *The Well-Tempered Clavier* (harpsichord or piano), Vol. 1: Fugue No. 1 in C Major (theme; short line)
Handel, George Frideric. *Largo* ("Ombra mai fù," from the opera *Serse*) (long line)
Schubert, Franz. *Die Winterreise* (The Winter Journey, a song cycle): No. 24, "The Organ Grinder" (short lines)

RANGE

Wide: Mozart, W. A. *Piano Concerto in C Major*, K.467: II

Schumann, Robert. *Kinderszenen* (Scenes from Childhood): No.7, "Träumerei" ("Reverie")

Varèse, Edgard. *Density 21.5* (solo flute)

*Narrow:*Sibelius, Jean. *Finlandia* (tone poem for orchestra): main theme

REGISTER

Mendelssohn, Felix. *Concerto in E Minor for Violin and Orchestra*, Op. 64: I, first theme (high register)
Stravinsky, Igor. *Firebird Suite* (orchestra): opening theme (low)
Tchaikovsky, Pyotr. *Symphony No. 6 in B Minor*, Op. 74: I, introduction (low)

DIRECTION (AT BEGINNING)

Brahms, Johannes. *Symphony No. 1 in C Minor*, Op. 68: I, introduction (up)

Puccini, Giacomo. *Madama Butterfly* (opera): "Un bel dì vedremo" ("One Fine Day") (down)

Strauss, Richard. *Also sprach Zarathustra* (tone poem for orchestra): beginning (up)

Wagner, Richard. *Die Meistersinger* (opera): "Prize Song" ("Morgenlich leuchtend") (down)

PROGRESSION

Chopin, Frédéric. *Ballade No. 3 in A-flat Major*, Op. 47 (piano): first theme (conjunct), second theme (disjunct)

Mozart, W. A. *Symphony No. 40 in G Minor*, K. 550: I, first theme (disjunct balanced by conjunct), bridge theme (mostly disjunct), second theme (conjunct), closing theme (mostly disjunct)

Wagner, Richard. *Die Meistersinger* (opera): "Prize Song" ("Morgenlich leuchtend") (conjunct)

Webern, Anton. *Concerto for Nine Instruments*, Op. 24 (disjunct)

6

Harmony and Tonality

Harmony is the musical element that results from the simultaneous sounding of two or more tones and encompasses the various ways in which such tone combinations interrelate. Whereas melody is a horizontal concept, because of its consecutively sounding pitches, harmony is a vertical concept. Harmony appeared comparatively late in the history of music (around the ninth century A.D.) and has been developed primarily in Western civilization.

ELEMENTS OF HARMONY

Intervals

As defined in chapter 2, an interval is the distance in pitch between two tones. Intervals may be sounded consecutively, as in a melody, or simultaneously, producing harmony. The numerical size of an interval is determined by counting the number of letter names encompassed by the two pitches, including both the bottom and top notes (e.g., C - D is a second, C - D - E is a third, etc.):

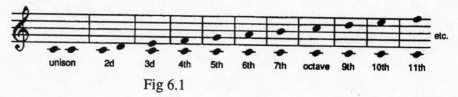

unison 2d 3d 4th 5th 6th 7th octave 9th 10th 11th etc.

Fig 6.1

Within each numerical size a finer distinction, known as the *quality* of the interval, may be specified by adding a qualifying term (perfect, major, minor, and so on). Figure 6.2 illustrates the most commonly used intervals that may be constructed above the pitch C. These same intervals may also be constructed above any other pitch. Each interval in figure 6.2 is identified by its size and quality and by the specific number of half steps it encompasses.

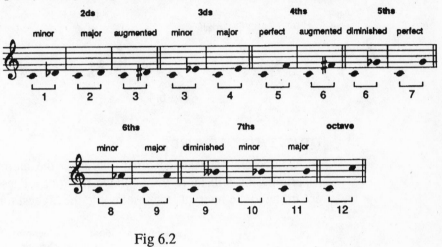

Fig 6.2

Chords

A group of three or more tones sounding together is called a *chord*. The most fundamental chord in Western harmony is the triad.

TRIAD

A triad is a chord containing three different tones arranged in superimposed thirds above a given pitch, known as the *root*. The tone that is a third above the root is called the *third* of the triad; the tone that is a fifth above the root is the *fifth*.

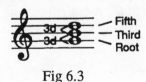

Fig 6.3

A triad may be constructed by selecting any tone as root and adding two more tones above it, using every other letter: C - E - G, D - F - A, E - G - B, F - A - C, and so on.

There are four types of triads: major, minor, augmented, and diminished. Each differs subtly from the others in intervallic content.

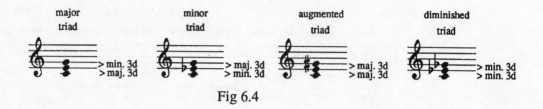

Fig 6.4

OTHER TYPES OF CHORDS

Composers have added other chords to the harmonic vocabulary by superimposing still more thirds above the root. These chords are named according to the interval from the root to the highest tone of the chord.

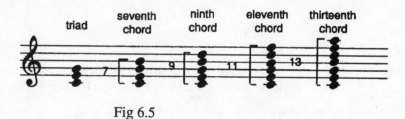

Fig 6.5

Triads and seventh chords constituted the basic harmonic vocabulary from the fifteenth century until about 1900. After that, ninth, eleventh, and thirteenth chords gained wider acceptance, particularly in the music of the French Impressionistic composers (around the turn of the century) and in jazz.

Composers of the twentieth century have also introduced more complex chords constructed from intervals other than thirds. These are discussed in chapter 25.

OTHER ASPECTS OF CHORDS

The tones of any chord may be arranged in different orders, and they may be duplicated in one or more higher or lower octaves without changing the essential nature of the chord:

Fig 6.6

The tones of a chord may also be sounded one after another, producing a *broken chord* or *arpeggio*, which combines the qualities of harmony and melody:

Fig 6.7

Consonance and Dissonance

Some intervals and chords produce a feeling of stability, called *consonance*, while others impart a feeling of instability, called *dissonance*. A dissonance creates a tension that demands an onward motion to a more stable sound; this motion from dissonance to consonance helps move music forward, enlivening it and making it more interesting. The sense of consonance and dissonance has changed over time; what formerly seemed dissonant now seems consonant. Nevertheless, consonance and dissonance have always provided the composer with a powerful tool: by carefully regulating the build-up of tension in a musical work and the timing of its release, it is possible to affect the listener's emotions deeply.

For roughly the past five centuries, the following intervals have been considered consonant:

unison major third, minor third

octave major sixth, minor sixth

perfect fifth perfect fourth (in some situations)

Other intervals (such as seconds and sevenths), and chords containing them, are considered dissonant.

During the twentieth century, as the language of music has continued to evolve, our concepts of consonance and dissonance have continued to evolve as well. These changes are discussed in chapter 25.

TONALITY

Tonality in the West is a musical property that, in a given segment of music, creates a sense of gravitation toward a focal pitch, called the *tonic* or *keynote*. Western tonality is tied to the diatonic scale (see below)—it arises from it and relies upon it. When the primacy of the diatonic scale was challenged in the late nineteenth and early twentieth centuries, tonality itself began to dissolve; however, the great bulk of Western art and popular music remains tonal.

All Western music from about 1650 to 1900 and most folk and popular music since 1900 exemplify a system known as **major-minor tonality**. The essential elements of major-minor tonality are major and minor scales, diatonic triads and seventh chords built upon the seven degrees of these scales, and principles that underlie the motion of diatonic chords from one to another. These elements are discussed below. Characteristics of harmony in music before 1650 and since 1900 are discussed at appropriate places in Part Two.

Scale and Key

A *diatonic* scale is a set of seven ascending or descending notes, each successive note written on the next most adjacent line or space of the staff; thus, each letter name is used only once. The first note is often repeated an octave higher after the seventh. Major-minor tonality is based upon two specific types of diatonic scales: the major scale and the minor scale.

MAJOR SCALE

A *major scale* divides the octave from the tonic pitch to its octave duplication using the following pattern of major seconds and minor seconds.

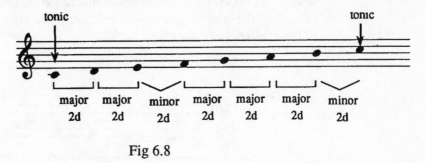

Fig 6.8

Scales are named according to their tonic pitch, and the tones of a scale are referred to as *scale degrees*. Thus, the major scale illustrated in figure 6.8 is the C major scale, and music written on the basis of this scale is said to be in the tonality or *key* of C major. One can build a major scale on any of the pitches of the chromatic scale by following the succession of intervals illustrated in figure 6.8 and by making sure that each letter name is represented only once.

The sound of the major scale is the familiar *do re mi fa sol la ti do*. Examples of songs in major keys include "Silent Night," "Joy to the World," "Twinkle, Twinkle, Little Star," "America," and "The Star-Spangled Banner." The great majority of popular music is written in major keys.

MINOR SCALE

The *minor scale* divides the octave from the tonic pitch to its octave duplication using the following interval pattern:

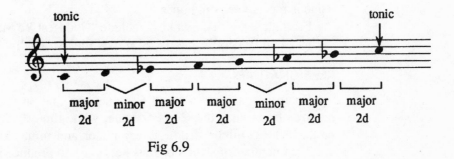

Fig 6.9

The distinguishing feature of the minor scale is the third tone of the scale, which is a half step rather than a whole step above the second tone. The sixth and seventh tones can vary depending upon the musical context. Figure 6.10 illustrates the two most common variants of the minor scale—the *harmonic minor* and the *melodic minor*—and also how the sixth and seventh degrees of these scales typically progress.

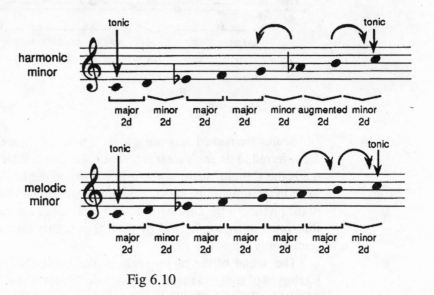

Fig 6.10

The minor scales illustrated in figures 6.9 and 6.10 are all different versions of the C minor scale because the tonic note is C, and music written on the basis of these scales is in the tonality, or key, of C minor. Like the major scale, the minor scale can be built on any of the pitches of the chromatic scale using the interval patterns illustrated, again making sure that each letter name is represented only once.

Familiar songs in minor keys include "God Rest Ye Merry, Gentlemen"; "What Child Is This?"; and the Beatles' "Eleanor Rigby."

KEY SIGNATURES

Comparing figures 6.8 and 6.9, one sees that no sharps or flats were required to produce the C major scale, while three flats were required to produce the C minor scale. Every major and minor key, in fact, has a specified number of sharps or flats necessary to produce its basic scale. In musical notation, these are shown in a *key signature*, a group of sharps or flats placed after the clef at the beginning of the staff. Each sharp or flat in the key signature applies to every appearance of that particular letter name throughout the composition unless the composer specifies otherwise.

The key signatures of all the major and minor keys are shown in figure 6.11. Note that each key signature is shared by a major key and a minor key. Thus, for example, both F major and D minor have a key signature of one flat.

Fig 6.11

Diatonic Chords

Triads and seventh chords may be constructed on each of the scale degrees of a major or minor key. These are referred to as *diatonic chords*, and they comprise the fundamental harmonic material of the key. Figure 6.12 illustrates the diatonic *triads* of C major and C minor; diatonic triads may be constructed similarly in all major and minor keys. Each chord is identified by a Roman numeral corresponding to its scale degree.

Diatonic Triads of C Major

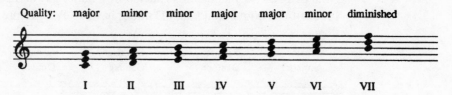

Diatonic Triads of C Minor

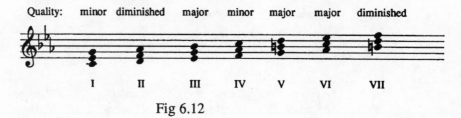

Fig 6.12

The principal triads are built on the first degree of the scale (I, the *tonic*), the fourth scale degree (IV, *subdominant*), and the fifth scale degree (V, *dominant*). Of these, the tonic triad is the most important. Like the tonic pitch, it acts as the home base of the other chords in the key, the chord toward which they gravitate. In major keys, the tonic triad is a major triad, while in minor keys it is a minor triad. The chords on II, III, VI, and VII, while of secondary importance, contribute to harmonic variety and interest.

Chord Motion

In major-minor tonality, the gravitation of chords toward the tonic triad is made possible in part by composers having developed certain conventional types of chord motions, or chord *progressions*, for "guiding" chords toward the tonic. Generally, chords descend by fifths toward the tonic; however, chords that share two or more chord tones (e.g., IV and II or VII and V) are often substituted one for the other. Figure 6.13 illustrates these points.

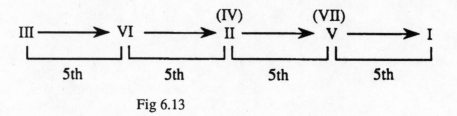

Fig 6.13

In their motion toward the tonic, chords sometimes skip over the next fifth in the series (e.g., III progressing directly to IV, VI progressing to V, or IV progressing to I); this hastens the gravitational motion back to the tonic. On the other hand, chords sometimes move further *away* from the tonic (e.g., V progressing to VI), temporarily defying its gravitational pull, as it were. Chords progressing as shown in figure 6.13 create a strong "pull" toward the tonic triad. In addition, they create subtle expectations on the part of the listener. As soon as we hear the progression I - IV - V, for example, we intuitively expect I to follow. The composer is thus provided with an effective tool for either satisfying our expectations or creating tension by temporarily thwarting them.

Progressions involving the tonic and those triads related to the tonic by fifth (i.e., IV-I, or V-I) are most common. The progression from V to I, for example, is the strongest, most key-defining of all chord motions, and progressions involving IV - V - I or IV - I are extremely frequent.

To be sure, composers do not always choose to have chords progress as in figure 6.13; in fact, they often take great care to devise new and colorful chord motions. However, even to this day, composers will often fall back on these standard progressions when they want to convey a clear sense of harmonic motion toward a goal.

Other Aspects of Major-Minor Tonality

CADENCE

In chapter 5 we found that phrases end with a pause or punctuation called a cadence. Both the melody and the harmony contribute to the establishment of a cadence. The melody generally has a longer note at a cadence and comes to rest on certain scale degrees, usually scale degree 1 for the most complete cadence or scale degree 3, 5, 7, 2 or 6 for a less conclusive one. Certain conventional harmonic formulas are also typically used at cadences. The most final cadence is the authentic cadence, which most often involves a V to I progression. Less final cadence formulas are the half cadence (a cadence pausing on the V chord), the plagal cadence (IV to I), and the deceptive cadence (most often V to VI).

Given the fact that a cadence can contain both melodic and harmonic elements, we may now broaden our definition of cadence: a cadence is a melodic or harmonic formula, more or less conclusive in nature, used to punctuate the end of a phrase.

MODULATIONS

The tonic key, with the tonic chord as its center of gravity, gives focus to all the harmonic activity in a musical composition and ultimately reigns supreme throughout the entire piece. However, composers frequently create harmonic variety and tonal interest by emphasizing areas of the key other than the tonic chord itself. One effective way of doing this is to treat other diatonic triads of the key (or even nondiatonic triads) as temporary tonics which, for a short time, replace the true tonic chord as the apparent center of gravity. Most often emphasized are the five major and minor keys whose key signatures differ from that of the tonic key by no more than one sharp or one flat. For example, if the tonic key is C major, other keys most commonly treated as temporary tonics are A minor, G major, E minor, F major, and D minor.

The process of changing from one key to another within the same piece of music—or more precisely, of having different scale degrees of the key act as temporary centers of tonal gravity—is known as *modulation*. Although modulations may be so subtle that the listener cannot consciously identify them, they contribute on a subconscious level to increased variety, interest, and enjoyment of music. Ventures into other areas of the key make returns to the tonic all the more effective.

Combination of the Elements

As a simple example of how the elements of major-minor tonality may be combined, figure 6.14 shows "Twinkle, Twinkle, Little Star," notated in C major.

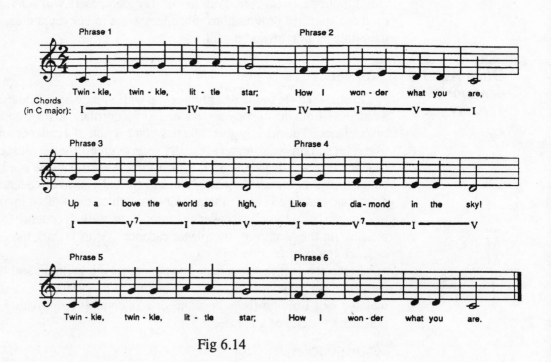

Fig 6.14

In phrases 1 and 2, the melody begins on the tonic pitch, arches up (defying gravity), then gradually gives in to gravity, descending smoothly back to the tonic (arriving on the word *are*). The cadence at the end of phrase 1 (a IV to I plagal cadence ending with scale degree 5 in the melody) is inconclusive, creating an expectation of more to come; this is balanced by the cadence in phrase 2, which creates a sense of finality through use of an authentic cadence (V to I) supporting the melodic return to the tonic pitch. In phrases 3 and 4, the melody, beginning on scale degree 5, descends *almost* to the tonic but stops short in both phrases on scale degree 2. These pauses just short of the tonic goal, supported by half cadences (pausing on the V chord), create a demand for the ultimate resolution of tension represented by a return to the tonic pitch in the melody and the tonic chord in the harmony. This resolution is provided in phrases 5 and 6, which, as before, begin and end on the tonic.

Even in a simple example such as this, we can get a good idea of how melody and harmony, working in combination, can contribute to that elusive feeling of gravitation known as tonality. In art music, the techniques used are normally more complex and sophisticated, but the principles remain the same, and the subconscious effects that they produce are comparable. Major-minor tonality is, therefore, like a nonverbal language that composers use to communicate such things as movement vs. stability, tension vs. relaxation, and open-endedness vs. finality in music, as well as an infinite variety of colorful and moving harmonic shadings.

GENERAL HARMONIC QUALITIES

Although it is possible to combine the various elements of harmony and tonality in an infinite number of ways, the overall style of the harmony in a composition will often reflect certain general harmonic qualities.

Major and Minor Harmony

The minor is of necessity more chromatic than the major, requiring as it does differing versions of itself for differing contexts. As a result, the minor often sounds "darker," more problematic—thus "sadder"—than the major. Since the eighteenth century, composers have often associated major keys with positive states, such as happiness and triumph, while using minor keys to depict sadness, struggle, and other negative states. To be sure, composers do not always use major and minor keys in these roles, but they do so often enough to warrant mention of it as a general harmonic quality.

Simple and Complex Harmony

A simple harmony is one in which chords consist of few tones (simple harmonic construction) and few chord changes (simple harmonic progression). "Twinkle, Twinkle, Little Star" is an example of simple harmony. A complex harmony consists of a large number of chord tones together with unconventional progressions. Rich musical sounds are frequently produced by means of a complex harmony. The harmony of the nineteenth century and especially of the twentieth century is characteristically complex. In fact, the whole history of Western art music shows an evolution from simple to more complex harmony.

Consonant and Dissonant Harmony

A harmonic style may be predominantly dissonant (e.g., Schoenberg's *String Quartet No. 4*, Op. 37) or comparatively consonant (e.g., Haydn's *Quartet in C Major for Strings*, Op. 76, No. 3, second movement). In general, the use of dissonance has increased gradually from earliest times to the present.

Diatonic and Chromatic Harmony

Somewhat related to simple and complex harmony are the attributes of diatonic and chromatic harmony. A diatonic harmony is one in which most of the notes conform to the key signature. Folk songs are typically diatonic. A chromatic harmony is one in which there are numerous altered tones (e.g., Wagner's Prelude to *Tristan und Isolde*). Chromatic harmony is especially typical of the late nineteenth century.

The elements and principles of harmony presented in this chapter apply primarily to the system of major-minor tonality, one of the great achievements of Western music. In the late nineteenth century, composers began to experiment with this system, introducing remotely related keys and rapid or prolonged modulations. The result of this experimentation was to obscure key feeling. Finally, in the twentieth century, some composers have arrived at new concepts of tonality or have done away with key feeling altogether, giving rise to such approaches as polytonality (the combination of two keys at once) and atonality (the complete avoidance of key feeling). These approaches are discussed in chapter 25.

For Additional Study

Harder, Paul O., and Greg A. Steinke. *Harmonic Materials in Tonal Music*. 6th ed. 2 vols. Boston: Allyn and Bacon. 1990.

Jones, George Thaddeus. *Music Theory*. The Barnes & Noble Outline Series. New York: Barnes & Noble. 1974.

Kostka, Stefan, and Dorothy Payne. *Tonal Harmony, with an Introduction to Twentieth-Century Music*. 2nd ed. New York: Alfred A. Knopf. 1989.

Sadie, Stanley, ed. *The New Grove Dictionary of Music and Musicians*. New York: Macmillan. 1980. S.v. "Harmony," by Carl Dahlhaus.

Recommended Listening

The following compositions have been selected to illustrate various aspects of harmony. In each composition, concentrate on the particular characteristic that it illustrates.

COMPARISON OF MAJOR AND MINOR KEYS:

Handel, George Frideric. *Messiah*: "Hallelujah" Chorus (major)

Popular Songs: *Stairway to Heaven* (Led Zeppelin); *Another Brick in the Wall, Part II* (Pink Floyd) (both minor)

Purcell, Henry. *Dido and Aeneas*: "Dido's Lament" (minor)

Schubert, Franz. *Erlkönig* (Erlking, a song) (The tragic narrative is mostly in minor, but the sections during which the Erlking woos the child are in major.)

DIATONIC HARMONY:

Byrd, William. *Laudate, pueri, Dominum* (motet, choir)

Copland, Aaron. *Appalachian Spring* (ballet suite for orchestra): " 'Tis the Gift to be Simple"

Haydn, Franz Joseph. *Symphony No. 94 in G Major* ("Surprise"): II

Popular songs: *The Wind Beneath My Wings* (Bette Midler); *We Didn't Start the Fire* (Billy Joel)

CHROMATIC HARMONY:

Bach, J. S. *Mass in B Minor*, BWV 232: "Crucifixus"

Chopin, Frédéric. *Prelude No. 4 in E Minor*, Op. 28, No. 4 (piano)

Ellington, Duke, Irving Mills, and Mitchell Parish. *Sophisticated Lady*

Gesualdo, Carlo. *Moro lasso al mio duolo* (madrigal)

Wagner, Richard. *Tristan und Isolde* (opera): Prelude to Act I

SIMPLE HARMONY:

Folk and Traditional Songs, such as *Auld Lang Syne*, *Down in the Valley*, *He's Got the Whole World in His Hands*, and *On Top of Old Smoky*

Haydn, Franz Joseph. *Symphony No. 94 in G Major* ("Surprise"): II

COMPLEX HARMONY:

Coltrane, John. *Naima*

Ravel, Maurice. *La valse* (orchestra)

Stravinsky, Igor. *Le sacre du printemps* (The Rite of Spring, a ballet)

CONSONANT HARMONY:

Morley, Thomas. *Now Is the Month of Maying* (madrigal, a cappella)

Palestrina, Giovanni Pierluigi da. *Missa Brevis* (a cappella choir): "Kyrie"

DISSONANT HARMONY:

Schoenberg, Arnold. *String Quartet No. 4*, Op. 37

Webern, Anton. *Concerto for Nine Instruments*, Op. 24

MODULATIONS:

Beethoven, Ludwig van. *Piano Sonata in C Minor*, Op. 13 ("Pathétique"): II (The keys are A-flat major, E-flat major, A-flat major, A-flat minor, E major, and A-flat major.)

Corelli, Archangelo. *Sonata da chiesa*, Op. 3, No. 7 (trio sonata): III (The keys are E minor, G major, A minor, and E minor.)

Schubert, Franz. *Erlkönig* (Erlking, a song) (Opens in G minor. Once the Erlking starts to woo the child, the music begins modulating to successively higher keys as the drama mounts: B-flat major, B minor, C major, C-sharp minor, D minor, and E-flat major, finally returning to G minor for the tragic close.)

7

Musical Texture

In the weaving of fabrics, the characteristic disposition or connection of threads is called texture. This term also refers to an important property of music.

Musical texture is the characteristic disposition and relationship of melodic (horizontal) and harmonic (vertical) factors in music. The three principal types of texture used in Western music are (1) monophonic, (2) homophonic, and (3) polyphonic. More broadly, the terms "thick" (or heavy) texture and "thin" (or light) texture are also used to refer to the total effect produced by the number of parts, spacing and register of tones, and timbre.

TYPES OF MUSICAL TEXTURE

Monophonic Texture

When music exists solely as a single melody with no accompaniment, the texture is *monophonic*. This term means literally a single sound, i.e., a single melodic line. Plainsong (see chapter 12) constitutes the largest body of monophonic music, but any instrument or voice performing a melody without an accompaniment is effecting a monophonic texture, as is a group of instruments or voices performing the same melody in unison or at the octave.

Homophonic Texture

When a single melody is accompanied by subordinate harmonic material (i.e., chords) the texture is *homophonic*. To give but a few examples, the harmonization of "Twinkle, Twinkle, Little Star" shown in chapter 6 (figure 6.14) illustrates homophonic texture, as does a folk song with guitar accompaniment or an operatic aria or a symphonic theme in which the melody is supported by chordal accompaniment.

Polyphonic Texture

When two or more melodies of more or less equal prominence sound simultaneously, the resulting texture is said to be *polyphonic*. The terms *polyphonic* and *contrapuntal* are nearly synonymous, as are the corresponding nouns *polyphony* and *counterpoint*.

There are two basic types of polyphony or counterpoint. *Imitative polyphony* (or more simply, *imitation*) occurs when the various instruments or voices echo the same or quite similar melodic material. Sometimes the imitation is exact, as in a round such as "Row, Row, Row Your Boat" or "Frère Jacques." More often, though, the imitation is freer, with the various lines beginning alike but then going their separate ways. *Nonimitative polyphony* occurs when each of the voices or instruments has a different melody. A number of musical forms are based on polyphonic (or contrapuntal) texture: fugue, canon, motet, madrigal, and so on. These forms will be discussed in Part Two.

Figure 7.1 illustrates these three types of texture with different versions of "Frère Jacques" (Brother John).

Fig 7.1

"THICK" AND "THIN" TEXTURE

Another attribute of texture is its quality of "thickness" or "thinness." This quality is determined by a number of factors.

Number of Parts   A polyphonic composition that consists of six or eight parts (i.e., separate simultaneous melodies) has a richer, thicker texture than one consisting of only two parts. Likewise, a homophonic composition with an elaborate accompaniment of full chords and many tones has a richer sound than one having an accompaniment of only a few tones. Because of the number of instruments that may be sounding simultaneously in different registers, the symphony orchestra has a thicker texture than the string quartet, for example, which consists of only four instruments.

Spacing of Tones   When voice parts or the tones of a chord are closely spaced, the result is apt to be a thick texture; when tones are widely spaced, the texture is apt to be thin.

Register of Tones   A thin texture is likely to result from music in which a high register predominates and a thick texture from music in which a low register predominates.

Timbre   Tone quality, or *timbre*, also affects texture. A quartet of flutes has a thinner sound than four horns. An extreme contrast of textural sonority can be observed by comparing a flute solo with a complex chord sounded by a full symphony orchestra. In the flute solo, we hear only a thin sound; in the symphonic chord, we hear a rich sound resulting from multiple timbres, a large number of tones, high and low registers, and a close spacing of tones throughout the entire orchestral register.

TEXTURAL VARIETY

The two categories of texture—(1) its classification into monophonic, homophonic, and polyphonic and (2) its relative thickness or thinness—operate independently of each other. That is to say, heavy textures may be found in homophonic and polyphonic music (but not in monophonic music, which is always thin in texture); and light, thin textures exist in all three types of music.

A single composition does not necessarily remain consistently in only one kind of texture. The texture may shift from a rich, heavy texture to a thin, clear one; moreover, it may change in any sequential order from one of the principal types of texture to another. A good example of this is the "Hallelujah" Chorus from Handel's *Messiah*, which changes constantly among monophonic, homophonic, and polyphonic textures.

*O*f *the three types of texture presented in this chapter, one or the other has usually predominated during a given period in the history of Western art music. During the early Middle Ages, music was largely monophonic. Polyphony emerged in the late ninth century, gradually becoming the predominant texture. After 1750 homophony gained the upper hand, though polyphony has also continued to be important.*

For Additional Study

Downey, Juan. Bachdisc. Distributed by Voyager Company (Santa Monica, CA). Videodisc. (Good introduction to polyphonic texture)

Kamien, Roger. *Music: An Appreciation*. 4th ed. New York: McGraw-Hill. 1988. (Pages 73–74 contain a good explanation of the various textures used in the "Hallelujah" Chorus from Handel's Messiah.)

The University of Delaware Videodisc Music Series. Distributed by the University of Delaware (Newark, DE). Interactive videodiscs. (Brahms's *Schaffe in Mir, Gott* is a good introduction to texture in general.)

Recommended Listening

MONOPHONIC TEXTURE:

Bach, J. S. *Suite No. 1 in G Major for Violoncello Solo*, BWV 1007: Minuets I and II
Debussy, Claude. *Syrinx* (solo flute)
Gregorian chant. Any example

HOMOPHONIC TEXTURE:

Chopin, Frédéric. *Nocturne in E-flat Major*, Op. 9, No. 2 (piano)
___. *Prelude in E Minor*, Op. 28, No. 4 (piano)
Grieg, Edvard. *From Holberg's Time,* Op. 40 (suite for piano or strings): "Air"
Handel, George Frideric. *Largo* ("Ombra mai fù," from the opera Serse)
Puccini, Giacomo. *La bohème* (opera): "Mi chiamano Mimi"
Satie, Erik. *Trois Gymnopédies* (Three Gymnopédies, piano or orchestra)

POLYPHONIC TEXTURE:

Bach, J. S. *Die Kunst der Fuge* (The Art of Fugue), BWV 1080
___. Cantata No. 140, *Wachet auf, ruft uns die Stimme*, BWV 140: "Wachet auf" (opening chorus); "Wenn kommst du" (duet for soprano and bass)
___. *The Well-Tempered Clavier* (harpsichord or piano): any of the 48 fugues in Vol. I or II
___. Two-Part *Inventions*, BWV 772–86 (harpsichord or piano)
Handel, George Frideric. *Messiah* (oratorio): "For unto Us a Child," "And with His Stripes"
Hindemith, Paul. *Ludus tonalis* (piano)
Palestrina, Giovanni Pierluigi da. *Missa Papae Marcelli* (a cappella choir)

TEXTURAL VARIETY:

Handel, George Frideric. *Messiah* (oratorio): "Hallelujah" Chorus

8

Musical Form

*T*he word form is used in music in both a general sense and a specific
sense. In its general sense, form refers to the overall organization of musical
elements within a composition and includes such elements as the
composition's external shape or outline, its internal structure, and the ways
in which its various parts fit together to create a unified whole. When we
speak of form in music or we say that a piece of music has form, we use the
term in this sense. The term may also denote a specific type of form, i.e., a
certain standardized formal pattern. When we say that a piece is in binary
form or rondo form, for example, we use the term in this more specific sense.

This chapter explores principles and characteristics of form in general
and introduces standard small forms.

PRINCIPLES AND ELEMENTS
OF MUSICAL FORM

Unity and Variety

A fundamental principle that underlies form in all the Western arts is the
balance between unity and variety. In music these are achieved by repetition,
contrast, and variation.

REPETITION

Unity in music is created by repetition. Repetition of musical ideas helps
us to remember them, establishes them in our minds as significant, and
contributes to the coherence of the form.

CONTRAST

Since incessant repetition would bore us, however, we also need variety to sustain our interest. Variety in music is provided by contrast. Whether the contrast is great or small, whether it results from the appearance of a new theme, a change of key or a different tempo, register, tone color, texture, meter, rhythmic pattern or dynamic level, it helps satisfy our need for change.

VARIATION

Midway between repetition and contrast is variation, the reappearance of a musical idea in an altered, but still recognizable, form. Variation combines unity and variety.

Inner Form and Outer Form

Repetition, contrast, and variation combine to give a piece of music "form" in its general sense; we may refer to this as the "inner form" of music. On the other hand, the specific external shapes or outlines that themes, sections or the composition as a whole exhibit make up its "outer form." Sometimes elements of the outer form of a composition are highly individualistic. Just as frequently, though, they may exhibit centuries-old standardized patterns that are familiar enough to give the listener a recognizable structure to hang on to yet general enough to allow the composer room for personal expression and adaptation. Several of these standardized patterns are introduced later in this chapter.

Motive and Phrase

Two of the most basic building blocks of inner form and outer form are the motive and the phrase. In chapter 5 a motive was described as a fragmentary musical idea, as opposed to a phrase, which is a more or less complete idea. A motive can be used as a segment of a phrase or, as William S. Newman has pointed out (in *Understanding Music*), motives and phrases can be used as completely separate entities, capable of producing vastly different types of musical structures.

Whenever the repetition, development or especially the imitation of a motive is a composer's main goal, *polyphonic* texture and forms tend to result. On the other hand, whenever a composer uses the phrase as the basic formal unit and proceeds to build a piece by joining together phrases into larger units, *homophonic* texture and forms tend to result. Typical forms resulting from these two processes are listed in figure 8.1.

TYPICAL POLYPHONIC FORMS PRODUCED BY THE IMITATION OF MOTIVES	TYPICAL HOMOPHONIC FORMS PRODUCED BY THE JOINING OF PHRASES
motet, madrigal, ricercar, fugue, invention, and canon	period, binary and ternary form, free part form, compound binary and ternary form, rondo form, and main theme areas of sonata allegro form

Fig 8.1

The history of Western music from the tenth century to c. 1900 divides roughly into two large eras: the "polyphonic age" (c. 900–1750), during which polyphonic texture and forms predominated, and the "homophonic age" (1750–c. 1900), during which homophonic texture and forms predominated. As an introduction to the latter, the remainder of this chapter will focus on common small homophonic forms.

SMALL HOMOPHONIC FORMS

Period

Phrases may be combined in various ways to form larger formal units, the most common of which is the *period*. A period may be defined as a two-phrase unit in which the two phrases stand in a "question" and "answer" relationship, normally with the first (the *antecedent*) ending in an incomplete cadence and the second (the *consequent*) ending in an authentic cadence:

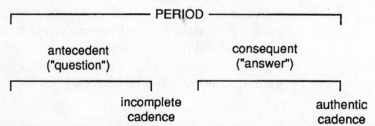

The first two phrases of "Twinkle, Twinkle, Little Star" (shown in musical notation in figure 6.14) illustrate this form:

antecedent: Twinkle, twinkle, little star;   ("question")
consequent: How I wonder what you are.   ("answer")

Other types of two-phrase units and combinations involving three, four or more phrases are also seen.

Strophic Form

A song containing two or more verses, each of which is set to the same music, is said to be in *strophic form*. Many hymns, Christmas carols, popular songs, and folk songs are in strophic form.

Two-Part (Binary) Form

A piece of music that consists of two main sections is considered to be in *binary form*. There are several possibilities within this one concept.

First, the form may consist of two sections of essentially the same material, the second being a modified repetition of the first. This form may be represented by the letters A A′. (The sign ′ designates modification of the same theme.)

Second, the sections may consist of essentially different thematic material, in which case the structure is represented by the formula A B. Without changing the essential binary form of the piece, either or both of these sections may be repeated with or without modification: A A B (called *barform*), A A′ B, A B B, A B B′, A A B B or A A′ B B′.

Each of the sections is usually at least two phrases in length, and one section may be longer than the other. In art music, binary form is associated most closely with the Baroque period (1600–1750), during which it was the normal form for dance movements in suites. (The specific characteristics of Baroque binary form are discussed in chapter 17.) Binary form is also used frequently for folk and popular songs, such as "Auld Lang Syne":

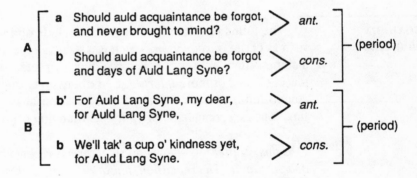

Three-Part (Ternary) Form

A composition in *ternary form* consists of *three* main sections, forming a pattern of statement (A), departure (B), and return (A). The return of the first section may be literal (A B A) or modified (A B A′).

The B section provides a contrast to the first A section, and it usually ends on a V (*dominant*) chord or other incomplete cadence to create a demand for the return of A. The amount of contrast between the A and B sections may vary from slight to extreme.

As in binary form, the A section in ternary form is usually at least two phrases in length, but the B section may range from a single phrase to longer segments. As with binary form, too, various repetitions of patterns may occur, the most common of which are A A B A (called *song form*) and A A B A B A. Song form is particularly common in popular and rock songs, which frequently have two verses set to the same music (A A), a contrasting section (B, known as a *bridge*), and a third verse (A), set to the music of the first verse.

Because of the symmetry inherent in the A B A pattern, ternary form is the most common musical form of all, used for folk and popular songs, art songs and arias, short instrumental compositions and themes of larger works, and, on a larger scale, for the da capo aria, minuet and trio, and other forms. A simple example of ternary form is "Twinkle, Twinkle, Little Star":

A	**a** **b**	Twinkle, twinkle, little star; How I wonder what you are,	*ant.* *cons.*	(period)
B	**c** **c**	Up above the world so high, Like a diamond in the sky!		(repeated phrase)
A	**a** **b**	Twinkle, twinkle, little star; How I wonder what you are.	*ant.* *cons.*	(period)

Auxiliary Elements

The forms just described may also include optional auxiliary elements, such as (1) an *introduction*, which is a section appearing at the beginning of a composition and serving as a prologue or preface to the main part of the piece; (2) one or more *interludes*, or digressions from the main ideas of the composition; and (3) a *coda*, a brief section at the end of the piece that functions as a conclusion or epilogue, rounding off the form.

As this chapter has shown, musical form is created by repetition, contrast, and variation. The repetition, imitation or development of motives tends to result in polyphonic forms, while the joining of phrases into larger units tends to result in homophonic forms. Small homophonic forms include such structural units as the period, strophic form, two-part (binary) form, and three-part (ternary) form. Larger homophonic forms and polyphonic forms will be discussed as they arise in Part Two.

For Additional Study

Berry, Wallace. *Form in Music.* 2d ed. Englewood Cliffs, NJ: Prentice-Hall. 1986.
Newman, William S. *Understanding Music.* 2d ed. New York: Harper & Row. 1961.

Recommended Listening

STROPHIC FORM:

Lennon, John, and Paul McCartney. *Day Tripper*
Schubert, Franz. *An Sylvia (Who Is Sylvia?)*, D. 891; *Heidenröslein* (Little Heath Rose), D. 257 (songs)

SMALL TWO-PART (BINARY) FORM:

Familiar songs and hymns:
Autry, Gene, and Dakley Haldeman. *Here Comes Santa Claus* (aa′ bb′ = A B)
Bates, K. L., and S. A. Ward. *America, the Beautiful* (aa′ bc = A B)
Lennon, John, and Paul McCartney. *All My Loving* (barform: A A B)
Traditional. *America* (A B); *Greensleeves* (aa′ bb′ = A B)
Bach, J. S. *French Suite No. 1*, BWV 812: "Sarabande," "Minuet I" (both A B)
Brahms, Johannes. *Wiegenlied* (Lullaby; aa′ bb′ = A B)
Purcell, Henry. *Dido and Aeneas* (opera): "Dido's Lament" (barform: A A B)

SMALL THREE-PART (TERNARY) FORM:

Brahms, Johannes. *Waltz in A-flat Major*, Op. 39, No. 15 (piano; A A B A′ B A′)
Chopin, Frédéric. *Mazurka 24 in C Major,* Op. 33, No. 3 (piano; A B A)
___. *Nocturne in E-flat Major*, Op. 9, No. 2 (piano; A A B A B A coda)
Grieg, Edvard. *From Holberg's Time*, Op. 40 (suite for piano or strings): "Air" (A A B A B A)

SONG FORM (ALL A A B A UNLESS OTHERWISE NOTED):

Familiar Songs:
Foster, Stephen C. *Old Folks at Home*
Gillespie, Haven, and J. Fred Coots. *Santa Claus Is Comin' to Town*
Harburg, E. Y., and Harold Arlen. *Over the Rainbow*
Lennon, John, and Paul McCartney. *And I Love Her*, *Blackbird*, *Eight Days a Week*, *A Hard Day's Night*, *Yesterday*
Traditional:
Deck the Hall (A A B A′); *Marine's Hymn*; *O Christmas Tree*
Brahms, Johannes. *Hungarian Dance No. 7* (piano)
Chopin, Frédéric. *Mazurka in A Minor*, Op. 17, No. 4 (piano): mm. 1–60 (introduction A A′ B A′)
Schubert, Franz. *Der Lindenbaum* (The Linden Tree, a song) (A A′ B A)

9

Musical Mediums: Voices

A musical medium is the intermediate agent between the composer's ideas on the printed page and their realization in actual musical sound. In other words, performers translate the written symbols into physical tone through the medium of one or more voices or instruments.

The human voice was perhaps the first musical medium, and it remains the most basic one. Because the voice emanates from the singer's body rather than from an external source, and because singing combines words and music, vocal music possesses an unsurpassed naturalness of expression, directness of communication, subtlety of emotional and musical shading, and general "human" quality. Vocal music was predominant in Western culture until the late seventeenth century, and even though instrumental music has come to equal it in importance, it retains a special place in the hearts of listeners.

Methods of singing vary widely from culture to culture, and, even within our own culture, there are great differences—for example, the difference in tone quality between rock singers and opera singers, or even between two different rock (or opera) singers. Every style of singing—folk, country, jazz, gospel, rock, classical or other—has its own standards and conventions; true appreciation of these styles comes from attempting to understand each on its own terms.

This chapter focuses on the main vocal classifications and mediums encountered in Western art music.

VOICE CLASSIFICATIONS

In jazz, folk, and popular music, voices are generally classified only as male or female, whereas in art music they are further classified by register and quality.

Vocal Registers

Male and female voices are generally divided into high, medium, and low registers, with each male register lying approximately an octave below the corresponding female register:

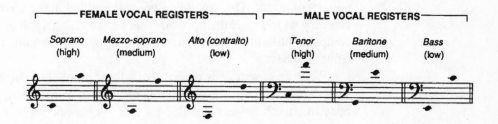

Fig 9.1

Vocal Qualities

Besides being divided into these six vocal registers, voices in art music are classified also according to certain styles of music for which they are specially qualified. The *coloratura soprano* can sing particularly high notes, rapid runs, trills, and light ornaments. The *dramatic soprano* and *dramatic* (or heroic) *tenor* have heavier voices and are capable of conveying intense emotions in dramatic situations. The *lyric soprano* and *lyric tenor* have voices especially suited to sweet, songlike melody in which beauty of tone is the predominant quality. A bass singer with a particularly strong low register is known as a *basso profundo*, while one specializing in comic roles is sometimes referred to as a *basso buffo*.

Lower voice registers, such as alto and bass, generally have a darker, richer "chest" sound than higher registers.

VOCAL MEDIUMS

Vocal mediums comprise solos and ensembles.

Vocal Solo

A large share of the Western world's great music is composed for solo singer, either with or without accompaniment. Such musical forms as the aria, Lied, folk song, troubadour song, and dramatic recitative are vocal solos.

Vocal Ensemble

When two or more voices are involved, the medium is called a *vocal ensemble*. An ensemble may consist of parts for two voices (*duet* or *duo*), three voices (*trio*), four voices (*quartet*), five voices (*quintet*), six voices (*sextet*) or more. The individual voice types that make up these ensembles can vary widely, and the only one that has anything approaching a standard complement is the vocal quartet, which typically contains a soprano, alto, tenor, and bass.

When an ensemble is made up of a large number of singers with several singers on each part, the medium is referred to as a *chorus*. A comparable body of church singers is called a *choir*. A chorus or choir may consist of male voices, female voices or a combination of both (called a *mixed chorus*). When two complete choruses (or choirs) are employed, the medium is referred to as a *double chorus*. (The opening chorus of J. S. Bach's *St. Matthew Passion* is for double chorus.) The term *a cappella* refers to a chorus without instrumental accompaniment.

In past centuries, boys with unchanged voices and adult males with soprano- or alto-range voices often sang the soprano and alto parts. An adult male capable of singing unusually high parts, either naturally or through the technique of falsetto, is referred to as a *countertenor*.

The voice classifications and vocal mediums presented in this chapter are the principal types encountered in Western art music. More specialized types will be introduced as they arise in Part Two.

For Additional Study

Stevens, Denis, ed. *A History of Song*. Rev. ed. New York: Norton. 1970.
The Chorus: A Union of Voices. Distributed by Educational Audio Visual, Inc. (Pleasantville, NY). Videocassette.
Voice: The Universal Instrument. Distributed by Educational Audio Visual, Inc. (Pleasantville, NY). Videocassette.

Recommended Listening

VOCAL SOLO

Coloratura Soprano:
Delibes, Léo. *Lakmé* (opera): "Bell Song"
Donizetti, Gaetano. *Lucia di Lammermoor* (opera): "Mad Scene"
Mozart, W. A. *The Magic Flute* (opera): "Queen of the Night" aria
Dramatic Soprano:
Puccini, Giacomo. *Tosca* (opera): "Vissi d'arte"
Verdi, Giuseppe. *Aïda* (opera): "O patria mia"
Wagner, Richard. *Die Götterdämmerung* (The Twilight of the Gods, opera): "Brünnhilde's Immolation"
Lyric Soprano:
Puccini, Giacomo. *La bohème* (opera): Mi chiamano Mimi," "Quando m'en vo' "
Mezzo-soprano:
Bizet, Georges. *Carmen* (opera): "Habanera" ("L'amour est un oiseau rebelle"), "Séguidille" ("Près des remparts")
Saint-Saëns, Camille. *Samson et Dalila* (Samson and Delilah, opera): "Amour, viens aider," "Mon coeur s'ouvre à ta voix"
Alto (Contralto):
Brahms, Johannes. *Alto Rhapsody*, Op. 53 (alto, male chorus, and orchestra)
Handel, George Frideric. *Messiah* (oratorio): "Then Shall the Eyes of the Blind" (recitative), "He Shall Feed His Flock" (aria)
Lyric Tenor:
Donizetti, Gaetano. *L'elisir d'amore* (The Elixir of Love, opera): "Una furtiva lagrima" (A Furtive Tear)
Handel, George Frideric. *Messiah* (oratorio): "Comfort ye" (recitative), "Every Valley" (aria)
Puccini, Giacomo. *La bohème* (opera): "Che gelida manina"
Dramatic Tenor:
Leoncavallo, Ruggiero. *I pagliacci* (The Clowns, opera): "Vesti la giubba"
Puccini, Giacomo. *Tosca* (opera): "E lucevan le stelle"
Wagner, Richard. *Lohengrin* (opera): "In fernem Land"
Baritone:
Bizet, Georges. *Carmen* (opera): "Toréador en garde" ("Toreador Song")
Rossini, Gioacchino. *Il barbiere di Siviglia* (The Barber of Seville, opera): "Largo al factotum"
Bass:
Handel, George Frideric. *Messiah* (oratorio): "The People That Walked in Darkness," "Thus Saith the Lord," "But Who May Abide"
Mozart, W. A. *Don Giovanni* (opera): "Madamina!" ("Catalog Aria")

VOCAL ENSEMBLE

In this list the following letters indicate the voices: S (soprano), mS (mezzo-soprano), A (alto), T (tenor), and B (baritone or bass)
Duet:
Verdi, Giuseppe. *Aïda* (opera): "O terra,addio" (ST)
Wagner, Richard. *Tristan und Isolde* (opera), Act 2: "Love Duet" (ST)

Trio:

Mozart, W. A. *Don Giovanni* (opera): End of Act 2 finale (BBB: Don Giovanni, Commendatore, Leporello)

Verdi, Giuseppe. *Requiem*: "Lux æterna" (mS T B), "Quid sum miser" (SmST)

Quartet:

Beethoven, Ludwig van. *Symphony No. 9 in D Minor* ("Choral"), Op. 125, IV: "Seid umschlungen, Millionen" (O ye millions; with chorus)

Mozart, W. A. *Requiem*, K. 626: "Tuba mirum," "Benedictus" (SATB)

Quintet:

Bizet, Georges. *Carmen* (opera): "Nous avons en tête une affaire" (SmSSTT)

Mozart, W. A. *The Magic Flute* (opera): "Hm! Hm! Hm!" (SSATB)

Sextet:

Donizetti, Gaetano. *Lucia di Lammermoor* (opera): "Sextet" (SmSTTBB)

Male Chorus:

Brahms, Johannes. *Alto Rhapsody*, Op. 53 (alto, male chorus, orchestra)

Female Chorus:

Brahms, Johannes. *Part Songs for Women's Voices*, Op. 17

Debussy, Claude. *Nocturnes*: "Sirènes" (orchestra and female chorus without text)

A Cappella Chorus:

Palestrina, Giovanni Pierluigi da. *Missa Papae Marcelli*

Mixed Chorus:

Bach, J. S. *Mass in B Minor*, BWV 232: "Kyrie," "Sanctus," "Dona nobis pacem"

Beethoven, Ludwig van. *Symphony No. 9 in D Minor* ("Choral"), Op. 125: IV

Brahms, Johannes. *Ein deutsches Requiem* (A German Requiem), Op. 45: "How Lovely is Thy Dwelling Place" ("Wie lieblich sind deine Wohnungen")

Handel, George Frideric. *Messiah* (oratorio): "Hallelujah" Chorus, "And the Glory of the Lord," "For unto Us a Child Is Born," "And with His Stripes We are Healed"

Mozart, W. A. *Requiem*, K. 626

Verdi, Giuseppe. *Requiem*: "Dies irae," "Sanctus" (double chorus)

10

Musical Mediums: Instruments

*T*here are six main categories of musical instruments: (1) string instruments, (2) woodwind instruments, (3) brass instruments, (4) percussion
instruments, (5) keyboard instruments, and (6) electronic instruments. (For
the purposes of this discussion, keyboard instruments are considered as a
separate class, even though several of them produce tone through the
vibration of strings.)

This chapter introduces the principal instruments within each of these
six categories and gives a survey of the main types of instrumental mediums.

CATEGORIES OF INSTRUMENTS

**String
Instruments**

String instruments, also called *stringed instruments*, produce tone
through the vibration of stretched strings. There are two types of string
instruments: (1) *bowed strings* and (2) *plucked strings*.

BOWED STRINGS

Bowed string instruments produce tone primarily by means of a bow
drawn across the strings. Instruments in this category usually have several
strings tuned to different pitches, and further differences of pitch are obtained
by pressing the strings against a fingerboard at different points along their
length. The four principal instruments in this category are the violin, viola,
violoncello (or simply cello), and string bass (or double bass):

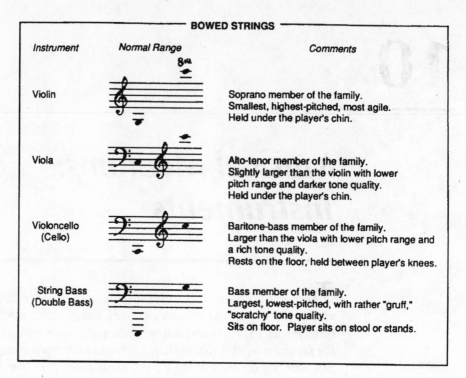

Fig 10.1

Because of their warm tone quality, the beautiful way in which their separate sounds blend, and their ability to play anything from slow, singing melodies to fast, technical passages, the bowed strings are among the most versatile of instruments, and they constitute the backbone of the orchestra. In addition, they are able to produce a wide variety of special effects: (1) *Pizzicato*—the technique of plucking a string instead of bowing it; (2) *Multiple stopping*—the production of intervals or chords by bowing on two (double stopping), three (triple stopping) or four (quadruple stopping) strings simultaneously; (3) *Muted (con sordino)*—the use of an attachment called a mute to produce a muffled, veiled sound; (4) *Tremolo*—an effect produced either by the rapid movement of the bow back and forth in short strokes across the string or by the rapid alternation between two tones on one string; (5) *Harmonics*—high, thin, almost flutelike tones produced by lightly touching the strings with the fingers of the left hand instead of pressing the string down firmly while bowing or plucking; (6) *Sul ponticello*—the act of bowing near the bridge of the instrument to produce a metallic, "ghostly" tone; (7) *Glissando*—an effect produced by sliding the finger along the string from one pitch to another; (8) *Col legno*—the technique of striking the string with the wood of the bow.

PLUCKED STRINGS

Although instruments of the bowed-string class can produce tone through the plucking of strings (pizzicato), plucked string instruments produce tone solely by this means. The player plucks the strings either with the finger or with a plectrum held in the hand. The three principal instruments in this category are the harp, lute, and guitar.

Harp. The harp is one of the oldest instruments still in use and the only plucked string instrument normally included in the orchestra. Each of its strings produces a different letter-name pitch (comparable to the white keys on a piano); pedals at the base of the instrument make it possible to raise or lower each pitch a half step.

Lute. A variety of plucked string instruments belong to the lute family. Lutes have pear-shaped bodies and flat necks. Although the instrument dates far back into pre-Christian times and is now not commonly used, music for the lute constitutes an important segment of sixteenth- and seventeenth-century musical literature.

Guitar. Instruments in the guitar family resemble the lute except that the guitar has a flat back and a "waist" shaped like that of a violin. Although the guitar today is associated most closely with folk and popular music, its history and literature have made their contributions to art music also, especially to that of Spain in the sixteenth century.

Others. Other plucked string instruments include the ukulele (Hawaiian), the banjo (African-American), the mandolin, and numerous exotic and ancient instruments of the same general type.

Woodwind Instruments

Tone on a woodwind instrument is produced when the air column inside the instrument is set into motion by air blown across a mouth hole (the flute and piccolo) or through a single reed (the clarinet and saxophone) or a double reed (the oboe, English horn, bassoon, and contrabassoon). By using the fingers and a key mechanism to open or close small holes along the side of the instrument, the player can produce higher or lower pitches. Unlike bowed strings, which have very similar tone qualities, each woodwind instrument has its own distinctive tone quality.

Figure 10.2 lists the woodwind instruments of the orchestra, arranged from highest to lowest in pitch register.

Another familiar woodwind instrument is the saxophone, which comes in several sizes and ranges (e.g., B-flat soprano saxophone, E-flat alto saxophone, B-flat tenor saxophone, E-flat baritone saxophone, and B-flat bass saxophone). Invented in 1840 by Adolphe Sax, it is a single reed woodwind instrument with a brass body. Though most closely associated with jazz and rock music, it is used also in concert and marching bands, in chamber ensembles, as a solo instrument, and occasionally in orchestras.

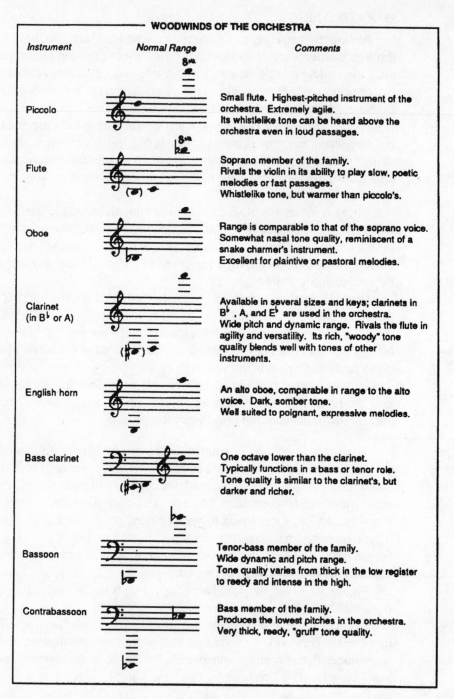

WOODWINDS OF THE ORCHESTRA

Instrument	Normal Range	Comments

Piccolo — Small flute. Highest-pitched instrument of the orchestra. Extremely agile.
Its whistlelike tone can be heard above the orchestra even in loud passages.

Flute — Soprano member of the family.
Rivals the violin in its ability to play slow, poetic melodies or fast passages.
Whistlelike tone, but warmer than piccolo's.

Oboe — Range is comparable to that of the soprano voice.
Somewhat nasal tone quality, reminiscent of a snake charmer's instrument.
Excellent for plaintive or pastoral melodies.

Clarinet (in B♭ or A) — Available in several sizes and keys; clarinets in B♭, A, and E♭ are used in the orchestra.
Wide pitch and dynamic range. Rivals the flute in agility and versatility. Its rich, "woody" tone quality blends well with tones of other instruments.

English horn — An alto oboe, comparable in range to the alto voice. Dark, somber tone.
Well suited to poignant, expressive melodies.

Bass clarinet — One octave lower than the clarinet.
Typically functions in a bass or tenor role.
Tone quality is similar to the clarinet's, but darker and richer.

Bassoon — Tenor-bass member of the family.
Wide dynamic and pitch range.
Tone quality varies from thick in the low register to reedy and intense in the high.

Contrabassoon — Bass member of the family.
Produces the lowest pitches in the orchestra.
Very thick, reedy, "gruff" tone quality.

Fig 10.2

Brass Instruments

Tone on a brass instrument is created when the player presses his or her lips into a cup- or funnel-shaped mouthpiece and vibrates them by blowing air through them. Change of pitch is effected both by variation in lip tension and by the manipulation of a slide (trombone) or valves (the other brasses). The characteristic tone quality of each brass instrument can be varied by inserting devices known as *mutes* (or, in the case of the French horn, also the hand) into the opening of the bell. Mutes also soften the dynamics of the instrument somewhat.

There are a great many instruments of this class, both ancient and modern. Figure 10.3 lists the four principal brass instruments of the orchestra from highest to lowest in pitch register.

Other common brass instruments include the cornet and flügelhorn, which are similar to the trumpet but have a mellower tone quality; the baritone horn and euphonium, which are small tubas; and the sousaphone, a coiled tuba used for marching bands.

Percussion Instruments

Percussion instruments, which have primarily rhythmic functions, are characterized by the performer's having to strike, rub, or shake the instrument to produce the tone or sound. Certain keyboard instruments such as the piano are excluded from the present classification, although they are often grouped with percussion instruments in the orchestral score. Percussion instruments are divided into two groups: (1) instruments of definite pitch and (2) instruments of indefinite pitch.

DEFINITE-PITCH INSTRUMENTS

The principal percussion instruments of definite pitch are the timpani (or kettledrums), bells (or glockenspiel), xylophone, celesta, marimba, vibraphone, and chimes. In ensembles, they have melodic as well as rhythmic functions.

INDEFINITE-PITCH INSTRUMENTS

The chief percussion instruments in this class are the snare drum (or side drum), bass drum, tambourine, cymbals, gong (or tam-tam), castanets, and maracas (rattle). A drum set (or trap set) is an arrangement of various indefinite-pitch percussion instruments, playable by a single performer, which consists typically of a pedal-operated bass drum, snare drum, tom-tom and other drums, a pair of pedal-operated cymbals called a *hi-hat*, and several suspended cymbals. The use of drum sets is particularly common in jazz and rock music.

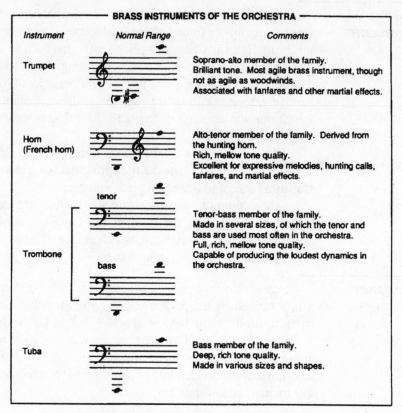

Fig 10.3

Keyboard Instruments

Instruments in this category are operated by means of a keyboard, which consists of a series of black and white keys. On all keyboard instruments a tone is produced when the performer depresses a key, but the precise way in which the key produces a tone varies from one instrument to another.

Keyboard instruments are both melodic and harmonic; thus, they can play a melody and its accompaniment at the same time. The three principal keyboard instruments are the piano, the harpsichord, and the organ.

PIANO

The piano came into prominence during the late eighteenth century. This instrument produces a tone by means of a felt hammer that strikes one or more strings when a key is depressed. The piano is capable of sustaining tone to a limited extent, and it can produce a wide range of dynamics and musical effects. In the twentieth century, several composers have experimented with the placement of metal, rubber, and other foreign objects among the strings of the piano to produce unusual timbres; this effect is known as *prepared piano*.

HARPSICHORD

An important instrument of the sixteenth, seventeenth, and eighteenth centuries was the harpsichord, which produces tone by means of strings that are plucked (by a mechanism called a *plectrum*) when a key is depressed. The harpsichord is incapable of accent or shaded dynamics, but its tone is clear and brilliant with a pleasantly "twangy" quality. Because its tones cannot be sustained very long, music for harpsichord typically contains many fast scales, arpeggios, trills, and other embellishments.

ORGAN

The organ has a history dating back to pre-Christian times. Its tones are produced when keys are depressed, releasing air into pipes of different lengths. An organ may have several keyboards (called *manuals*) as well as a pedalboard, which the player presses with the feet. Sets of pipes, differing in size, shape, and material, give the organ a vast range of pitch and color, and what is called a *swell pedal* makes possible gradual changes in dynamics. The organ is capable of sustaining tones indefinitely.

OTHER KEYBOARD INSTRUMENTS

Among other instruments that are played by means of a keyboard, several may be mentioned. The piano accordion has a melody keyboard for the right hand. The celesta, usually classified as a percussion instrument (see above), produces a bell-like tone by means of hammers that strike steel bars. The clavichord, which flourished from about 1400 to 1800, has a tone that is produced by brass wedges that strike the strings when the keys are depressed. It does not have the volume or flexibility of tone of the harpsichord, but it can produce subtle gradations of tone and mild accents. Because of its limited volume of tone, the clavichord was intended for use in a small room rather than a large hall.

Electronic Instruments

An electronic instrument is one on which sound is produced or amplified by electronic means. Perhaps the simplest instruments in this category are electronically amplified conventional instruments, such as the electric guitar, bass guitar, and steel guitar. These instruments also often employ various sound-altering devices, such as wah-wah, distortion, and reverberation units, making possible many new effects not available on their purely acoustical counterparts.

EARLY ELECTRONIC INSTRUMENTS

Early attempts at producing sound directly by electronic means resulted in the development of a class of electronic instruments that produce tones by oscillation through vacuum tubes. Instruments of this class, most of them operated by keyboard, include such devices as the theremin (or aetherophone), ondes martenot, trautonium, Hammond organ, Baldwin electronic organ, Novachord, and Solovox, several of which are now obsolete.

TAPE RECORDER

Shortly before 1950, the tape recorder became a means of creating music. Tape recorder music employs several techniques. Conventional media, both vocal and instrumental, as well as unconventional media and natural sounds can be recorded on electromagnetic tape and then distorted by reversing the direction of the tape, altering the speed (thus changing the pitch level), splicing sections of the tape, and combining different recordings simultaneously. The composer creates his or her compositions directly onto the tape. Tape recorder technique may also be combined with synthesizer and computer techniques.

ELECTRONIC SYNTHESIZER

The production of sound by electronic means entered a new age with the appearance of the synthesizer. Introduced in the 1950s, the synthesizer has evolved through several stages to its present form, a highly efficient, compact, and economical instrument based upon digital (i.e., computer) technology that is capable of generating virtually any sound imaginable, from those of nature or of conventional instruments (through a process called *sampling*) to the most unique, "space age" sounds.

Although the most common types of synthesizers used today are operated by keyboard, digital technology has been applied to other instruments as well. Of these, the drum machine has been the most successful and widely used, although advances continue to be made in the areas of guitar synthesizers, wind controllers (i.e., wind instrument synthesizers), and even voice controllers (i.e., voice-activated synthesizers).

The development of synthesizer technology has been facilitated greatly by the industry-wide adoption of MIDI (Musical Instrument Digital Interface) as a standard language for digitizing music and for enabling different kinds (and different brands) of computers and synthesizers to be coupled to each other. Rock musicians especially have been quick to exploit this technology, using synthesizers both to duplicate conventional instrumental timbres and to create new sounds.

Instrumental Mediums

Instrumental Solo

A large body of music exists for *solo*, or single, instruments. Although the piano and other keyboard instruments are particularly favored, solo literature has been written for virtually all the other instruments as well.

Chamber Ensembles

Chamber music, a medium that calls for only a few performers, is usually played with one performer to a part. Music in which two instruments have equal importance is called a *duo*; music for three instruments is a *trio*; for four, a *quartet*; for five, a *quintet*; for six, a *sextet*; for seven, a *septet*; for eight, an *octet*; for nine, a *nonet*. These ensembles may consist of any combination of instruments. The most common chamber music ensembles are listed below.

COMMON CHAMBER ENSEMBLES

Duo sonata	any solo instrument plus piano or other accompaniment
Piano trio	piano, violin, cello
String trio	violin, viola, cello or 2 violins and cello
String quartet	2 violins, viola, cello
Piano quartet	piano, violin, viola, cello
String quintet	string quartet plus another viola or cello
Piano quintet	piano plus string quartet
Woodwind quintet	flute, oboe, clarinet, French horn, bassoon
Brass quintet	2 trumpets, horn, trombone, tuba (or bass trombone)

Fig 10.4

Chamber Orchestra and Chamber Winds

The terms *chamber orchestra* and *chamber winds* are applied to small instrumental ensembles in which there are only a few performers to a part. These ensembles fall midway between chamber ensembles and large ensembles.

Large Ensembles

The two main types of large ensemble are the *orchestra* and the *band*.

ORCHESTRA

An orchestra is any sizable group of instrumental performers, usually including strings plus woodwind, brass, and percussion as needed. In the orchestral ensemble, several string instruments of the same kind normally play the same part, whereas woodwind, brass, and percussion players all play separate parts. An orchestra may vary in size from a relatively small group (see chamber orchestra above) to an ensemble of a hundred players or more. A typical *symphony orchestra* complement is as follows:

STRINGS: 8-18 first violins, 6–16 second violins, 4–12 violas, 6–12 cellos, 3–10 string basses, and 1–2 harps

WOODWINDS: 2–4 flutes (including 1 piccolo), 2–4 oboes (including 1 English horn), 2–4 clarinets (including 1 bass clarinet), 2–4 bassoons (including 1 contrabassoon)

BRASS: 4–6 French horns, 2–4 trumpets, 3 trombones, 1 tuba

PERCUSSION: 2-5 players (including 1 timpani player)

BAND

A band is an instrumental ensemble consisting mainly or exclusively of woodwind, brass, and percussion instruments. The *marching band* is closely associated with outdoor events, such as parades and football games, while the *concert band* (also referred to as a *symphonic band* or *wind ensemble*) performs concert music on the stage.

Mixed Ensembles

A considerable literature of music exists for large mixed ensembles, which include instruments and voices. Such musical types as opera, oratorio, cantata, Mass, and even some symphonies may employ vocal soloists, chorus, and orchestra. Mixed chamber ensembles have become important in the twentieth century (e.g., Schoenberg's *Pierrot* lunaire).

Instrumental Groups in Popular Music

Many types of instrumental ensembles are used in popular music. A few of the most common types are listed below, together with their typical complements.

TYPICAL POPULAR MUSIC ENSEMBLES

Big Band:

Reeds: 2 alto saxophones, 2 tenor saxophones, 1 baritone saxophone.
Some of the saxophone players usually also play clarinet and/or flute
Brass: 3-5 trumpets, 3-5 trombones
Rhythm: piano, string bass, drum set, sometimes guitar

Jazz Combo:

piano, string bass, drum set, and often one or more other instruments
(e.g., trumpet, saxophone, guitar, vibraphone)

Rock Band:

1 or 2 electric guitars, 1 bass guitar, drum set, often 1 or more keyboard
instruments (e.g., electric piano, electric organ or synthesizer), and sometimes
1 or more other instruments (e.g., trumpet, saxophone, trombone or additional
percussion)

Fig 10.5

This chapter has presented the principal musical instruments and instrumental mediums used in Western music. This list is by no means exhaustive, however, and the listener may expect to encounter instruments or mediums not covered in this chapter, particularly in folk and non-Western music. The listener should also regard this information as only a starting point; real understanding of the instruments comes from listening and learning to distinguish each instrument's distinctive tone quality.

For Additional Study

BOOKS:

Baines, Anthony, ed. *Musical Instruments through the Ages*. 2d ed. New York: Walker. 1976.

Marcuse, Sibyl. *A Survey of Musical Instruments.* New York: Harper & Row; Newton Abbot: David & Charles. 1975.

Newquist, H. P. *Music & Technology.* New York: Billboard Books; an imprint of Watson-Guptill Publications. 1989.

Sadie, Stanley, ed. *New Grove Dictionary of Musical Instruments.* 3 vols. London: Macmillan. 1984.

AUDIOVISUALS:

The University of Delaware Videodisc Music Series. Distributed by the University of Delaware (Newark, DE). Interactive videodiscs.

Various titles distributed by Educational Audio Visual, Inc. (Pleasantville, NY): *The Orchestra* (videocassette), *Instruments of the Symphony Orchestra* (2 videocassettes), *Keyboard Instruments* (videocassette), *The Pipe Organ* (audiocassettes and filmstrips), *An Introduction to the Guitar and Lute* (audiocassette and filmstrip), *The Guitar: From Stone Age through Solid Rock* (videocassette), and *An Overview of Electronic Music with Don Muro* (videocassette).

Recommended Listening

GENERAL INTRODUCTIONS TO THE INSTRUMENTS

Britten, Benjamin. *The Young Person's Guide to the Orchestra*
Saint-Saëns, Camille. *The Carnival of the Animals* (orchestra)
The Instruments of the Orchestra (Vangard VSD 721–722)
The Orchestra and Its Instruments (Scholastic FT 3602)

BOWED STRINGS

Violin: Bach, J. S. *Sonatas and Partitas for Solo Violin*, BWV 1001–06
 Jazz violinists: Stuff Smith, Sven Asmunssen, Stephane Grappelli, and Jean-Luc Ponty (all on the album *Violin Summit*)
Viola: Bartók, Béla. *Viola Concerto*
Cello: Bach, J. S. *Six Suites for Solo Violoncello*, BWV 1007–12
Fauré, Gabriel. *Élégie for Cello and Orchestra*, Op. 24
String Bass: Dittersdorf, Karl Ditters von. *Concerto in E for Double Bass*
 Jazz and rock bassists (including electric bass): Jeff Berlin (the album *Road Games* with Allan Holdsworth); Stanley Clarke (the album *Stanley Clarke*); Ron Carter (albums such as *Patrão* and *VSOP, the Quintet/VSOP Live*); Tony Levin (albums such as *So*, with Peter Gabriel, and *Discipline* and *Three of a Perfect Pair* with King Crimson); Charles Mingus (the albums *The Black Saint and the Sinner Lady* and *Mingus at Carnegie Hall*); and Jaco Pastorius (Weather Report albums such as *Night Passage*)

PLUCKED STRINGS

Harp: Mozart, W. A. *Concerto in C for Flute and Harp*, K. 299
Guitar: Rodrigo, Joaquín. *Concierto de Aranjuez* (guitar and orchestra)
 Jazz and rock guitarists (including electric guitar): Al Di Meola, John McLaughlin, and Paco de Lucia (the album *Friday Night in San Francisco*); Edward Van Halen (the albums *Van Halen I* and *Fair Warning*); Jimi Hendrix (the album *Band of Gypsies*); Stanley Jordan (the album *Magic Touch*); Wes Montgomery (the albums *Beginnings* and *Wes and Friends*); Joe Pass (the

albums *Virtuoso* and *Virtuoso 2*); Joe Satriani (the album *Flying in a Blue Dream*); Andy Summers (albums with The Police such as *Reggatta de Blanc* and *Ghost in the Machine*)

WOODWINDS

Piccolo: Sousa, John Philip. *The Stars and Stripes Forever*

Flute: Bach, J. S. *Sonatas for Flute and Harpsichord*, BWV 1030–35

Oboe: Poulenc, Francis. *Sonata for Oboe and Piano*

English Horn: Sibelius, Jean. *The Swan of Tuonela*

Clarinet: Copland, Aaron. *Clarinet Concerto* (clarinet, strings, harp, and piano)
        Mozart, W. A. *Concerto in A Major for Clarinet and Orchestra*, K. 662

Bass Clarinet: Tchaikovsky, P. I. *Nutcracker Suite* (orchestra): "Dance of the Sugar-Plum Fairy"

Bassoon: Hindemith, Paul. *Sonata for Bassoon and Piano*

Contrabassoon: Ravel, Maurice. *Ma mère l'oye* (*Mother Goose Suite*; orchestra): "Beauty and the Beast"

Saxophone: Debussy, Claude. *Rhapsodie for Saxophone and Orchestra*
        Jazz saxophonists: John Coltrane (the albums *Meditations* and *A Love Supreme*); Charlie Parker (the albums *The Savoy Sessions* and *The Definitive Charlie Parker*, Vols. 1–4); David Sanborn (the album *Voyeur*); and various saxophonists (Gerry Mulligan, Ben Webster, Johnny Hodges, Zoot Sims, Stan Getz, Paul Desmond, and others) on the compact disc *The Silver Collection: Gerry Mulligan Meets the Saxophonists*

BRASS

Trumpet: Bach, J. S. *Brandenburg Concerto No. 2 in F Major*, BWV 1047 (solo instruments: high trumpet, recorder, oboe, violin)
        Jazz trumpeters: Louis Armstrong (the compact disc *Great Original Performances*); Clifford Brown (the albums *Study in Brown* and *In Concert* [with Max Roach]); Miles Davis (the albums *Kind of Blue*, *Sketches of Spain*, *Bitches Brew*, and *You're Under Arrest*); Dizzy Gillespie (the albums *In the Beginning*, *The Greatest of Dizzy Gillespie*, and *The Giant*); and Wynton Marsalis (the albums *Think of One*, *Black Codes*, and *J Mood*)
        Kennan, Kent. *Sonata for Trumpet and Piano*

Horn: Mendelssohn, Felix. *A Midsummer Night's Dream* (orchestra): "Nocturne"

Trombone: Rimsky-Korsakov, Nikolay. *Concerto for Trombone and Military Band*

Tuba: Vaughan Williams, Ralph. *Bass Tuba Concerto*

PERCUSSION

Bartók, Béla. *Sonata for Two Pianos and Percussion*
        Jazz and rock drummers (drum set): Ginger Baker (albums with Cream such as *Wheels of Fire* and *Live Cream*); Art Blakey (the albums *Night in Tunisia* and *Free for All*); Bill Bruford (the album *Discipline* with King Crimson); Neil Peart (albums with Rush, such as *Permanent Waves* and *Exit . . .Stage Left*); Max Roach (the albums *Percussion Bittersweet*; *Speak, Brother, Speak*; and *Historic Concerts*); Tony Williams (the album *Foreign Intrigue* and earlier albums with Miles Davis and Lifetime)

Saint-Saëns, Camille. *Danse macabre* (xylophone)

Tchaikovsky, P. I. *Nutcracker Suite* (orchestra): "Dance of the Sugar-Plum Fairy" (celesta)

Varèse, Edgard. *Ionisation* (percussion ensemble)

KEYBOARD

Piano: Cage, John. *Bacchanale* (prepared piano)

Chopin, Frédéric. *Polonaise No. 6 in A-flat Major*, Op. 53

Jazz and rock keyboardists: Tony Banks (albums with Genesis, such as *Duke* and *Abacab*); Bill Evans (the albums *The Village Vanguard Sessions* and *Conversations with Myself*); Herbie Hancock (the album *Future Shock*); Keith Jarrett (the albums *The Köln Concert* and *Standards Live*); Thelonius Monk (the albums *Thelonius Monk with John Coltrane* and *Brilliance*); Oscar Peterson (the albums *In Russia* and *A Salle Pleyel*)

Harpsichord: Bach, J. S. *English Suites*, BWV 806–11; *French Suites*, BWV 812–17

Organ: Bach, J. S. *Toccata and Fugue in D Minor*, BWV 565

ELECTRONIC INSTRUMENTS

Appleton, John. *Syntrophia*

Hammer, Jan. *Miami Vice* soundtrack

Subotnik, Morton. *Silver Apples of the Moon*

CHAMBER ENSEMBLES

Duo: Bartók, Béla. *Duos for Two Violins*

Trio: Beethoven, Ludwig van. *Trio in B-flat Major* ("Archduke"), Op. 97 (piano trio)

Bartók, Béla. *Contrasts* (violin, clarinet, and piano)

Quartet: Haydn, Franz Joseph. *Quartet in C Major*, Op. 76, No. 3 (string quartet)

Kronos Quartet. Albums such as *Winter Was Hard* and *Black Angels*

Quintet: Arnold, Malcolm. *Quintet* (brass quintet)

Ibert, Jacques. *Trois pièces brèves* (woodwind quintet)

Schubert, Franz. *Quintet in A Major*, D. 667 ("Trout," for piano, violin, viola, cello, string bass)

Other : Gabrieli. *Canzonas for Brass Choirs*

Schoenberg, Arnold. *Pierrot lunaire* (voice and chamber ensemble)

Stravinsky, Igor. *L'Histoire du soldat* (The Soldier's Tale, ballet for narrator and 7 instruments)

___. *Octet for WInd Instruments*V

illa-Lobos, Heitor. *Bachiana brasiliera No. 5* (8 cellos and soprano)

ORCHESTRAL ENSEMBLES

String Orchestra: Barber, Samuel. *Adagio for Strings*

Mozart, W. A. *Eine kleine Nachtmusik* (A Little Night Music), K. 525

Penderecki, Krzysztof. *Threnody to the Victims of Hiroshima*

Symphony Orchestra:

Bach, J. S. *Suite No. 3 in D Major*, BWV 1068

Bartók, Béla. *Concerto for Orchestra*

Beethoven, Ludwig van. 9 symphonies

Berlioz, Hector. *Symphonie fantastique* (Fantastic Symphony)

Brahms, Johannes. 4 symphonies; *Academic Festival Overture*, Op. 80

Debussy, Claude. *La Mer* (suite); *Nocturnes* (3 pieces)
Haydn, Franz Joseph. *Symphony No. 104 in D Major* ("London"), H. I/104
Hindemith, Paul. *Mathis der Maler*
Ligeti, György. *Atmosphères*
Mahler, Gustav. *Symphony No. 1 in D Major*; *Symphony No. 5 in C-sharp Minor*
Mendelssohn, Felix. *A Midsummer Night's Dream*
Mozart, W. A. *Symphony No. 40 in G Minor*, K. 550; *Symphony No. 41 in C Major*, K. 551 ("Jupiter")
Prokofiev, Sergey. *Romeo and Juliet* (ballet); *Symphony No. 5*
Ravel, Maurice. Suite No. 2 from *Daphnis et Chloé*; *Bolero*
Rimsky-Korsakov, Nikolay. *Scheherazade* (suite); *Capriccio espagnol*
Schubert, Franz. *Symphony No. 8 in B Minor*, D. 759 ("Unfinished")
Shostakovich, Dmitry. *Symphony No. 5 in D Minor*, Op. 47
Still, William Grant. *Symphony No. 1* ("Afro-American")
Strauss, Richard. *Also sprach Zarathustra*, *Don Quixote*, *Ein Heldenleben*, and *Till Eulenspiegels lustige Streiche* (symphonic poems)
Stravinsky, Igor. *Firebird Suite* (ballet suite); *Petrushka* (ballet suite); *Le sacre du printemps* (The Rite of Spring; a ballet), *Symphony in C*
Tchaikovsky, P. I. *Nutcracker Suite*; *Symphonies No. 4, 5, 6*
Wagner, Richard. *Die Meistersinger von Nürnberg* (opera): Prelude to Act 1
Webern, Anton. *Five Pieces for Orchestra*, Op. 10

BAND

Hindemith, Paul. *Symphony in B-flat Major*
Holst, Gustav. *Suite No. 1 in E-flat Major*, Op. 28
Persichetti, Vincent. *Divertimento for Band*
Sousa, John Philip. *The Stars and Stripes Forever*

INSTRUMENTAL GROUPS IN POPULAR MUSIC

Big band: Basie, Count. Albums such as *The Atomic Mr. Basie* and *Basie Big Band*
Ellington, Duke. Albums such as *The Works of the Duke*, Vols. 1–18
Jones, Thad, and Mel Lewis. Albums such as *Thad Jones & Mel Lewis: Monday Night at the Village Vanguard* and *Thad Jones - Mel Lewis*
Kenton, Stan. Albums such as *Stan Kenton's Greatest Hits* and *Artistry in Jazz*
Jazz combo and rock band:
(see earlier entries for string bass, guitar, saxophone, trumpet, percussion, and keyboard.)

Part Two

An Introduction to Western Art Music

11

Musical Style

The word "style" in music refers to a characteristic synthesis of the various musical elements and properties that distinguishes a particular musical category, medium, form, genre, composer, group of composers, geographical region, nation, civilization or historical period. This chapter surveys the principal areas of musical style.

BROAD MUSICAL CATEGORIES

Broad musical categories, such as jazz, rock, folk, and classical, have distinctive stylistic traits that enable us to tell them apart. In addition, each of these categories has subcategories. Thus, in the area of rock music, for example, it is possible to differentiate the styles of 1950s rock, heavy metal, folk rock, rap, and so forth, and it is possible even to break down these subcategories into further subdivisions on the basis of stylistic traits. If we continue this process, eventually we arrive at the styles of individual mediums, forms, genres, composers, groups of composers, and performers.

Styles of Mediums, Forms, and Other Aspects of Music

MEDIUMS

Every musical medium has certain style characteristics that are determined by its special properties, capacities, and limitations. In mediums, the broadest distinction of style is between instrumental and vocal music. Although stylistic differences between the two mediums are not always emphasized, instrumental music generally has, for example, a wider melodic range and more disjunct melodic style than does vocal music. Solo mediums (both instrumental and vocal) tend to display greater flexibility in regard to ornamentation, improvisatory style, and personal expression than large ensembles. The physical properties of instruments also affect the style of music written for instrumental mediums. The flute, for instance, can play rapid scale passages and figuration, but it cannot play very loudly; the trombone, on the other hand, is capable of very loud dynamics but cannot compare with the flute in agility. Composers writing for these instruments must take these qualities into account.

FORMS AND GENRES

Certain musical forms and genres also have characteristic musical styles. The fugue, for example, has a distinctive texture of imitative polyphony; the toccata and étude are characterized by virtuosity; an aria is more lyric than a recitative, while the latter is more declamatory; and an opera is more highly dramatic than a cantata or an oratorio.

RELIGIOUS AND SECULAR MUSIC

The serious purpose of religious music in general and church music in particular makes it typically more restrained in style than secular music.

FUNCTIONAL MUSIC

The function for which a piece of music is written sometimes influences its style. Funeral music, for example, is more sober than wedding music; dance music is more exuberant than processional music; and work songs correspond in mood and style to the nature of the task.

VIRTUOSO MUSIC

A performer (singer or instrumentalist) who has exceptional technical ability and who is prone to display that skill is known as a *virtuoso musician*, and music that is composed in a style that exploits the technical dexterity of the performer is *virtuoso music*. Although virtuosity is sometimes overemphasized, because uncritical audiences are often impressed and entertained more by showmanship than by the more subtle aspects of musical art, virtuoso composers and performers have nevertheless contributed to musical art insofar as they have advanced the technical resources of a particular medium. Moreover, mastery of technical difficulties in one period has often enabled a later composer to widen horizons of expression.

Styles of Individual Composers and Performers

Individual composers and performers often develop distinctive styles that set them apart from their peers. The style of a composer is manifested in his or her characteristic way of handling the various musical elements, such as Stravinsky's strong irregular rhythms, complex metric schemes, and brilliant orchestration; Wagner's chromaticism and long melodic lines; and Schoenberg's atonality, strong dissonance, and disjunct linear style.

Groups of composers can sometimes share stylistic traits. The Burgundian school of composers of the early fifteenth century, the Viennese masters of the eighteenth century (Haydn, Mozart, and Beethoven), and Italian opera composers of the nineteenth century are a few examples of such groups.

Individual performers can also have distinctive styles. This is especially true in popular music, as exemplified by the immediately recognizable styles of such performers as Frank Sinatra, Bob Dylan, Ray Charles, and Louis Armstrong. Classical performers also develop individual styles, although the differences between one performer and another tend to be more subtle than in popular music.

Regional and National Styles

Musical styles distinctive of ethnic groups, regions, countries, and even entire civilizations (for example, the musical style of the West as opposed to that of the East) constitute still another significant area of musical style. Composers often draw upon their native folk songs, dances, folklore, and national legends to reflect the spirit of their countries in their music.

Period Styles

Although history is continuous and composers and other artists living at any given time may differ greatly in their individual styles, art and music historians have found it possible to divide Western cultural history into broad periods, or ages, based upon certain shared stylistic characteristics over a given number of years. The style of a particular period is influenced by such things as political, economic, social, and religious developments of the age; nationalistic concerns; important intellectual and artistic ideas; the status of the artist in society; the nature of the contemporary audience; and the ways in which art is disseminated to the public.

Because changes in style are very gradual and because progressive and conservative traits exist side by side at any given time, the division between stylistic periods can only be approximate. Furthermore, the dates for similarly named style periods in the different arts do not always coincide exactly, because the arts do not always develop at a uniform rate.

The principal style periods of Western art music and their approximate dates are given below. These will be refined and qualified further in the remaining chapters of Part Two

The Middle Ages	450–1450
The Renaissance	1450–1600
The Baroque Period	1600–1750
The Classical Period	1750–1820
The Romantic Period	1820–1900
The Modern Period	1900–present

A knowledge of the characteristics of style periods can help the listener appreciate better the aims and accomplishments of individual composers and musical works of a particular period. It can also give the listener a better idea of what to listen for in the music of a given period.

This chapter has explored the principal areas of musical style. There is no short cut for developing stylistic perception, however; it comes only with listening experience. If you listen perceptively to a quantity of music in any category of music literature, you will acquire a familiarity with the style of that particular category. If, for example, you hear a number of Beethoven's compositions, you will learn to distinguish his music from that of other composers. In the same way, after hearing a good deal of music of the late eighteenth century, you can distinguish that music from the literature of other periods. In this way, it is possible gradually to learn to differentiate music of all styles and style periods.

The remainder of Part Two will summarize the main characteristics of each of the principal style periods in Western art music.

For Additional Study

The list that follows is an introductory "sampler" of books pertaining to the main areas of musical style discussed in this chapter. Additional sources and recommended listenings appear under appropriate headings in chapters 12 through 28.

GENERAL:

Sadie, Stanley, ed. *The New Grove Dictionary of Music and Musicians.* 20 vols. London: Macmillan. 1980.

Shapiro, Meyer. "Style." In *Aesthetics Today*, edited by Morris Philipson and Paul J. Gudel. New York: Meridian. 1961.

BROAD MUSICAL CATEGORIES:

Abrahams, Roger D., and George Foss. *Anglo-American Folk Song Style.* Englewood Cliffs, NJ: Prentice-Hall. 1971.

Gridley, Mark C. *Jazz Styles: History and Analysis.* 3d. ed. Englewood Cliffs, NJ: Prentice-Hall. 1988.

Malone, Bill C. *Country Music, U.S.A.* Rev. ed. Austin: University of Texas Press. 1985.

Mates, Julian. *America's Musical Stage: Two Hundred Years of Musical Theatre.* Westport, CT: Greenwood. 1985.

Pielke, Robert G. *You Say You Want a Revolution: Rock Music in American Culture.* Chicago: Nelson-Hall. 1986.

MEDIUMS, FORMS, AND GENRES:

Cuyler, Louise Elvira. *The Symphony.* New York: Harcourt Brace Jovanovich. 1973.

Gillespie, John. *Five Centuries of Keyboard Music: An Historical Survey of Music for Harpsichord and Piano.* Belmont, CA: Wadsworth. 1965.

Grout, Donald Jay. *A Short History of Opera.* 2d ed. New York: Columbia University Press. 1965.

Horsley, Imogene. *Fugue: History and Practice.* New York: Free Press. 1966.

Newman, William S. *The Sonata in the Baroque Era* (Chapel Hill, NC: University of North Carolina Press, 1959; 4th ed. New York: Norton, 1983); *The Sonata in the Classic Era* (Chapel Hill, NC: University of North Carolina Press, 1963; 3d ed. New York: Norton, 1983); and *The Sonata Since Beethoven* (Chapel Hill, NC: University of North Carolina Press, 1970; 3d ed. New York: Norton, 1983).

Smither, Howard E. *A History of the Oratorio.* 3 vols. Chapel Hill, NC: University of North Carolina Press. 1977–87.

Stevens, Denis, ed. *A History of Song.* Rev. ed. New York: Norton. 1970.

Ulrich, Homer. *Chamber Music.* 2d ed. New York: Columbia University Press. 1966.

REGIONAL, NATIONAL, AND ETHNIC STYLES:

Béhague, Gerard. *Music in Latin America: An Introduction.* Englewood Cliffs, NJ: Prentice-Hall. 1979.

Collaer, Paul, ed. *Music of the Americas: An Illustrated Music Ethnology of the Eskimo and American Indian Peoples.* New York: Praeger. 1971.

Hitchcock, H. Wiley, ed. *Music in the United States: A Historical Introduction.* 3d ed. Englewood Cliffs, NJ: Prentice-Hall. 1988.

Idelson, A. Z. *Jewish Music in Its Historical Development.* New York: Schocken Books. 1967.

Leonard, Richard A. *A History of Russian Music.* New York: Macmillan, 1956; reprint, London: Minerva Press, 1968; reprint, Westport, CT: Greenwood Press, 1977.

Malm, William. *Music Cultures of the Pacific, the Near East, and Asia.* 2d ed. Englewood Cliffs, NJ: Prentice-Hall. 1977.

May, Elizabeth, ed. *Music of Many Cultures: An Introduction.* Berkeley, Los Angeles, and London: University of California Press. 1980.

McGee, Timothy. *The Music of Canada.* New York: Norton. 1985.

Nketia, J. H. Kwabena. *The Music of Africa.* New York: Norton. 1974.

Southern, Eileen. *The Music of Black Americans.* 2nd ed. New York: Norton. 1983.

Titon, Jeff Todd, ed. *Worlds of Music: An Introduction to the Music of the World's Peoples.* New York: Schirmer. 1984.

Wade, Bonnie C. *Music in India: The Classical Traditions.* Englewood Cliffs, NJ: Prentice-Hall. 1979.

Wiant, Bliss. *The Music of China.* Hong Kong: Chinese University of Hong Kong. 1965.

PERIOD STYLES IN WESTERN ART MUSIC:

Grout, Donald Jay, and Claude V. Palisca. *A History of Western Music.* 4th ed. New York and London: Norton. 1988.

Rosenstiel, Léonie, et al, eds. *Schirmer History of Music.* New York: Schirmer. 1982.

Stolba, K. Marie. *The Development of Western Music: A History.* Dubuque, IA: Wm. C. Brown Publishers. 1990.

12

The Middle Ages

A.D.313	Edict of Milan makes Christianity a lawful religion; broad expansion of Christianity begins
c. 375–c. 570	The Great Migrations
476	Fall of Western Roman Empire
590–604	Pope Gregory I (the Great) codifies church liturgy and music, establishes Roman papacy as final authority in church
768–814	Reign of Charlemagne
c. 850–900	Earliest descriptions of polyphonic music
c. 1050–1200	Romanesque period in architecture and art
1066	Norman conquest of England
c. 1086–c. 1300	Troubadours and trouvères flourish in France
1096–1291	Crusades
c. 1140–1450	Gothic period in architecture and art
c. 1150–c.1250	Notre Dame school of organum composers active in Paris
1307	Dante, *The Divine Comedy*
1309–1377	Popes in exile at Avignon
c. 1315–c. 1375	French *ars nova*, led by Machaut
1330s–1374	Rise of humanism in Petrarch's study of ancient Greek and Roman classics
1330s–1410	Italian *ars nova*, led by Landini
1337–1453	Hundred Years' War
1348–1350	The Black Death
1378–1417	Papal schism (the "Great Schism")
1386	Chaucer, *Canterbury Tales*
1453	Constantinople conquered, ending Eastern Roman Empire

1454   Gutenberg invents printing from movable type

The Middle Ages encompasses a period of roughly 1,000 years between the fall of the Western Roman Empire in 476 and the dawn of the Modern age around 1450, a period during which a distinctively "European" culture emerged from its roots in antiquity and came to flower. For much of the Middle Ages, the Christian church was the center of social life, learning, and the arts. However, with the rise of feudalism and the age of chivalry, courts also began to share in this role, particularly after the eleventh century, joined later by towns as they grew in size and power. Courts and towns, in turn, brought increased interest in secular (i.e., nonreligious) matters; thus, it is natural that the music and the other arts of the early Middle Ages are primarily sacred while those of the later Middle Ages are increasingly secular.

SACRED MONOPHONY

The roots of Western music lie in the music of ancient Greece and Rome and in the traditions of the Hebrew and other Mediterranean cultures. From them we derived ideas about the role of music, traditions of musical performance and instrumental construction, musical and acoustical terminology and theory, views concerning the relationship of words and music, and a long tradition of music that is primarily monophonic in texture. Yet, since only a few fragments of the actual music of these cultures survive, the history of Western music "proper" begins with the earliest music that has descended to us, that of the early Christian church.

The Mass

The principal types of service in the Roman Catholic church are the *Mass* and the *Offices* (or *Canonical Hours*). We will focus on the Mass because of its importance both to the music of the Middle Ages and to that of later eras.

The Mass, a symbolic reenactment of the Last Supper of Christ and His disciples, derives its name from the closing phrase of the service, *Ite, missa est* ("Go, [the congregation] is dismissed"). It attained its historically settled format in about 1014, although various regional variations continued in use.

The texts of certain sections of the Mass, called the **Ordinary**, are invariable; these include the *Kyrie, Gloria, Credo, Sanctus-Benedictus,* and *Agnus Dei.* Other texts, called the **Proper**, vary according to the season and the particular feast or commemoration being celebrated. Figure 12.1 outlines the principal sections of the Mass.

A special type of Mass is the Mass for the Dead, or **Requiem Mass**, which derives its name from its opening section, *Requiem aeternam dona eis Domine* ("Rest eternal grant them, O Lord"). The Requiem Mass omits the Gloria and Credo and has its own Proper, which includes a vision of the Last Judgment, the *Dies irae* ("Day of wrath"). Musical settings of the Requiem Mass have formed an important part of the repertory since the fifteenth century.

As a result of the Second Vatican Council (1962–1965), the liturgies of the Mass and the Requiem Mass were altered in some respects, and the use of the vernacular (i.e., native languages) has largely replaced Latin texts.

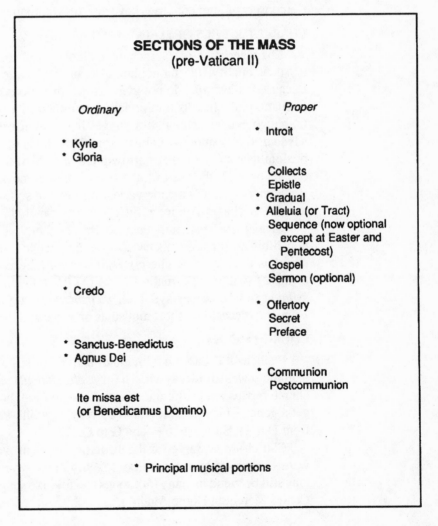

Fig 12.1

Plainchant

The music of the early church is known by several names: *plainchant*, *plainsong*, *ecclesiastical chant*, and *Gregorian chant*. The last of these names derives from the role that Pope Gregory I (pope from 590 to 604) played in codifying the church music of his time. However, since several non-Gregorian chant repertories are extant and the majority of the more than 3,000 "Gregorian" melodies were composed between 600 and 1300, perhaps a more general term such as plainchant serves better to denote this music.

Plainchant constitutes one of the great treasures of Western music. In addition to its importance as the earliest body of Christian music and the official music of the Catholic church for over 1,000 years, it provided the basis for many secular songs in the Middle Ages and for numerous polyphonic compositions throughout the later Middle Ages and Renaissance. Composers of later centuries have also drawn upon these timeless melodies.

CHARACTERISTICS OF PLAINCHANT

Characteristics of plainchant include (1) a cool, impersonal, almost mystical quality; (2) monophonic texture; (3) free, unmeasured rhythm. Because manuscripts do not give explicit directions concerning the rhythm of chant, plainchant is traditionally performed in a free, nonmetric manner (although recent scholarship suggesting a metrical approach is gaining advocates); (4) smooth, undulating melodic lines in which conjunct motion predominates; (5) a rather narrow pitch range; (6) the use of church modes (see below); (7) the use of Latin texts (although now the use of translations is common); and (8) a wide variety of melodic styles, ranging from almost monotonic chanting to long, fully developed melodies.

Chants are characterized also by (1) their type of text: Biblical or non-Biblical, prose or poetry; (2) the manner in which the chant is sung: *antiphonal* (alternating choirs), *responsorial* (alternating soloist and choir) or *direct* (without alternation); and (3) the relation of notes to syllables: *syllabic* (one note per syllable), *melismatic* (many notes per syllable) or *neumatic* (occasional short melismas on some syllables).

CHURCH MODES

Plainchant is based not on major and minor scales but on other types of diatonic scales known as *church* (or *ecclesiastical*) *modes*. A discussion of church modes is beyond the scope of this outline; however, the reader can get a general idea of their sound by playing white-key scales on the piano from D to D, E to E, F to F, and G to G.

Church modes served as the theoretical basis of Western music until they were superseded by major-minor tonality in the seventeenth century. They may still be found in many folk songs and folklike songs (e.g., "When Johnny Comes Marching Home Again").

SECULAR MONOPHONY

In addition to plainchant, composers of the Middle Ages also produced a large body of secular monophony, which appears primarily in manuscripts dating from the eleventh century and after. The most characteristic examples of this are the vernacular songs of the troubadours and trouvères.

The Troubadours and Trouvères

The troubadours and trouvères were poet-composers, respectively from regions that are now southern and northern France, who flourished from c. 1086 to c. 1300. They were active mainly in courtly circles, an early example of non-Church patronage, and many of them were from the nobility. Most, however, were professional musicians, sometimes of humble birth, who gained acceptance and social status because of their musical and poetic talents. Aristocratic women troubadours of southern France, the *trobairitz*, were also active at this time, as were male counterparts in Germany, the *Minnesänger* (singular, *Minnesinger*, "love singer") and, later, the *Meistersinger*.

Jongleurs

Some troubadours and trouvères performed their music themselves, while others entrusted it to minstrels, or *jongleurs* (jugglers), a class of wandering musicians who went from town to town singing, playing instruments, dancing, miming, performing acrobatics and magic tricks, and even displaying trained animals. Often social outcasts, they nevertheless did much to disseminate the popular secular songs of their day.

Poetic and Musical Characteristics

POETIC TYPES

Troubadour and trouvère poems reflect nearly every aspect of medieval life, although most favored are poems dealing with the courtly love of the age of chivalry.

TEXTURE

Like plainchant, these songs appear in manuscripts as monophonic melodies. However, from literary and pictorial evidence, it seems likely that they were sung with some kind of instrumental accompaniment.

RHYTHM

As is the case with chant, relative note values are not indicated. Modern editors often transcribe these pieces in triple meter, based upon rhythmic practices seen in polyphonic music of the time; however, this is somewhat conjectural, and some scholars prefer a free, unmeasured rhythm.

MELODY

Melodies have a narrow range, seldom more than an octave, and trouvère melodies, in particular, have short, clear-cut phrases, easily remembered tunes, and a simplicity that resembles that of folk song.

TEXT SETTING AND FORM

Melodic settings are largely syllabic with occasional short melismatic figures. Typically, the songs are strophic, repeating the same melody for different stanzas of the text, and many of them have refrains (recurrent sections of text and melody). Both musical and poetic forms show infinite variety.

THE RISE OF POLYPHONY

The emergence of polyphony, first described in the late ninth century, ranks as the most significant single event in the history of Western music, because it is the exploitation of this technique that most sets Western music apart from that of other cultures.

Early Organum

Polyphony written from the late ninth century to c. 1250 was called *organum*. The earliest organum consisted simply of a second line of music added below a given chant melody that followed the chant note for note in parallel or nearly parallel motion at the interval of a fifth or fourth (figure 12.2). Either or both parts could also be doubled at the octave to create three- or four-part music.

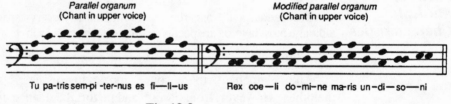

Fig 12.2

During the next 250 years, composers learned how to give the voices greater melodic independence, through the use of crossed voices and contrary motion (i.e., motion in which the voices move in opposite directions), and some degree of rhythmic independence by writing several notes in the newly composed melody for each note of the chant melody.

Notre Dame Organum

After 1150 a group of composers associated with the Cathedral of Notre Dame in Paris assumed leadership in the writing of organum. Led by Léonin (active c. 1163–1190) and Pérotin (active c. 1190–c. 1225), these composers introduced new techniques and brought organum to its highest point of development.

One of their most important innovations was the introduction of a method for notating relative rhythmic values. Although limited to a few rhythmic patterns (called *rhythmic modes*), all of which were divisible by three, symbolic of the Holy Trinity, this new method of notation provided, for the first time, a means of indicating the rhythm of music with some precision.

THE THIRTEENTH CENTURY

In many ways, the thirteenth century was the "golden age" of the Middle Ages, a century that witnessed the building of soaring Gothic cathedrals, the church at its peak of spiritual and worldly power, the culmination of medieval Scholastic philosophy, the flourishing of towns, the age of chivalry, an increase in scientific studies, and lasting contributions to the arts. In music the thirteenth century saw also the emergence of the most characteristic polyphonic form of the Middle Ages, the *motet*.

The Motet

The motet, from the French *mot* ("word"), originated in the practice by early thirteenth-century Notre Dame composers of adding words to textless upper voices of organum. During the second half of the century, the new form spread throughout western Europe, becoming the principal polyphonic genre of the time.

GENERAL CHARACTERISTICS

Most thirteenth-century motets are written for three voices (called, from bottom to top, the *tenor*, *motetus*, and *triplum*). A motet was composed in three steps. First, the composer selected a preexisting melody for the lowest voice (the tenor); usually this was a plainchant, although after 1250 secular songs and instrumental tunes were also used. Next, the composer set the tenor melody in precise rhythmic values, usually in fairly long durations. Finally, the composer added the two upper voices above the tenor melody in faster moving notes, based on the rhythmic modes. The three voices were usually all in the same general vocal register and, as they all moved about in the same musical space, crossing of voices was common. *Nonimitative* polyphony (see chapter 7) was the norm.

A preexisting melody used as the basis of a polyphonic composition is known as a *cantus firmus* (fixed song), and the thirteenth-century composer's practice of constructing a motet upon the "scaffolding" of a cantus firmus was nothing new. Since the earliest examples of organum, the traditional way of writing polyphony had been to select a preexisting melody (usually a chant) and to add one or more newly composed melodies to it. Composers would continue to use cantus firmus technique, in fact, throughout the later Middle Ages and Renaissance.

The two upper parts usually had different texts, which might be sacred, secular or both. Both parts might be in Latin or in French, or one might be in Latin, the other in French. The tenor part usually had no text other than the initial word or words (called an *incipit*) of its plainsong melody; thus, it was probably played on an instrument. Because of the different texts in each of the three parts, the standard way of identifying a motet is by a composite title made up of the incipit of each of the parts, from highest to lowest.

Figure 12.3, a fragment of a motet praising the Virgin Mary, illustrates the characteristics just described. (NOTE: the small 8 below the treble clefs indicates that the parts are to be sung an octave lower than written.)

Motet, Salve, salus hominum - O radians stella - nostrum

Triplum: Hail, safety of men, hope of pity,
Duplum: O shining star, outshining all others, Mother and
Daughter of the highest God,

Source: Anderson, Gordon, ed. *The Latin Compositions of Fascicules VII and VIII of the Notre Dame Manuscript Wolfenbüttel Helmstedt 1099.* 2 vols. Brooklyn: Institute of Medieval Music. 1968. Used by permission of the Institut für Mittelalterliche Musikforschung.

Fig 12.3

HARMONY

Consonant Intervals. For medieval musicians, the consonant intervals were the unison, octave, perfect fifth, and perfect fourth (with the perfect fourth gradually beginning to lose this status in the late Middle Ages). These intervals were used for beginnings, endings, cadences, and other points of emphasis, such as the chords that appear on the first beats of the measure in modern transcriptions. Other intervals serve as elements of motion, moving toward or around these consonant intervals.

In three-part music, typical combinations of consonant intervals were as follows:

octave and
fifth above
tenor

both upper
voices a fifth
above tenor

one upper voice a
fifth above tenor, the
other in unison with
the tenor

Fig 12.4

These "open fifth" harmonies, which sound somewhat hollow to modern ears used to the fuller sound of triads, account in large part for the distinctive sound of medieval harmony.

Dissonant Clashes. Between the occurrences of consonant chords, the voices often momentarily form seconds or other dissonant intervals, as seen in measures one and five of figure 12.3. These dissonant clashes, plus the still-frequent progression of voices in parallel fifths and octaves (a carry-over from early organum technique), give the music a certain primitive quality that is nevertheless charming in its own way.

THE FOURTEENTH CENTURY

In the fourteenth century, the fabric of medieval society began to unravel. Devastating events, such as the Black Death and the Hundred Years' War, coupled with a weakening of the feudal system, a papal crisis, corruption in the church, a loss of confidence in Scholastic philosophy, and a rise in secular interests and humanism, shook the very foundations of the medieval order.

Characteristic of the age, composers produced far more secular than sacred music. As chivalry degenerated into flowery conventions, this music grew increasingly intricate and manneristic, a characteristic that is shared also by the painting, architecture, and poetry of the time. Composers and theorists began also to look upon the music of the past 150 years as the "old art" (*ars antiqua*), in contrast to their "new art" (*ars nova*). This "new art" represents both a last phase of the Middle Ages in music and the beginning of trends that were to shape the music of the Renaissance.

The French ars nova

The French *ars nova* (c. 1315–c. 1375) introduced a number of technical and stylistic changes into the musical language inherited from the thirteenth century.

MUSICAL CHARACTERISTICS

Rhythm. Perhaps the most far-reaching innovation of the *ars* nova in the area of rhythm was the introduction of duple division; now all note values could be divided into two parts as well as the traditional three parts. In addition, more diversified rhythms replaced the rhythmic modes, faster note values were introduced, and rhythmic writing in general became increasingly complex. By the end of the century, rhythmic complexity reached a level not equaled until the twentieth century.

Melody. Melodic and rhythmic interest began to be centered in the top voice, particularly in works in the "cantilena" style (see below), and melodies exhibited a higher degree of refinement and lyricism than before.

Harmony. The harmony of the fourteenth century stands midway between the practices of the Middle Ages and those of the Renaissance. On the one hand, there were still frequent parallel fifths and octaves and occasional dissonant clashes, and the unison, octave, and perfect fifth were still considered the primary ("perfect") consonances. However, thirds and sixths were now also gaining acceptance as "imperfect" consonances, and their increased use gives the harmony a sweeter, less hollow sound. There is also a greater sense of harmonic "order;" even the distant beginnings of a chordal concept can be glimpsed in the music.

Texture. Nonimitative polyphony was still the norm, and composers continued to write many pieces having the same general texture as the thirteenth-century motet. However, the progressive texture of the time was the "cantilena" (or "ballade") style, in which a high solo voice was supported by two or more lower, more slowly moving instrumental parts (in effect a solo with accompaniment).

Polyphonic Forms. The motet reached its peak of development in the fourteenth century. An important innovation in this form was the *isorhythmic motet*, which employed a reiterated rhythmic and/or melodic pattern (usually in the tenor but occasionally in the upper voices as well). The progressive tendencies of the period appear most clearly, though, in the polyphonic French song forms —the *virelai* (or *chanson balladée*), *rondeau*, and *ballade*—which typically employ the new cantilena style.

Monophonic Forms. Composers also continued to write monophonic French songs, employing such forms as the monophonic *virelai* and the *lai*.

MACHAUT

The leading composer of the French *ars nova* was Guillaume de Machaut (c. 1300–1377), who was also a poet. Typical of the period, his secular compositions outnumber his sacred works, and they represent all the French forms of the time. His most celebrated work, however, is a sacred composition, *La Messe de Nostre Dame*, a work of great sophistication and skill, notable for its four-part texture (unusual for the time), its spacious dimensions, and because it is the first setting of the Ordinary of the Mass in which all the movements were conceived as a unified whole.

The Italian ars nova

Although there are subtle differences between Italian and French polyphony of the fourteenth century, the two share the same general musical style. In Italy as in France, secular music predominated; favored forms were the *madrigal* (no relation to the later sixteenth-century madrigal), the *caccia*, and the *ballata*. The leading fourteenth-century Italian composer was Francesco Landini (c. 1325–1397).

Instrumental Music

Literary and pictorial sources document widespread use of instruments in the Middle Ages, yet only a few pieces of purely instrumental music, all monophonic in texture, have survived. Of these, the most common type of piece is the *estampie* (also *estampida* or *istampida*), a dance form with repeated sections. Other compositions are identified by such names as *danse real*, *trotto*, and *saltarello*.

It is not possible to determine exactly how instruments were used during the Middle Ages because manuscripts almost never specify even whether a given part is instrumental or vocal, much less the specific instruments intended; apparently composers simply left the choice of instruments and voices to the performers. Most likely, though, instruments were used (1) to accompany dancing or solo singing, (2) to play textless parts in polyphonic compositions, (3) to double or substitute for one or more vocal parts in polyphonic compositions, (4) to perform purely instrumental arrangements of vocal works, and (5) to accompany the solo voice in cantilena-style polyphonic works.

*T*he Middle Ages brings to mind the Roman deity Janus, the god of beginnings, whose double-faced head looked both backward and forward. Early Christian and Byzantine art and early medieval music clearly looked back toward their roots in antiquity; in music, this is evident particularly in the development of the modal system and in the monophonic texture of plainchant and secular song. With the rise of Romanesque art and polyphony in music, however, Western art and music began to turn toward future, more distinctly "Western," practice. The climax of the Middle Ages in the thirteenth century is seen in the Gothic style in art and in the most characteristic of all late medieval musical forms, the motet.

During the fourteenth century, the medieval order began to crumble as new developments such as the rise of humanism and secularism and the inventions of gunpowder (which rendered medieval military tactics obsolete) *and the printing press signaled the dawn of a new era. The music of the fourteenth century also reflects this transitional stage, foreshadowing many Renaissance trends. By the end of the Middle Ages, Western polyphony had progressed far from its primitive beginnings in organum and stood at the threshold of the golden age of polyphony that awaited in the High Renaissance.*

For Additional Study

Caldwell, John. *Medieval Music.* Bloomington: Indiana University Press. 1978.

The EAV Art and Music Series. "Medieval Art and Music." *Distributed by Educational Audio Visual, Inc. (Pleasantville, NY). Videocassette.*

The EAV History of Music. Part 1: "Origins and Overview"; Part 2: "The Middle Ages and Renaissance." Distributed by Educational Audio Visual, Inc. (Pleasantville, NY). Videocassette.

Hoppin, Richard H. Medieval Music. New York and London: Norton. 1978.

Reese, Gustave. Music in the Middle Ages. New York: Norton. 1940.

Seay, Albert. Music in the Medieval World. 2d ed. Englewood Cliffs, NJ: Prentice-Hall. 1975.

Yudkin, Jeremy. Music in Medieval Europe. Englewood Cliffs, NJ: Prentice-Hall. 1989.

Recommended Listening

GREGORIAN CHANT:

Alleluia, *Vidimus stellam* (We have Seen His Star)

Hymn, *Veni Creator Spiritus* (Come, O Creator Spirit), for the Second Vespers of Whitsunday

Sequence, *Victimae paschali laudes* (To the Paschal Victim), for the Solemn Mass of Easter Day

SECULAR MONOPHONY:

Halle, Adam de la. *Le Jeu de Robin et de Marion* (The Play about Robin and Marion): Rondeau, *Robins m'aime* (Robin Loves Me; trouvère song)

Reuenthal, Neidhart von. *Willekommen Mayenschein* (Welcome, May's Bright Sun; Minnelied)

Ventadorn, Bernart de. *Can vei la lauzeta mover* (When I See the Lark Beating; troubadour song)

ORGANUM AND 13TH-CENTURY MOTET:

Benedicamus Domino (Let Us Bless the Lord; 12th-century melismatic organum, School of St. Martial)

Léonin. *Alleluia Pascha nostrum* (Alleluia, Our Paschal Lamb; organum duplum, School of Notre Dame)

Pérotin. *Sederunt* (Gradual for St. Stephen's Day; organum quadruplum, School of Notre Dame)

Pucelete-Je languis-Domino (13th-century motet)

Fourteenth-Century and Instrumental Music:

Danse Royale (Royal Dance; 13th-century instrumental music)

Firenze, Giovanni da. *Con brachi assai* (With Hounds Aplenty; caccia)

Landini, Francesco. *Chi più le vuol sapere* (Who Wishes to Know Them More; ballata)

Machaut, Guillaume de. *S'il estoit nulz* (If There Is Anyone) (isorhythmic motet)

___. *La Messe de Nostre Dame* (The Mass of Our Lady)

13

The Renaissance

1305–1306	Giotto's frescoes for Arena Chapel, Padua, foreshadow Renaissance trends
1330s–1374	Rise of humanism in Petrarch's study of ancient Greek and Roman classics
1413–1425	Early Renaissance style established in sculpture (e.g., Donatello), architecture (Brunelleschi), and painting (Masaccio)
1420s–c. 1450	Formation of the early Renaissance style in music (Dunstable, Dufay, and Binchois)
1453	End of the Hundred Years' War; fall of Constantinople, ending the Eastern Roman Empire
1454	Gutenberg invents printing from movable type
1469–1494	Ficino's translations and commentaries on the writings of Plato generate the Florentine Platonist Renaissance
1486	Pico della Mirandola, *Oration on the Dignity of Man*
1486–1522	Era of great sea explorers: Diaz, Columbus, da Gama, Balboa, Magellan, and Cortez
1490-1560	High Renaissance in music
c. 1495–c. 1527	High Renaissance art flourishes in works by Leonardo da Vinci, Michelangelo, and Raphael
1501	First collection of polyphonic music printed from movable type
1509	Erasmus, *In Praise of Folly*
1513	Machiavelli, *The Prince*
1517	Beginning of the Reformation with Martin Luther's ninety-five theses
c. 1525–1620	Madrigals flourish in Italy
1528	Publication of Castiglione's *The Book of the Courtier* (written 1513–1518)
1543	Copernicus, *On the Revolutions of the Celestial Spheres*
1545–1563	Council of Trent, an important facet of the Counter Reformation

1550s-1594	Palestrina active in Rome
1558–1603	Reign of Elizabeth I in England
1580	Montaigne, *Essays* (Books I and II)
c. 1584–1612	Shakespeare (1564–1616) active in England
1587	Monteverdi, first book of madrigals
1588	War between Spain and England; defeat of Spanish Armada
1590s–c. 1625	Golden age of English secular song and instrumental music

*R*enaissance, a term borrowed from art history, has come to denote the period in European history extending from the end of the Middle Ages through the sixteenth century. Historians traditionally date the Renaissance in music from c. 1450 to 1600, although some place its beginnings as early as 1400.

The term "renaissance" means "rebirth," and many people of the time did feel that the world was awakening out of a deep sleep. An important factor in this rebirth was humanism, an intellectual movement that began in the fourteenth century as a revival of interest in the philosophy and arts of ancient Greece and Rome and came to embody a general rebirth of the human spirit, engendering an age characterized by individuality, a striving for excellence ("virtu"), and a new-found confidence in the possibilities of human thought and creations.

Beginning in Italy, the Renaissance movement spread throughout Europe, bringing far-reaching social and cultural changes. A brilliant and exciting age that produced such men as Michelangelo, Leonardo da Vinci, Copernicus, Columbus, Shakespeare, and Martin Luther, the Renaissance laid the foundations of the world we know today.

THE FIFTEENTH CENTURY

The Renaissance in music began in the first half of the fifteenth century, not in Italy as was the case with the other arts, but in England and in the courts of the dukes of Burgundy, whose lands stretched from the Rhône River in east central France to the North Sea. The entire fifteenth century may be regarded as a transitional era, during which composers gradually transformed the inherited medieval musical language into the High Renaissance style of the sixteenth century.

The First Half of the Fifteenth Century

The music of the first half of the fifteenth century exhibits such an even mixture of medieval and progressive tendencies that some historians consider this period the last phase of the Middle Ages, while others consider it the first stage of the Renaissance. The three principal composers of this time were the Englishman John Dunstable (c. 1385–1453) and the Burgundian composers Guillaume Dufay (c. 1400–1474) and Gilles Binchois (c. 1400–1460). Dufay, the most prolific and innovative of the three, may not actually have served at the Burgundian court, but he is traditionally linked to the Burgundian "school" of composers because of stylistic similarities in his music.

MUSICAL CHARACTERISTICS

Texture. Nonimitative polyphony was still the rule, although scattered examples of imitation appear. Three-voice texture, in which the top voice predominates (as was the case in the older cantilena style), also continued to be popular, particularly in the chanson. However, four-voice writing began to gain favor around 1450, bringing with it a gradual replacement of treble-dominated writing with a texture in which all voices were equal in importance and similar in melodic style and rhythmic character.

Melody. Composers of the early fifteenth century, especially Dufay, introduced a new type of melody that was to form the basis of later Renaissance style: warmly expressive, with gracefully arching contours and frequent melismas at cadences.

Rhythm. Rhythmic complexities of the fourteenth century gave way to simpler rhythms. Triple meter was more common than duple.

Harmony. Composers of this period made much more extensive use of full triads than ever before; in fact, this period marks the real beginning of triadic harmony in Western music. Composers now also began to control dissonance and voiceleading very carefully; gone were the dissonant clashes, parallel fifths, and other archaic elements of medieval harmony. In addition, close attention to harmonic direction and a fuller understanding of the roles of tonic and dominant presage later tonal practices.

FORMS

Composers of the fifteenth century continued to employ musical forms inherited from the fourteenth century—principally the chanson, motet, and Mass—which they adapted to their new style and techniques.

Chanson. Chansons of the period normally exhibit the treble-dominated three-voice texture of the time and were, in essence, solo songs with accompaniment.

Motet. Motets often exhibit the treble-dominated texture of the chanson; in these, the top voice may be freely composed or an ornamentted chart melody. Composers still occasionally wrote isorythmic motets also, but this had now become a consciously archaic form that was gradually abandoned.

Mass. Although polyphonic settings of the Mass (or portions of it) were not new, it was composers of the fifteenth century who first established the regular practice of setting the Ordinary of the Mass as a unified whole. Composers explored various techniques for achieving musical unity, but the one that came to prevail was the *cantus firmus Mass* (or *tenor Mass*), in which the same cantus firmus (either a chant or secular melody) appeared in each movement. The *cantus firmus* typically appeared in the tenor, but now composers often placed a fourth voice below it. The resulting four voices—called, from top to bottom, the *discantus* (or *superius*), *altus*, *tenor*, and *bassus*—began to establish four-voice texture as the norm and foreshadowed the later adoption of soprano, alto, tenor, and bass as the four principal voice registers. The Masses of Dufay also reveal a genius for large-scale structural planning, and his use of four voices of equal importance in his late Masses influenced his successors greatly.

The Second Half of the Fifteenth Century

Musical leadership had shifted to the north with Dufay and Binchois, and "Netherlanders"—from territories that now include the Franco-Belgian region, Belgium, and portions of Holland—continued to dominate musical life until at least 1550, holding most of the important musical positions throughout Europe. The leading composer of the Netherlands between the generation of Dufay and Binchois and the rise of the High Renaissance style was Johannes Ockeghem (c. 1410–1497).

In Ockeghem's music, forward-looking tendencies include (1) the rise of four-voice writing as the norm, with all voices nearly equal in importance and similar in character; (2) the use of a chorus rather than solo voices; (3) the downward extension of the range of the bass voice; (4) the use of overlapped phrase endings in the various voices, which produced an almost continuous flow of sound; and (5) the introduction of occasional passages for two voices, three voices, or alternating pairs of voices to provide variety and relief from the prevailing four-voice texture. The principal forms were still the Mass, motet, and chanson, with the Mass now becoming the main form in which a composer was expected to demonstrate his skill. Among Ockeghem's Masses is the earliest extant polyphonic setting of the *Requiem Mass*.

THE HIGH RENAISSANCE (1490–1560)

The decades surrounding the beginning of the sixteenth century brought many important events, such as the era of great sea explorations, the rise of the High Renaissance style in art, and the beginning of the Reformation. This period witnessed also the completion of the transition to the High Renaissance style in music, seen first in the works of the generation of Netherlanders led by Josquin des Prez (c. 1440–1521), Heinrich Isaac (c. 1450–1517), and Pierre de la Rue (c. 1460–1518) and brought to its "classic" phase by Netherlanders of the succeeding generation, particularly Nicolas Gombert (c. 1495–c. 1560). Josquin stands out especially as a composer of genius, whom some music historians rank among the greatest composers of all time.

Music culture grew tremendously during the High Renaissance, facilitated greatly by the rise of music printing. The ability to read and perform music now became one of the marks of an educated person, resulting in widespread amateur music making. Influenced by a wider public and by humanist ideals, composers strove to make their music more accessible in style and structure and more immediately appealing to the senses.

Crucial to the formation of the High Renaissance musical style were the rise and gradual blending of two important new developments: (1) the perfection of the "classic" Netherlands contrapuntal style based on pervading imitation and (2) the growth of national styles.

The Netherlands Contrapuntal Style

Although examples of imitation may be found in polyphonic music prior to the sixteenth century, nonimitative counterpoint was the normal practice. However, during the late fifteenth century, Josquin and his contemporaries established imitative counterpoint as the predominant polyphonic texture. Furthermore, at this time, *pervading* imitation (i.e., imitation in which all voices participate) became the rule. Developed further by composers of the succeeding generation, such as Gombert, imitative counterpoint became the basis of Renaissance polyphony throughout the sixteenth century.

MAIN CHARACTERISTICS

In this style, each phrase of the text has its own musical motive, which is presented in imitation by each voice entering one at a time. Each phrase so presented is called a *point of imitation*. As one point of imitation ends, another begins, based on the next phrase of the text. Points of imitation and cadences usually overlap, so that while some voices are completing one point of imitation, others are beginning the next, and the music continues without obvious breaks.

Figure 13.1 illustrates this style, with separate points of imitation on "Ave Maria" and "Gratia plena." Note how the superius begins the second point of imitation (in m. 8) while the bassus is completing the first; this is the overlapping technique described earlier.

Josquin des Prez, *Ave maria . . . virgo serena* (motet)

(Notes values are halved.)

Source: *Werken van Josquin des Pres.* Uitgegeven door Dr. A. Smijers. Vereeniging voor Nederlandsche Muziekgeschiedenis. Tweede Aflevering. *Motetten.* Tweede Druk. Amsterdam: G. Alsbach & Co. 1935. Used by permission.

Fig 13.1

SOURCES OF VARIETY

In theory, this technique would produce pieces that have an almost seamless texture of continual pervading imitation. In practice, though, composers developed techniques for providing variety and relief, such as (1) intentionally breaking the continuous flow of the music by cadencing simultaneously in all voices and then restarting, (2) changing the meter and/or tempo in various sections, (3) writing some sections for two voices, three voices or alternating pairs of voices as a relief from the full four-voice or five-voice texture, and (4) introducing some sections in homophonic texture or simple chordal style as a relief from the prevailing imitative texture.

National Styles

Imitative counterpoint lay at the center of polyphonic music throughout the Renaissance, in large part because Netherlanders continued to dominate music during the sixteenth century as they had in the fifteenth. It was not until the very end of the sixteenth century that northern leadership was toppled—by Italian composers, who led the way into a new era, the Baroque.

As a result of the widespread demand for northern musicians, most Netherlands composers of the sixteenth century traveled widely, serving first in one country and then in another. A consequence of this was not only that they spread the Netherlands contrapuntal style all over Europe but also that they were in turn influenced by native styles they encountered, in such forms as the Italian frottola, the new French chanson, the German *Lied* and the Spanish *villancico*.

Most of these native forms had certain characteristics in common: (1) strong, lively rhythms that often make use of repeated patterns; (2) a clear presentation of text (often syllabic); (3) simple, folklike melodies that make much use of repeated notes; (4) a preference for chordal writing and homophonic texture, in which the role of counterpoint and imitation is slight and in which the main melody is often in the topmost voice, supported by a harmonically oriented bass and inner voices that are often merely "fillers"; (5) clear-cut phrases; (6) four-voice texture; and (7) harmony that clearly foreshadows practices of later major-minor tonality. Figure 13.2 illustrates these characteristics.

The Blending of Styles

Because many Netherlanders found employment in Italy, Italian native music exerted an especially strong influence on northern composers. Gradually, the northerners' style itself changed as a result of this contact with Italian music, showing more chordal orientation, a heightened sense of tonality, and a greater interest in the relation of text to music.

All the musical forms of the High Renaissance show this blending of Netherlands contrapuntal technique with the more homophonic, chordal texture of native styles. Composers became amazingly adept at shifting effortlessly between these two styles, from section to section—or even from phrase to phrase—as the setting of the text demanded.

Philippus de Lurano, *Se me e grato*

Source: Schwartz, Rudolf, ed. *Ottaviano Petrucci Frottole, Buch I und IV*. Publikationen älterer
Musik, No. 8. © Hildesheim: Georg Olms; Wiesbaden: Breitkopf & Härtel. 1967. Used by permission.

Fig 13.2

Other Characteristics

In general, the music of the High Renaissance, like High Renaissance painting and the architecture of Palladio, reflects the classic (and humanist) ideals of balance, restraint, and clarity of structure. High Renaissance music can be quite expressive, yet seldom in the overtly dramatic manner of later music.

MUSIC AND TEXT

Polyphonic composers of earlier centuries had shown little interest in how the music and text fit together. However, during the sixteenth century, even northern composers began to take greater care in the setting of texts, perhaps influenced by Italian music or by humanist ideals. High Renaissance composers generally strove simply for clear declamation of the text, that is, they set their words so that melodic and rhythmic accents corresponded properly with accented syllables of the text and approximated normal speech patterns. Later Renaissance composers attempted to capture also the emotion and even the meaning of the words; for example, *run* might be set to fast-moving notes or *cruel* to a dissonant harmony. This type of text setting is known as *word painting*. Although word painting could be carried to silly extremes, handled sensitively it could add greatly to the expressiveness of the music.

MELODY

Melodies typically exhibit long, arching phrases, a serene beauty, and an extremely "singable" quality. They show a careful balance between conjunct and disjunct motion and between ascending and descending motion.

HARMONY

Although the theoretical basis of harmony was still the church modes, the approaching age of major-minor tonality is foreshadowed even more strongly than in the music of Dufay by the predominance of full triadic harmonies, the rising importance of the major and minor modes, the frequent function of the bass voice as a harmonic foundation even when it was imitating the other voices, the use of cadence formulas that approximate modern plagal (IV–I) and authentic (V–I) cadences, and a greater percentage of what would later become typical harmonic progressions. Composers also continued to handle dissonances with great care, maintaining a judicious balance between tension and repose.

RHYTHM

Rhythms are fluid and generally lack strong accents. In imitative passages, the rhythmic placement of dissonances and their resolutions typically produces an overall alternation of strong and weak beats, while individual voices proceed in more flexible rhythms that often run contrary to this implied duple meter. Chordal passages, on the other hand, often exhibit strongly marked rhythmic patterns.

SONORITY

Five- or even six-voice writing gradually gained favor over four-voice writing, giving Renaissance music a fuller, richer sonority than before. A cappella performance (i.e., unaccompanied voices) was the ideal sound of the time; yet, in practice, instrumental accompaniment was common.

Forms

High Renaissance composers continued to employ the three principal forms inherited from the fifteenth century (motet, Mass, and chanson), but the motet now replaced the Mass as the principal form in which the composer was expected to display his skill. A new development was the *imitation Mass*, a Mass in which an entire preexisting composition (as opposed to a single cantus firmus melody) was used as the basis for polyphonic development. Motets, Masses, and chansons all exhibit the blending of Netherlands imitative counterpoint and the more chordal texture of native styles described earlier.

THE LATER SIXTEENTH CENTURY

The second half of the sixteenth century brought a flowering of secular vocal forms such as the madrigal, important developments in sacred vocal music resulting from the Reformation and Counter Reformation, the rise of instrumental music, and developments that foreshadowed the coming Baroque era.

The Madrigal

THE ITALIAN MADRIGAL

The most important and popular secular vocal form of the late Renaissance was the madrigal, which flourished first in Italy and later in England. The madrigal was a setting of a short vernacular poem that was usually amorous in nature and often contained pastoral allusions. The form of the madrigal resembled that of a motet in that it consisted of several overlapping or interlocking sections, each based on a single phrase of the text, which might be set in either imitative or homophonic style. Unlike the motet, however, madrigals were written for a small ensemble of singers rather than a chorus, and they tended to be more vivid and dramatic in their musical language.

Most early Italian madrigals (c. 1525–c. 1545) were for four voices; later, five voices became the norm, and madrigals for six or more voices were not uncommon. During the late sixteenth century, the madrigal replaced the motet as the most progressive Renaissance musical form, as madrigal composers developed word painting to an unprecedented degree and experimented with chromaticism and other bold harmonic techniques.

The history of the Italian madrigal illustrates the gradual changeover from northern to Italian leadership in music, in that the leading first- and second-generation madrigalists were mostly northerners (e.g., Philippe Verdelot, Jacob Arcadelt, Adrian Willaert, Cipriano de Rore, Philippe de Monte, and Giaches de Wert), while the most progressive madrigalists at the end of the sixteenth century were Italians: Luca Marenzio (c. 1553–1599); Carlo Gesualdo (c. 1561–1613); and, above all, Claudio Monteverdi (1567–1643), whose madrigals represent the culmination of the genre.

Chromaticism in the Italian madrigal reached its peak in the works of Gesualdo. Figure 13.3 at the top of the following page, a fragment from his madrigal *Io pur respiro*, illustrates his chromaticism (mm. 4–9). This example also illustrates the ease with which Renaissance composers were able to shift between chordal texture (mm. 1–3) and imitative texture (mm. 4–9), and it offers insights into typical Renaissance word painting: the bright C major chords on "A la vita" (to life), the use of a cadence on "fin" (end), and the wrenching chromaticism on "et (&) al gran duolo" (and to [my] great pain).

THE ENGLISH MADRIGAL

During the last decade of the sixteenth century and the early years of the seventeenth, Elizabethan England experienced a golden age in literature (most notably in the plays of Shakespeare) and in secular music. Stimulated by the popularity of Italian madrigals in England, a school of English madrigalists arose, including Thomas Morley (c. 1557–1602), Thomas Weelkes (1576–1623), and John Wilbye (1574–1638).

English madrigalists tended to emphasize musical features over depiction of text, and the English madrigal is typically lighter and more humorous than its Italian counterpart, with simpler melody and harmony. Related forms are the *ballett* and *canzonet*, derived from similarly named Italian forms and characterized by homophonic texture, dancelike rhythms, and "fa-la" refrains.

Carlo Gesualdo, *Io pur respiro* (madrigal)

... give an end to life and to [my] great pain.

Source: Davison, Archibald T., and Willi Apel. *Historical Anthology of Music*. Vol. 1, *Oriental, Medieval, and Renaissance Music*. Revised edition. Cambridge, MA: Harvard University Press. ©1946, 1949; 9th printing, 1968. Reprinted by permission.

Fig 13.3

Sacred Vocal Music

The critical event in religion during the sixteenth century was the Reformation (1517–c. 1555), a religious revolution that had far-reaching political, economic, and social effects and that led to the breaking away of the Protestant church from the Roman Catholic. By the latter part of the century, an important new body of Protestant music was flourishing alongside Roman Catholic church music, which now rose to new splendor in the works of Lasso, Palestrina, and Byrd.

REFORMATION MUSIC

Germany. The most important musical contribution of the Lutheran Reformation was the *chorale*, a strophic congregational hymn. Some chorales were newly composed tunes or secular songs with new religious texts (known as *contrafacta*); others were based on plainchant melodies or nonliturgical sacred songs. Originally monophonic, chorales were later set to four-part harmony with the chorale melody in the uppermost part. Lutheran composers also wrote elaborate polyphonic settings of chorale tunes for chorus, including *chorale motets*, and contrapuntal arrangements for organ, called *chorale preludes*; these works established a tradition of Lutheran church music that was to culminate in the works of J. S. Bach (1685–1750).

England. The Church of England separated from the Roman Catholic church in 1534, during the reign of Henry VIII. The two principal types of Anglican music were (1) the *Service*, which included music for the unchanging Morning and Evening Prayers and for Communion, and (2) the *anthem*, which is similar to the Latin motet. Psalm singing was also common in England, inspired by Calvinist models (see below). The leading composers of Anglican music were William Byrd (c. 1543–1623), who also wrote Catholic music, and Orlando Gibbons (1583–1625).

Other Countries. The development of church music was somewhat limited in the Protestant regions of France under Calvin (1509–64) and Switzerland under Zwingli (1484–1531), neither of whom favored its use in worship. The only important musical contributions from these areas were the Psalters, which were rhymed metrical translations of the Psalms set to newly composed, popular or chant melodies. Translations of the French Psalter were adopted in several European countries and, in turn, influenced the creation of new Psalters in England and Scotland.

THE COUNTER REFORMATION

In an effort to correct abuses exposed by the Reformation and retain the loyalty of its people, the Catholic church began a broad series of reforms known collectively as the Counter Reformation. Of its many manifestations, the most important for music were the deliberations of the Council of Trent (1545–1563, with interruptions). The Council was concerned especially about increased secularism in church music, imitative polyphony that obscured the words, excessive use of instruments, and the irreverent attitude of church musicians. In the end, though, the Council made only general recommendations against impurity and lasciviousness.

The composer whose music best exemplifies the ideals of the Counter Reformation is **Giovanni Pierluigi da Palestrina** (c. 1525–1594), an Italian who served nearly his entire career in Rome. Although Palestrina composed a fairly large amount of secular music, he is most noted for his sacred vocal music, which includes over 100 Masses, more than 375 motets, and numerous other works.

The basis of Palestrina's style is the High Renaissance technique of imitative counterpoint, which he brought to its height of perfection in a balanced, restrained polyphony devoid of any secular suggestion. The avoidance of secular suggestion is also apparent in Palestrina's harmony, which eschews all traces of the type of chromaticism associated with the madrigal. Cool and impersonal, his music expresses an almost medieval mysticism within a deliberately conservative Renaissance musical language.

Other leading composers of Catholic church music during the later sixteenth century were Orlando di Lasso (1532–1594), the Spanish composer Tomás Luis de Victoria (1548–1611), and the English composer William Byrd (c. 1543–1623).

Instrumental Music

Although vocal music continued to predominate during the Renaissance era, serious composers began to show rising interest in instrumental music, and we can see the beginnings of independent instrumental forms and styles of writing for instruments.

INSTRUMENTS

During the Renaissance, instruments were classified as *haut* (loud) and *bas* (soft) and were grouped into families, called *consorts*. An ensemble consisting entirely of instruments from the same family constituted a *whole consort*, while one made up of instruments from several families was known as a *broken consort*.

Popular wind instruments were the flute; the recorder, an end-blown wooden flute; double-reed instruments such as the shawm and cromorne (or Krummhorn); the cornett, a wooden instrument with a cup-shaped mouthpiece; the trumpet; and the trombone.

The principal bowed string instrument was the viol, which came in six sizes and was frequently included in consorts. Instruments of the violin family—violin, viola, and violoncello—were also in use in the sixteenth century. The lute, a pear-shaped plucked string instrument, was the most popular household solo instrument of the Renaissance; its Spanish counterpart was the *vihuela de mano*, which, however, had a guitarlike body.

Keyboard instruments included the organ, the harpsichord, and the clavichord. A large variety of percussion instruments was used as well, including anvil and hammer, bells, chimes, small cymbals, triangle, tambourine, xylophone, and several kinds of drums.

INSTRUMENTAL FORMS

At the beginning of the sixteenth century, instruments were still used much in the same way that they had been used in the Middle Ages, that is, to accompany dancing and solo singing, to double or replace parts in polyphonic vocal compositions, and to perform instrumental arrangements of vocal pieces. Most publications of vocal music, in fact, stated that the pieces were suitable either for singing or playing. Gradually, though, independent instrumental forms began to emerge; the principal types are discussed below.

Canzona and Ricercar. The *canzona* and the *ricercar* evolved respectively from the French chanson and the motet. The canzona, which was lighter and more rhythmic than the ricercar, became the leading type of contrapuntal instrumental music in the late sixteenth century, but both exerted important influences on seventeenth-century instrumental music (see chapter 17).

Dance Pieces. The popularity of social dancing during the Renaissance led to an increase in dance pieces for lute, keyboard instruments, and ensembles, which generally exhibited regular rhythmic patterns and repeated sections. Composers often grouped dances in pairs (e.g., the slow *pavane* and the faster *galliard*) or threes, foreshadowing the later grouping of dances into suites.

Improvisatory Works. Improvisation played an important role in all Renaissance music; however, certain instrumental forms specifically exploited this technique. The most important improvisatory form in the second half of the sixteenth century was the *toccata* (from the Italian *toccare*, to touch), in which the prevailing free, improvisatory texture is sometimes broken by imitative passages.

Variations. The theme and variations form, which may have originated with Spanish lute and keyboard composers of the first half of the sixteenth century, experienced an extraordinary popularity in the late sixteenth century, especially among the English *virginalists* (from *virginal*, the English generic term for all string keyboard instruments). Composers typically based sets of variations upon dance tunes, popular songs or folk melodies, and they displayed great ingenuity in the way they varied the melody each time they repeated it. The leading English virginalists were William Byrd, Giles Farnaby, John Bull, Thomas Tomkins, and Orlando Gibbons.

The Venetian School

During the sixteenth century, the church of St. Mark in Venice emerged as the center of a distinguished school of musicians who included many of the leading composers of the Renaissance. Like their Venetian contemporaries in painting and architecture, Venetian composers cultivated a flamboyant, colorful style, which manifested itself in full, rich textures, colorful and varied timbres, and a tendency toward homophony and chordal harmonies rather than intricate polyphony. Evidence of their interest in color was their use of cornetts, trombones, and viols, as well as the organ, to accompany voices.

Stimulated by the presence of two choir lofts in St. Mark's, each with its own organ, Venetian composers developed *polychoral* singing, in which two or more choirs, placed in the balconies and at other points in the basilica along with various instruments and vocal soloists, either echoed each other back and forth or joined together for massive climaxes. In addition to providing the listener with a splendid spectacle for the eye and ear, polychoral writing introduced the element of space as a factor in music and the principle of contrast and opposition of sonorities, a principle that would become the basis of the *concertato* style of the Baroque.

The Venetian school reached its high point in the works of Giovanni Gabrieli (c. 1553–1612). One of his works, the *Sonata pian' e forte*, was one of the first compositions to designate specific instrumentation; it was also the earliest known ensemble work to indicate dynamics.

In their increased interest in instrumental color, their tendency toward homophonic texture, and their introduction of the principle of opposing sonorities, the Venetian school of composers represents music at the threshold of a new age.

The High Renaissance style in music embodies the classic ideals of balance, restraint, and clarity of structure favored by the humanists. It also struck a balance between the Netherlanders' continued reliance on the medieval modal system and vocal polyphony (now expressed as imitative counterpoint within a homogeneous texture of equal voices) and more progressive Italian influences, such as the tendency toward homophonic texture and harmonic practices that foreshadow major-minor tonality. Developments in the second half of the sixteenth century—particularly the increased use of homophony (as seen in the works of Venetian composers and others) and the continued coalescence of the eight-mode modal system into the two-mode system of major-minor tonality—may perhaps represent, then, the triumph of Italian practices over northern, paralleling the toppling of northern musical leadership by Italian composers.

It is interesting to note, though, that the event that traditionally marks the beginning of the Baroque era, the rise of opera and monody, resulted from an attempt to rediscover ancient Greek solo song. Thus, the Renaissance in music ended as the Renaissance movement in other fields had begun: with a humanistic desire to revive the glories of classical antiquity.

For Additional Study

Blume, Friedrich. *Renaissance and Baroque Music: A Comprehensive Survey.* Translated by M. D. Herter Norton. New York: Norton. 1967.

Brown, Howard Mayer. *Music in the Renaissance.* Englewood Cliffs, NJ: Prentice-Hall. 1976.

The EAV Art and Music Series. "Renaissance Art and Music." Distributed by Educational Audio Visual, Inc. (Pleasantville, NY). Videocassette.

The EAV History of Music. Part 2: "The Middle Ages and Renaissance." Distributed by Educational Audio Visual, Inc. (Pleasantville, NY). Videocassette.

Kerman, Joseph, et al. *The New Grove High Renaissance Masters.* New York: Norton; London: Macmillan. 1984.

Munrow, David. *Instruments of the Middle Ages and Renaissance.* London: Oxford University Press. 1976.

Music & Man Series. "Out of the Darkness." Distributed by Films for the Humanities & Sciences (Princeton, NJ). Videocassette.

Reese, Gustave. *Music in the Renaissance.* rev. ed. New York: Norton. 1959.

Recommended Listening

SACRED VOCAL MUSIC

Mass: Dufay, Guillaume. *Missa Se la face ay pale* (If My Face is Pale; cantus firmus Mass)

Josquin des Prez. *Missa Fortuna desperata* (imitation Mass)

___. *Missa de Beata Virgine* (Mass of the Blessed Virgin; cantus firmus Mass)

Ockeghem, Johannes. *Missa Fors seulement*

Palestrina, Giovanni Pierluigi da. *Missa Papae Marcelli* (Pope Marcellus Mass)

Motet:

Byrd, William. *Laudate, pueri, Dominum* (Praise, O Servants of the Lord)

Dufay, Guillaume. *Alma Redemptoris Mater* (Gracious Mother of the Redeemer)

Dunstable, John. *Quam pulchra es* (How Fair Thou Art)

Gabrieli, Giovanni. *Plaudite* (Clap Your Hands; polychoral motet)

Josquin des Prez. *Ave Maria . . . virgo serena* (Hail, Mary . . . serene Virgin)

___. *Absalon fili mi* (Absalom, my Son)

Lasso, Orlando di. *Cum essem parvulus* (When I Was Little)

Victoria, Tomás Luis de. *O magnum mysterium* (O Great Mystery)

Other: Chorales: *O Sacred Head Now Wounded; Now Thank We All Our God; A Mighty Fortress Is Our God*

Tomkins, Thomas. *When David Heard that Absalom Was Slain* (English anthem)

SECULAR VOCAL MUSIC

Chanson: Binchois, Gilles. *Adieu m'amour et ma maistresse* (Farewell My Love and My Dear Lady)

Janequin, Clément. *Le Chant des oiseaux* (The Song of Birds)

Lasso, Orlando di. *Bon jour mon coeur* (Good Day, My Heart)

Sermisy, Claudin de. *Vivray je tousjours en soucy* (Shall I Live Ever in Worry [for You])

Madrigal: Gesualdo, Carlo. *Moro lasso al mio duolo* (I Die, Alas! from My Pain)

Gibbons, Orlando. *The Silver Swan*

Marenzio, Luca. *S'io parto, i' moro* (If I Leave, I Shall Die)

Monteverdi, Claudio. *Ohime! se tanto amate* (Alas, if You So Love . . .)

Morley, Thomas. *April Is in My Mistress' Face*

Weelkes, Thomas. *As Vesta Was from Latmos Hill Descending*

Other: Dowland, John. *Flow My Tears* (song for voice and lute)

Lasso, Orlando di. *Ich armer Mann* (I, Poor Man; German Lied)

Marco, Cara. *Io non compro più speranza* (I'll Buy No More Hope; frottola)

Morley, Thomas. *Now Is the Month of Maying* (English ballett)

INSTRUMENTAL MUSIC

Farnaby, Giles. *Loth to Depart* (variations for virginal)

Gabrieli, Andrea. *Ricercar in the Twelfth Mode* (Venetian school)

Gabrieli, Giovanni. *Canzonas*

___. *Sonata pian' e forte*

Gibbons, Orlando. *In Nomine* (piece for consort of viols)

Merulo, Claudio. *Toccata Quinta, Secondo Tuono*

Susato, Tilman. *La Mourisque* and *Pavane "La Bataille"*

14

The Baroque Period:
An Introduction

1597–1623	Rise, in Rome, of the Baroque style in painting (Caravaggio and Carracci), architecture (Maderno), and sculpture (Bernini)
c. 1600–c. 1650	Early Baroque period in music; earliest operas, cantatas, oratorios, and several new instrumental forms appear
1601–1627	Kepler makes important advances in astronomy and optics
1605	Cervantes, part I of *Don Quixote* (part II, 1615); Monteverdi introduces the concept of the two practices
1607–c. 1702	Founding of the English colonies in America
1610	Rubens's *The Raising of the Cross* establishes the Baroque style in the north
1618–1648	Thirty Years' War
1620	Bacon presents his scientific method in *Novum Organum*
1628	Harvey, *On the Motion of the Heart and Blood in Animals*
c. 1631–1669	Rembrandt, the great Dutch artist, produces his mature works
1632	Galileo, *Dialogue Concerning the Two Chief World Systems—Ptolemaic and Copernican*
1637	Descartes, *Discourse on Method*
1648	Treaty of Westphalia, ending the Thirty Years' War, raises France to first place in Europe and lays the foundation for the modern concept of Europe as a community of sovereign states
1649	King Charles I of England beheaded, Commonwealth established (until 1660); civil wars begin in France (until 1653)
c. 1650–c. 1700	Middle Baroque period in music
1660	Restoration of the monarchy in England
1661–1715	Absolute reign of Louis XIV in France

1662–1673	Molière writes masterful comic plays
1666	Great fire of London
1667	Milton, *Paradise Lost*; Bernini, colonnade of St Peter's, Rome
1675	Spinoza completes his *Ethica* (published 1677)
1677	Racine, *Phèdre*
1678	Bunyan, *The Pilgrim's Progress*
1687	Newton, in *Principia mathematica*, formulates the law of universal gravitation
1690	Locke, *Essay Concerning Human Understanding*
1690s–c. 1754	Baroque architecture flourishes in southern Germany and Austria
1692	Salem witchcraft trials
1696–1725	Peter the Great reigns as sole ruler in Russia
c. 1700	"Balance of power" becomes the prevailing theory of international relationships
c. 1700–c. 1750	Late Baroque period in music: Vivaldi, Telemann, Rameau, J. S. Bach, and Handel
c. 1709	First pianoforte built
1715–1774	Reign of Louis XV in France; Rococo style in art flourishes
1719	Defoe, *Robinson Crusoe*
c. 1720–c. 1770	Rise of pre-Classical styles in music
1726	Swift, *Gulliver's Travels*
1735–1754	Linnaeus produces pioneering studies in botany
1738	Excavation of Herculaneum (discovered in 1709), and later of Pompeii, contributes to a neoclassical revival
1740	Reign of Frederick the Great begins, first of the "enlightened despots"
1740–1748	War of Austrian Succession
1750	Death of J. S. Bach

The term "Baroque" denotes both the chronological period extending from c. 1600 to c. 1750 and the style that prevailed in the arts of western Europe during that period. The word itself, probably derived from the Portuguese "barroco" (irregularly shaped pearl), was used originally in the derogatory sense of "unnatural, over-blown, and grotesque" by writers who saw the period as a type of "dark ages" between the more classically oriented Renaissance and Classical periods. Gradually, though, people began to recognize the positive qualities of Baroque art and music, and today the term has lost its earlier negative connotations.

Whereas Renaissance artists strove to attain the classical ideals of balance, restraint, and clarity, Baroque artists sought to arouse the passions and stir the soul. As a result, Baroque art and music teem with energy, drama, movement, and contrast. Allied with this, too, is a love for monumental conceptions, ornate decoration, spectacular effects, and the illusion of boundlessness.

By the beginning of the Baroque era, the terrible religious wars of the sixteenth century had ended, leaving south and central Europe largely Roman Catholic and northern countries largely Protestant; yet wars continued almost without break throughout the period as nations jockeyed for power. The Baroque period was an age of great contrasts: a time of strong religious faith alongside unprecedented secularism, incredible scientific advances alongside rampant superstition and belief in witches, and extravagant luxury alongside dismal poverty. The period also witnessed the rise of absolute monarchies, epitomized by Louis XIV, accompanied by the emergence of a powerful middle class. Both played a significant role in art and music patronage, as did princes and lesser nobles, state and city governments, the papacy, and individual churches.

The Baroque arose in Italy, and from there it spread rapidly to the north, becoming an international style. In music, elements of the new style began to appear during the 1560s and by 1580 were widespread in northern Italy. However, the beginning of the period is traditionally dated from the appearance of opera and monody around 1600. The Baroque period in music divides into three smaller phases of approximately fifty years each: early (1600–1650), middle (1650–1700), and late (1700–1750).

GENERAL MUSICAL CHARACTERISTICS

Although each of the three divisions of the Baroque period brought changes in style and form, there are certain traits that characterize Baroque music in general and set it apart from Renaissance music.

DISTINCTION BETWEEN OLD AND NEW PRECTICES

Well before the end of the sixteenth century, composers began to search for ways to infuse their music with greater emotional content. This led some to radically new techniques, most notably that of *monody* (accompanied solo song; see chapter 15). Like composers in centuries before them, these innovators hailed their work as the "new music." Unlike earlier composers, however, they did not reject the older style but preserved it as a second language. Thus, for the first time in music history, composers consciously acknowledged and cultivated two distinct musical practices, which they used for different purposes.

PRIMA PRATTICA

The older practice (the *prima prattica* or *stile antico*) was based on the Renaissance style of imitative counterpoint as perfected by Palestrina. In this style, the composer's main concern was the writing of beautiful counterpoint. The music was, thus, more important than the words, which easily became obscured in the web of imitative entrances.

SECONDA PRATTICA

In the newer practice (the *seconda prattica or stile moderno*), on the other hand, the setting of the text was paramount, and this both suggested a homophonic texture (so that the words could be heard clearly) and justified the use of harmonic and melodic techniques that had been forbidden during the Renaissance. In a sense, these two practices represent a polarization of the influences from the Netherlands and Italy that had been blended in the High Renaissance style.

Representations of the Affections

A theory widely held during the Baroque period was that the passions—or *affections*, to use the term of that time—were caused by an imbalance of bodily fluids, an imbalance that could be brought about by both internal and external sensations. Baroque composers concluded that, if they wanted to arouse a certain affection within the listener, they simply had to devise a musical setting associated with that affection and the listener would automatically respond.

Early seventeenth-century composers of vocal music, continuing the Renaissance practice of word painting, often tried to capture the affection implied by each phrase—or even by individual words—of the text, resulting sometimes in an almost kaleidoscopic succession of rapidly changing musical textures. Later Baroque composers preferred to project a *single* overall affection for each section or movement. In doing this, they typically chose a musical pattern that expressed the desired affection and then based the entire section or movement on this pattern, continuing it in a virtually unbroken stream from beginning to end.

Rise of Idiomatic Writing

Whereas in Renaissance music voices and instruments had been largely interchangeable, during the Baroque period composers developed idiomatic ways of writing for each vocal and instrumental medium. As a result, instrumental music at last came into its own and, by the end of the period, was equal to vocal music in quantity and quality. With the development of idiomatic writing came also the possibility of deliberately *interchanging* these idioms (e.g., transferring lute ornaments to the harpsichord). Composers even interchanged entire forms, as in their use of the late Baroque instrumental concerto format for the vocal aria.

Harmony and Tonality

One of the most important developments in the Baroque period—in fact, in the history of Western music—was the final triumph of major-minor tonality over the modal system. Interestingly, the triumph of this system of musical "gravitation" (see chapter 6) came at the end of the seventeenth century at almost exactly the same time that Newton published his formulation of the laws of universal gravitation. In the new system, the earlier conception of harmony as the by-product of the intervals formed by the various voices in a contrapuntal texture was replaced with a conception of the chord as a self-contained entity whose motion was conditioned by the gravitational pull toward the tonic chord. As a result, Baroque harmony exhibits a much stronger goal-orientedness than does the older modal harmony. This harmonic and tonal stability, in turn, enabled Baroque composers to incorporate dissonance and chromaticism more freely than before, to introduce new chord types (e.g., seventh chords), and to explore modulation more fully.

Texture

COUNTERPOINT

As noted earlier, Baroque composers continued to employ imitative counterpoint, which ultimately reached new heights of perfection in the works of J. S. Bach. But their use of counterpoint differed from that of the Renaissance because it was now *harmonically* based counterpoint, in which the melodic lines were regulated to a large extent by the harmonic scheme.

BASSO CONTINUO

The most characteristic texture of the Baroque period was not imitative counterpoint, however, but rather a texture that emphasized the two outer voices—the melody and bass—held together by "filler" harmonies. In about 1600 the preference for this texture led to the rise of a musical shorthand known as *basso continuo* or *thoroughbass*, in which the composer wrote out only the melody and bass in full and simply indicated the desired harmonies by numerals or accidentals placed above or below the bass part (a practice known as *figured bass*). One or more performers playing instruments capable of producing harmony (e.g., the harpsichord, organ or lute) improvised (or *realized*) the harmonies implied by the figured bass, while another performer reinforced the bass line on a sustaining melodic instrument such as a violoncello or bassoon. The use of the basso continuo throughout the period was such an important feature of the Baroque style that some historians have referred to the period itself as the "thoroughbass period."

Rhythm

Contrapuntal music still tended to exhibit the evenly flowing rhythms associated with Renaissance polyphony. More typical of the period, however, are two other types of rhythmic organization: either the rhythm is decidedly more regular and strongly metrical than in past centuries (illustrated by the standard use, for the first time, of meter signatures and barlines) or, at the other extreme, it makes use of free, unmeasured rhythm, as in recitative (see chapter 15).

Tempo and Dynamics

Composers now also began to indicate tempo and dynamics, although this practice was by no means universal. In terms of dynamics, Baroque music tends to proceed at fairly constant levels, with a passage uniformly loud being followed by one uniformly soft. This sudden shift in dynamics is known as *terraced dynamics*. Crescendo and diminuendo are not characteristic features of Baroque music, although singers and instrumentalists probably made some use of them for expressive purposes.

Improvisation

Although improvisation had been used before, it played a more important part in the performance of Baroque music than in that of any preceding period. In addition to using improvisation in basso continuo realizations, musicians were trained in the art of improvising melodic ornaments, variations on a theme, and cadenzas.

Concertato Style

A final general characteristic of Baroque music is concertato style (*stile concertato*). This style arose in the early seventeenth century and is characterized by the juxtaposition of one voice or instrument timbre against another, one group against another or a group against a solo. Originating in the polychoral works of the Venetian school and in certain late sixteenth-century madrigals, concertato style was an important feature of Baroque music throughout the period.

OVERVIEW OF THE PERIOD

The Early Baroque (c. 1600–1650)

The first half of the seventeenth century was a period of great experimentation as composers attempted to reconcile polyphonic techniques inherited from the Renaissance with developments that came to the fore around 1600, such as monody, basso continuo, concertato style, and idiomatic writing. By midcentury composers had begun to fuse these elements into a coherent new musical language.

There was also much experimentation in the area of harmony as composers began the transition from modality to major-minor tonality. The harmony of the early Baroque lies midway between the two systems: chordal in concept, yet lacking the organizing force of tonality with its goal-oriented harmonic progressions. As a result, it can sometimes seem crude and lacking in direction, although it does have a certain "anything goes" charm.

MUSICAL FORMS

Many important new musical forms made their first appearances during the early Baroque. Of these, the principal new vocal forms were the opera, oratorio, and cantata (see chapters 15 and 16), while the main instrumental forms were the sonata, dance suite, and fugue (see chapter 17). In addition, several forms inherited from the Renaissance continued to develop, such as the madrigal, motet, Mass, theme and variations, chaconne (passacaglia), toccata, ricercar, and canzona. Important schools of French lute and harpsichord music and German organ composition also arose.

Italy dominated the early Baroque, with nearly every new form originating and flourishing first in that country. Exceptions include the dance suite, which arose in Germany (with the French contributing the characteristic style and idiom of the individual dance movements), and the fugue, which also flourished earliest in northern countries. For the most part, musical form was in constant flux throughout the period. By midcentury, opera had assumed a standard format based upon the alternation of recitatives and arias (with occasional choruses interspersed). Other forms, however, generally did not settle into their characteristic Baroque formats until the second half of the century.

REPRESENTATIVE COMPOSERS

The two leading composers of the early Baroque period are (1) Claudio Monteverdi (1567–1643), the composer whose works best illustrate the transition from the Renaissance to the Baroque style and who most clearly fused the disparate musical elements of the early seventeenth century into the new Baroque musical language; and (2) Heinrich Schütz (1585–1672), the greatest German composer of the mid-seventeenth century , whose fusion of the Italian and German styles laid the foundation for later German Baroque music.

Other prominent composers include Giulio Caccini (c. 1545–1618), Jacopo Peri (1561–1633), Stefano Landi (c. 1591–c. 1655), Luigi Rossi (c. 1597–1653), Pietro Francesco Cavalli (1602–1676), Antonio Cesti (1623–1669), and Giacomo Carissimi (1605–1674) in the area of vocal music, and Girolamo Frescobaldi (1583–1643), Samuel Scheidt (1587–1654), Johann Jakob Froberger (1616–1667), Jan Pieterszoon Sweelinck (1562–1621), Jacques Champion de Chambonnières (1602–1672), and Biagio Marini (c. 1587–1663) in the area of instrumental music.

The Middle Baroque (c. 1650–1700)

During the second half of the seventeenth century, the Baroque style reached its maturity as major-minor tonality came into full bloom and the various vocal and instrumental genres settled into standardized formats.

VOCAL FORMS

Opera. Opera, which had flourished primarily in Italy during the early Baroque, now spread to other countries, where national styles emerged. Italian opera, with its center in Venice, still led the way, however. The most important new development was the bel canto style (see chapter 15). Toward the end of the century, Naples emerged as an important center, bringing a new style that was to dominate opera of the late Baroque. During this period, also, the opera overture began to crystallize; the two main types were the French overture and the Italian sinfonia.

Cantata. Composers of cantatas, most of whom also wrote operas, adapted the operatic format of alternating recitatives and arias, and the Italian cantata spread to other countries.

Sacred Music. The oratorio emerged as a major new form, adapting opera's alternating recitatives and arias as its standard format. The motet became the favored form at the Royal Chapel of Louis XIV, while in England the anthem and Service continued as the principal sacred vocal forms. As Germany recovered from the Thirty Years' War, the period from 1650 to 1750 became a golden age of Lutheran music. Composers also continued to write Passions, Masses, and other types of sacred music.

INSTRUMENTAL FORMS

Keyboard Music. The most important developments in organ music during this period took place in Germany, where the main forms were the toccata, fugue (which had almost entirely replaced the older ricercar), and compositions based upon chorales. The two most important forms of clavier (i.e., harpsichord and clavichord) music were the theme and variations and the suite. In Germany the suite assumed its standard core of four dances: *allemande*, *courante*, *sarabande*, and *gigue*.

The Sonata. Italians still reigned supreme in instrumental chamber music, and an age of great string music in Italy began, corresponding to an era of great violin makers in Cremona (e.g., Amati, Stradivari, and Guarneri). The characteristic texture of the period was that of the trio sonata, consisting of two treble instruments (usually violins or flutes) and basso continuo. Yet composers also began to write solo sonatas during this period, establishing a genre that was to become increasingly important after 1700. During this period, too, the sonata crystallized into two basic types, the *sonata da chiesa* (church sonata) and the *sonata da camera* (chamber sonata). The leading sonata composer of the time was Arcangelo Corelli.

The Concerto. The concerto emerged in the 1680s and became the most important Baroque instrumental form after 1700. The two main types of concerto were (1) the *concerto grosso*, which pitted a small group of solo instruments against the orchestra, and (2) the *solo concerto*, for a single solo instrument and orchestra. In the works of Giuseppe Torelli, the concerto attained a standard three-movement plan (fast-slow-fast) and a format of alternating *ritornellos* and solo passages within individual movements (see chapter 17).

REPRESENTATIVE COMPOSERS

The leading Italian composer of the middle Baroque was Arcangelo Corelli (1653–1713), who brought Italian chamber music to its "classic" Baroque phase and whose works provide the earliest examples of major-minor tonality in full bloom. The leading composer in France was Jean-Baptiste Lully (1632–1687), an Italian by birth, who established the characteristic types of French Baroque opera and ballet. England's greatest composer of the period was Henry Purcell (1659–1695), who produced many fine instrumental and vocal works, among them incidental music for forty-nine plays and one immortal opera (*Dido and Aeneas*).

Of the many other important composers of the period, ones most closely associated with vocal music include Antonio Sartorio (1630–1680), Giovanni Legrenzi (1626–1690), Carlo Pallavicino (1630–1688), Agostino Steffani (1654–1728), Alessandro Stradella (1644–1682), John Blow (1649–1708), Marc-Antoine Charpentier (c. 1645–1704), and Antonio Caldara (1670–1736). Composers of instrumental music include Georg Böhm (1661–1733), Johann Christoph Bach (1642–1703), Dietrich Buxtehude (c. 1637–1707), Johann Pachelbel (1653–1706), Juan Bautista José Cabanilles (1644–1712), Heinrich Ignaz Franz Biber (1644–1704), G. B. Vitali (1632-1692), and Giuseppe Torelli (1658–1709).

The Late Baroque (c. 1700–1750)

By the beginning of the eighteenth century, the various Baroque vocal and instrumental forms had all settled into fairly standardized formats. Yet, *within* these forms we can see in the works of certain composers progressive approaches that clearly presage a new era. Thus, at the same time that the Baroque style was reaching its culmination, the pre-Classical style was emerging, and composers were able to choose from among imitative techniques inherited from the Renaissance, approaches developed during the seventeenth century, and more progressive tendencies. The late Baroque style is therefore an amalgam of these practices, with the specific blend varying from composer to composer.

Because the majority of Baroque music performed today dates from the late Baroque, many listeners think of the late Baroque style as "the" Baroque style.

GENERAL CHARACTERISTICS OF STYLE

At the beginning of the eighteenth century, progressive tendencies can be seen most clearly in the solo concertos of Antonio Vivaldi (see chapter 17). His concertos exhibit a mastery of major-minor tonality and a full awareness of its possibilities, great rhythmic energy, a "popular" orientation, and a typical Italian flair for simple yet dramatic statement. Vivaldi's concerto style was to have profound influence on later Baroque concertos and instrumental music and on vocal music as well.

Melody. The most characteristic type of late Baroque melody is one in which the line is long and the composer's interest is centered more on the elaboration of a motive than on the breaking up of the melody into short, regular phrases. In such melodies, it is not uncommon for the line to spin forth in one continuous flow for an entire section before coming to rest on a cadence. On the other hand, there are also melodies—seen particularly in dance movements—that do fall into regular phrases (often four measures in length) and ones that are based upon simple triadic or scalewise progression; it is these that presage more clearly the approaching Classical style. Baroque melodies are characterized also by frequent use of sequences (see chapter 6), florid ornamentation, and wide range.

Rhythm. Reflecting the late Baroque practice of projecting a single basic affection for an entire movement or section, there is a strong tendency in late Baroque music for a rhythmic pattern, once established, to continue from the beginning to the end of a movement or section. This does not make it boring, however. In Vivaldi's fast movements, for example, this regularity manifests itself in an almost machinelike rhythmic drive that generates a great amount of energy and motion.

Harmony. The bedrock upon which late Baroque harmony rests is the perfection of major-minor tonality. Within this system composers soon developed a complete musical grammar, capable of expressing every possible emotional and musical nuance. Secure within this system, they were also able to explore modulations and chromaticism in ways that are both compelling and entirely logical.

Texture. Texture varies greatly in late Baroque music. In some genres, such as the fugue or invention, imitative counterpoint predominates. In others a homophonic texture prevails. Yet even in music that is primarily homophonic, a distinctive "Baroque" type of homophony is the general rule, one that Bukofzer (*Music in the Baroque Era*) has called *continuo-homophony*. Originating in the concerto style of Vivaldi, continuo-homophony is homophonic in the sense that there is one main melody. Yet there is much incidental use of counterpoint as well, and the bass voice, in particular, has a much greater melodic character and importance than in later homophony. Thus continuo-homophony—like the basso continuo texture in general— tends to emphasize the two outer voices. Fast-changing chords are another characteristic of continuo-homophony.

Passages in which all the voices or instruments proceed in unison (producing monophonic texture) are also common.

VOCAL FORMS

Opera. In the late Baroque, two main trends emerged in opera: (1) the presence of the new Neapolitan style of opera alongside the older Baroque style of opera inherited from the seventeenth century and (2) the separation of serious opera (*opera seria*) from comic opera (*opera buffa*). Important, too, were the application of the concerto style to the operatic aria and the prevalence of the da capo aria form (chapter 15).

Cantata. The Italian chamber cantata retained the general outlines established during the seventeenth century. Alessandro Scarlatti, with over 600 cantatas, was the leading composer in this genre.

The Lutheran Church Cantata. The late Baroque period did produce one important new genre, the Lutheran church cantata (chapter 16), which combined the chorale, the solo song, and the concertato style with the operatic recitative and aria. J. S. Bach's cantatas represent the culmination of this genre.

Oratorio and Other Sacred Music. The oratorio reached its peak in the works of George Frideric Handel. Composers also continued to write Passions, Masses, motets, and other forms of sacred music; most of these reached their culmination in the works of J. S. Bach.

INSTRUMENTAL FORMS

Concerto. The solo concertos of Vivaldi, which built upon the format and style of Torelli, set the standard for the late Baroque concerto. Other notable contributions to the genre were made by later Italian composers and by Bach (e.g., his *Brandenburg Concertos*) and Handel (particularly his twelve *Grand Concertos*, Op. 6).

Sonata. The same developments that revolutionized the concerto in the early eighteenth century also touched the sonata to some extent, resulting in an increased use of homophonic texture, more regular phrase structures, and greater rhythmic vitality. In addition, sonatas increasingly adapted the three-movement plan of the concerto, and solo sonatas began to predominate over ensemble sonatas.

Suite. The keyboard suite continued to flourish, particularly in the works of François Couperin and J. S. Bach. Also important during this period were orchestral suites, such as the four by J. S. Bach as well as Handel's *Water Music* and his *Music for the Royal Fireworks*.

Other Instrumental Forms. Other forms, such as the toccata, fugue, chorale prelude, theme and variations, and passacaglia, also continued to thrive. Many of these found their highest expression in the hands of J. S. Bach, who created masterpieces in every instrumental form of the period.

REPRESENTATIVE COMPOSERS

The four giants of the late Baroque period are (1) Antonio Vivaldi (1678–1741), the Italian composer whose concerto style revolutionized early eighteenth-century musical style; (2) Jean-Philippe Rameau (1683–1764), the leading French musician of the period, who was notable both as a composer and as a music theorist; (3) George Frideric Handel (1685–1759), a German who studied in Italy but spent most of his career in London and whose operas and oratorios epitomize the grand style in late Baroque music; and (4) Johann Sebastian Bach (1685–1750), revered today as one of the greatest composers who ever lived, who developed contrapuntal techniques to unsurpassed heights and produced sublime masterpieces in virtually every Baroque form except opera.

Other important composers of vocal music include Alessandro Scarlatti (1660–1725), Reinhard Keiser (1674–1739), Giovanni Battista Pergolesi (1710–1736), Johann Adolf Hasse (1699–1783), and Georg Philipp Telemann (1681–1767). Representative composers of instrumental music include François Couperin (1668–1733), Francesco Geminiani (1687–1762), Francesco Veracini (1690–c. 1750), Pietro Locatelli (1695–1764), Jean-Marie Leclair (1697–1764), and Tomaso Albinoni (1671–1750).

Developments in music during the Baroque period may be summarized as follows. During the seventeenth century, which encompassed the early and middle phases of the Baroque period, composers explored the radical new developments in harmony, style, and musical form that arose c. 1600. By the end of the century, the new Baroque musical language had crystallized in the perfection of major-minor tonality, and virtually every Baroque vocal and instrumental form had settled into a format that was to remain standard for the rest of the period. During the late Baroque, composers such as Vivaldi, Rameau, Handel, and Bach developed these forms to their highest level of perfection while at the same time influencing and being influenced by emerging pre-Classical trends.

For Additional Study

This list contains only general sources. Works related to specific genres and composers appear in the reading lists at the end of chapters 15 through 17.

Anthony, James, et al. *The New Grove French Baroque Masters*. New York: Norton; London: Macmillan. 1986.

Arnold, Denis, et al. *The New Grove Italian Baroque Masters*. New York: Norton; London: Macmillan. 1984.

Blume, Friedrich. *Renaissance and Baroque Music: A Comprehensive Survey*. Translated by M. D. Herter Norton. New York: Norton. 1967.

Bukofzer, Manfred F. *Music in the Baroque Era*. New York: Norton. 1947.

The EAV Art and Music Series. "Baroque Art and Music." Distributed by Educational Audio Visual, Inc. (Pleasantville, NY). Videocassette.

The EAV History of Music. Part 3: "The Baroque Era." Distributed by Educational Audio Visual, Inc. (Pleasantville, NY). Videocassette.

Man & Music Series. "The Age of Reason"; "Music at the Court of Louis XIV." Distributed by Films for the Humanities & Sciences (Princeton, NJ). Videocassettes.

Palisca, Claude V. *Baroque Music.* 3d ed. Englewood Cliffs, NJ: Prentice-Hall. 1991.

Rifkin, Joshua, et al. *The New Grove North European Baroque Masters.* New York: Norton; London: Macmillan. 1985.

15

Baroque Opera

1539–89	The *intermedio*, madrigal comedy, and other forerunners of opera flourish in Italy
1570s	The Florentine Camerata begins to meet, considers ancient Greek drama
1597	Jacopo Peri, *Dafne*, the first opera (largely lost)
1600	First published examples of basso continuo; *Euridice*, the earliest surviving opera
1607	Monteverdi's *L'Orfeo* is produced in Mantua, the first great opera
1629	Lope de Vega, *La selva sin amor*, the first Spanish drama set completely to music
c. 1631–c. 1653	Roman school of early Baroque opera flourishes
1637	First public opera house opens in Venice; its success generates others, influencing composers to write for the broader public rather than the aristocratic few
1639	Mazzocchi and Marazzoli, *Chi soffre, speri*, the first comic opera
c. 1639–c. 1700	Venice reigns as the leading center of Italian opera
1644	S. T. Staden, *Seelewig*, the earliest surviving German opera
1648	Pedro Calderón de la Barca invents the Spanish *zarzuela* form
1671–83	French opera arises under Louis XIV and flourishes in the works of Lully
1678–1738	Hamburg opens the first public opera house in Europe outside of Italy and serves as a center for a national school of German opera
1683–1740	Rise of *intermezzi* and other developments in comic opera
1684–1702	Rise of Naples as an important center of opera (e.g., Scarlatti)
1689	Purcell, *Dido and Aeneas*
1705–41	Handel composes operas in Hamburg, Venice, and London
1728	The success of the ballad opera *The Beggar's Opera* signals that England is tiring of Italian opera
c. 1730	Rise of the Neapolitan "pre-Classical" style of opera
1733–49	Rameau raises French opera to new heights

Every age has produced forms that combine drama with music, from the tragedies of ancient Greece to the liturgical plays of the Middle Ages and the intermedi (entertainments performed between the acts of a play), madrigal comedies, and other genres of the Renaissance. Since the beginning of the seventeenth century, however, the principal type of musical drama in Western art music has been the opera.

An opera is a drama set to music. It embraces such arts as poetry, scenic and costume design, acting, and dancing, in addition to vocal and instrumental music. Operas may be serious, comic, or a combination of the two, and, though they may contain spoken dialogue, most are sung in their entirety.

Opera was one of the first and greatest of the new musical forms to appear at the beginning of the Baroque period. Arising in Italy c. 1600, it soon spread throughout Europe, becoming the leading form of musical entertainment. Better than any other musical genre, opera—with its unique blend of music, theater, virtuosity, nobility, spectacle, and emotional expressiveness—captures the spirit of the Baroque age.

Later in this chapter, we will survey developments in Baroque opera. But first, by way of introduction, we will explore the various components of opera.

COMPONENTS OF OPERA

Acts and Scenes

Like a play, an opera is customarily divided into main sections, or *acts*. These are usually subdivided into shorter sections, or *scenes*. A scene may end definitely, and provide an opportunity for applause, or it may proceed directly into the following scene to form a continuous flow of music.

Libretto

The text of an opera is called the *libretto*. The libretto is sometimes adapted from a novel or play; most often, though, it is written specially for a particular composer (e.g., Lorenzo da Ponte's libretti for Mozart); and sometimes, though less often, it is created by the composer himself (e.g., Wagner and Menotti).

The performance of an opera in a foreign language may constitute a barrier to appreciation. As an aid to understanding the dialogue, most recordings of complete operas are issued with the libretto and its translation printed side by side. In addition, television and other video productions normally provide running translations at the bottom of the screen. In many live productions, the translation is projected onto a screen above the stage.

Lacking these, a synopsis of the plot, easily obtained from libraries, can provide a general idea of the story line.

Recitative

Recitative is sung dialogue, that is, a type of singing that is midway between speech and true song and in which the vocal line imitates the rhythmic inflections and the natural rise and fall of speech. Recitative is used mainly for monologues, dialogues, the advancement of the plot, and other situations in which the composer is interested more in making the words intelligible than in constructing a beautiful song.

The two main types of recitative are (1) *recitativo secco* (dry recitative), in which the voice, supported only by sparse accompaniment in the continuo, moves quickly through dialogue; and (2) *recitativo accompagnato* (accompanied recitative), used for more dramatic situations, in which the voice is accompanied by the orchestra.

Aria

An *aria* is an extended song for solo voice accompanied by orchestra, in which the action typically stops while the singer pauses to reflect on, and react emotionally to, events. An aria has a more elaborate melody and a more structured formal design than does a recitative. It has a strict metrical pattern and a steady beat, and the repetition of words for dramatic emphasis is common. Arias constitute an important literature for solo voice. Familiarity with famous arias is one basis for developing an appreciation of opera.

Duo, Trio, and Other Small Ensembles

Small vocal ensembles (see chapter 9) also play an important part in opera. The "Quartet" from *Rigoletto* and the "Sextet" from *Lucia di Lammermoor* are famous examples.

Chorus

Operas that include scenes involving crowds of people make use of large choral ensembles. Examples of famous operatic choruses are the "Anvil Chorus" from *Il trovatore and the "Pilgrim's Chorus" from Tannhüser*.

Orchestra

In opera, the voices are normally accompanied by orchestra. The orchestra is also heard alone in the overture (see below) and in instrumental interludes. In some operas, the orchestra provides merely the accompaniment to singing and dancing, while in others it plays a more significant role. The orchestra occupies a particularly prominent position in Wagner's operas.

Overture

The instrumental composition that is played before an opera begins is called an *overture*, or, sometimes, a *prelude*. Two types of overture that were common during the Baroque period were the *French overture* and the *Italian sinfonia*; both are discussed later in this chapter. Mention should be made also of the *potpourri* or *medley* overture used in light operas. This type of overture consists of chains of themes from the opera. In general, composers are more concerned in the overture with presenting the prevailing mood of the opera than with introducing its themes.

Ballet

Dances of a formal and stylized nature are sometimes introduced into opera as interludes not essential to the plot. Ballet is particularly important in French opera.

APPRECIATION OF OPERA

It is possible to enjoy opera merely by listening to it. To grasp the full experience of opera, however, it must be seen as well as heard. Therefore, it is recommended that the listener attend live opera productions, if possible, or view performances on television, videotape, videodisc or film. When listening to audio recordings, it can be helpful to visualize the action, scenery, and costuming as the music is playing.

Appreciation of opera depends also in large part on our accepting the convention that characters sing instead of talk.

BAROQUE OPERA

Baroque opera developed along two general lines. Many operas of the period were composed for presentation at court and tended toward formality and grandeur; the French operas of Lully and Rameau exemplify this style. Beginning with the opening of the first public opera house in Venice in 1637—followed soon by others in Italy and, during the early 1700s, by important ones in Hamburg, Leipzig, and London—we also see operas written for the general public, with a resulting attempt to appeal to broader tastes; this is particularly evident in Italian operas of the middle and late Baroque. Some composers, such as Handel, were able to combine the grand manner with popular appeal.

Baroque opera plots were based most often on tales drawn from Greek and Roman mythology or on historical subjects. Like the other Baroque arts, opera sought above all to arouse the passions, and extremes of emotion were the rule.

Opera brought with it, too, the rise of the virtuoso singer. Especially prominent throughout the period were the *castrati* (singular, *castrato*), male singers who had undergone castration before their voices changed in order to preserve their soprano or alto register throughout adulthood.

Early Baroque Opera (c. 1600–1650)

FLORENTINE OPERA

Opera arose as the result of attempts by a group of Florentine humanists, known as the Camerata, to rediscover the method of performance used in ancient Greek drama. These men concluded that Greek drama was sung to a type of melody that was midway between speech and song and that served simply to enhance the effect of the words, which were the more important element. They decided that, in order not to obscure the text in modern settings, homophonic rather than polyphonic texture was required. Thus, they invented a new type of homophonic solo song called monody, in which a solo voice sang the melody, accompanied by simple chords that supported, but in no way obscured, the vocal delivery of the text. Further, for the presentation of dramatic music, they invented a special style of monody in which the melody, fashioned on the Greek model, was midway between speech and song—a type of melody similar to what we know today as recitative. This style underlay the earliest operas, such as Euridice (1600), set jointly by Jacopo Peri and Giulio Caccini but published a year later in separate versions by each (figure 15.1).

Jacopo Peri, Excerpt from *L'Euridice* (1601)

O mio core o mio spe-me, o pace o vi-ta Oi- me chi- mi t'ha tol- to,

O my heart, O my hope, O peace, O life,
Alas, who has taken you from me?

Source: Peri, Jacopo. *Le Musiche di Jacopo Peri nobil Fiorentino sopra L'Euridice del Sig. Ottavio Rinuccini . . . .* Venice: Alessandro Raverii. 1608. Transcription of the full printed score at the British Museum. 1915. (Washington, DC: Library of Congress)

Fig 15.1

Orfeo. The first *great* opera was Monteverdi's *L'Orfeo* (Orpheus), written in 1607 for the Gonzaga court in Mantua, the first of three operas by Monteverdi that survive. Like Josquin a century earlier, Monteverdi was the greatest composer of his time. He occupied a position in the creation of the Baroque style comparable to Josquin's in the creation of the High Renaissance style. When he turned his genius toward the fledgling operatic genre, he transformed it immediately into a true art form.

In *Orfeo*, Monteverdi's handling of the recitative style far surpassed anything written earlier, particularly in such passages as Orpheus's lament, "Tu se' morta" (You Are Dead). In addition, he used every other musical resource available to produce a varied and imaginative work: solo airs, duets, madrigal-like choruses, dances, and all kinds of instrumental music. For Monteverdi, the music was every bit as important as the words. *Orfeo* shows, moreover, a more organized formal structure, more expressive uses of harmony, and a stronger and more varied representation of emotions than did the earlier operas.

OPERA IN ROME AND VENICE

In the 1630s and 1640s, first Rome and then Venice emerged as centers of opera, led by Stefano Landi and Luigi Rossi of Rome and Pietro Francesco Cavalli and Antonio Cesti of Venice. Monteverdi also wrote his last two surviving operas for Venice, *Il ritorno d'Ulisse in patria* (The Return of Ulysses to His Native Country, 1641) and his greatest opera, *L'incoronazione di Poppea* (The Coronation of Poppea, 1642).

The Rise of Public Opera. The opening of the first public opera house in Venice in 1637, followed shortly by others in Venice and elsewhere, was a milestone whose importance cannot be overemphasized. For the first time, Western music was to be written for the broader public rather than the aristocratic few. The need to appeal to this broader audience forced composers to develop a more popular style. As a result, operas soon became public spectacles, with elaborate scenery, much use of stage machinery for special effects, and a more accessible style of music.

Emphasis on Solo Singing. During this period, the libretto came to be viewed as no more than a framework for the music and spectacle, and plots were filled with complex and improbable situations. More and more, interest came to be centered on the solo voice, bringing both an increase in virtuosic singing (as seen particularly in writing for the castrato) and the rise of the bel canto ("beautiful singing") tradition that was to remain important in Italian opera for centuries. Accompanying this increased emphasis on solo singing was a drastic reduction in the roles of the chorus and orchestra. On the other hand, we do see in this period the earliest examples of full-fledged overtures.

Bel Canto. The bel canto style is characterized by (1) smooth, graceful melodies well suited to the voice; (2) simple rhythms, often based on dance patterns; (3) the frequent use of triple meter; (4) short phrases punctuated by clear cadences; (5) simple harmonies that often make use of stereotyped chord progressions; and (6) the projection of one main affection per movement or section rather than many. Figure 15.2 illustrates this new style of singing, which took the opera world by storm.

The Rise of Recitative and Aria. Another vitally important development during this period was the separation of solo singing into recitative and aria. This reconciled once and for all the *prima prattica–seconda prattica* controversy by giving words and music each their separate domains. Recitative would be used whenever clear declamation of text was more important, whereas the aria, with its greater emphasis on musical values, would be used whenever the characters pause to reflect on events. At this time a standard format thus arose that was to predominate in opera for the remainder of the Baroque period and be applied to the oratorio and cantata as well: the regular alternation of recitatives and arias, with an occasional small ensemble, chorus or instrumental piece interspersed as the action dictated.

Cavalli, Aria from *Egisto* (1643), Act 3, scene 7

Source: Cavalli, Francesco. *Opera L'Egisto di Fran.ᶜᵒ Cavalli.* Transcription, 1907. (Washington, DC: Library of Congress)

Fig 15.2

Middle Baroque Opera (c. 1650–1700)

During the second half of the seventeenth century, national styles of opera developed throughout Europe. Italy still led the way, however.

ITALIAN OPERA

Venice remained the center of Italian opera during the middle Baroque period, led by Antonio Sartorio and Giovanni Legrenzi , who continued the trends present at midcentury. In their works, the aria assumed more importance than ever before, and both virtuosic and bel canto writing were developed further.

Toward the end of the century, Naples emerged as another important center of opera, bringing a new style that would predominate in the eighteenth century. The Neapolitan composer most associated with the transition to this newer style is Alessandro Scarlatti. Other important Italian composers of the time were Alessandro Stradella and two who worked mainly in Germany, Agostino Steffani and Carlo Pallivicino.

OPERA IN OTHER COUNTRIES

France. Although Italian opera had been presented in France earlier, France did not develop a national style of its own until the 1670s, during the reign of Louis XIV. The composer most responsible for establishing a French opera style was Jean-Baptiste Lully.

Lully created a form of opera, which he called the *tragdie lyrique* (tragedy in music), by blending Italian opera characteristics, the pastoral tradition, French classic tragedy as exemplified by Racine and Corneille, and French court ballet. Compared with Italian opera, French opera (1) made greater use of ballet as an integral part of the genre, (2) made less distinction between recitative and aria, (3) made more use of the chorus and orchestra, and (4) placed greater importance on dramatic integrity and less on virtuosic display. Lully also established the French overture (see below) as the standard overture form for French opera.

England. The principal forerunner of opera in England was the *masque*, a form of court entertainment that combined dialogues, songs, dances, and instrumental music. Toward the end of the seventeenth century, two works appeared that may be classified as true operas: *Venus and Adonis* (1684), by John Blow, and *Dido and Aeneas* (1689), by Henry Purcell.

Purcell. Purcell was one of the greatest English composers of all time, and many consider his *Dido and Aeneas* (based on Virgil's *Aeneid*) to be the finest opera ever written on an English text. Particularly beautiful is "Dido's Lament" ("When I Am Laid in Earth") and the chorus which follows it ("With Drooping Wings"). Typical of Baroque laments, "Dido's Lament" is based upon a *ground bass*, or *basso ostinato* (obstinate, or persistent, bass), a device in which the bass repeats a short musical idea over and over while the other upper voices constantly change. The particular ground bass used by Purcell, a chromatically descending line (figure 15.3), was a stock Baroque lament figure. Yet in his hands the repetitions of the bass become powerful symbols both of Dido's growing resolve to kill herself and of the inevitability of the outcome. With each repetition tension mounts until a heartbreaking climax is reached on the words "remember me."

Ground Bass of "Dido's Lament" from Purcell's *Dido and Aeneas* (1689)

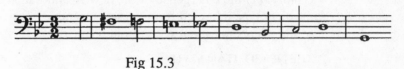

Fig 15.3

Purcell and other English composers also wrote a significant amount of incidental music to accompany plays. Some of this music is so extensive that it approaches opera.

Germany and Spain. For most of the seventeenth century, opera in Germany was dominated by Italian composers living in the country. However, with the opening of the Hamburg opera house in 1678—the first public opera house in Europe outside of Italy—a school of native German opera composers began to emerge, culminating in Reinhard Keiser. In Spain a national form, the *zarzuela*, arose in 1648 in the works of Pedro Caldern de la Barca; this form combined singing and dancing with spoken dialogue.

THE OPERA OVERTURE

From the very beginning, composers had used instruments by themselves in various places in their operas. Most often these passages took the form of a *ritornello* (an instrumental passage that recurs again and again in the manner of a refrain) or a *sinfonia* (a short instrumental piece used as an interlude or to facilitate a scene change).

As early as Monteverdi's *Orfeo*, composers had also used instrumental pieces to introduce the opera. Gradually during the seventeenth century, two main types of overture crystallized: the *French overture* ("ouverture") and the *Italian sinfonia*. Although both types had been foreshadowed earlier, Lully is usually credited with establishing the French overture as an important form, while Alessandro Scarlatti is given credit for the Italian sinfonia.

The French overture consists of two main sections, each usually repeated: a slow, majestic opening section, which is usually homophonic and features dotted rhythms; and a faster second section, which is usually imitative and concludes with a brief return to the slow tempo and dotted rhythms of the first section. The Italian sinfonia typically consists of three sections: an imitative section in fast tempo, a short interlude in slow tempo, and a fast, dancelike section in binary form. This form of overture was the forerunner of the classical symphony.

French and Italian overture types were used not only in operas of the Baroque period but also as opening movements to oratorios, cantatas, suites, and other instrumental forms.

LATE BAROQUE OPERA (c. 1700–c. 1750)

Two main trends characterize opera during the first half of the eighteenth century: (1) the emergence of the new Neapolitan style of opera alongside the older type inherited from the seventeenth century and (2) the separation of serious opera (*opera seria*) from comic opera (*opera buffa*).

THE NEAPOLITAN STYLE

During the late seventeenth and early eighteenth centuries, a new style of opera began to appear in the works of the Neapolitan composer Alessandro Scarlatti. This style was developed further by Scarlatti's successors in Naples, such as Leonardo Vinci (c. 1690–1730), Nicola Porpora (1686–1768), Giovanni Battista Pergolesi (1710–1736), and other composers.

During the eighteenth century, the Neapolitan style superseded the Venetian and soon dominated not only Italian opera but also that of every European country except France.

General Musical Characteristics. Neapolitan composers preferred tuneful melodies that often fell into short, symmetrical phrases; a thinner homophonic texture in which the melody clearly predominated; and simple harmonies. In addition, four other distinct practices characterize Neapolitan opera: (1) the establishment (by Scarlatti) of the Italian sinfonia as the preferred overture type; (2) the division of recitative into the two now-common classes of *recitativo secco* and *recitativo accompagnato*; (3) the adaptation of the Vivaldi concerto style (see chapter 17) to the opera aria, with the result that arias began to exhibit the general musical character and the pattern of alternating instrumental ritornellos and solo passages heard in the concerto; and (4) the establishment of the A B A da capo aria as the prevailing aria form.

The Da Capo Aria. The da capo aria is so designated because composers often wrote out only the A and B sections and, at the end of the B section, simply directed the performer to go back to the beginning (*da capo*, the "head") for the return of the A section. This form permitted performers to improvise all sorts of embellishments during the return of the A section. The da capo aria became so popular that composers soon used it to the virtual exclusion of other aria forms.

Figure 15.4 shows the formal outline of a typical Scarlatti *da capo aria*, illustrating how the A B A da capo form and the alternating instrumental ritornellos (labeled R) and vocal solos (labeled S) derived from the concerto style might be coordinated. It also illustrates how composers might modulate through various keys before returning to the home key (here, C minor). The specific number of ritornello-solo alternations in each section was subject to infinite variation, and later composers such as Handel often greatly expanded each of the three main sections. However, this general approach was used for countless arias in operas, oratorios, cantatas, and other vocal genres of the late Baroque period.

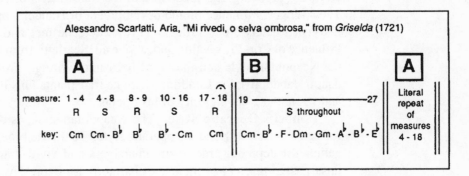

Fig 15.4

Changes in the Libretto. Given the decline in the quality of libretti during the seventeenth century, it was inevitable that a reform movement would begin. This manifested itself during the early eighteenth century in a neoclassical revival championed in opera by the poets Apostolo Zeno (1668–1750) and Pietro Metastasio (1698–1782). From a neoclassical belief that tragedy and comedy should not be mixed, Zeno purged serious opera of all comic elements; this, in turn, gave rise to an increased distinction between serious opera and comic opera, which thereafter tended to develop along different paths.

Ultimately, the reforms of Zeno and Metastasio were not successful, in part because of their continued reliance on outmoded traditions such as the rigid alternation of recitatives and arias rather than on more flexible approaches and because composers continued to stress excessive vocal virtuosity over a more equal balance of dramatic and musical elements. Nevertheless, the new style pointed opera in a new direction that would lead eventually through the reforms of Christoph Gluck to a culmination in the operas of Mozart. For this reason the Neapolitan style, particularly from about 1730 on, is sometimes referred to as the pre-Classical style.

THE OLDER STYLE

At the same time that the Neapolitan style was emerging, the older form of Baroque opera was reaching its culmination in the works of such composers as Reinhard Keiser in Germany, George Frideric Handel in England,

and in the French operas of Jean-Philippe Rameau, who carried the operatic tradition of Lully to greater heights.

Handel. The leading figure of this group, and perhaps the greatest of all late Baroque opera composers, was Handel. Handel was an extremely cosmopolitan composer, whose operas show a blend of German polyphonic craft, the French grand manner, and the innovations of Neapolitan opera. The strongest influence on the development of Handel's operatic style was his visit to Italy from 1706 to 1710, where he met and came under the influence of Corelli, Vivaldi, and, above all, Scarlatti, from whom he learned the Neapolitan style and the art of bel canto writing. From 1712 until his death, Handel lived in London, where he transplanted his Italian opera style and wrote the great majority of his operas.

Handel's Operatic Style. The Neapolitan style, as described earlier, formed the basis of Handel's operatic style. To this he brought an incredible genius for depicting true-to-life characters and vivid dramatic effects, an unsurpassed mastery of the use of harmony for expressive purposes, and a typically German command of polyphony. He also favored the French overture form over the Italian sinfonia. Typical of the late Baroque, each of his arias normally expresses a single main affection. As a result, a Handel opera as a whole gives the general effect of a series of separate moods strung together. Late Baroque opera was, in many ways, a highly artificial and convention-bound genre. Yet, in the hands of Handel and Rameau, it was capable of great expressive power.

In 1728 the success of the lighter ballad opera *The Beggar's Opera* was a sign that the English public was beginning to tire of Italian opera. As a result, in the 1730s, Handel began to turn more and more to oratorio (see chapter 16), though he continued to write operas until 1741.

COMIC OPERA

Zeno's abolition of comic elements from serious opera brought about a complete separation of the two types, and comic opera thereafter began to develop as a separate genre. A number of different national forms developed, such as the Italian *opera buffa*, the French *opra comique*, the English *ballad opera*, and the German *Singspiel*. These forms are discussed in relation to Classical opera in chapter 20.

*O*pera *arose in aristocratic circles from an attempt to rediscover the method of performance used in Greek drama. Following Greek ideals, early composers of opera invented monody and a recitative style in which the music served simply to enhance the words, which were considered the more important element. By the middle of the seventeenth century, the opposite situation prevailed: opera had become an art for the public, and music and spectacle were more important than the libretto, which was now often filled with complex* *and improbable situations. During the middle and late Baroque, this type of opera hardened into a rigid alternation of recitatives and arias, and the solo voice and vocal virtuosity reigned supreme, to the relative neglect of ensembles, choruses, and the orchestra. Yet in the hands of composers like Handel and Rameau, this artificial form was still capable of tremendous expressive power.*

At the same time that this older style was reaching its culmination in the first half of the eighteenth century, the Neapolitan style emerged. This type of opera was based on new ideas concerning the libretto and new developments in musical style. While this new opera was weakened by its ties with outmoded traditions of the past, it pointed the way toward the opera of the Classical Period.

For Additional Study

Arnold, Denis, and Nigel Fortune, eds. The New Monteverdi Companion. London: Faber. 1985.

Dean, Winton, with Anthony Hicks. *The New Grove Handel*. New York: Norton. 1983.

Grout, Donald Jay. *Alessandro Scarlatti: An Introduction to His Operas*. Berkeley: University of California Press. 1979.

___. *A Short History of Opera*. 2d ed. New York and London: Columbia University Press. 1965.

Music & Man Series. "Monteverdi in Mantua"; "The Italian Connection." Distributed by Films for the Humanities & Sciences (Princeton, NJ). Videocassettes.

Newman, J. E. W. *Jean-Baptiste de Lully and His Tragedies lyriques*. Ann Arbor, MI: UMI Research Press. 1979.

Westrup, Jack A. *Purcell*. New York: Collier Books. 1962.

Recommended Listening

Although specific excerpts are cited for each opera listed below, try to listen to at least one or two complete operas to get an idea of the overall structure. Multiple works by a given composer are listed chronologically.

Early Baroque:
Cavalli, Pietro Francesco. *Egisto* (1643): Aria, "Rallegratevi"
Monteverdi, Claudio. *L'Orfeo* (1607): "Tu se' morta"; "Possente spirto"
___. *L'incoronazione di Poppea* (1642): "Coronation Scene" (Act 3, scene 7)
Middle Baroque:
Lully, Jean-Baptiste. *Perse*: "Lament of Merope"
Purcell, Henry. *Dido and Aeneas* (1689): "Dido's Lament" and the chorus "With Drooping Wings"
Late Baroque:
Handel, George Frideric. *Rinaldo* (1711): Recitative, "Al valor del mio brando," sinfonia, and aria, "Cara Sposa"
___. *Giulio Cesare* (1724): "Empio, dir, tu sei"; "V'adoro"; "Se piet di mi non senti"; "Pianger la sorte mia"
___. *Serse* (1741): "Ombra mai f" (the "Largo from Xerxes")
Rameau, Jean-Philippe. *Castor et Pollux* (1737): Scene, "Sjour de l'ternelle paix"
Scarlatti, Alessandro. *Griselda* (1721): Aria, "Mi rivedi, o selva ombrosa"
Opera Overtures:
Lully, Jean-Baptiste. Overture to *Armide* (French overture)

16

Other Baroque Vocal Genres

1600	Emilio de' Cavalieri, *Rappresentatione di Anima, et di Corpo*, a forerunner of the oratorio
1602	Caccini, *Le nuove musiche*, influential in establishing the popularity of monody in Italy
1605–1638	Growth of the concertato style in Monteverdi's madrigals (Books V to VIII)
1610	Monteverdi, *Vespers*
c. 1619	Alessandro Grandi, *Cantade ed arie*, first use of the term *cantata*
1619–1666	Schütz lays the foundation of German Baroque music
c. 1650	Carissimi, *Jephte* (Jephtha), the best-known early oratorio
c. 1679–1722	Scarlatti active in Italy; his more than 600 secular cantatas represent a climax in the genre
1698	*Orpheus Britannicus*, a large collection of Purcell's vocal music
1701–1767	Telemann active in Germany (some 4,000 surviving works, including at least 1,100 cantatas plus other vocal works in all genres)
1705	J. S. Bach walks over 200 miles to hear Buxtehude's music
1712	Handel settles in London
1718–1720	Handel, *Chandos* anthems
1723–1750	Bach, in Leipzig, composes the majority of his great vocal works
1727	Bach, *St. Matthew Passion* (revised 1729, 1736, 1740s)
1742	Handel, *Messiah*
c. 1747–1749	Bach, *Mass in B Minor*

*I**n addition to opera, many other types of vocal music flourished during the Baroque period, including several important new genres such as the secular cantata, oratorio, and church cantata. In both secular and sacred music, the first half of the seventeenth century was a period of great experimentation as composers worked to fuse monody, the basso continuo, concertato style, bel canto style, operatic recitative and aria, and polyphonic techniques inherited from the Renaissance into a coherent musical language. By 1650 this had been largely accomplished, preparing the way for the gradual standardization of vocal genres between 1650 and 1700, most of which adopted the operatic format of alternating recitatives and arias.*

Not surprisingly, Italy—the birthplace of the new Baroque techniques—led in the early development of both secular and sacred vocal music. Nevertheless, other countries developed their own distinctive national styles and, in the area of sacred music, eventually surpassed Italy. This chapter surveys several of the most representative types of Baroque nonoperatic vocal music.

SECULAR VOCAL MUSIC

Early Developments

In Italy during the first half of the seventeenth century, solo songs in the new monodic style became extremely popular following the appearance of Giulio Caccini's *Le nuove musiche* (The New Music, 1602), the first important collection of monodies. Also important were Monteverdi's madrigals, books V to VIII (1605–1638), which contributed to the establishment of the concertato style.

Meanwhile, in France, the *air de cour* flourished, and a school of Lied composers arose in Germany. After 1650, however, composers in these two countries, as well as in Italy, began to focus increasingly on the secular cantata.

Secular vocal music in England developed along somewhat different lines, drawing more on national traditions than foreign influences. Important collections include the first volume of *Orpheus Britannicus* (1698), which contains vocal music by Henry Purcell, and *Amphion Anglicus* (1700), a collection of works by John Blow.

English composers also wrote large works for chorus, soloists, and orchestra for special occasions (e.g., Purcell's *Ode for St. Cecilia's Day*, 1692). These works were important forerunners of Handel's oratorios.

The Secular Cantata

After 1650 the principal type of Baroque secular vocal chamber music was the cantata. Like the opera, it originated in Italy and then spread to other countries, chiefly France and Germany.

ITALY

The first composer to use the term *cantata* (literally, a piece "to be sung") appears to have been Alessandro Grandi (c. 1575–1630) in his *Cantade ed arie* (Cantatas and Arias; c. 1619). At first the term implied no definite structure or content. Between 1650 and 1670, however, the cantata came to denote more specifically a short, nonstaged chamber composition usually for solo voice (less often for two or more voices) accompanied by continuo, which was based typically on a lyrical, amorous or quasi-dramatic text and was organized normally into a series of alternating recitatives and arias.

The leading composer of cantatas was Alessandro Scarlatti, with some 600 surviving cantatas, mostly for solo voice (usually soprano) and continuo. Like scenes from operas, his cantatas typically contain two or three arias separated by *secco* recitatives. Most often these arias use the da capo form (chapter 15). Some are written in a style midway between recitative and aria, known as *arioso*. Scarlatti's cantatas feature the light texture, clearly focused harmonies, and flowing bel canto style characteristic of his Neapolitan operas.

FRANCE

The cantata flourished in France during the first quarter of the eighteenth century, influenced by Italian models. The leading composers were Marc-Antoine Charpentier, André Campra (1660–1774), Nicolas Bernier (1665–1734), Nicolas Clérambault (1676–1749), and Jean-Philippe Rameau.

GERMANY

German composers of secular cantatas include Reinhard Keiser, Georg Philipp Telemann, and J. S. Bach, who composed some twenty secular cantatas, the best known of which were the *Coffee Cantata* (c. 1734) and the *Peasant Cantata* (1742).

SACRED VOCAL MUSIC

The contrast between the older Renaissance polyphonic techniques and the new Baroque techniques was particularly strong in the area of sacred music during the first half of the seventeenth century. Some composers continued to write in the Palestrina style (particularly those in the Roman Catholic church) or in the Venetian polychoral style. Others embraced monody and other progressive elements. The greatest composers, however, worked to blend the old and new techniques; of these, the most important were Claudio Monteverdi (e.g., his 1610 *Vespers*) and Heinrich Schütz.

Schütz is known particularly for his works in concertato style (e.g., the *Symphoniae sacre*, Sacred Symphonies, of 1629, 1647, and 1650), which united northern counterpoint and the new Italian innovations in a way that laid the foundations for the German tradition of concerted sacred music that found its highest expression in the Lutheran church cantata.

Two important new sacred music genres arose during the Baroque period, the *oratorio* and the *Lutheran church cantata*. Yet composers also continued to develop older forms, which were raised to unparalleled heights, particularly in the works of J. S. Bach.

Mass

The Mass became a relatively less important genre during the Baroque period, partly because it was overshadowed by newer forms and partly because much of the greatest Baroque sacred music was being written for Protestant churches. However, particularly those composers who worked in the Roman Catholic church still continued to write Masses and other liturgical compositions.

GENERAL CHARACTERISTICS

Settings of the Mass became longer and more elaborate than in the Renaissance. Composers often divided the five main sections—the Kyrie, Gloria, Credo, Sanctus, and Agnus Dei—into contrasting sections or movements and scored the individual sections in a wide variety of moods, tempos, textures, and styles.

The Lutheran church also continued to use parts of the Latin Ordinary during the Baroque period, but musical settings were generally limited to the Kyrie and Gloria. A shortened setting of this type was called a *Missa brevis* (short Mass). J. S. Bach, for example, wrote four of these.

REPRESENTATIVE COMPOSERS

Among numerous composers of Masses were Monteverdi, Orazio Benevoli (1605–1672), Johann Josef Fux (1660–1741), Alessandro Scarlatti, Giovanni Pergolesi, Antonio Caldara, and Georg Philipp Telemann.

The greatest achievement in the Baroque Mass was J. S. Bach's *Mass in B Minor*, which Bach compiled between c.1747 and 1749 from Mass sections written earlier, arrangements of movements from cantatas, and newly composed music. Too long and elaborate for use in church services, it is not really a typical Baroque Mass; Bach probably wrote it simply as a model of what could still be done with the ancient form. The "Crucifixus" section of the Credo is possibly the most beautiful use in all music of the *basso ostinato*, and the work as a whole is a transcendent musical expression of Christian faith.

Oratorio

Around the middle of the seventeenth century an important new type of sacred music arose, the *oratorio*. Its name derived from the place in which such compositions were first performed, the Oratorio (oratory, prayer room) of a church. Since most early oratorio composers also composed operas, the oratorio is quite similar to the opera. Like an opera, an oratorio is a large-scale dramatic composition for solo voices, chorus, and orchestra. It has acts, scenes, dialogue, characters, and (usually) a plot; and its music is organized into a succession of recitatives, arias, vocal ensembles, and orchestral interludes. Unlike an opera, however, an oratorio is almost always based on a sacred or semisacred subject; it is normally presented in a concert hall or church without scenery, costumes, or acting; it makes far greater use of the chorus; and it often features a narrator (*testo* or *historicus*), who relates the outlines of the story in recitative. Oratorios were not intended for use in religious services but for presentation in concert performances.

ORIGIN AND RISE

The oratorio arose in Rome, evolving from a number of sources: medieval and Renaissance religious dramas with music, dramatic presentations of the Passion (see below), motets with narrative biblical texts, sacred songs called *laude*, religious dialogues presented in the oratories of Roman churches, and sacred operas of the Roman school. An important forerunner of the oratorio, considered by some to *be* the first oratorio, was Emilio de' Cavalieri's allegorical opera *Rappresentatione di Anima, et di Corpo* (The Play about Soul and Body), presented in Rome in 1600.

The text of early oratorios could be in Latin (*oratorio latino*) or Italian (*oratorio volgare*). Latin oratorio reached its climax during the mid-seventeenth century in the works of Giacomo Carissimi, whose best-known oratorio was *Jephte* (Jephtha, c. 1650), but died out in the second half of the seventeenth century as composers came to prefer vernacular oratorio. Scarlatti was particularly influential in the rise of vernacular oratorio in Italy, and Schütz helped establish the oratorio in Germany. J. S. Bach also wrote three works that he called oratorios (*Christmas Oratorio, Easter Oratorio*, and *Ascension Oratorio*). The genre reached its greatest heights in the incomparable English oratorios of Handel.

HANDEL'S ORATORIOS

When the English public started to tire of Italian opera, Handel began to look for another form that audiences might take to. He found it in the oratorio. During the 1730s, when he first began to explore the possibilities of oratorio, he continued to write operas. However, after 1741 he abandoned opera completely in favor of the new genre.

Handel's switch from opera to oratorio involved a change from a genre favored by the English aristocracy to one aimed at appealing to the broader middle class. To make his oratorios more accessible to this new audience, Handel used English libretti. Furthermore, because the English middle class liked their entertainment to be morally uplifting as well as diverting, and because they were intimately familiar with stories from the Bible, particularly the Old Testament, he based nearly all his oratorios on stories from the Old Testament. He also made the chorus—symbolic of the people—the focus of his oratorios. Handel was a shrewd businessman, and his oratorios were commercial ventures, composed not for church services but for the public concert hall and paying customers. Yet in spite of this, he produced some of the most exalted music ever written, epic monuments of the "grand" Baroque style.

General Characteristics. Handel's oratorios adhere generally to the standard format described earlier, including the use of characters and plots, and their overall musical style is virtually indistinguishable from that of his operas. Their most important innovation by far lies in the use of the chorus. Drawing from the choral writing of Carissimi, from the Lutheran choral music of Schütz and his successors, and especially from the long tradition of English choral writing, Handel made the chorus a main "character" in the drama, one that could participate in the narrative or comment on the action in the manner of a Greek chorus. Using a free mixture of chordal homophony, imitative polyphony, and unison writing, he used the chorus to project effects ranging from utmost delicacy to overwhelming power. Other notable features of Handel's oratorios include his imaginative use of the orchestra to create atmosphere and pictorial allusions, his larger-than-life characters, and his unerring genius for finding just the right musical expression for every nuance of the text.

Representative Works. Handel's first true oratorio was *Esther* (1732), a revision of a masque, but it was *Saul* and *Israel in Egypt* (both written in 1739) that first showed the possibilities inherent in the genre. He continued to build interest in the oratorio with his *Messiah* (1742), *Samson* (1743), and other works of the mid-1740s such as *Judas Maccabaeus* (1746), at last winning over the British public. In his later oratorios, which culminate in *Jephtha* (1752), Handel kept largely to the proven formula of religious subjects.

Handel's most famous and well-loved oratorio is his *Messiah*, written in twenty-four days and premiered in Dublin in 1742. It is somewhat untypical in that its text is meditative rather than dramatic, and it lacks a plot and specific characters. The libretto, a compilation of verses from the Bible, is in three parts. The first part deals with the birth of Christ; the second, with His death and resurrection; and the third, with the certainty of eternal life through faith in Christ. Each part contains numerous immortal musical moments. The "Hallelujah" Chorus, which ends Part Two, for example, is perhaps the most famous chorus of all time. At the first London performance of *Messiah* in 1743, King George II was so moved by this chorus that he rose to his feet; in remembrance of this, audiences today traditionally stand whenever this chorus is performed.

Lutheran Church Cantata

Following Germany's recovery from the Thirty Years' War (1618–1648), the years 1650 to 1750 became a great age of Lutheran church music. Building upon the achievements of Heinrich Schütz and other German composers of the early Baroque period, Lutheran composers of the middle and late Baroque composed splendid new music that combined the chorale, solo song, and concertato style with operatic recitative and aria and Renaissance imitative polyphony.

The chorale (see chapter 13) provided a rich heritage for all Lutheran composers. By the late seventeenth century, chorales served not only as the basis for congregational singing but also as the foundation for many elaborate vocal and instrumental works, and composers wove them into their musical textures in much the same way that medieval and Renaissance composers had used Gregorian chant.

Important Lutheran composers of the late seventeenth century include Dietrich Buxtehude and Johann Pachelbel. In 1705 J. S. Bach walked over 200 miles to hear Buxtehude's music.

RISE OF THE CANTATA

At the end of the seventeenth century, the poet Erdmann Neumeister (1671–1756) and others began to write a new kind of devotional poetry for musical setting called *cantatas*. These cantatas were published in cycles, each cycle containing texts for all the Sundays and holidays of the church year. Their purposes were to correspond with and expand upon the prescribed biblical passages and hymns used in the Lutheran service. This new cantata type became very popular, initiating the greatest of all Lutheran genres, the church cantata.

General Characteristics. In essence, the Lutheran church cantata was a short oratorio, that is, an unstaged composition for vocal soloists and chorus, accompanied by organ and usually a small orchestra. Like an oratorio, it consisted of several movements that were organized as a series of recitatives, arias, ensemble numbers, and choruses. Because it was intended for use in church services, the cantata was generally more restrained in style than an oratorio. It was also shorter, typically about twenty-five minutes long. It was based on a religious text sung in the vernacular, either newly written or drawn from the Bible or a hymn. Frequently, the music of the cantata was based upon a chorale tune, and the congregation often joined the choir in singing the chorale in the last movement of the cantata.

During the first half of the eighteenth century, the cantata became an integral part of the Lutheran church service. The cantor, or music director, was required to provide separate cantatas for every Sunday and holiday—about sixty per year. Some composers wrote several complete cycles of cantatas. Telemann, for example, wrote at least 1,100 cantatas!

Representative Composers. Representative composers of church cantatas during the first half of the eighteenth century include Johann Philipp Krieger (1649–1725), Johann Kuhnau (1660–1722), Friedrich Wilhelm Zachow (1663–1712), Telemann, and the greatest master of them all, J. S. Bach. The term *cantata* is also applied loosely to earlier concertato works by Lutheran composers such as Schütz and Buxtehude.

Bach's Church Cantatas. The great majority of Bach's sacred music, including his cantatas, dates from his last position as cantor at St. Thomas's School and music director in Leipzig (1723–1750). There is evidence that he composed five complete cycles of about 60 cantatas each, but only about 195 survive, scored normally for chorus, vocal soloists, continuo, and an orchestra of strings and winds as needed. The cantatas show great structural variety, but a typical format consists of from five to eight movements, of which the first and last movements, and sometimes a middle movement, are for chorus. The remaining movements normally consist of recitatives, arias or arioso movements, and small vocal ensembles. Many incorporate one or more chorale tunes, which are used in an infinite variety of ways; in such cantatas, the final movement is frequently a simple four-voice setting of the chorale, which the congregation probably sang with the choir.

In Bach's cantatas, technical perfection is wedded to a spirit of profound religious devotion.

Passion Music

A *Passion* is the story of the events leading up to the crucifixion of Christ as recorded by the Gospels. Musical presentations of the Passion had existed for centuries, from simple plainsong chanting of the Gospels in the early medieval period to motet settings of the entire text (the *motet Passion*) during the Renaissance.

CHARACTERISTICS

During the Baroque period, the most characteristic type of Passion setting was the *oratorio Passion*, patterned on the general format of the oratorio and featuring recitatives, arias, vocal ensembles, chorus, and orchestra. Gospel texts were extended to include (1) inserted non-Biblical meditations of the events of the story, usually set as arias; and (2) chorales related to the story, usually sung by the chorus or congregation.

By Bach's time, a Passion setting usually included a narrator (Evangelist); soloists to portray the roles of Christ, Pilate, Peter, and other characters; a chorus to portray the crowd (the *turba*); and an orchestra. As the Evangelist related the story in recitative, the characters reacted with their parts, and the action was often interrupted for meditative arias, small ensembles, or chorales.

REPRESENTATIVE COMPOSERS

Important Baroque composers of Passion settings include Heinrich Schütz, whose *Resurrection Story* (1623), *The Seven Last Words* (1645), and the three Passions of 1665–1666 (*St. John*, *St. Matthew*, and *St. Luke*) set the standard for Baroque German Passion settings; Johann Sebastiani (1622–1683); Johann Theile (1646–1724); Georg Philipp Telemann; G. F. Handel; and J. S. Bach. Bach's two complete Passions, the *St. John Passion* (1724) and *St. Matthew Passion* (1727; revised 1729, 1736, 1740s), represent the culmination of the genre.

Other Sacred Music

In addition to the major forms just discussed, Baroque composers also wrote other types of sacred music. The most important of these were the motet and anthem.

MOTET

The motet, adapted to the new techniques, continued to thrive during the Baroque period. Among early Baroque composers, Monteverdi and Schütz made important contributions to the genre. During the absolute reign of Louis XIV (1661–1715) in France, the motet based on a biblical text became the preferred form at the Royal Chapel, and composers such as Lully, Charpentier, and Michel-Richard de Lalande (1657–1726) produced notable examples. In the late Baroque, J. S. Bach wrote six motets.

ANTHEM

The anthem and Service continued to be the principal forms of Anglican church music. John Blow, Henry Purcell, and Pelham Humpfrey (1647–1674) were outstanding composers in this area. Handel's *Chandos* anthems (1718–1720) are also notable examples.

OTHER FORMS

Baroque composers also continued to set other traditional Latin texts, such as the *Te Deum laudamus* (We Praise Thee, O God), the *Stabat Mater* (By the Cross the Mother Standing), and the *Magnificat* (Mary's hymn of praise, based on Luke I: 46–55). Many of these traditional texts had received settings since the early Middle Ages. An outstanding Baroque example is J. S. Bach's setting of the *Magnificat* (1728–1731), for five-part chorus, soloists, and orchestra.

*F*ollowing a period of experimentation during the first half of the seventeenth century, Baroque secular and sacred vocal genres settled into standardized formats based on the operatic pattern of alternating recitatives and arias. The principal secular vocal genre was the secular cantata, which reached its culmination in the works of Alessandro Scarlatti. The principal sacred vocal genres were the oratorio, Mass, and Lutheran church cantata;

Handel was the outstanding composer in the first of these genres, Bach in the latter two. Other important sacred vocal genres included the Passion, motet, and anthem.

For Additional Study

Boyd, Malcolm. *Bach*. London: Dent. 1983.

Dent, Edward J. *Alessandro Scarlatti: His Life and Work*. London, 1905. Revised with additions by Frank Walker. London: Edward Arnold, 1960; reprint, 1962.

Moser, Hans Joachim. *Heinrich Schütz*. Trans. C. F. Pfatteicher. St. Louis: Concordia. 1959.

Smither, Howard E. *A History of the Oratorio*. Vol. 1: *The Oratorio in the Baroque Era: Italy, Vienna, Paris*; vol. 2: *The Oratorio in the Baroque Era: Protestant Germany and England*. Chapel Hill, NC: University of North Carolina Press. 1977.

Recommended Listening

SECULAR VOCAL MUSIC:

Caccini, Giulio. *Le nuove musiche* (The New Music; 1602): "Perfidissimo volto" (O, Most Perfidious Face") (monody)

Monteverdi, Claudio. *Madrigals*, Book VII (entitled *Concerto*; 1619): "Chiome d'oro" (Golden Hair) (duet for soprano, bass, 2 violins, continuo)

Purcell, Henry. *Ode for St. Cecilia's Day* (1692)

Scarlatti, Alessandro. *Lascia, deh lascia* (Cease, O Cease) (secular cantata)

SACRED VOCAL MUSIC:

Bach, J. S. Cantata No. 4, *Christ lag in Todesbanden* (Christ Lay in Death's Bonds, c. 1707), BWV 4 (Lutheran church cantata)

___. Cantata No. 80, *Ein' feste Burg ist unser Gott* (A Mighty Fortress Is Our God, 1715), BWV 80 (Lutheran church cantata)

___. Cantata No. 140, *Wachet auf, ruft uns die Stimme* (Awake, a Voice Is Calling Us, 1731), BWV 140 (Lutheran church cantata)

___. *Jesu meine Freude* (Jesus, My Joy, 1723) (motet)

___. *Magnificat in D* (1728–31), BWV 243

___. *Mass in B Minor* (compiled c. 1747–1749), BWV 232

___. *Passion According to St. Matthew* (1727; revised 1729, 1736, 1740s), BWV 244

Carissimi, Giacomo. *Jephte* (Jephtha, c. 1650) (oratorio)

Handel, George Frideric. Oratorios: *Israel in Egypt* (1739); *Messiah* (1742)

Monteverdi, Claudio. *Vespers* (1610)

Purcell, Henry. *Thou Knowest, Lord, the Secrets of Our Hearts* (anthem)

Schütz, Heinrich. *Symphoniae sacrae III* (Sacred Symphonies, vol. 3, 1650): "O Herr, hilf" (O Lord, Help); "Saul, was verfolgst du mich?" (Saul, Why Persecutest Thou Me?)

17

Baroque Instrumental Music

1557	First known use of the term *suytte* (suite) for a group of dance pieces
1561	First use of *sonata* as a title (lute pieces by Gorzanis)
1587	Andrea and Giovanni Gabrieli, *Concerti*, first use of *concerto* as a title
1597–1650	Rise of the sonata in Italy (e.g., G. Gabrieli, Marini, Fontana)
1620s–1693	Development of the standard core of dances in the suite (e.g., Froberger)
1635	Frescobaldi, *Fiori musicali*, organ music
c. 1660	*Sonata da chiesa* and *sonata da camera* become standard designations of types of sonatas
1668–1707	Buxtehude active as organist and composer at Lübeck
1681–1700	Corelli establishes the "Classic phase" of the Baroque sonata
c. 1682	Corelli, *Concerti grossi* (published 1714)
1686–1709	Torelli's concertos establish the Baroque concerto format
1695	Pachelbel writes early examples of true fugues
1703–17	J. S. Bach composes many of his organ works while serving in Arnstadt (1703–1707), Mühlhausen (1707–1708), and Weimar (1708–1717)
c. 1712–c. 1730	Vivaldi's concerto publications
1713–1730	Couperin, *Pièces de clavecin* (4 volumes), important collections of keyboard suites (called *ordres*)
c. 1717	Handel, *Water Music*
1717–1723	Bach, in Cöthen, composes many of his clavier and chamber works
1721	Bach, *Brandenburg Concertos*
c. 1722	Bach, *Well-Tempered Clavier*, Part I (Part II, c. 1742)
1723–1750	Bach, in Leipzig, composes several of his most mature instrumental works as well as the majority of his vocal works

c. 1725   Vivaldi, *The Four Seasons*

1749   Handel, *Music for the Royal Fireworks*

*O*ne of the most far-reaching developments in Baroque music was the rise of instrumental music as an independent medium, which brought advances in idiomatic writing, the emergence of virtuoso instrumentalists, the appearance of important new genres, and, by the end of the period, a body of instrumental music equal in quantity and quality to that of vocal music. In instrumental music as in vocal, the seventeenth century was a period of experimentation that led, by the end of the century, to the relative standardization of forms. Italy led in the development of string music, while Germany and France were the leaders in keyboard writing.

INSTRUMENTS AND TUNING

Baroque Instruments

Baroque composers continued to use the instruments that had been popular during the Renaissance (see chapter 13). However, a number of developments may be noted. (1) The harpsichord rose to prominence as the backbone of the continuo ensemble and perhaps the favorite solo instrument. Its distinctive timbre is an important aspect in all Baroque ensemble music. During the Baroque period, it was known by several names: *clavecin* (French), *clavicembalo* (Italian), *virginal* (English), and *clavier* or *Klavier* (German; also used for clavichord). (2) The piano was invented around 1709; however, it did not come into general use until the Classical period. (3) The organ was perfected and reached its greatest popularity. The greatest development in organ music occurred in Germany, culminating in the works of J. S. Bach. (4) Although viols continued in use, they were being superseded by members of the violin family (violin, viola, violoncello). (5) Literature for the lute declined and, in Spain, the guitar replaced the vihuela. (6) A great tradition of high-register (*clarino*) trumpet playing emerged. (7) The oboe and bassoon became the favorite double-reed woodwind instruments. (8) The timpani was the only percussion instrument that continued to be used with any frequency, and then only in orchestral music. (9) The modern orchestra had its beginnings.

Tuning

Musicians had experimented with a number of methods for tuning keyboard and fretted string instruments in previous centuries. During the late Baroque period, *equal-tempered tuning*, or *equal temperament*, came into general use. In this system, the octave is divided into twelve equal semitones; thus, an instrument sounds equally in tune in any key. This system is still in use today.

INSTRUMENTAL GENRES INHERITED FROM THE RENAISSANCE

Some of the instrumental genres inherited from the Renaissance merged with newer forms and lost their separate identity, while others continued to thrive throughout the period. The ricercar and organ canzona merged with the fugue; the ensemble canzona evolved into the *sonata da chiesa*; and dance pieces came increasingly to be grouped into suites. Of the genres that continued to thrive, improvisatory works and variations were the most important.

Improvisatory Works

Given the importance of improvisation in Baroque music, it is not surprising that pieces written to convey a sense of improvisation continued to flourish throughout the period. The three main types were the *toccata*, *fantasia*, and *prelude*, which were written most often for organ or clavier. These pieces typically exhibit a free, unstructured form; irregular rhythms and phrase lengths; sudden changes of texture; and a deliberate uncertainty of harmonic style.

The toccata (from the Italian *toccare*, to touch) became a vehicle for showing off the performer's technical skill. It thus emphasized rapid scales, arpeggios, melodic ornamentation, and massive chords. The fantasia was also marked by virtuosic brilliance and structural freedom. The prelude, which evolved from short introductions improvised by lutenists and keyboard players, came to denote simply a short instrumental piece, that could stand alone as an independent composition or serve as an introduction to a group of dances or a fugue.

The outstanding Baroque composer in all three of these genres was J. S. Bach. Among his most famous works in these categories are the *Toccata and Fugue in D Minor*, BWV 565 (c. 1707), for organ; the *Fantasia and Fugue in G Minor*, BWV 542 (c. 1720), for organ; the *Chromatic Fantasia and Fugue in D Minor*, BWV 903 (c. 1720), for clavier; and the forty-eight preludes and fugues that constitute *Das wohltemperirte Clavier* (The Well-Tempered Clavier; vol, I, c. 1722; vol. II, c. 1742). Other important Baroque composers who contributed to these genres include Girolamo Frescobaldi, Johann Pachelbel, and Dietrich Buxtehude.

Variations   The theme and variations form, which had enjoyed a golden age in the works of the English virginalists of the late sixteenth century, continued to be popular throughout the Baroque period. Two famous examples are Handel's set of variations (known as "The Harmonious Blacksmith") from his *Suite No. 5 in E Major* for harpsichord (1720) and J. S. Bach's "Goldberg Variations" from Part IV of the *Clavier-Übung* (1742).

Variation technique also underlies several new Baroque forms (e.g., the passacaglia, chaconne, and chorale partita), and much vocal music (e.g., strophic variations and arias over a ground bass) and is often found in ricercars, canzonas, and dance suites.

NEW BAROQUE INSTRUMENTAL GENRES

Suite   As noted earlier, dance pieces came increasingly to be grouped into sets, called *suites* (or *partitas*). Because suites were normally intended for listening rather than dancing, the dances were often written in a stylized manner, with much elaboration and refinement; however, each dance usually retained the meter, tempo, and characteristic rhythmic figures associated originally with its dance steps.

German composers were among the first to conceive of the suite as a musical unity, but it was the French who established the distinctive character of each of the individual dances. Suites were written for small chamber ensembles, orchestra, and solo instruments such as the harpsichord or lute.

GENERAL CHARACTERISTICS

Although there was no set "form" for suites during the Baroque period, by the late seventeenth century a type of clavier suite that many consider to be "the" characteristic Baroque suite had crystallized in Germany. It consisted normally of four core dances in the order *allemande, courante, sarabande,* and *gigue.* To these the composer might add an introductory movement (e.g., a prelude or French overture) or one or more optional dances, placed most often between the sarabande and gigue. All movements were normally in the same key, and most were written in binary form. Figure 17.1 outlines the main characteristics of the four movements.

CORE MOVEMENTS OF THE BAROQUE SUITE				
Dance	*Meter*	*Tempo*	*Comments*	*Origin*
Allemande	4/4	Moderate	Quick upbeat. Flowing. Usually polyphonic.	Germany
Courante	3/4, 3/2 or 6/4	Moderately fast	Sometimes replaced by livelier, more homophonic Italian *corrente*.	France
Sarabande	3/4 or 3/2	Slow	Stately. Often a secondary accent on beat two. Often homophonic.	Spain
Gigue	Compound time (6/8, 12/8, etc.)	Fast	Short upbeat. Wide melodic skips. Often imitative. Sometimes in 2/2.	England or Ireland

Fig 17.1

FORM IN INDIVIDUAL MOVEMENTS

The individual dance movements in a Baroque suite are most often written in binary form, consisting of two sections of roughly the same length, **a** and **b**, each of which ends with a cadence and is then repeated immediately (thus, **aa bb**). The first part usually moves from the tonic key to a contrasting key. If the movement is in a major key, the second key will most often be the dominant. If the movement is in a minor key, the second key will probably be the relative major (a minor third higher than the tonic—the key with the same key signature as the tonic key). The second part works its way back to the tonic. Both parts use closely related thematic material. Using the symbol ‖: to represent repeats, this form may be diagrammed as follows:

‖: a :‖: b :‖

major: I ⟶ V ⟶ I

minor: I ⟶ III ⟶ I

Sometimes, during the second half of the movement, the **a** material and the tonic key return, producing a type of **aba** form within the overall two-part outer structure:

‖: a :‖: b   a :‖

major: I ⟶ V ⟶ I

minor: I ⟶ III ⟶ I

This is sometimes referred to as a *rounded binary*. Both the regular binary form and the rounded binary were to have great influence on the development of form during the Classical period, giving rise to both small part-forms and larger forms such as the sonata form.

Within each of the two sections, the music may flow in a virtually unbroken stream from beginning to end, or it may fall into short, regular phrases. The latter type of organization clearly foreshadows the phrase structure of the Classical period, particularly when the movement is also homophonic in texture.

REPRESENTATIVE COMPOSERS

The German composers J. H. Schein (1586–1630) and especially Johann Jakob Froberger were important in the early history of the suite. Later composers of suites include, among others, Johann Pachelbel, Georg Böhm, Johann Kuhnau (1660–1722), Georg Muffat (1653–1704), J. K. F. Fischer (c. 1670–1746), Purcell, Telemann, Rameau, J. S. Bach, and Handel. Notable suites for orchestra include Bach's four *Ouvertures* (BWV 1066–69; 1725–31) and Handel's *Water Music* (c. 1717) and *Music for the Royal Fireworks* (1749).

Sonata

Terms similar to *sonata* had been used in connection with instrumental music since the Middle Ages and as the title of instrumental pieces since the sixteenth century. However, it was not until the seventeenth century that the sonata first emerged as an important musical genre. The rise of the sonata during the Baroque period is significant not only because the literature for this genre constitutes an important body of Baroque music but also because the sonata exerted a strong influence on other genres, such as the concerto, and because as a genre it has continued to occupy an important place in music literature down to the present. Broadly defined, a sonata is a composition for a solo instrument or a small group of instruments that consists of several relatively extended movements in contrasting tempos, textures, forms, and sometimes keys.

ORIGIN AND SPREAD

Originally, the term *sonata* (from *sonare*, to sound, play) implied simply a piece of instrumental music (in contrast to *cantata*, a vocal composition), and for much of the seventeenth century, it was used somewhat interchangeably with *canzona*, *sinfonia*, and even *concerto* and *toccata*. Only gradually did a characteristic Baroque sonata "form" emerge, and this form owed most to the ensemble canzona, the many short sections of which were gradually reduced in number and extended in length to become true movements.

As William Newman (*The Sonata in the Baroque Era*) has documented, the sonata arose in Italy at the beginning of the seventeenth century and spread to Austria and Germany by the 1620s, to England by about 1660, and to France by the end of the century. As the Baroque period ended, the sonata was just taking root in Spain and Portugal, and it did not reach the United States until the Classical period. Sonatas were played in church, at court, in homes, and in public meeting places.

INSTRUMENTS AND SETTINGS

From shortly after 1670 the favorite sonata setting was the *trio sonata*, which actually required four performers: two solo instruments (usually violins or flutes) and two continuo players (a harpsichord or other chording instrument and a reinforcing instrument such as a violoncello or bassoon). After 1700 the trio sonata was superseded by the *solo sonata*—for three players (one solo instrument and two continuo players). Sonatas were also written for other small instrumental ensembles (with or without continuo), for unaccompanied solo string instruments, and for solo organ, harpsichord, lute or guitar.

FORM

By the end of the seventeenth century, standard Baroque sonata formats had become established. The sonata's now-characteristic formats are seen most clearly in the sixty sonatas of Arcangelo Corelli, who brought the Baroque sonata to its "Classic" phase. The two main classes of this genre are the *sonata da chiesa* (church sonata) and the *sonata da camera* (chamber sonata).

Sonata da chiesa. The sonata da chiesa usually (but not always) has four movements in the order slow-fast-slow-fast. Typically, the movements are as follows:

The *Sonata da chiesa*			
Movement	Meter	Tempo	Characteristics
First	4/4	Slow	Intertwining melodic lines over a bass of running eighth notes. Weighty, polyphonic. Highly irregular phrases. Often dotted rhythms.
Second	4/4	Fast	Imitative texture. Often the musical center of gravity for the sonata.
Third	3/4 or 3/2	Slow	Short. Often homophonic.
Fourth	Compound	Fast	In the nature of a French gigue.

Fig 17.2

In practice, a lot of variety was possible; for example, many church sonatas end with one or more dance movements, overlapping the sonata da camera.

Sonata da camera. This is essentially a suite of dances. Occasionally, nondance movements (e.g., a prelude) are included as well, overlapping the sonata da chiesa.

EIGHTEENTH-CENTURY DEVELOPMENTS

The same developments that revolutionized the concerto in the eighteenth century (see below) also touched the sonata to some extent, resulting in an increased use of homophonic texture, more regular structures, greater rhythmic vitality, a rise in the use of the three-movement plan of the concerto, and the predominance of solo sonatas over ensemble sonatas.

REPRESENTATIVE COMPOSERS

A few of the many outstanding composers of sonatas are listed below by country.

Italy. Biagio Marini, G. B. Fontana (died c. 1630), Maurizio Cazzati (1620–1677), G. B. Vitali, Arcangelo Corelli, Antonio Vivaldi, Francesco Maria Veracini, G. B. Somis (1686–1763), and Giuseppe Tartini (1692–1770).

Austria and Germany. Heinrich Ignaz Franz Biber, Georg Muffat, Johann Jakob Walther (c. 1650–c. 1717), Johann Kuhnau, J. S. Bach, Telemann, and Handel.

England. Henry Purcell, Jean Baptiste Loeillet (1688–c.1720), and Francesco Geminiani.

France. François Couperin and Jean-Marie Leclair.

Concerto

Like several other terms, *concerto* was used during the sixteenth and most of the seventeenth centuries in a rather loose sense, referring to compositions for voices, instruments, or combinations of the two, in the process overlapping other terms such as *sonata* and *sinfonia*. By the late seventeenth century, however, it had come to denote a purely instrumental composition consisting of several movements that pitted the sound of a solo instrument or a small group of solo instruments against that of the orchestra. An excellent manifestation of the Baroque concertato style, the concerto both united dissimilar and unequal bodies of sound into harmonious agreement and deliberately juxtaposed these sounds to produce contrast and variety. Ultimately, a sense of "competition" also entered the picture, especially in the solo concerto, in which the solo instrument came to symbolize the individual striving against the mass.

The two most important types of Baroque concerto were the *concerto grosso*, the earliest type to emerge, and the *solo concerto*. A third and less important type was the *orchestral concerto*.

THE CONCERTO GROSSO

The concerto grosso opposes a small group of solo instruments (the *concertino*) against the orchestra (the *ripieno* or *tutti*). In Baroque concerti grossi, the concertino consisted usually of the standard trio sonata ensemble (two violins and continuo), while the orchestra was most often a small string orchestra. Composers sometimes added winds to either of these groups. Arcangelo Corelli's *Concerti grossi*, Op. 6 (published in 1714 but written earlier), the first significant works in the genre, were little more than church or chamber sonatas with musical material divided between the smaller and larger groups. Like the sonata, they typically contained four or more movements, and they made little distinction between the two groups.

Torelli. More important for the later development of the concerto were the concerti grossi and solo concertos of Giuseppe Torelli. Torelli established a three-movement pattern (fast-slow-fast) and a *ritornello form* for the allegro movements that became standard in later Baroque concertos. He also made a greater distinction between the tutti and solo passages and wrote vigorous allegro themes that influenced many later composers, particularly Vivaldi.

Ritornello Form. A movement in ritornello form usually begins with a complete statement of a theme (the ritornello) by the orchestra. Alternating with passages for the solo instrument(s), the ritornello recurs several times during the movement, usually in an incomplete form and in different keys. It usually appears also at the very end, in the tonic key and usually complete, to round off the movement. Sometimes the material of the solo passages is related thematically to the ritornello, sometimes not; in either case, the recurrences of the ritornello give the music a sense of unity. Ritornello form may be diagramed as follows:

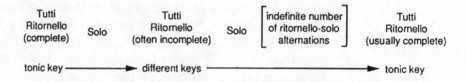

Ritornello form became standard in vocal arias (see chapters 15 and 16) as well as in later Baroque concertos.

SOLO CONCERTO

The solo concerto opposes a single solo instrument against the orchestra. Although most Baroque solo concertos are for violin, other instruments could be used also. The most important Baroque composer of solo concertos was Antonio Vivaldi.

VIVALDI

Vivaldi wrote over 500 concertos, of which about 350 are solo concertos. Building upon the three-movement plan and ritornello form of Torelli, he developed a concerto style that was to influence both instrumental and vocal music of the late Baroque period. In a sense, Vivaldi's concerto style is the instrumental counterpart of Neapolitan opera, which arose at the same time. Like Neapolitan opera, it emphasizes homophonic texture, virtuosity, rhythmic energy, and clarity of harmony and form, and it, too, was important in the transition from the Baroque to the Classical style. Among Vivaldi's best-loved concertos are the first four concertos of his Op. 8 (published c. 1725), known collectively as *The Four Seasons*.

Vivaldi's Concerto Form. Vivaldi adhered essentially to the three-movement (fast-slow-fast) pattern established by Torelli. The first movement is typically an allegro in ritornello form. The slow movement, not always in the same key, is like an operatic aria or arioso. (Vivaldi was the first composer to make the slow movement equal in importance to the two fast movements.) The last movement is usually shorter and livelier than the first.

Vivaldi's Concerto Style. Vivaldi's concerto style is characterized by (1) "catchy" melodies that often feature outlined triads and fast, scalewise passages; (2) great rhythmic vitality; (3) continuo-homophony (see chapter 14); (4) skillful use of solo and orchestral colors; (5) mastery of major-minor tonality and a full awareness of its possibilities; (6) frequent use of square-cut, regular phrase forms; (7) much use of melodic and harmonic sequences (see chapter 6); (8) a clear delineation of form; and (9) emphasis on the solo instrument as the dominant musical "personality."

Several of these characteristics may be seen in two excerpts from a Vivaldi concerto (figure 17.3), the first a tutti passage that leads into a solo section, and the second a passage in which short fragments of the tutti ritornello material alternate with rapid scales in the solo violin. Note in particular the driving rhythms, the continuo-homophony with its characteristic active bass line, the extensive use of scales and outlined triads in the melody, and the virtuosic writing for the solo violin. Passages like these revolutionized late Baroque music.

Fugue

A *fugue* is a polyphonic work for two or more voice or instrument parts that develops, by contrapuntal means, a melodic phrase known as a *subject*. The fugue of the late Baroque period represents the most mature stage of the centuries-old tradition of imitative counterpoint.

A fugue may be an independent piece or a movement of a larger work, and it may be written for a group of instruments or voices, for a solo instrument such as organ or harpsichord or for a combination of voices and instruments. Whether a fugue is written for voices or instruments, it contains a set number of melodic lines or parts, which are called *voices*. Fugues for three or four voices are the most common, although there are fugues for two, five, or more voices.

GENERAL CHARACTERISTICS

The fugue is a way of writing rather than a form, and the exact manner in which a composer develops the subject varies from piece to piece. However, virtually every fugue begins with a relatively standardized section known as the *exposition*.

Vivaldi, excerpts from *The Four Seasons*, Op. 8, No. 3: "Autumn" (first movement)

Source: Vivaldi, Antonio. *Il Cimento dell' Armonia e dell' Inventione. Concerti a 4 e 5 ...*
Opera ottavo. Libro primo. Amsterdam: Michele Carlo le Cene. [1725]. (Washington, DC:
Library of Congress)

Fig 17.3

Exposition. The *subject* enters alone in the tonic key at the beginning
of the exposition. As it ends, a second voice enters with an *answer*, an
imitation of the subject at a different pitch level (usually in the dominant
key). The remaining voices then enter one at a time with alternating statements of the subject or answer until all have made their appearances. While
the subject or answer is being stated, the voice or voices that have already
entered continue with other counterpoint. If a particular contrapuntal line
appears consistently with the subject or answer, it is called a *countersubject*.

When all voices have entered, the exposition ends. The exposition may be repeated; if so, the voices normally enter in a different order.

Sections Following the Exposition. Without pause the fugue continues with a variable number of sections that restate and further develop the subject (often in different keys), alternating with other sections, called *episodes*, in which the subject is not present. Episodes typically function as transitions, modulating from the key of one statement of the subject to the key of the next statement. The melodic material in the episodes may be derived from motives taken from the subject or countersubject or from different material, and both melodic and harmonic sequences are extremely common. As the fugue unfolds, there is a sense of motion toward a climax that is ultimately resolved in the final measures in the tonic key. A typical fugue format is as follows:

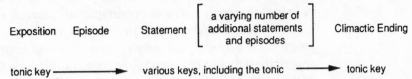

Contrapuntal Techniques. Composers employed a number of contrapuntal techniques in their development of the subject and other important thematic material: statement in longer note values (*augmentation*) or shorter note values (*diminution*); presentation of themes upside down (*inversion*), backwards (*retrograde*), or both (*retrograde inversion*); and presentation of the subject in overlapped statements (*stretto*), so that before one voice completes the subject the next voice enters with it. Composers showed great ingenuity and skill in manipulating these techniques.

Other Types of Fugue. Besides the fugue on a single subject described above, there are also fugues based on two subjects (*double fugue*) or on three (*triple fugue*). In addition, many composers often adopted a loose, quasifugal texture in works that are not, strictly speaking, fugues. Handel used this type of texture frequently in his choral writing, and examples of it abound in Baroque sonatas.

REPRESENTATIVE COMPOSERS

Some of the canzonas of Giovanni Gabrieli and the ricercars and fantasias of Sweelinck and Frescobaldi represent early stages in the development of the fugue. At the end of the seventeenth century, German composers such as Johann Krieger, Johann Pachelbel, and J. K. F. Fischer were writing true fugues, and this tradition was continued by many composers of the early eighteenth century. The undisputed master of the fugue was J. S. Bach. In addition to his numerous individual fugues (often coupled with toccatas, fantasias or preludes), he also composed two monumental collections that sum up with great mastery all the techniques and possibilities inherent in the genre: (1) *Das wohltemperirte Clavier* (The Well-Tempered Clavier; Part I,

c. 1722; Part II, c. 1742), each part of which contains twenty-four preludes and fugues, one pair for each of the twelve major and minor keys; and *Die Kunst der Fugue* (The Art of Fugue; 1749–1750), left unfinished at his death, a collection of fugues (all on the same subject) and canons that demonstrate all types of fugal writing.

Other Instrumental Genres

THE PASSACAGLIA OR CHACONNE

In the theme and variation form (see above), there are usually short pauses between each variation. In contrast to this are *continuous variations*, which flow from one into the other without interruption. Continuous variations are designated by three terms: *ground bass* (chapter 15), *passacaglia*, and *chaconne*.

The terms *passacaglia* and *chaconne* refer to a type of continuous variation in which either (1) contrapuntal material is superimposed on a recurrent bass melody as in a ground bass, or (2) there is a recurrent chord progression above which varying melodies and contrapuntal material are superimposed. The bass melody or chord progression that serves as the basis of the variations is usually four or eight measures in length, in a stately triple meter, and often in the minor mode. If a bass melody is used, it may sometimes be embellished slightly during the course of its repetitions, and it may occasionally move from the bass register to a higher one.

Some writers identify the passacaglia with the type of variation based on a recurrent bass melody and the chaconne with the type of variation based on a recurrent chord progression. During the Baroque period, however, the two terms were virtually interchangeable. J. S. Bach wrote outstanding examples of both types: the *Passacaglia in C Minor* (BWV 582, before 1708?) for organ, variations on a bass melody; and the "Chaconne" from the *Partita No. 2 in D Minor* (BWV 1004, 1720) for unaccompanied violin, variations on a recurrent chord progression.

CHORALE COMPOSITIONS

An important class of Baroque organ compositions based on chorale melodies arose in the early seventeenth century and flourished in middle and northern Germany in the late seventeenth and early eighteenth centuries. Such works are often grouped loosely under the general heading of *chorale prelude*, perhaps in reference to the probable origin of the genre in the practice by organists of playing a chorale tune through as a prelude before the congregation sang it. However, other names are used for specific types of chorale compositions; among these are *chorale partita*, *chorale fugue*, and *chorale fantasia*.

Representative composers of chorale compositions include Samuel Scheidt and J. P. Sweelinck of the early Baroque period; Dietrich Buxtehude, Johann Pachelbel, and Georg Böhm of the middle Baroque period; and, above all, J. S. Bach, whose works represent the culmination of the genre.

*D*uring the Baroque period, instrumental music came into its own and, by the end of the period, was equal to vocal music in quantity and quality. In vocal and instrumental music alike, the seventeenth century was a period of experimentation, during which some genres inherited from the Renaissance were developed further while others gradually merged with newer ones; by the end of the century, most had settled into standardized formats.

The most important new instrumental genres were the suite, the sonata, the concerto, and the fugue. Others include the passacaglia, the chaconne, and chorale compositions. Vivaldi's concertos were particularly important for the future development of music, clearly presaging the approaching Classical style in their emphasis on homophonic texture, their conspicuous use of outlined triads and scalewise passages in melodies, their tendency toward regular phrase structures, and their clarity of form and harmony.

For Additional Study

Dickinson, A. E. F. *Bach's Fugal Works, with an Account of Fugue before and after Bach.* London: Pitman & Sons, 1956; reprint, Westport, CT: Greenwood Press. 1979.

Downey, Juan. *Bachdisc.* Santa Monica, CA: Voyager Company. Videodisc.

Gillespie, John. *Five Centuries of Keyboard Music: An Historical Survey of Music for Harpsichord and Piano.* Belmont, CA: Wadsworth, 1965: reprint, New York: Dover. 1972.

Hutchings, Arthur. *The Baroque Concerto.* 3d ed. London: Faber and Faber. 1973.

Kolneder, Walter. *Vivaldi.* Translated by B. Hopkins. Berkeley: University of California Press. 1971.

Newman, William S. *The Sonata in the Baroque Era.* Chapel Hill, NC: University of North Carolina Press, 1959. 4th ed. New York: Norton. 1983.

Pincherle, Marc. *Corelli: His Life, His Music.* Translated by Hubert E. M. Russell. New York: Norton, 1956; reprint, 1968.

Recommended Listening

TOCCATA, FANTASIA, PRELUDE, RICERCAR, AND FUGUE:

Bach, J. S. *Chromatic Fantasia and Fugue in D Minor*, BWV 903 (c. 1720; clavier)
___. *Fantasia and Fugue in G Minor*, BWV 542 (c. 1720; organ)
___. *Die Kunst der Fuge* (The Art of Fugue), BWV 1080 (1749–1750)
___. *Toccata and Fugue in D Minor*, BWV 565 (c. 1707; organ)
___. *Das wohltemperirte Clavier* (The Well-Tempered Clavier), I: Prelude in C Major; Prelude and Fugue in C Minor
Frescobaldi, Girolamo. *Fiori musicali* (Musical Flowers; 1635): "Ricercare dopo il Credo" from *Messa della Madonna* (organ)

VARIATION, PASSACAGLIA, CHACONNE, AND CHORALE COMPOSITIONS:

Bach, J. S. Chorale Preludes (organ): *Jesu, meine Freude*, BWV 610; *Wenn wir in höchsten Nöten sein*, BWV 641; *Vor deinen Thron tret' ich hiermit*, BWV 668
___. *Clavier-Übung*, IV (1742): "Goldberg Variations" (clavier)
___. *Partita No. 2 in D Minor*, BWV 1004 (1720; unaccompanied violin): "Chaconne"
___. *Passacaglia and Fugue in C Minor*, BWV 582 (before 1708?; organ)

Handel, George Frideric. *Suite No. 5 in E Major* (1720; harpsichord), IV: "The Harmonious Blacksmith" (variations)

Pachelbel, Johann. *Kanon in D Major*

SUITE:

Bach, J. S. Clavier Suites: "Six Partitas," BWV 825–30, from *Clavier-Übung*, I (1731); *English Suites*, BWV 806–11 (c. 1715); *French Suites*, BWV 812–17 (c. 1722–1724)

___. *Suite No. 3 in D Major*, BWV 1068 (c. 1731; orchestra)

Couperin, François. *Pièces de clavecin*, I (1713; harpsichord): "Second ordre"

Froberger, Johann Jakob. *Suite in E Minor* (harpsichord)

Handel, George Frideric. Orchestral suites: *Water Music* (c. 1717); *Music for the Royal Fireworks* (1749)

SONATA:

Bach, J. S. *Musikalisches Opfer* (Musical Offering), BWV 1079 (1747): "Trio Sonata in C Minor" (flute, violin, continuo)

Corelli, Arcangelo. *Sonata da chiesa*, Op. 3, No. 7 (1689; trio sonata)

Handel, George Frideric. *Sonata in F Major for Flute and Continuo*, Op. 1, No. 11

Tartini, Giuseppe. "Devil's Trill" *Sonata in G Minor* (after 1735; violin and continuo)

CONCERTO:

Bach, J. S. *Six Brandenburg Concertos*, BWV 1046–51 (1721)

Handel, George Frideric. *Twelve Grand Concertos*, Op. 6 (1739)

Torelli, Giuseppe. *Concerto grosso*, Op. 8, No. 7

Vivaldi, Antonio. *Concerto in A Minor*, Op. 3, No. 6 (1712; violin and orchestra)

___. *Le quattro stagione* (The Four Seasons), Op. 8, Nos. 1–4 (c. 1725)

18

The Classical Period: An Introduction

1690	Locke, *Two Treatises on Civil Government*
c. 1700–c. 1750	Late Baroque period in music
c. 1709	First pianoforte built
1715–1774	Reign of Louis XV in France; Rococo style flourishes
c. 1720–c. 1770	Emergence of pre-Classical styles in music
1720s	Rise of public concerts
1734	Voltaire, *Lettres philosophiques*
1738	Excavation of Herculaneum (discovered in 1709), and later of Pompeii, contributes to a neoclassical revival
1740	Richardson, *Pamela*
1740–1796	Era of "enlightened despots": Frederick the Great of Prussia (r. 1740–1786), Charles III of Spain (r. 1759–1788), Catherine the Great of Russia (r. 1762–1796), Joseph II of Austria (r. 1765–1790), and Gustav III of Sweden (r. 1771–1792)
1749	Fielding, *Tom Jones*
1750	Death of J. S. Bach; Montesquieu, *L'Esprit des lois* (The Spirit of Laws)
1751–1772	Diderot oversees publication of the French *Encyclopédie*
c. 1760	Beginning of Industrial Revolution in England
c. 1760–c. 1785	*Sturm und Drang* (Storm and Stress) movement in Germany
1761	Haydn enters service for the Esterházys
1762	Rousseau, *Émile* and *Du contrat social*; young Mozart (b. 1756) begins touring Europe as a child prodigy
1769	Watt patents the steam engine

1770	Hargreaves patents the spinning jenny; Gainsborough, *The Blue Boy*
1770s	Emergence of the Classical style in music
1774	Priestley discovers oxygen
1774–1793	Louis XVI reigns in France
1776	Adam Smith, *An Inquiry into the Nature and Causes of the Wealth of Nations*
1776–1783	American Revolution
1781	Mozart moves to Vienna
1781–1790	Kant publishes his three "Critiques"
1785	Cartwright patents the power loom
1789–1795	French Revolution
1791	Mozart dies in poverty; U.S. Bill of Rights is ratified
1792–1827	Beethoven active in Vienna
1794	Whitney patents the cotton gin
1795–1815	Napoleonic era
1796	Jenner discovers a vaccine for smallpox
1798	Coleridge and Wordsworth help launch the English Romantic movement with their *Lyrical Ballads*; Malthus, *An Essay on the Principle of Population*, a study in economic pessimism
1798–1827	Laplace publishes the five volumes of his *Celestial Mechanics*
1800	Volta demonstrates the first electric battery
1802	Beethoven, "Heiligenstadt Testament," writes of his growing deafness
1804	Schiller, *Wilhelm Tell*
1806	End of the Holy Roman Empire; Lewis and Clark reach the Pacific
1807	Fulton builds the first commercial steamboat
1808	Goethe, *Faust*, Part I (Part II, 1832)
1809	Napoleon enters Vienna; death of Haydn
1811–1830	Revolts in South America lead to independence for Paraguay (1811), Mexico (1821), the La Plata region (1816), Chile (1818), Peru (1821), Brazil (1822), and Venezuela (1830)
1812	War of 1812 between United States and England; Napoleon retreats from Moscow
1815	Napoleon defeated at Waterloo; Congress of Vienna establishes post-Napoleonic reorganization of Europe
1819	Keats, Odes
1820	Shelley, *Prometheus Unbound*

1821   Faraday constructs the first electric motor

1827   Death of Beethoven

Music historians traditionally date the Classical period in music from 1750 to 1820 or 1825. Yet as we saw in chapters 14 through 17, the pre-Classical style had already begun to emerge in the early eighteenth century, even as the Baroque style was reaching its culmination. At the other end of the period, musical Romanticism was well under way by 1820. Thus, as with all other stylistic periods, the beginning and ending dates are only approximations.

The Classical period in music took place during a time of momentous intellectual, social, political, and scientific developments. The first of these was the Age of Enlightenment (or the Age of Reason), a European intellectual movement of the seventeenth and eighteenth centuries (among whose exponents were Locke, Voltaire, Diderot, Rousseau, and Kant) that was based on the premise that reason, not tradition or emotion, was the best guide to human conduct. Underlying the Enlightenment was a faith in the unlimited possibility of human understanding and in human perfectability, plus the belief that religions, political systems, the arts, and education should all be judged by how they contributed to the well-being of the individual.

Intellectuals of the period were convinced that not just the natural sciences but all aspects of life and society were governed by fixed natural laws that could be discovered through scientific investigation. Once discovered, these laws could be used to guide human action, bringing continuous progress. Two important proponents of this school of thought were John Locke, whose ideas contained in his "Second Treatise on Civil Government" (1690) found direct echoes in the Declaration of Independence, and Adam Smith, whose concept of laissez-faire economics outlined in "An Inquiry into the Nature and Causes of the Wealth of Nations" (1776) laid the foundations of modern capitalism.

Since Europe at the beginning of the Enlightenment was ruled by absolute monarchs, the initial practical application of the new theories in the areas of politics and economics rested in the hands of so-called "enlightened despots." Ultimately, though, the new democratic ideals led to an Age of Revolution, which manifested itself in the American war of independence, the French Revolution, and revolts in South America. Following the French Revolution, the Napoleonic era brought nearly all of Europe under French control until Napoleon was finally defeated at Waterloo. By the time all this had ended, intellectuals had begun to dismiss the concept of human perfectability as naive and to accept the idea that scientific laws are inadequate to explain the ethical and spiritual nature of humankind.

Continued advances in science and technology led to still another momentous development during this period—the Industrial Revolution, which began in England and was centered in that country for most of the period. The period also witnessed the rise of the novel and other notable events in literature, culminating in the work of the great German writer Goethe (1749–1832).

The tumultuous age of the Classical period in music was, thus, one in which an old world was dying and a new one was being born.

FROM BAROQUE TO CLASSIC

Rococo

During the reign of Louis XV from 1715 to 1774, French tastes shifted away from the grandiose Baroque style to that of the Rococo (from *rocaille*, a shell, referring to the ornate scroll-and-shell work that was characteristic of Rococo). A lighter, more intimate style than the Baroque, Rococo was more appropriate for the salon than for the palace. It retained the ornate quality of the Baroque but had a more delicate, playful manner. For over fifty years the style flourished in France and elsewhere until, in the years preceding the French Revolution, it began to seem frivolous and excessively ornate.

Pre-Classical Music

During this same period, there was a similar turning away from the ponderousness and complexity of Baroque music toward a lighter, simpler way of writing, even as the Baroque style was reaching its culmination in the works of J. S. Bach and Handel. This pre-Classical subperiod, which extended from c. 1720–c. 1770, constituted a transitional phase between the Baroque and mature Classical styles, combining the ornateness of Baroque music with the lighter textures of the Classical period. Two general styles emerged within the pre-Classical subperiod: the French and Italian *galant* style (French, *style galant*; Italian, *galante*) and the German *Empfindsamer Stil* (sensitive, or expressive, style).

Although these two styles differ in some respects, they have several traits in common: (1) a preference for thin-textured homophony over contrapuntal texture; (2) a tendency toward simple melodies that are organized hierarchically into short phrases and sections as opposed to the older Baroque forth-spinning melodies; (3) uncomplicated harmonies and a slower rate of chord changes than in Baroque music; (4) a preference for major keys over minor; and (5) the gradual abandonment of the basso continuo and its rhythmically active and contrapuntally independent bass lines in favor of settings in which the bass simply provides support for the melody and the inner voices are mere "fillers."

Eventually, both the *galant* style and the *Empfindsamer Stil* were absorbed into the Classical style. But, before they were, pre-Classical composers made important contributions to the development of existing genres, such as the opera and concerto, and they also initiated several extremely important new instrumental forms and genres that were to reach perfection during the Classical period, notably the sonata cycle and the symphony (see chapter 19).

GALANT STYLE

The *galant* style arose c. 1720 and flourished primarily in aristocratic circles. Elegant, witty, and ornate, it is the perfect counterpart of Rococo art. Representative examples of the style may be found in the works of the French *clavecin* school (e.g., François Couperin) and other late Baroque composers (e.g., Rameau, Telemann, Leclair, Tartini, and Pergolesi).

EMPFINDSAMER STIL

After 1750 in Germany, a form of *galant* style known as *Emfindsamer Stil* became important. Emphasizing expressiveness and sensitivity and reflecting middle class rather than aristocratic tastes, this new style strongly influenced the later Classical style and, in fact, came to fullest flower in the music of the Romantic period. Composers writing in this style typically explored a variety of moods within a movement, as opposed to the Baroque composers, who normally projected only a single affection. In doing this, they used all possible dynamic shadings, subtle changes of harmony and rhythm, and a more unadorned "natural" melody in place of the highly ornamental type favored in the *galant* style.

A later phase of the *Empfindsamer Stil* was the *Sturm und Drang* (Storm and Stress) movement, influenced by the similarly named movement in German literature (c. 1760–c. 1785) and the other arts. Proponents of this movement, whose major figures included Goethe and Schiller (in their early works), exalted nature and human individualism in opposition to the Enlightenment cult of rationalism, and they often sought to shock their audiences or overcome them with emotion. Sturm und Drang elements may be seen in numerous dramas of the period, in "Gothic" novels, and in paintings of macabre scenes and nightmares (e.g., Fuseli's *The Nightmare*). In music elements of Sturm und Drang appear, for example, in several of Haydn's works written during the early 1770s.

The leading composer in the *Empfindsamer Stil* was Carl Philipp Emanuel Bach (1714–1788), the second son of J. S. Bach. Also important was J. S. Bach's youngest son, Johann Christian Bach (1735–1782).

OTHER PRE-CLASSICAL COMPOSERS

Among other important pre-Classical composers are several who were instrumental in the rise of the symphony (besides C. P. E. Bach and other north German composers): Giovanni Battista Sammartini (1701–1775) in Milan; Johann Stamitz (1717–1757) and Christian Cannabich (1731–1798) in Mannheim; Georg C. Wagenseil (1715–1777) and Georg Monn (1717–1750) in Vienna; and François-Joseph Gossec (1734–1829) in France. Other representative composers include Johann Quantz (1697–1773), Johann Gottlieb Graun (1703–1771), and Domenico Alberti (c. 1710–1740).

EIGHTEENTH-CENTURY CLASSICISM

The term *classical* is used with a number of connotations. It may refer to the art or culture of ancient Greece and Rome or to later creations that embody the classical values of balance, restraint, and clarity of form. It may serve as an antonym of "popular" (as in "classical" vs. "popular" music) or of "romantic" (see chapter 21). It may refer to that phase in the development of a style in which the style is at its fullest and most harmonious expression. It may also refer in general to any supreme achievement of lasting appeal.

During the last half of the eighteenth century, the Enlightenment brought a desire for a more "natural" and "reasonable" means of expression. Coupled with a revived interest in antiquity, this led to a neoclassical revival in the arts, which manifested itself in buildings (e.g., Thomas Jefferson's Monticello), paintings (e.g., those of Jacques-Louis David), sculpture (e.g., that of Jean-Antoine Houdon), china (e.g., Wedgewood china), and other artifacts patterned on classical models or principles. At the same time, though, there was a parallel movement that foreshadowed the coming Romantic age. Before these romantic tendencies gained predominance, however, eighteenth-century Classicism produced, in the area of music, three of the greatest composers of all time: Franz Joseph Haydn (1732–1809), Wolfgang Amadeus Mozart (1756–1791), and Ludwig van Beethoven (1770–1827)—all three of whom made their careers primarily in and around Vienna.

General Characteristics of Classical Music

TEXTURE

The Classical period represents a milestone in the history of music, for it was in this period that homophonic texture finally triumphed over contrapuntal texture, which had predominated since the Middle Ages. Furthermore, composers of this period favored thin, light sonorities in which the melody clearly stands out above the accompaniment. Counterpoint did not simply disappear, however. Composers still occasionally wrote fugues and other contrapuntal forms, and they drew heavily upon contrapuntal techniques in transition and development sections of large forms. In addition, they continued to use counterpoint in many subtle, unobtrusive ways to enliven predominantly homophonic passages.

FORM

Together with the rise of homophonic texture, the Classical period also saw the rise of forms based on the hierarchical arrangement of sections within sections. The new popularity of these so-called homophonic forms represents another watershed in the history of Western music: whereas forms based on polyphonic techniques (motet, madrigal, fugue, and so forth) had predominated in music dating from the rise of organum through the end of the Baroque period, forms based on homophonic practices would be preeminent from the beginning of the Classical period to at least the end of the Romantic.

In the music of the Classical period, phrases are characteristically short (typically four measures) and have well-defined cadences. They often group themselves into larger units that, in turn, combine to form still larger sections. Large forms exhibit a high degree of symmetry and long-range structural planning.

MELODY

Classical melodies and themes are generally more compact than Baroque melodies and are more tuneful and easier to remember. Sometimes even folklike in quality, they are typically organized into symmetrical phrases with clear-cut cadences and easily grasped thematic relationships. In the transition and development sections of larger forms, on the other hand, composers often adopted a less well-defined melodic style, concentrating instead on the development of short motives, on contrapuntal imitation, and on scales and other figuration.

HARMONY

On the whole, Classical harmony is less complex than Baroque harmony. It is more diatonic, places more emphasis on the principal triads of the key (the tonic, subdominant, and dominant), and has slower rates of chord changes. On the other hand, Classical composers show a much more dramatic and purposeful approach to modulation. Whereas Baroque music typically glides effortlessly from one key to another, most Classical music emphatically moves to and establishes broad tonal "plateaus." Particularly important in large forms is the initial establishment of the tonic key at the beginning of a movement, followed by an equally emphatic juxtaposition of a secondary key. A secondary key established in such an emphatic manner creates a type of structural tension that can only be resolved by an equally emphatic motion back to the tonic key later in the movement. As a result, modulations are more of an "event" in Classical music than in Baroque. Only in the transition and development sections of large forms do Classical composers typically fall back on the faster, less emphatic modulations found in Baroque music.

RHYTHM

Classical rhythm is similar to Baroque rhythm in that it has a clear, strong metrical pulse. However, in other ways it is strikingly different. Whereas in Baroque music a single rhythmic pattern established at the beginning of a movement typically repeats itself continuously throughout the movement with little or no change, in Classical music the rhythm is much more flexible and unpredictable. It is full of unexpected starts and stops, and it uses a far greater variety of rhythmic patterns. Furthermore, Classical rhythm shares more fully with harmony and melody in the role of making clear the phrase-and-cadence structure. Rhythmic variety also helps make clear the contrasting moods within a movement.

DYNAMICS

The desire to express ever-changing shades of emotion led also to a more flexible and subtle use of dynamics. In place of the rigid terraced dynamics of Baroque music, Classical music makes much greater use of crescendos, diminuendos, expressive accents, and other dynamic nuances. This desire for greater dynamic variety led, in turn, to a gradual abandonment of the harpsichord, which is incapable of producing crescendos and diminuendos, in favor of the piano.

TIMBRE

The Classical period brought the standardization of the symphony orchestra (see chapter 19). Composers explored the many subtle shades of tone color available from the various combinations of instruments, establishing the modern concept of orchestration.

Patronage and Public Concerts

As in the Baroque period, courts, opera houses, and churches continued to be important patrons of the arts. However, the rise of a new forum for the composer—the public concert—was to have far-reaching significance. To be sure, opera houses and churches had long provided the composer with opportunities for public performance, but concert music had generally been performed at court or at private functions. Beginning in the 1720s, however, public performances of concert music increasingly became a regular part of musical life. As had been the case in opera, the rise of public concerts produced fundamental changes in music. Now writing for the broader public rather than for the cultured aristocracy, composers had to adapt their music to the tastes and musical understanding of this new audience. Thus, their music took on an increasingly popular flavor.

The rise of public concerts at this time owed much to the increased influence of the middle class and its desire to hear good music on a regular basis. Middle class music lovers also took musical lessons and participated in making music in their homes. As a result, composers were able to augment their income by giving music lessons, writing music that amateurs could perform, and performing private concerts in homes.

The careers of Haydn, Mozart, and Beethoven reflect the gradual changes brought about by these new developments. Haydn thrived under the old patronage system, even though he was treated essentially as a servant. Mozart, rebelling against patronage, left his position in Salzburg and tried to make an independent living in Vienna, only to die in poverty. Beethoven, on the other hand, succeeded in establishing himself as an independent artist while also receiving gifts from nobles who treated him as an equal.

Haydn, Mozart, and Beethoven

HAYDN

Life. Franz Joseph Haydn (1732–1809), born in Rohrau, Lower Austria, and trained as a choirboy at St. Stephen's Cathedral, Vienna, spent most of his career (from 1761) in the service of the Esterházys, a family of wealthy princes with castles in Eisenstadt, near Vienna, and later also at Eszterháza, in present-day Hungary. Generous patrons of the arts, the Esterházy family maintained an opera company, a marionette theater, a chapel, and an orchestra, for which Haydn conducted performances, composed new music as required, trained the musicians, and took care of the instruments.

During the 1770s and 1780s, Haydn's fame began to spread throughout Europe. During the 1780s he also met Mozart and established an association that benefitted both of them as composers. In 1790 a new Esterházy prince who was not a music lover disbanded the orchestra, and Haydn, though still nominally employed by the Esterházys, was permitted to move to Vienna. When he resumed service with the family in 1795, it was on a more limited basis. Freedom from his palace duties enabled Haydn to pursue other activities, the most notable of which were two spectacularly successful trips to London, in 1791–92 and 1794–95, during which he presented new compositions (e.g., the twelve "London" symphonies) and concertized. In 1792 he met the young Beethoven in Bonn and encouraged him to come to Vienna, where Beethoven studied with him for about a year. In his later life, Haydn was esteemed as the leading composer of his time and received numerous honors. He died May 31, 1809, shortly after Napoleon conquered Vienna. Kind, humble, and beloved by those who knew him, Haydn, more than any other person, was responsible for the transformation of the pre-Classical style into the mature Classical style and particularly for the development of the Classical approach to the sonata cycle (see chapter 19).

Works. Haydn's principal works include (1) over 100 symphonies, plus concertos for various instruments and other orchestral music; (2) string quartets, piano trios, and numerous other works for chamber ensembles; (3) keyboard works, including some 49 sonatas; (4) Masses (including the *Mass in Time of War*, 1796, and the *Lord Nelson Mass*, 1798), oratorios (e.g.,*The Creation*, 1798, and *The Seasons*, 1801), and other choral music; (4) operas; and (5) solo songs, cantatas, vocal quartets and trios, arrangements of folk songs, and other vocal music.

MOZART

Life. Wolfgang Amadeus Mozart (1756–1791) was born in Salzburg, Austria, the son of Leopold Mozart, a noted violinist-composer attached to the chapel of the Archbishop of Salzburg. Perhaps the most gifted musical prodigy of all time, Mozart began composing before age six, was a harpsichord virtuoso by age six, and even in his youth had the ability to reproduce complete works after hearing them only once. He received excellent training from his father, who also took him and his almost equally talented sister on extended tours of the musical capitals of Europe, where the children displayed their talents and young Mozart absorbed the leading musical trends of the time.

Mozart served at the archbishop's court in Salzburg for a while, but resigned in 1781 while on a court visit to Vienna, remaining there to establish himself as an independent musician. In 1782 he married Constanze Weber. Things went well at first, and he reached the high point of his success from 1784 through 1786. Following increasing financial difficulties in the last five years of his life, however, Mozart died in poverty.

Mozart's natural gifts and the ease with which he composed are considered marvelous. His works are models of clarity and grace, yet they are also filled with profound emotional expressiveness, singing melodies, and warm, subtly chromatic harmonies. They epitomize that perfect balance of rational and emotional elements that we think of as "classic."

Works. Mozart's principal works include (1) symphonies (over fifty, counting fragments and *sinfonie* in other works), concertos, and other orchestral music; (2) operas, including such masterworks as *Die Entführung aus dem Serail* (The Abduction from the Seraglio, 1782), *Le nozze di Figaro* (The Marriage of Figaro, 1786), *Don Giovanni* (Don Juan, 1787), *Così fan tutte* (Thus Do They All, 1790), and *Die Zauberflöte* (The Magic Flute, 1791); (3) choral music, including eighteen Masses, the *Requiem* (K. 626; incomplete, 1791), and other liturgical music; (4) chamber music, including twenty-six string quartets, string quintets, piano trios and quartets, sonatas for violin and piano, and other works for small ensembles; keyboard works, including twenty-one piano sonatas, variations, fantasias, and other works; and (5) concert arias for voice and orchestra and songs for voice and piano.

BEETHOVEN

Life. Ludwig van Beethoven (1770–1827), who was born and began his career in Bonn, Germany, moved to Vienna in 1792 at the urging of Haydn. There he studied with Haydn and others and soon took the Viennese public by storm with his piano playing. A brash young man with a fiery temperament and independent spirit, he was able to establish himself as a free-lance musician and to win acceptance and financial support from the aristocracy, who regarded him as an equal. When he was in his late twenties he began to lose his hearing. Faced with the end of his concert career, he considered suicide, but emerged determined to continue as a composer. Thereafter, the idea that human beings could triumph over whatever fate dealt them became an epic theme in his music (e.g., in his *Symphony No. 5 in C Minor*, Op. 67). In his later years, however, his deafness caused him to retreat more and more into himself and to become more suspicious and irritable. His later years were also plagued by family problems and deteriorating health. When he died in 1827, some 10,000 persons attended his funeral.

Beethoven, like Napoleon, was a child of the Age of Revolution, those turbulent times when the old social order was passing and the new was emerging. With demonic energy and heroic passion, Beethoven carried music from the Classical period to the Romantic, in the process becoming the model for later Romantic composers. He was a master of musical architecture, where his genius expressed itself most fully in such forms as the sonata and symphony, which he expanded to unprecedented proportions and transformed into vehicles for intensely personal expression.

Works. Beethoven's principal works include (1) nine symphonies, overtures, and incidental music to accompany plays; (2) concertos, including five for piano, one for violin, and one triple concerto for piano, violin, and cello; (3) chamber music, including sixteen string quartets plus the *Grosse Fuge* (Op. 133, 1826), nine piano trios, ten violin sonatas, five cello sonatas, serenades, and other chamber music works for winds and other ensembles; (4) works for piano, including thirty-two sonatas with opus numbers, at least twenty sets of variations (e.g., the *Thirty-three Variations on a Waltz by Diabelli*, Op. 120, 1823), and other compositions; (5) the opera *Fidelio* (1805, revised 1806, 1814); (6) choral music, including two Masses (e.g., *Missa Solemnis*, Op. 123, 1823) and the oratorio *Christus am Ölberge* (Christ on the Mount of Olives, 1803); and (7) songs, including the song cycle *An die ferne Geliebte* (To the Distant Beloved, Op. 98, 1816) and many other arrangements of folk songs with piano trio.

*T*he creation of the mature Classical style in music was largely the work of Haydn, who absorbed and transformed elements from pre-Classical music into a compelling new musical language. This new style was taken over by Mozart and Beethoven, who transformed it further through the force of their *genius.   While Mozart's music remains well within Classical bounds, Beethoven's approaches more closely (and perhaps even crosses in some ways) the borderline between the Classical and Romantic styles.*

Straddling the Enlightenment and the Age of Revolution, the music of the Classical period holds rational and emotional elements in an exquisite balance.   Shortly afterwards, the scale would be tipped toward the emotional.

For Additional Study

Abert, Hermann. *W. A. Mozart.* 2 vols. Leipzig: Breitkopf & Härtel, 1956; revised 1975.

Blume, Friedrich. *Classic and Romantic Music: A Comprehensive Survey.* Translated by M. D. Herter Norton. New York: Norton. 1970.

The EAV Art and Music Series. "Eighteenth-Century Art and Music." Distributed by Educational Audio Visual, Inc. (Pleasantville, NY). Videocassette.

The EAV History of Music. Part 4: "Into the Classical Period." Distributed by Educational Audio Visual, Inc. (Pleasantville, NY). Videocassette.

Landon, H. C. Robbins. *Haydn: Chronicle and Works.* 5 vols. Bloomington, IN: Indiana University Press. 1976–80.

___, and David Wyn Jones. *Haydn: His Life and Music.* Bloomington, IN: Indiana University Press. 1988.

Man & Music Series. "London: The Musical Capital"; "Haydn and the Esterházys"; "Music of an Empire"; "Mozart: Dropping the Patron"; "Mozart: A Genius in His Time"; "Beethoven: The Age of Revolution"; "Beethoven: The Composer as Hero." Distributed by Films for the Humanities & Sciences (Princeton, NJ). Videocassettes.

Pauly, Reinhard G. *Music in the Classic Period.* 3d ed. Englewood Cliffs, NJ: Prentice-Hall. 1988.

Ratner, Leonard. Classic Music: Expression, Form, and Style. New York: Schirmer. 1980.

Rosen, Charles. *The Classical Style: Haydn, Mozart, Beethoven.* New York: Viking Press, 1971; New York: Norton, 1972.

Sadie, Stanley. *The New Grove Mozart.* New York: Norton. 1983.

[A. W.] Thayer's Life of Beethoven. Revised and edited by Elliot Forbes. 2 vols. Princeton: Princeton University Press, 1969; 1-vol. paperbound ed., 1970.

Tyson, Alan, and Joseph Kerman. *The New Grove Beethoven.* New York: Norton; London: Macmillan. 1983.

19

Instrumental Music in the Classical Period

c. 1709	First pianoforte built
1720s	Rise of pre-Classical styles and public concerts
1722	J. S. Bach, *Well-Tempered Clavier*, Part I
c. 1725	Vivaldi, *The Four Seasons*
1730s	Rise of symphony (e.g., Sammartini)
1732	Birth of Haydn
1742	J. S. Bach, *Well-Tempered Clavier*, Part II; C. P. E. Bach, *"Prussian" Sonatas*
c. 1745	Rise of the string quartet
1745–1765	Reign of Emperor Francis I and Maria Theresa in Vienna
1750	Death of Bach
c. 1750	Haydn dismissed as choirboy from St. Stephens, Vienna
1756	Birth of Mozart
1759	Death of Handel
1761	Haydn enters service of the Esterházys
1762	Young Mozart begins touring Europe as a child prodigy
1763–1777	Publication of J. C. Bach's keyboard concertos
1764	Mozart's first published compositions and first symphonies
1765–1780	Emperor Joseph II reigns with Maria Theresa, his mother, in Vienna
1768–c. 1773	Haydn's *Sturm und Drang* period (e.g., symphonies 44, 49, 52 and string quartets Opp. 17 and 20); Mozart also influenced by the *Sturm und Drang* movement (e.g., *Symphony in G Minor*, K. 183)
1770	Birth of Beethoven; Mozart's first string quartets

1770s	Rise of Classical style in music
1780	Death of Maria Theresa; Joseph II reigns as an "enlightened despot" (until 1790)
1781	Mozart moves to Vienna
1782	Beethoven's earliest publications
1782–1785	Mozart, *Haydn Quartets*
c. 1785	Harpsichord begins to disappear in titles
1788	Mozart's last three symphonies (K. 543, 550, 551)
1789–1795	French Revolution
1791	Mozart's last piano concerto (K. 595) and *Clarinet Concerto* (K. 622); death of Mozart
1791–1792	Haydn's first set of "London" Symphonies
1792	Beethoven moves to Vienna
1793–1795	Haydn's second set of "London" Symphonies
1793–1803	Haydn's final string quartets (Opp. 71, 74, 76, 77, 103)
1798–1800	Beethoven's first string quartets (Op. 18)
1799	Beethoven, *Symphony No. 1 in C Major*, Op. 21
1802	Beethoven in "Heiligenstadt Testament" writes of his growing deafness
1803–1808	Beethoven, symphonies 3–6 and the string quartets, Op. 59
1806	Final dissolution of the Holy Roman Empire
1809	Napoleon occupies Vienna; death of Haydn
1811–1812	Beethoven, symphonies 7 and 8
1820–1822	Beethoven's last piano sonatas (Opp. 109, 110, 111)
1823	Beethoven completes his *Symphony No. 9*
1824–1826	Beethoven's final string quartets (Opp. 127, 130, 131, 132, 133, 135)
1827	Death of Beethoven

*A*lthough opera and other types of vocal music continued to be important during the Classical period, it was in the area of instrumental music that the most characteristic new forms and genres emerged. For this reason, we reverse the order of presentation used for the Baroque period and begin with an exploration of developments in instrumental music during the Classical period. This chapter begins with an examination of the sonata cycle, a new format for organizing multimovement works, and ends with a survey of developments within the principal instrumental genres.

THE CLASSICAL SONATA CYCLE

Pre-Classical and Classical composers developed a new format, the *sonata cycle*, which they used to organize the structure not only of the sonata but also of the symphony, concerto, string quartet, and other instrumental genres. The basis of the sonata cycle was the following four-movement plan:

SONATA CYCLE: GENERAL FORMAT

Movement	Key	Tempo	Character	Form
First	Tonic	Allegro	Epic or dramatic	Sonata
Second	Contrasting	Andante, Adagio, Largo	Slow and expressive	Sonata, Rondo or Theme and variations
Third	Tonic	Allegretto or Allegro	Minuet (dancelike 3/4) or Scherzo (whimsical or demonic 3/4)	Minuet and trio or Scherzo and trio
Fourth	Tonic	Allegro, Vivace, Presto	Lively and spirited, dramatic or triumphal	Sonata, Rondo, Sonata-rondo, or Theme and variations

Fig 19.1

In certain genres, such as the sonata and concerto, composers often omitted the third of these four movements, creating a three-movement cycle (fast-slow-fast) that resembled the Italian sinfonia, solo concerto, and solo sonata of the late Baroque period.

First Movement   As figure 19.1 indicates, the first movement of the sonata cycle is usually an Allegro movement in the tonic key. It employs a form that is referred to variously as *sonata form*, *sonata-allegro form* or *first-movement form*. We will use the term *sonata form* (not to be confused with *sonata cycle*, which refers to the entire three- or four-movement structure). Sonata form is one of the most ingenious and durable musical forms ever devised for the large-scale presentation and development of musical ideas.

A movement in sonata form consists of three main sections: (1) an *exposition*, in which the main musical ideas of the movement are presented; (2) a *development* section, which explores these ideas further; and (3) a *recapitulation*, which rounds off the movement with a modified restatement of the exposition. An optional slow *introduction* may precede the exposition, and an optional *coda* may follow the recapitulation.

INTRODUCTION

Sometimes a movement in sonata form begins with a slow introduction that sets the stage for the exposition. The introduction may be short or fairly extended, and it may or may not include thematic material used in the exposition. The introduction is not an essential part of the sonata form; consequently, it is not usually restated if the exposition is repeated, nor is it typically included in the recapitulation.

EXPOSITION

The primary role of the first main section, the exposition, is to establish the tonic key and then to oppose it with another key of almost equal importance. Many of the details of the internal construction of the exposition stem from the conflict of these two opposing keys.

The Tonic Key Area. The exposition begins with a theme in the tonic key, known as the *first theme*. This theme is often vigorous or forceful in character, and it may be a self-contained tune or more motivic in nature. In larger works, several ideas may be presented in the tonic key, in which case the term *first theme group* is appropriate.

Transition. Following the first theme is a *transition*, or *bridge*, which modulates to the second main key of the exposition. In music from the Classical period, if the movement is in a major key, the second key will most often be the dominant. If the movement is in a minor key, the second key will probably be the relative major (a minor third higher than the tonic—the key with the same key signature as the tonic key). As noted in chapter 18, composers of the Classical period had a much more dramatic conception of modulation than did Baroque composers. Rather than slide effortlessly into the second key, Classical composers preferred to create a *polarity* between the two keys, to set the second key in strong relief against the tonic as if it were an opposing character in a drama. Consequently, in the transition section of a sonata form, the composer makes the establishment of the second key an "event" by moving forcefully to the dominant of the new key and often extending that dominant for some time to build anticipation for the arrival of the new key itself. During the transition section, there is less use of real "tunes" than in the first theme area; more often this section features the development of short motives or the use of rapid scales or other figuration.

The Second Key Area. Following the transition, the remainder of the exposition is in the second main key. Often the composer marks the arrival of the second key with a new contrasting theme, so that the opposition of the two main keys is paralleled by the opposition of two main themes. If the first theme has been vigorous, this new theme, the *second theme*, is most often lyrical and expressive. As with the first theme, there may be more than one theme, in which case the term *second theme group* is appropriate. The appearance of a new theme or themes in this section is not in any way an essential feature of sonata form, however; the firm establishment of the second key as an opposite tonal pole is all that is required. Thus, early Classical composers such as Haydn, still influenced by the Baroque idea that a movement should present only one affection, often simply reworked the first theme in this section.

The second key area generally concludes with a short *codetta* (a small coda) or a *closing theme* that is cadential in nature and brings the exposition to a strong close in the second key. Beethoven and later composers sometimes used a variant of the first theme as the closing theme.

In sonata forms of the Classical period, the exposition is usually repeated.

DEVELOPMENT

In the development section, the composer has free rein to explore and exploit the latent possibilities of the materials of the exposition. Themes are typically broken down into their constituent motives, which are then passed around among different registers (and by various instruments in ensemble compositions), combined and recombined contrapuntally with other motives, and placed into new and unexpected contexts. Sometimes material not included in the exposition is introduced as well. Like the characters in a drama, themes are played off against one another in different situations, each of which reveals new insights into their natures. In contrast to the exposition, which is characterized by broad stable "plateaus" in the same key, rapid modulations through a variety of keys are the rule in the development section, creating a sense of activity and excitement. At the end of the development, there is usually a *retransition* that leads to the triumphant reappearance of the tonic key at the beginning of the recapitulation.

RECAPITULATION

The recapitulation is essentially a modified restatement of the exposition. As Charles Rosen (*The Classical Style*) has observed so astutely, the one fixed rule of the sonata recapitulation is that material originally exposed outside of the tonic key (i.e., that which appeared originally in the second key area of the exposition) must be restated in the tonic key fairly completely, even if it is rewritten and reordered. The reason for this, he explains, is that material presented outside the tonic key must have created, in the eighteenth century, a feeling of instability that demanded to be resolved. On the other hand, material that originally appeared in the tonic key (i.e., first theme material) could be restated, altered or omitted as the composer saw fit. Thus, although many recapitulations exhibit a fairly literal restatement of the entire exposition, with the transition altered and the second key area transposed into the tonic key, most exhibit a good bit of reworking and reordering, especially of first theme material.

CODA

The movement may end at the conclusion of the recapitulation, or the recapitulation may lead into a *coda*. The coda may be a brief epilogue, or it may be more extended. Beethoven's codas were particularly elaborate, often functioning virtually as a second development section.

EVOLUTION OF SONATA FORM

Sonata form evolved from the binary and rounded binary forms of the Baroque period (see chapter 17), and it went through several stages of development before reaching the mature stage just described. Even in its mature stage, however, the relationship between the sonata form and the rounded binary form is easily seen:

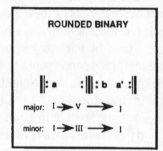
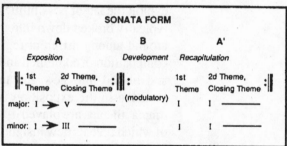

Fig 19.2

In early Classical sonata forms, both halves of the movement are often marked to be repeated, as shown above. In such cases, the feeling of an overall two-part structure (exposition, development-recapitulation) is strong. In later Classical sonata forms, while the repeat of the exposition is still normally (though not always) marked, the repeat of the second half is usually not indicated. In these cases, the movement acquires more of a three-part feeling (exposition, development, recapitulation).

Second Movement

The second movement of the Classical sonata cycle is normally in a slow tempo and in a different key from that of the first movement (most commonly the subdominant key). Usually songlike and expressive, it provides an effective contrast to the more dramatic first movement. Like the first movement, it may be in sonata form. If it is, however, it normally uses an abbreviated version known as *sonatina form*, or *slow-movement sonata form*, in which the development section is either omitted altogether or replaced by a brief episode between the exposition and recapitulation. The slow movement may also employ binary form, ternary form, one of the rondo forms (discussed below) or theme and variations form.

Third Movement

If a composition employing the Classical sonata cycle has four movements, the third is almost invariably a *minuet and trio* or *scherzo and trio* in the tonic key. The minuet is a dancelike section in 3/4 meter that usually exhibits a binary or rounded binary form. Coupled with the minuet is another dancelike section in binary or rounded binary form known as the *trio* (so called because the earliest examples were scored for three instruments), which is usually lighter in texture. Following the trio, the minuet repeats, creating an overall A B A form. Often the return of the minuet is a literal da capo, but with internal repeats omitted. The form is as follows:

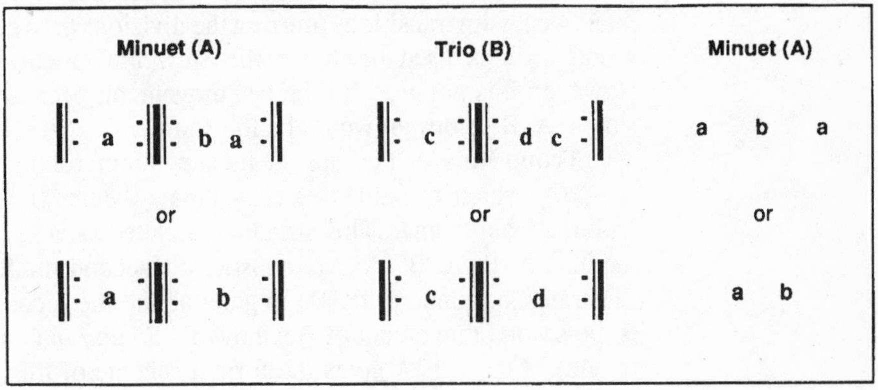

Fig 19.3

In the nineteenth century, the *scherzo* often replaced the minuet, producing the form scherzo-trio-scherzo. Like the minuet, the scherzo is usually in the tonic key, in 3/4 meter, and cast in binary or rounded binary form. However, the scherzo (Italian for "joke") is faster in tempo and is marked by more abrupt changes of mood, ranging from whimsical to demonic. Beethoven, in particular, is noted for his scherzos.

If one of the movements of the four-movement cycle is omitted, it will most often be this movement. Also, this movement and the second are sometimes reversed in order of appearance.

Fourth Movement

The final movement of the sonata cycle is in a fast tempo and in the tonic key. It may be light and lively in nature or dramatic with a triumphant ending. Typical forms include sonata form, theme and variations, rondo, and sonata-rondo.

RONDO FORMS

General Characteristics. Several structural plans come under the heading of *rondo forms*. The essential feature of all rondo structures is the recurrence of a main theme that alternates with one or more subordinate themes. Each theme may in itself be a short part-form or a simple binary or ternary structure. Whereas the main theme (A) almost always appears in the tonic key, the other themes (B, C, and so on) usually appear in contrasting keys. The themes of a rondo structure may be separated by episodes or transitions consisting of nonthematic (or less thematic) material. Typical rondo designs include:

First Rondo: A B A

Second Rondo: A B A C A   (less often A B A B′ A)

Third Rondo: A B A C A B′ A   (less often A B A C A D A)

First Rondo. The first rondo form (A B A) shares the same formal scheme as the three-part A B A form. However, where the A B A part-form tends to be more sectional, the first rondo form is more thoroughly integrated, with transitions blurring the divisions between the parts. The first rondo form is used often for the slow movement in the sonata cycle. However, it is not used for the last movement; because of the fast tempo, a simple A B A design would be too short.

Second Rondo. Perhaps the most common rondo form is the plan A B A C A, which contains two subordinate themes (B and C) in alternation with the main theme. This structure is called *second rondo*. (More rarely, the plan A B A B′ A may constitute a second rondo.) An example that illustrates the rondo principle in general and the second rondo in particular is the second movement of Beethoven's *Sonata in G Major*, Op. 49, No. 2 (piano). Figure 19.4 gives the formal scheme of this movement. Note in particular that all appearances of the main theme (A) are in the tonic key (G major), while the two subordinate themes (B and C) are in contrasting keys (D major and C major, respectively).

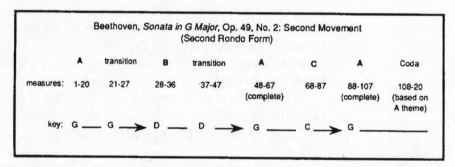

Fig 19.4

Third Rondo. The most elaborate and extended of the rondo forms is the plan A B A C A B′ A. Like the second rondo, it has two subordinate themes (B and C), but it also has further statements of A and B. The main theme (A) usually appears all four times in the tonic key. The second theme (B) appears first in a contrasting key and the second time usually in the tonic key. The third (C) theme is usually in a third key. In the third rondo structure, when the middle section (C) is not essentially a different theme but rather a development of A and/or B, the form is referred to as a sonata-rondo because of its resemblance to a sonata form. The biggest difference between the two forms is the return to the tonic key after the first B section, before the beginning of the developmental C section.

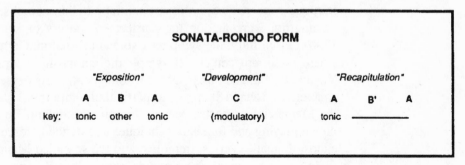

Fig 19.5

PRINCIPAL INSTRUMENTAL GENRES

The Symphony   The Classical period saw the rise of the modern orchestra and the invention of a new genre, the symphony, which has retained its importance to the present day. A symphony is a multimovement composition for orchestra that during the Classical period was based on the four-movement sonata cycle as described earlier. The rise of the symphony coincided with the rise of public concerts. Because of its appeal to audiences of the time, the symphony soon became a regular feature on concert programs and gradually replaced the concerto as the most important genre for large instrumental ensembles.

THE CLASSICAL ORCHESTRA

Whereas Baroque orchestras varied widely in instrumentation, the orchestra of the Classical period became standardized as a four-section ensemble consisting of strings, woodwinds in pairs (two flutes, two oboes, two bassoons, and, later, two clarinets), brass (two horns and two trumpets), and percussion (timpani). (Although trombones were used in opera orchestras, they were not included in the symphony orchestra until Beethoven introduced them in his *Symphony No. 9*.) The Classical orchestra was small, consisting usually of about twenty-five to forty members.

THE EARLY SYMPHONY

The symphony evolved from the Italian opera *sinfonia* of the late seventeenth century, the three sections (fast-slow-fast) of which were gradually expanded into true movements. The Baroque trio sonata and the late Baroque concerto were also influential. Italian composers such as G. B. Sammartini were among the earliest composers of symphonies (around 1730). From Italy, the symphony spread to Austria, Germany, and France, where important centers of symphonic composition arose in Mannheim, Vienna, Berlin, and Paris. Of the leading composers in these cities (listed in chapter 18), Johann Stamitz was particularly important. Under his direction, the Mannheim orchestra became famous throughout Europe for its disciplined playing and for such techniques as extended crescendos and diminuendos, dramatic pauses, tremolos, and the so-called Mannheim "rocket," a rapid upward arpeggio over a wide range. Stamitz was also the first composer to use the four-movement scheme on a consistent basis, and he was one of the first to introduce a contrasting theme in the second key area of sonata-form expositions. Also important were the composers of the Berlin, or northern German, school, who introduced the use of contrapuntal techniques and a dramatic approach to thematic development. Composers such as these paved the way for Haydn, Mozart, and Beethoven, in whose hands the Classical symphony reached its culmination.

Haydn. More than any other single composer, Haydn deserves credit for transforming the experimental pre-Classical symphony into its mature Classical form. Of his first eighty-one symphonies, all but five were written for the Esterházys, and it was in these that Haydn gradually evolved his mature style. Haydn's most mature symphonies, however, were commissioned by others: Nos. 88–92 (1787–1788), composed for private individuals; and his culminating works in the genre, the two sets of "London" Symphonies, Nos. 93–98 (1791–1792) and 99–104 (1793–1795), composed for his two trips to London.

Mozart. Forty-one complete symphonies of Mozart survive, plus fragments of others and several *sinfonie* related to other works. Mozart began writing symphonies at age eight, and his early development was influenced successively by such composers as J. C. Bach, composers of the Viennese school, Sammartini, Stamitz and other composers of the Mannheim school, and Haydn. Ultimately all these influences coalesced into his mature symphonic style. The most-performed of his symphonies are his last six: No. 35 in D major, K. 385 ("Haffner"; 1782); No. 36 in C major, K. 425 ("Linz"; 1783); No. 38 in D major, K. 504 ("Prague"; 1786); and his greatest masterpieces in the genre, written in a six-week period in 1788, No. 39 in E-flat major, K. 543; No. 40 in G Minor, K. 550; and No. 41 in C major, K. 551 ("Jupiter").

The last two symphonies in particular show not only Mozart at the height of his craft but also the two sides of his musical personality. The *Symphony No. 40 in G Minor*, like several other works by Mozart in that key, illustrates his dark, "romantic" side, especially in the three fast movements: the brooding first movement with its haunting air of pathos, the stern Minuet, and the impetuous finale with its Mannheim "rocket" first theme. The *Symphony No. 41 in C Major*, on the other hand, is a prime example of Mozart's sunny, "classical" style. In addition, its final movement is a masterful demonstration of his contrapuntal skill.

Beethoven. In his nine symphonies, Beethoven brought the Classical symphony to its culmination and gradually transcended the bounds of Classical form and style by greatly expanding the lengths of movements, adding instruments (and even vocal soloists and a chorus in the Ninth Symphony), introducing programmatic elements (e.g., in No. 6, the "Pastoral" Symphony), and, in general, infusing the genre with his fiery, dynamic personality. All nine of his symphonies have remained at the core of the modern symphonic repertoire, but the most popular are No. 3 in E-flat major, Op. 55 ("Eroica;" 1803); No. 5 in C minor, Op. 67 (1807–1808); No. 6 in F major, Op. 68 ("Pastoral"; 1808); No. 7 in A major, Op. 92 (1811–1812); and No. 9 in D minor, Op. 125 ("Choral"; 1817–1823).

Beethoven's *Symphony No. 5 in C Minor* is perhaps the most popular of all symphonies. Though not explicitly programmatic, it has come to symbolize Beethoven's triumph over his deafness and, by extension, the idea that humans can triumph over their problems in life. The stormy first movement, with its famous short-short-short-long motive (see figure 5.3) symbolizes fate knocking at the door. Following the calmer second movement, the struggle with fate resumes in the Scherzo, which begins softly and mysteriously only to erupt into a theme characterized by the same short-short-short-long rhythmic motive of the first movement. The Scherzo is linked to the Finale by a ghostlike bridge passage which gives the impression that the struggle, still in doubt, is reaching a climax. Out of this the triumphant Finale emerges, bringing the symphony to a jubilant close in C major. The struggle-to-triumph theme of this symphony was often imitated by composers of the Romantic period.

The Concerto

During the eighteenth century, the solo concerto supplanted the concerto grosso. In their solo concertos, Classical composers retained the three-movement (fast-slow-fast) scheme of the late Baroque concerto but adapted it to their new techniques and aims.

CONCERTO FORM

Composers of the Classical period were fully aware of the individual-against-the-mass symbolism inherent in the concerto relationship and of the dramatic possibilities this opposition offered. Aware, too, of the public's love of virtuoso soloists, they made the soloist in the concerto a "star." Yet they managed also to retain the orchestra as a true partner by giving both the soloist and the orchestra important passages alone and by letting first one and then the other predominate when both were playing simultaneously.

First Movement. The first movement is normally an Allegro movement in the tonic key. Its form represents a fusion of the Baroque ritornello principle with Classical sonata form. Though a great deal of structural variety was possible, the general outlines of the first movement can be delineated as follows:

(1) *Exposition 1*: The orchestra, playing alone, sets the stage for the soloist by presenting a preliminary exposition of some (or all) of the principal themes in the tonic key. The length of this opening section establishes the orchestra as a true partner in the proceedings; yet, at the same time, a sense of anticipation for the soloist's entrance is maintained.

(2) *Exposition 2*: The soloist enters like the main character in a drama, symbolically replacing the orchestra in the spotlight. Together with the orchestra, the soloist presents the "real" exposition, in which several additional themes are often introduced and the modulation to the second main key occurs. By saving this modulation—the big event of the exposition—for the soloist to make, the composer avoids a sense of anticlimax in this second exposition. When all of the themes have been presented, the orchestra rounds off the exposition (in the second key) with a codettalike extension.

(3) *Development or Fantasia*: Following the second exposition, the soloist and orchestra may develop the themes of the exposition or they may engage in a freer, fantasylike dialogue. In either case, this section is generally modulatory.

(4) *Recapitulation*: A recapitulation follows, for orchestra and soloist, with all themes in the tonic key. Quite often some further development also occurs. At the end of the recapitulation, the orchestra states another codettalike extension, which typically comes to a dramatic pause on the tonic six-four chord (i.e., the tonic chord with the fifth of the chord in the bass).

(5) *Cadenza*: At this point the soloist enters with a free, unaccompanied virtuosic section known as a cadenza. Often during the Classical period, cadenzas were improvised by the soloist-composer (e.g., Mozart or Beethoven); but, even when they are written out, they retain an improvisatory quality, drawing freely upon the thematic material of the movement together with fast scales, arpeggios, and other figuration aimed at showing off the soloist's technique. Eventually, the soloist comes to rest on a long trill over the dominant chord, signaling that the cadenza is completed.

(6) *Coda*: Upon the completion of the cadenza, the orchestra reenters with a coda in the tonic key, usually without the soloist.

Figure 19.6 illustrates how, in its alternation of orchestral and soloist sections, the Classical concerto first-movement form retains the Baroque ritornello principle while fusing this with Classical sonata form.

THE CLASSICAL CONCERTO: FIRST MOVEMENT FORM							
ORCHESTRA ALONE	SOLOIST & ORCHESTRA	ORCHESTRA ALONE	SOLOIST AND ORCHESTRA		ORCHESTRA ALONE	SOLOIST ALONE	ORCHESTRA ALONE
Exposition 1 (May or may not be complete)	Exposition 2 (Complete)	Extension	Development or Fantasia	Recapitulation	Extension	Cadenza	Coda
	Th.1 Th.2						
Tonic ———	Tonic 2d key	———————	(modulatory) Tonic	———	$I\,^6_4$	—— V	Tonic

Fig 19.6

Second Movement. The second movement of the Classical concerto, in a contrasting key and slow tempo, usually has the quality of an instrumental aria and often reaches great heights of lyricism (e.g., Mozart's poignant F major Andante in his *Piano Concerto in C Major*, K. 467). A variety of forms are employed, the most common of which are A B A form, various types of rondos, and abbreviated first-movement form.

Third Movement. The concerto finale, a lively movement in the tonic key, is typically a rondo or sonata rondo, although other forms, such as theme and variations, may appear. The movement is often lighter in character and shorter than the first movement, and it may contain folklike themes, virtuosic display for the soloist, and one or more cadenzas.

REPRESENTATIVE COMPOSERS

The Pre-Classical Concerto. Of the many composers who contributed to the development of the pre-Classical concerto (e.g., C. P. E. Bach, J. C. Bach, Sammartini, Quantz, Wagenseil, and so on), Johann Christian Bach deserves special mention. He was the first to introduce the piano to public performances, and his concertos show the Classical concerto form complete in most of its essentials (though he still favored a fantasylike middle section rather than a true development). The influence of his concertos on Mozart's cannot be overestimated.

Haydn. Although Haydn's concertos are not as important as his symphonies and string quartets, he did contribute examples for keyboard, violin, cello, trumpet, and other instruments, which range in style from pre-Classical (before 1765) to Classical. Among the most popular of Haydn's concertos today is the *Trumpet Concerto in E-flat Major* (1796).

Mozart. It was Mozart who, more than anyone else, perfected the Classical concerto, particularly the piano concerto. Unmatched even by his symphonies, his concertos became a vehicle for some of his most profound musical ideas. His more than forty concertos include twenty-one original concertos for solo piano, plus arrangements, rondos, and cadenzas; one for two pianos; one for three pianos; one for bassoon; five for violin, plus others that are incomplete or of uncertain authenticity; two for flute; one for clarinet; three for horn, plus fragments of others; a double concerto for flute and harp; and the *Concertone* (K. 190) for two violins. Among his most-loved concertos today are the piano concertos in D minor (K. 466; 1785), C major (K. 467; 1785), and B-flat Major (K. 595); the *Clarinet Concerto in A major*, K. 622 (1791, his last concerto); and the last three violin concertos (K. 216, 218, 219; all 1775).

The Piano Concerto in C Major, K. 467, is one of Mozart's most appealing concertos. The first movement (Allegro maestoso, C major), cast in a spacious double exposition sonata form, demonstrates Mozart's command of long range tonal and structural planning, and it features rich, virtuosic figuration in the piano set against broad phrases in the strings and winds. In the second movement, a heartbreakingly beautiful Andante in F major, the piano spins out an arching aria-like melody over poignant harmonies and a continuously throbbing accompaniment in the orchestra—an unforgettable example of the combination of formal elegance and restrained, yet profoundly moving, lyrical expressiveness at which Mozart excelled. A lively sonata rondo (Allegro vivace assai) in the tonic key rounds off the concerto.

Beethoven. Beethoven wrote five concertos for piano: Op. 15 in C major (1798), Op. 19 in B-flat major (1795; revised 1798), Op. 37 in C minor (1800), Op. 58 in G major (1806), and Op. 73 in E-flat major (the "Emperor;" 1809); a violin concerto in D major, Op. 61 (1806); and a triple concerto in C major, Op. 56, for piano, violin, and cello (1804–1805). In the last analysis, Beethoven's concertos retain the form and the spirit of the Classical concerto as described above. Still, they do contain elements that foreshadow developments in the Romantic concerto. For example, Beethoven took the first steps toward doing away with the double exposition of the first movement by bringing in the soloist briefly prior to the orchestral exposition (e.g., Opp. 58, 73) and by exploring various modulatory effects within the first exposition or at the end of the second exposition (e.g., Opp. 15, 37, 58, 61). However, in none of his concertos did he actually abandon the double exposition; that step was left for Mendelssohn to accomplish. Also, by interlocking or merging the last two movements in several of his concertos (Opp. 58, 56, 61, and especially Op. 73), he foreshadowed the eventual one-movement concerto of Liszt.

Chamber Music

Chamber music is music for a small number of performers, usually two to ten, with one player to a part and no conductor. Chamber music derives its name from its suitability for performance in a small chamber or salon.

Chamber music cannot match the sheer mass of sound or timbral variety of orchestral music; rather it proceeds from a different premise, as an *intimate dialogue among equals* that features a subtle, evenly balanced give and take among instruments. As such, chamber music is aimed at pleasing the performers as much as the listener. During the Classical period, in which clarity of thought and texture were highly appreciated, chamber music experienced a golden age.

The most important chamber music genre of the period was the string quartet, but composers wrote numerous works for other chamber ensembles as well. For all of these, composers generally used the four-movement sonata cycle seen earlier in the symphony.

STRING QUARTET

The string quartet (two violins, viola, and violoncello) developed from the practice of adding a viola to the Baroque trio sonata ensemble and omitting the keyboard. An important early composer of string quartets was Franz Xaver Richter (1709–1789). The principal composers of Classical string quartets were Luigi Boccherini (1743–1805), who composed about one hundred quartets, Haydn, Mozart, and Beethoven.

Haydn composed some sixty-four string quartets with opus numbers, the most mature of which are Opp. 64 (six, 1790), 71, 74 (three each, 1793); 76 (six, 1797); and 77 (two, 1799). Mozart contributed twenty-six works to the genre, the finest of which are the six *Haydn Quartets* (K. 387, 421, 428, 458, 464, 465), published in 1785 and dedicated to Haydn in gratitude for what Mozart had learned from the older master.

Beethoven's sixteen quartets and the *Grosse Fuge* (Great Fugue, Op. 133) are at the very center of the string quartet repertoire. Written over the greater part of his career, they reflect the various stages of his development as a composer, showing the early influence of Haydn (Op. 18, 1798–1800) as well as his final, most abstract and experimental style (Opp. 127, 130, 131, 132, 133, and 135; 1824–26). These final quartets were, in fact, his musical testament.

A late example, such as the *String Quartet in C-sharp Minor*, Op. 131, illustrates how far Beethoven's conception of form had progressed in his final period from the traditional four-movement Classical format. This quartet has seven movements, all performed without a break: (1) an Adagio fugue in the tonic key; (2) an Allegretto molto vivace sonata form in D major; (3) a short (eleven-measure) transitional movement in recitative style; (4) an Andante theme and variations in A major; (5) a Presto scherzo and trio in E major; and (6) an Adagio in G-sharp minor which functions as an introduction to (7) a final Allegro sonata form in the tonic key.

OTHER CHAMBER ENSEMBLES

In addition to the string quartet, Classical composers also wrote for many other chamber ensembles: piano trios, string trios, piano quartets, string quintets, quintets of mixed instruments, sextets, and larger ensembles. Among the masterworks in these genres are Mozart's string quintets K. 515 in C major (1787) and K. 516 in G minor (1787), the *Clarinet Quintet in A Major*, K. 581 (1789), the piano quartets K. 478 in G minor (1785) and K. 493 in E-flat major (1786), the piano trios K. 502 in B-flat major (1786) and K. 542 in E major (1788), and Beethoven's *Archduke Trio* in B-flat major, Op. 97 (1811).

Sonata

The Classical sonata was a sonata cycle, usually for one or two instruments, that consisted most often of three movements (fast-slow-fast, omitting the minuet) or less often of two or four movements. Most Classical sonatas were for solo piano or for piano and another instrument, usually violin or cello.

THE PRE-CLASSICAL SONATA

The majority of pre-Classical sonatas were for keyboard, although some were for other instruments. Among pre-Classical composers who contributed to the development of the genre were Domenico Alberti (c. 1710–1740), Baldassare Galuppi (1706–1785), G. B. Sammartini, and Luigi Boccherini in Italy; Domenico Scarlatti (1685–1757) in Italy and on the Iberian Peninsula; Johann Stamitz, M. G. Monn, Wagenseil, Wilhelm Friedemann Bach (1710–1784), Johann Christoph Friedrich Bach (1732–1795), and C. P. E. Bach in Austria and Germany; Johann Schobert (c. 1735–1767) in France; and J. C. Bach in England.

Haydn. Haydn contributed approximately forty-nine sonatas for keyboard, plus numerous sonatas for small ensembles. Although some of the later keyboard sonatas, in particular, are excellent examples of his mature style, his sonatas as a whole are of lesser significance than his symphonies and string quartets.

Mozart. Mozart left some twenty-one sonatas for keyboard, one for bassoon and cello, and numerous others for keyboard and violin, for four hands at one or two keyboard instruments, and for organ with other instruments. Although these rank below his symphonies and concertos, they represent the Classical sonata at its "classic" stage and include several true masterpieces, such as the keyboard *Sonata in C Minor* (K. 457; 1785), the four-hand *Sonata in F Major* (K. 497; 1786); and the sonatas for keyboard and violin in B-flat major (K. 481; 1785) and A major (K. 526; 1787).

Beethoven. Although Haydn and Mozart both made outstanding contributions to the genre, it was in the sonatas of Beethoven (particularly his piano sonatas) that the Classical sonata—perhaps even the sonata genre as a whole—reached its culmination. Beethoven's sonatas include thirty-two piano sonatas with opus numbers, plus five other student sonatas; one for piano duet; ten for violin and piano; five for cello and piano; and four for other instruments and piano. Beethoven's piano sonatas span his entire career and reflect every stage of his development. Among the most popular are Op. 13 ("Pathétique," C minor; 1798); Op. 27, No. 2 ("Moonlight," C-sharp minor; 1801); Op. 53 ("Waldstein," C major; 1803–1804); Op. 57 ("Appassionata," F minor; 1804–1805); and Op. 106 ("Hammerklavier," B-flat major; 1817–1818).

Among his greatest violin and cello sonatas are the deeply expressive *Cello Sonata in A Major*, Op. 69 (1807–1808), and the violin sonatas in A major ("Kreutzer," Op. 47; 1802–1803) and G major (Op. 96; 1812).

Other Instrumental Genres

DIVERTIMENTO

After the concerto grosso went out of fashion, the concertato principle was retained in light, entertaining compositions variously called divertimento, serenade, cassation, notturno, and (after 1765) symphonie concertante. These compositions, usually composed as background music for social events, were scored in groups ranging from small chamber ensembles to small orchestras and consisted typically of from three to ten movements. Haydn and Mozart were among the many composers who wrote music of this type. Mozart's most important divertimenti are K. 247, K. 287, and K. 334, all for two horns and solo strings. His most famous serenade is Eine kleine Nachtmusik, K. 525 (A Little Night Music; 1787).

SYMPHONIE CONCERTANTE

The symphonie concertante, a work for two or more solo instruments and orchestra, arose in the late 1760s and flourished until c. 1830. Most surviving works in this genre are three-movement compositions. J. C. Bach, Christian Cannabich, Karl Stamitz (1745–1801), Haydn, and Mozart are among the composers who wrote symphonies concertantes. Of Mozart's six, the *Sinfonia Concertante in E-flat Major*, K. 364 (1779), for violin and viola with orchestra, is a masterful example.

The development of the sonata cycle gave composers a new way of organizing multimovement instrumental compositions that they applied to virtually every instrumental genre. For individual movements, sonata form provided an ideal format for the presentation, development, and summarization of musical ideas that was comparable to the organization of essays or speeches. Important new instrumental genres arose, such as the symphony, solo keyboard sonata, duo sonata, and the string quartet and other chamber ensembles. Even established forms such as the concerto were reorganized with new aims and structures.

Haydn and Mozart brought instrumental forms and genres to a mature Classical phase. Beethoven expanded these forms and, in his later works, experimented with new techniques within individual movements and with new ways of organizing the cycle as a whole. Beethoven's works, and also some of Mozart's late works, also exhibit a more intensely personal emotional quality. Once again, the pendulum was swinging from classical restraint to more emotionally expressive "romantic" approaches.

For Additional Study

Barrett-Ayres, Reginald. *Joseph Haydn and the String Quartet*. New York: Schirmer Books. 1974.

Beethoven by Barenboim. Distributed by Films for the Humanities & Sciences (Princeton, NJ). 13-part videotape series.

Dearling, Robert. *The Music of W. A. Mozart: The Symphonies*. Rutherford, NJ: Fairleigh Dickinson University Press. 1982.

Girdlestone, Cuthbert M. *Mozart's Piano Concertos*. London: Cassell, 1958; 3d ed., 1978.

Grove, Sir George. *Beethoven and His Nine Symphonies*. London: Novello, 1884; reprint, New York: Dover, 1962.

Kerman, Joseph. *The Beethoven Quartets*. New York: Alfred A. Knopf, 1967; reprint, New York: Norton, 1979.

King, A. Hyatt. *Mozart Chamber Music*. London: British Broadcasting Corporation, 1968; Seattle, WA: University of Washington Press, 1969.

Landon, H. C. Robbins. *The Symphonies of Joseph Haydn*. London: Universal Edition, 1955; supplement, Barrie & Rockliff, 1961.

___, and Donald Mitchell, eds. *The Mozart Companion*. New York: Norton. 1969.

Newman, William S. *The Sonata in the Classic Era*. Chapel Hill, NC: University of North Carolina Press, 1963; 3d ed., New York: Norton, 1983.

Rosen, Charles. *The Classical Style: Haydn, Mozart, Beethoven*. New York: Viking Press, 1971; New York: Norton, 1972.

___. *Sonata Forms*. New York: Norton. 1980.

Schulenberg, David. *The Instrumental Music of C. P. E. Bach*. Ann Arbor, MI: UMI Research Press. 1984.

Terry, Charles Sanford. *John Christian Bach*. London: Oxford University Press, 1929; 2d rev. ed., by H. C. Robbins Landon, 1967, Westport, CT: Greenwood Press, 1980.

Tovey, Donald F. *A Companion to Beethoven's Pianoforte Sonatas*. London: Associated Board of the Royal Schools of Music, 1931; reprint, New York: AMS Press, 1976.

The University of Delaware Videodisc Music Series. Discs 1 and 4. Distributed by the University of Delaware (Newark, DE). Interactive videodiscs. (Excellent for the introduction of Classical forms.)

Recommended Listening

SYMPHONY:

Bach, C. P. E. *Symphony No. 3 in F Major*, H. 665
Beethoven, Ludwig van. 9 symphonies (particularly Nos. 5, 6, 7, and 9)

Haydn, Franz Joseph. Symphony No. 45 in F-sharp Minor ("Farewell"); Symphony No. 92 in G Major ("Oxford"); Symphony No. 94 in G Major ("Surprise"); Symphony No. 102 in D Major ("Clock"); Symphony No. 104 in D Major ("London")

Mozart, W. A. *Symphony No. 35 in D Major*, K. 385 ("Haffner"); *Symphony No. 40 in G Minor*, K. 550; *Symphony No. 41 in C Major*, K. 551 ("Jupiter")

Stamitz, Johann. *Sinfonia a8 in D Major* (*La Melodia Germanica*, No. 1; c. 1775)

CONCERTO:

Bach, J. C. *Concerto in E-flat Major for Harpsichord or Piano and Strings*, Op. 7, No. 5

Beethoven, Ludwig van. Piano concertos: No. 3 in C minor, Op. 37; No. 4 in G major, Op. 58; and No. 5 in E-flat major, Op. 73 ("Emperor"); *Violin Concerto in D Major*, Op. 61

Haydn, Franz Joseph. *Trumpet Concerto in E-flat Major*

Mozart, W. A. Piano concertos: D minor, K. 466; C major, K. 467; A major, K. 488; and C minor, K. 491; *Clarinet Concerto in A Major*, K. 622

SONATA:

Bach, C. P. E. *Sonata No. 4 in A Major*, W55/4 (harpsichord or clavichord)

Beethoven, Ludwig van. Piano sonatas: C minor, Op. 13 ("Pathétique"); C-sharp minor, Op. 27, no. 2 ("Moonlight"); C major, Op. 53 ("Waldstein"); F minor, Op. 57 ("Appassionata"); and A-flat major, Op. 110; *Sonata in A Major*, Op. 69 (cello and piano)

Haydn, Franz Joseph. *Piano Sonata in E-flat Major*, H. XVI/52

Mozart, W. A. Piano sonatas: A major, K. 331; C major, K. 545; C minor, K. 457; *Sonata in B-flat Major for Violin and Piano*, K. 481

Scarlatti, Domenico. *Sonata in D Major*, K. 119 (L. 415)

STRING QUARTET:

Beethoven, Ludwig van. *String Quartet in C Major*, Op. 59, No. 3; *String Quartet in C-sharp Minor*, Op. 131

Boccherini, Luigi. *String Quartet No. 90 in F Major*, (1804)

Haydn, Franz Joseph. *String Quartet in C Major*, Op. 76, No. 3; *String Quartet in F Major*, Op. 77, No. 2

Mozart, W. A. *String Quartet in D Minor*, K. 421 (from the "Haydn" quartets)

Richter, Franz Xaver. *String Quartet in B-flat Major*, Op. 5, No. 2

OTHER:

Beethoven, Ludwig van. *Piano Trio in B-flat Major*, Op. 97 ("Archduke")

Mozart, W. A. *Clarinet Quintet in A Major*, K. 581

___. *Eine kleine Nachtmusik*, K. 525 (serenade, string orchestra)

___. Piano Trios: B-flat major, K. 502; E major, K. 542

___. *Sinfonia Concertante in E-flat Major*, K. 364 (violin, viola, and orchestra)

___. String Quintets: C major, K. 515; G minor, K. 516

20

Opera, Oratorio, and Mass in the Classical Period

1709	Antonio Orefice, *Patrò Calienno de la Costa*, the earliest known full-length 18th-century *opera buffa*
c. 1720	Benedetto Marcello, *Il teatro alla moda*, satirizes current Italian opera
1724	Handel, *Giulio Cesare*
1728	Tremendous success in London of *The Beggar's Opera*, a ballad opera, signals that the London public is tiring of Italian *opera seria*
1730s	Rise of the Neapolitan "pre-Classical" style of opera
1733	G. B. Pergolesi, *La serva padrona*
1737	Rameau, *Castor et Pollux*
1741	Handel abandons opera
c. 1747–1749	Bach, *Mass in B Minor*
1752	Handel, *Jephtha*; success of *La serva padrona* in Paris sets off *guerre des bouffons*
1762–1779	Gluck's "reform" operas: *Orfeo ed Euridice* (1762), *Alceste* (1767), *Iphigénie en Aulide* (1774), *Iphigénie en Tauride* (1779)
1781	Mozart's *Idomeneo, rè di Creta*, his first mature opera
1782	Giovanni Paisiello, *Il barbiere di Siviglia*; Mozart, *Die Entführung aus dem Serail*
1784	A. E. M. Grétry, *Richard Coeur-de-lion*
1786–1790	Mozart's three Italian operatic masterpieces on librettos by Da Ponte: *Le nozze di Figaro* (1786), *Don Giovanni* (1787), *Così fan tutte* (1790)
1791	Mozart, *Requiem* (unfinished) and *Die Zauberflöte*, his last opera
1792	Domenico Cimarosa, *Il matrimonio segreto*
1796	Napoleon invades Austrian territory; Haydn, *Mass in Time of War*

1796–1798 Haydn, *The Creation*

1798 Haydn, *Lord Nelson Mass*

1801 Haydn, *The Seasons*

1805 Beethoven, *Fidelio* (revised 1806, 1814)

1823 Beethoven, *Missa solemnis*

Although the most characteristic new Classical forms and genres emerged in the area of instrumental music, composers of the period also made significant contributions in the area of vocal music, particularly in opera and sacred choral music. This chapter surveys major developments in these two areas.

OPERA

The Enlightenment brought growing dissatisfaction with the artificiality of Baroque opera and a desire for opera that was simpler and more true-to-life. Attempts by Zeno and Metastasio to reform opera librettos in accordance with neoclassic ideals (see chapter 15) led to the purging of comic elements from serious opera, giving rise to the categories of serious opera (*opera seria*) and comic opera (*opera buffa*). Yet Metastasio's rigid format of alternating recitatives and arias, coupled with excessive ornamentation and other abuses by singers, soon led men of letters such as Benedetto Marcello (*Il teatro alla moda*, The Fashionable Theater, c. 1720) to criticize this type of opera as well. Ultimately, the demand for more natural opera led both to further reforms in opera seria and to a phenomenal rise in the popularity of comic opera.

Opera Seria

Serious attempts by Italian composers to reform opera seria began in the mid-1740s, led by Niccolò Jommelli (1714–1774) and Tommaso Traetta (1727–1779). The culminating figure in this reform movement was the Bohemian composer Christoph Willibald Gluck (1714–1787).

GLUCK

Gluck's earliest operas were written in the older Italian style, but gradually he was drawn to the reform movement. In his later operas he sought to achieve, in his words, "a beautiful simplicity" and "to confine music to its true function of serving the poetry" without "useless and superfluous ornaments."

Gluck's "Reform" Operas. Gluck's new ideas led him to write a series of "reform" operas, the most important of which were *Orfeo ed Euridice* (1762) and *Alceste* (1767), produced in Vienna in collaboration with the librettist Raniero Calzabigi (1714–1795); *Iphigénie en Aulide* (Iphigenia in Aulis), produced in Paris in 1774; and his last and greatest operatic masterpiece, *Iphigénie en Tauride* (Iphigenia in Tauris), presented in Paris in 1779.

Gluck's Reforms. Among Gluck's reforms (some of which had been predated by such composers as Jommelli and Traetta) were: (1) the establishment of a more equal balance between music and drama; (2) an abandonment of the rigid pattern of alternating recitatives and arias in favor of more flexible methods of organizing scenes; (3) a reduction in the use of da capo arias in favor of more diversified forms; (4) the replacement of *secco* recitative by accompanied recitative, to reduce the "unnatural" and jarring change of texture between recitatives and arias; (5) an elevation of the orchestra from the role of mere accompanist to a more equal partnership with the singers; (6) an increased use of small vocal ensembles; (7) a reinstatement of the chorus, long neglected in Italian opera, to a central role in the proceedings (here following the lead of Jommelli); (8) a lessening of the differences between recitative and aria; and (9) the use of expressive melodies with little or no ornamentation. In addition, Gluck brought to his operas a genius for creating warm and believable characters and a sure sense of what "works" on the stage.

Gluck's Influence. Gluck directly influenced several composers who wrote operas for the Paris stage, such as Niccolò Piccini (1728–1800), Antonio Salieri (1750–1825), and Antonio Sacchini (1730–1786). He indirectly influenced other composers of opera seria, including Haydn and Mozart, and his artistic ideals also found spiritual descendents in such nineteenth-century French composers as Gaspare Spontini (1774–1851) and Hector Berlioz (1803–1869).

OTHER COMPOSERS

Other representative composers of opera seria include Leonardo Vinci; Nicola Porpora; G. B. Pergolesi; Johann Adolph Hasse (1699–1783), the most successful opera composer of his time; Karl Heinrich Graun (1704–1759); Johann Christian Bach; and Giuseppe Sarti (1729–1802).

Comic Opera

Comic opera emerged as an important independent genre during the first half of the eighteenth century (see chapter 15) and continued to grow until, by the late eighteenth century, it dominated the operatic scene. The new genre offered an entertaining, down-to-earth alternative to the formality of opera seria, and it answered well the demand for a more "natural" form of opera. Moreover, its fast-paced action was ideally suited to the flexible style of Classical music, particularly to the sonata form with its dramatic developmental methods. By the time of Haydn and Mozart, comic opera was every bit the rage in Vienna that opera seria had been in London in Handel's day.

Distinct national forms of comic opera arose in Italy, France, England, and Germany. In all these countries, comic opera originated as broad, low-class comedy but gradually acquired romantic, sentimental, and semi-serious qualities, so that, by the end of the century, a certain merging of serious opera and comic opera had occurred.

ITALY

Two types of comic opera, the *intermezzo* and *opera buffa*, flourished in Italy during the first half of the eighteenth century before merging around 1750.

Intermezzo. The intermezzo arose from the practice of performing comic musical interludes between the acts of an opera seria. Often these interludes themselves formed a continuous plot, thus creating a miniature comic opera that ran parallel to the main opera. Intermezzi typically required only two singing roles, plus one or two nonsinging parts. An innovation was the prominent use of the bass voice, which had rarely been used in opera seria. Intermezzi became so popular that they were frequently staged as independent works; a famous example that is still performed today is G. B. Pergolesi's *La serva padrona* (The Maid as Mistress; 1733). A spectacularly successful production of this work in Paris in 1752 touched off the famous *guerre des bouffons* (War of the Buffonists), a debate between French intellectuals over whether French or Italian opera was superior.

Opera Buffa. At the same time, opera buffa, a full-length comic opera with a larger cast of singing characters, also flourished. One of its chief innovations was the *ensemble finale*, a musical number at the end of an act in which the plot is constructed so as to bring all or most of the characters gradually to the stage until they all join in together at the end.

Although light farces predominated at first, around 1750 plots began to appear that, while remaining basically comic, contained serious or even tragic elements; this type of comic opera was called *dramma giocoso* (jocular drama). Examples include Niccolò Piccini's *La buona figliuola* (The Good Girl; 1760), based on Samuel Richardson's novel *Pamela*; Giovanni Paisiello's *Il barbiere di Siviglia* (The Barber of Seville; 1782); and Domenico Cimarosa's *Il matrimonio segreto* (The Secret Marriage; 1792). Dramma giocoso reached its culmination in the works of Mozart.

FRANCE

French comic opera, known as *opéra comique*, arose in the early eighteenth century as a form of low-brow popular theater. At first the music consisted primarily of popular tunes (*vaudevilles*), to which the authors adapted new words. Gradually, however, original songs (known as *ariettes*) replaced the vaudevilles. Unlike Italian comic opera, opéra comique used spoken dialogue instead of recitative. After 1750 plots began to acquire more serious qualities and sometimes dealt with the social issues of the day. The leading composer in the genre was André-Ernest-Modeste Grétry (1741–1813), whose *Richard Coeur-de-lion* (Richard the Lion-hearted; 1784) was an early example of "rescue" opera (discussed below).

ENGLAND

The English national comic opera form was the *ballad opera*, which interspersed dialogue with popular tunes, parodies of familiar operatic arias, and original music. Plots dealt with political, social, historical or other subjects, often in a satirical manner, and, like those of opera buffa and opéra comique, showed an evolution from broad comedy to more serious, sentimental qualities. Following the success of *The Beggar's Opera* in London in 1728, ballad opera enjoyed great popularity throughout England during the 1730s.

GERMANY

German comic opera, the *Singspiel* (song play), arose in the mid-eighteenth century with librettos adapted from English ballad operas and French operás comiques, to which composers added new music. Like its models, the Singspiel interspersed spoken dialogue with music in a popular style. The Singspiel in northern Germany, represented by Johann Adam Hiller (1728–1804), acquired serious, sentimental qualities and gradually merged with nineteenth-century German Romantic opera, while, in southern cities such as Vienna, Karl Ditters von Dittersdorf and other composers cultivated a lighter, more farcical type. Mozart raised the Singspiel to the level of great art in his operas *Die Entführung aus dem Serail* (The Abduction from the Seraglio; 1782) and *Die Zauberflöte* (The Magic Flute; 1791).

Mozart's Operas

Mozart is the supreme master of eighteenth-century opera, the composer in whose works the ideals of the century are most fully realized and in whose hands opera seria, Italian comic opera, and German opera find their highest expression.

CHARACTERS

Mozart's characters are no longer archetypes (as in Baroque opera) or stereotypes (as in earlier eighteenth-century opera), but living, breathing human beings whose strengths and foibles he reveals with astonishing psychological insight. Above all, the *individual*, not the abstract affection, is the constant focus of Mozart's attention, to the point that the individuality of each character stands out even in ensemble numbers. Mozart's complex, fully realized characters speak to today's audiences as directly as they did to the audiences of his time, which is one reason that, of all eighteenth-century operas, Mozart's are the only ones to have found a permanent place in the modern operatic repertoire.

VOICE TYPES

As part of the desire for more natural means of expression, the vogue of the castrato was gradually dying out in the second half of the eighteenth century, and new conventions arose in the assignment of voice parts. The heroine is almost always a soprano, her protagonist or lover typically a tenor. The heroine's servant, rival or older relative is often cast as a lower voice, such as a mezzo-soprano or contralto. Mezzo-sopranos sometimes also sing the parts of young men; such roles are called "trouser" or "pants" roles. Bass voices typically sing the roles of older men, authority figures (kings, priests, etc.), villains, and comic characters. Various types of male roles are assigned to baritone voices.

MUSICAL FORMS

By Mozart's time the rigid alternation of recitative and da capo arias was a thing of the past. Although Mozart continued to use recitatives, both *secco* and accompanied, his arias and other musical numbers show a wide variety of forms, ranging from simple strophic and A B A patterns to fully developed sonata forms and, in larger sections such as finales, multimovement structures. Whether the structure is small or large, however, Mozart shows great sensitivity to unity, variety, and symmetry.

THE ENSEMBLE

One of the great innovations of Classical composers, particularly Mozart, was their emphasis on ensemble numbers. Unlike the aria, which was dramatically static as characters paused to reflect on events, the ensemble number could be used to *advance* the plot. As a result, ensembles tend to be more dynamic, with dramatic situations in constant flux and characters entering and exiting frequently. The ensemble also permitted the composer to juxtapose the thoughts and feelings of several characters simultaneously, another important advance.

MOZART'S FINALES

A special type of ensemble, mentioned earlier, is the *ensemble finale*, in which characters gradually appear until virtually the whole cast is on stage. Mozart was the master of this form. Fast-paced and full of unexpected turns of events, his finales provide countless memorable musical and comedic moments. One of his greatest finales of this kind is the finale to Act 2 of *Le nozze di Figaro* (The Marriage of Figaro), which begins with two characters and builds until, at the end, seven characters are involved.

The finale to Act 1 of *Die Zauberflöte* (The Magic Flute), another of Mozart's great finales, provides a glimpse of his sense of symmetry. In this finale the climax of the action occurs when the heroine (Pamina) is saved from danger by the playing of magic bells. Interestingly, the bells enter in measure 293—the exact midpoint of the finale. Thus the action to and from this climax is balanced symmetrically.

WORKS

Most of Mozart's operas are comic operas, yet ones that blend both humorous and serious elements. Of his mature works, *Idomeneo, rè di Creta* (Idomeneus, King of Crete; 1781), his first fully mature opera, is perhaps the greatest opera seria of the late eighteenth century. The last three of his Italian comic operas, written on librettos of Lorenzo da Ponte, represent the culmination of this genre. These include *Le nozze di Figaro* (The Marriage of Figaro; 1786), *Don Giovanni* (Don Juan; 1787), and *Così fan tutte* (Thus Do They All; 1790). His German opera *Die Entführung aus dem Serail* (The Abduction from the Seraglio; 1782) raised, in one stroke, the Singspiel to the level of high art. His last opera, *Die Zauberflöte* (The Magic Flute, 1791) is on a still higher plane. Outwardly a Singspiel with many comic moments, it also contains much solemnity and symbolism which mark it as an important forerunner of German Romantic opera.

Haydn and Beethoven

As part of his duties for the Esterházys, Haydn composed both comic and serious operas that are largely forgotten today. Beethoven's only opera was the rescue opera *Fidelio* (1805; revised 1806, 1814), that is, an opera in which the hero, in peril of death, is rescued through the efforts of a friend. Although Beethoven was not totally at ease in the operatic genre, *Fidelio* contains much sublime music, particularly in sections that deal with the loftier emotions.

ORATORIO AND MASS

After the death of Bach and Handel, Protestant music declined, though several notable figures may be cited (e.g., C. P .E. Bach and K. H. Graun). However, Catholic composers such as Haydn and Mozart continued to build on the tradition inherited from the Baroque period of writing Masses, oratorios, and other sacred music for church and for concert performance.

Classical composers favored a manner of writing that combined Italian operatic influences (particularly for recitatives, arias, and small ensembles), the choral tradition of Handel, the Bach fugal style, recent advances in orchestral writing, and symphonic structures, particularly sonata form. Writing in a generally more conservative style than that of secular music, composers produced large-scale vocal works for soloists, chorus, and orchestra that were true counterparts of the Classical opera, symphony, and concerto.

Haydn

The last six of Haydn's Masses, written between 1796 and 1802, are his finest. Of these, the best known are the *Missa in tempore belli* (Mass in Time of War; 1796) and the *Missa in angustiis* (Lord Nelson Mass; 1798). Haydn composed three oratorios, of which the last two are masterpieces: *Die Schöpfung* (The Creation; 1796–1798) and *Die Jahreszeiten* (The Seasons; 1801). He was inspired to write these last two oratorios after being deeply moved by performances of Handel's oratorios, which he attended in London. Abounding in countless touches of genius, these oratorios reveal the aged composer still in full command of his creative powers.

Mozart

As part of his duties at Salzburg, Mozart composed sacred works fairly regularly from 1766 to about 1781; most of these, however, are not major works. Mozart's Masses, like Haydn's, are written in a symphonic-operatic style for soloists, chorus, and orchestra, and they range from short, simple works to more extended ones. His finest sacred works are the "Coronation" Mass in C major, K. 317 (1779); the unfinished Mass in C minor, K. 427 (1782); and the *Requiem*, K. 625, left unfinished at his death but completed by his pupil Franz Xaver Süssmayr.

The *Requiem*, in particular, is an outstanding example of Mozart's late style and of the combination of Baroque and Classical approaches favored by composers of the period in their oratorios and Masses. On the one hand, the *Kyrie*, a double fugue, recalls the contrapuntal mastery of J. S. Bach, and the dramatic, impassioned choral writing in such sections as the *Dies irae*, *Rex tremendae majestatis*, and *Confutatis* is truly Handelian in grandeur. On the other hand, sections such as the *Recordare* are pure Italianate opera, and, underlying everything, is his supreme command of Classical orchestral writing and formal symmetry. Imbued throughout with the expressive profundity of a genius at his peak contemplating the mysteries of the eternal, Mozart's *Requiem* has remained one of the most-loved works in the choral repertory.

Beethoven and Others

Beethoven's greatest sacred work is the Mass in D (*Missa solemnis*), Op. 123 (1819–1823). Too long and elaborate for use in church, it was intended for concert performance. Other representative composers of sacred music include C. P. E. Bach (e.g., the oratorio *The Israelites in the Wilderness*), K. H. Graun (the oratorio *Der Tod Jesu*), Johann Adolph Hasse, Paisiello (over 100 church compositions), Sarti, and Nicola Zingarelli (1752–1837), with over 500 works.

The Enlightenment brought a desire for more natural and true-to-life opera, which was met by Gluck's reforms in opera seria; by the rise of national comic opera forms in Italy, France, England, and Germany; and, above all, by Mozart's incomparable operatic masterworks. Composers of the period also contributed significantly to the continued development of the Mass, oratorio, and other sacred choral music.

For Additional Study

Bauman, Thomas. *North German Opera in the Age of Goethe.* Cambridge, Eng.: Cambridge University Press. 1986.

Charlton, David. *Grétry and the Growth of Opéra-comique.* Cambridge, Eng.: Cambridge University Press. 1986.

Dent, E. J. *Mozart's Operas.* 2d ed. London: Oxford University Press. 1960.

Gagey, Edmond M. *Ballad Opera.* New York: Columbia University Press. 1937.

Grout, Donald Jay. *A Short History of Opera.* 2d ed. New York and London: Columbia University Press. 1965.

Rosen, Charles. *The Classical Style: Haydn, Mozart, Beethoven.* New York: Viking Press, 1971; New York: Norton, 1972.

Steptoe, Andrew. *The Mozart-Da Ponte Operas.* Oxford: Clarendon Press. 1988.

Recommended Listening

OPERA:

As in chapter 15, specific excerpts are cited for each opera listed below. As before, however, it is recommended that you listen to at least one complete opera (or, preferably, see a live production or a performance on television or videotape).

Beethoven, Ludwig van. *Fidelio*: Quartet, "Mir ist so wunderbar"; Aria, "Abscheulicher! wo eilst du hin!"; "Prisoners' Chorus"; Aria, "In des Lebens Frühlingstagen"; Duet, "O namenlose Freude"

Gluck, C. W. *Orfeo ed Euridice*: Act 2, Scene 1; Aria, "Che farò senza Euridice?"

Grétry, A. E. M. *Richard Coeur-de-lion*: Romance, "Une fièvre brûlante"; Air, "O Richard, ò mon Roi"

Mozart, W. A. *Così fan tutte*: Aria, "Come scoglio"; Aria, "Per pietà, ben mio"; Duet, "Fra gli amplessi"

___. Don Giovanni: Overture; Act I, Introduction; Aria, "Dalla sua pace"; Aria, "Madamina!" (Leporello's Catalog Aria); Duet, "Là ci darem la mano"; Act 2, Finale

___. *Die Entführung aus dem Serail*: Aria, "Hier soll ich dich denn sehen, Konstanze"; Aria, "Ach, ich liebte"; Aria, "Martern aller Arten"; Act 3, Finale

___. *Le nozze di Figaro*: Overture; Aria, "Non più andrai"; Arietta, "Voi, che sapete"; Act 2, Finale; Recitative, "E Susanna non vien!" and Aria, "Dove sono"; Act 4, Finale

___. *Die Zauberflöte*: Song, "Der Vogelfänger bin ich ja"; Aria, "Dies' Bildnis ist bezaubernd schön"; Aria, "Zum Leiden bin ich auserkoren"; Quintet, "Hm! Hm! Hm!"; Act 1, Finale; Aria, "In diesen heil'gen Hallen"; Act 2, Finale

Pepusch, Johann, and John Gay. *The Beggar's Opera*: Scenes 11 to 13

Pergolesi, G. B. *La serva padrona*: Recitativo and Recitativo obbligato, "Ah quanto mi sa male"; Aria, "Son imbrogliato io"

MASS, ORATORIO, AND OTHER:

Beethoven, Ludwig van. Mass in D (*Missa solemnis*), Op. 123

Haydn, Franz Joseph. Masses: *Missa in angustiis* ("Lord Nelson Mass"); *Missa in tempore belli* ("Mass in Time of War")

___. Oratorios: *Die Schöpfung* (The Creation); *Die Jahreszeiten* (The Seasons)

Mozart, W. A. *Mass in C Minor*, K. 427

___. *Requiem*, K. 626

21

The Romantic Period: An Introduction

1760s	Precursors of Romanticism in English literature: Macpherson's pseudomedieval "Ossian" poems (1760–1763); Percy's *Reliques of Ancient English Poetry* (1765); and Walpole's medieval horror tale *The Castle of Otranto* (1765), which initiates a vogue for Gothic romances
c. 1760–c. 1785	*Sturm und Drang* movement in Germany, e.g., Goethe's *The Sorrows of Young Werther* (1774) and Friedrich Schiller's *The Robbers* (1781)
1778	Copley, *Watson and the Shark*
1788	Bernardin de Saint-Pierre, *Paul et Virginie*
1789–1795	French Revolution
1790	Fuseli, *The Nightmare*
1791	U. S. Bill of Rights is ratified
1794	Whitney patents the cotton gin
1798	Coleridge and Wordsworth, *Lyrical Ballads*
1808	Goethe, *Faust*, Part I
1811	Schubert's earliest Lieder
1812–1822	Publication of *Grimm's Fairy Tales*
1813	Austen, *Pride and Prejudice*
1814–1815	Goya, *The Third of May, 1808*
1815	Napoleon defeated at Waterloo; Congress of Vienna establishes post-Napoleonic reorganization of Europe
1816	Rossini, *The Barber of Seville*
1818	Byron, *Childe Harold's Pilgrimage* completed; Mary Wollstonecraft Shelley, *Frankenstein*

1818–1819   Géricault, *The Raft of the "Medusa"*

1819   Scott, *Ivanhoe*; Keats, Odes; Schopenhauer, *The World as Will and Idea*

1820   Percy Bysshe Shelley, *Prometheus Unbound*

1821   Weber, *Der Freischütz*; Constable, *The Hay-Wain*

1822   Schubert, *"Unfinished" Symphony*

1824   Friedrich, *The Polar Sea*

1827   Death of Beethoven; Heine, *Buch der Lieder*; Delacroix, *Greece Expiring on the Ruins of Missolonghi*

1830   Democratic revolts in France and other countries; Berlioz, *Symphonie fantastique*

1830s   Railroad era begins

1831   Bellini, *La sonnambula* and *Norma*; Faraday observes electromagnetic induction; Schumann's Op. 1 published

1832   Goethe, *Faust*, Part II

1836   Houses of Parliament begun in London (neo-Gothic)

1836–1839   Chopin, *Preludes*, Op. 28

1837   Coronation of Queen Victoria in England begins "Victorian era" (until 1901)

1838   First telegraph line built in the United States

1839   First commercially successful photographic process; Turner, *The Slave Ship*; Dickens, *Oliver Twist*

1840–1841   Wagner, *The Flying Dutchman*

1842   Mendelssohn, *A Midsummer Night's Dream*

1842–1846   Poe publishes his most popular works

1847   Emily Brontë, *Wuthering Heights*; Charlotte Brontë, *Jane Eyre*

1848   Marx and Engels, *The Communist Manifesto*; revolts in France, Germany, Italy, and other countries; Liszt, *Les Préludes*

1849   Courbet, *The Stone Breakers*

1850   Hawthorne, *The Scarlet Letter*

1851   First World Exposition in London; Heine, *Romanzero*; Melville, *Moby Dick*

1853   Verdi, *Il trovatore* and *La traviata*

1853–1856   Crimean War

1854   Thoreau, *Walden*

1855   Whitman, *Leaves of Grass*

1857   Flaubert, *Madame Bovary*

1859   Darwin, *Origin of Species*; Wagner completes *Tristan und Isolde*; Tennyson, *Idylls of the King*; Dickens, *A Tale of Two Cities*

1861   Serfs emancipated in Russia; American Civil War begins; unification of Italy

1862   Hugo, *Les Misérables*

1863   Emancipation Proclamation in the United States; Longfellow, "Paul Revere's Ride"

1865   U.S. Civil War ends; Lincoln assassinated

1866   First permanently successful transatlantic cable

1867   Marx, *Das Kapital*, vol. 1

c. 1867-c. 1886   "Impressionism" movement in painting (Manet, Monet, Pissarro, Renoir, Degas, etc.)

1869   First transcontinental railroad in U.S. completed; Suez Canal opens; Tolstoy, *War and Peace*

1870–1871   Franco-Prussian War

1871   German Empire established and "Bismarck era" begins; Verdi, *Aïda*

1871–1872   George Eliot, *Middlemarch*

1874   First performance of Musorgsky's opera *Boris Godunov*

1875   First performance of Bizet's opera *Carmen*

1876   Bell invents the telephone; Brahms, *Symphony No. 1*; Wagner's Bayreuth Theater opens and the *Ring* cycle (composed 1848–1874) is performed in its entirety; Mallarmé, *Afternoon of a Faun*

1877   Edison invents the phonograph

1879   Edison demonstrates the carbon-filament lamp; Ibsen, *A Doll's House*

1880   Smetana, *Má vlast*; Irish insurrection; Zola, *Nana*; Dostoyevsky, *The Brothers Karamazov*

1881   Tsar Alexander II killed; President Garfield shot

1882   Koch discovers the tuberculosis germ

1883   Stevenson, *Treasure Island*

1883–1884   Nietzsche, *Also sprach Zarathustra*, pts.1 through 3 (pt. 4, 1891)

1884   Twain, *Huckleberry Finn*

1885   Brahms, *Symphony No. 4*; Pasteur uses vaccination for first time against rabies

1885–1886   Daimler and Benz build early automobiles

1886   Statue of Liberty dedicated

1887   Verdi, *Otello*

1888   Mahler, *Symphony No. 1*

1889   Strauss, *Don Juan*; Paris International Exhibition; Eiffel Tower opens; Rodin, *The Thinker*; Van Gogh, *The Starry Night*

1890   James, *The Principles of Psychology*; Ibsen, *Hedda Gabler*

1892   Tchaikovsky, *The Nutcracker*

1893   Verdi, *Falstaff*

1894   Debussy, *Prelude to "The Afternoon of a Faun"*

1895   Roentgen discovers X-rays; Crane, *The Red Badge of Courage*

1896   Puccini, *La bohème*; Strauss, *Also sprach Zarathustra*; Marconi patents the wireless telegraph; first modern Olympic Games

1898   Spanish-American War; the Curies discover radium; Rodin, *The Kiss*

1899   Schoenberg, *Verklärte Nacht*; Debussy, *Nocturnes*

1900   Planck's fundamental work on the quantum theory; Ferdinand Graf von Zeppelin begins building large dirigibles; Freud, *Interpretation of Dreams*; Puccini, *Tosca*; Mahler, *Symphony No. 4*

The Romantic period in music (c. 1820–1900) was part of a larger cultural movement that swept Europe from the late eighteenth to the mid-nineteenth centuries. The era was characterized by such qualities as individualism; emotional subjectivity; nationalism; a sense of boundlessness; a yearning for the unattainable; an affinity with nature; and a love of remote times and places, the strange, the mysterious, and the supernatural. Romanticism is often considered the opposite of Classicism, which stresses emotional restraint, clarity of expression, and tradition. In a sense, Classicism and Romanticism represent opposite poles of human nature, the rational and the emotional, which are both always present to some degree. At times the rational "classical" side gains precedence, as in the High Renaissance and the Classical period; at other times the emotional "romantic" side predominates, as in the Gothic era, the Baroque period, and the Romantic period. In the late eighteenth and early nineteenth centuries, the two currents ran parallel as opposite reactions to the late Baroque aesthetic. At first Classicism predominated in the arts, but gradually Romanticism supplanted it as the leading force.

The word "romantic" derives from romance, a medieval literary form written in a romance language, that dealt typically with events of classical history or legend, the adventures of King Arthur and the Knights of the Round Table, or the deeds of Charlemagne and his knights, and that showed a fascination with mystery, the supernatural, and miraculous acts of chivalry and loyalty. In the late eighteenth century, the middle class found in these medieval tales of romance qualities that spoke powerfully to their own developing "romantic" spirit.

The Romantic spirit emerged first in literature, inspired by the medieval-oriented writings of James Macpherson, Thomas Percy, and Horace Walpole and by the philosophy of Jean-Jacques Rousseau, who stressed sensibility and the natural goodness of humanity. Romanticism proper began in Germany with the Sturm und Drang movement (c. 1760–1785) and the writings of von Schlegel, Tieck, Novalis, Holderlin, and Wackenroder. Among other early Romantic writers were Coleridge and Wordsworth in England and Bernardin de Saint-Pierre in France. During the first half of the nineteenth century, Romanticism became the leading literary movement, initiating an age of great achievements in poetry and novel writing. By the mid-nineteenth century, other movements arose to counter Romanticism, such as Parnassianism (Gautier and Heredia), Realism (Flaubert, Balzac, Dickens, Tolstoy, Turgenev, Dostoyevsky, and Ibsen), Naturalism (Zola and Guy de Maupassant), and Symbolism (Verlaine, Mallarmé, and Rimbaud).

In architecture, Romanticism manifested itself primarily in neo-Gothic, neo-Baroque, and neo-Renaissance revivalist styles. In painting, early Romantics such as Copley, Fuseli, and William Blake were followed by Constable and Turner in England, Delacroix and Géricault in France, Goya in Spain, and Friedrich in Germany. As in literature, countermovements also developed, the most important being Realism (Courbet, Millet, and Daumier), Impressionism (Manet, Monet, Pissarro, Renoir, and Degas), Postimpressionism (Cézanne, Van Gogh, Gauguin), and Art Nouveau (Beardsley and Morris). These later movements paved the way for more radical developments in twentieth-century art.

In music, Romantic tendencies were present throughout the Classical period, for example, in the pre-Classical expressive style and its extension as the Sturm und Drang movement, in some of Mozart's more passionate works (e.g., the Symphony in G Minor, K. 550), and in the heroic style of Beethoven. Its emergence in the 1820s as the leading style may thus be seen as a natural outgrowth of trends already present. Romanticism remained the dominant force in music until the end of the nineteenth century.

Romanticism in the arts flourished against the backdrop of a rapidly changing society. The Industrial Revolution spread throughout Europe, leading to the growth of great cities, the depopulation of the countryside, and the creation of often appalling working and living conditions for the working class. In response to these conditions the new science of sociology arose, social and labor reforms were enacted, and various economic systems emerged as alternatives to capitalism, the most important being socialism, a proponent of which was Karl Marx (1818–1883).

Although the nineteenth century was not plagued by the almost constant warfare that had characterized earlier centuries, there were several conflicts, such as the Crimean War, the Civil War in the United States, and the Franco-Prussian War. Also, the French Revolution had echoes in a number of smaller democratic revolts that swept through Europe (e.g., those in 1830 and 1848). The period also witnessed the "Victorian era" in England (1837–1901), the "Bismarck era" in Germany (1871–1890), continued advances in science and technology, and the appearance of numerous inventions that made life easier and brought society to the threshold of the world we inhabit today.

CHARACTERISTICS OF NINETEENTH-CENTURY ROMANTICISM

We turn now to a more detailed examination of several of the important characteristics of nineteenth-century Romanticism.

Individualism

A fundamental trait of Romanticism is its emphasis on individual freedom and worth. Since individual freedom is often in direct conflict with the institutions of society, Romantic artists often found themselves in the roles of rebels against established conventions and critics of society and its institutions. The conflict between the individual and society becomes a major theme in the nineteenth-century novel, a conflict that found symbolic expression in music in the concerto, in the "struggle" between the soloist and the orchestra, observed in the Classical period but now carried to even greater heights. Romantic individualism also manifested itself in new concepts of the artist and in the rise of nationalism.

New Concepts of the Artist

Now free from the patronage of the church and the aristocracy, artists became socially and economically more independent than ever before. They developed a growing awareness of themselves as "artists"—that is, as individuals different from ordinary people, with a special and somehow exalted mission in life. Various new concepts of the artist arose: (1) the artist as visionary or "seer," who transmits the flame of truth to mere mortals; (2) the artist as "bohemian," who starves in an attic, suffering and misunderstood but continuing to create works of art "for posterity" and who strives to shock the "bourgeois" with unusual dress and behavior; and (3) the artist as "Byronic hero," a tormented soul who feels more deeply and suffers more greatly than ordinary people and who is often driven by violent (or even fatal) passions. In short, the Romantic artist held a romanticized conception of himself or herself.

Emotional Subjectivity

Also fundamental to Romantic art is emotional subjectivity, that is, an attitude that imagination and personal expression are ends in themselves, at least as important as clarity of form. While in some respects this represents a departure from Classical ideals, in others it represents an intensification of tendencies already present but held in check.

Boundlessness

Related to emotional subjectivity is another quality common to Romanticism, the sense of boundlessness, the desire to break the bounds of established forms and conventions and give the imagination free rein. Allied with this, too, was an attempt to encompass the totality of experience and even to suggest the infinite. The Romantic artist yearned for the unattainable, forever suffering from an indefinable longing that can never be satisfied.

Connectedness of the Arts

Romantic boundlessness manifested itself also in a close connectedness of the various arts and an attempt to break down the boundaries between them. Romantic music, for example, shows an unprecedented affinity with poetry and painting. Thus, it is not surprising that two of the most characteristic new genres of the period are the *art song*, with its intimate marriage of music and text, and the *symphonic poem*, which paints a musical picture or depicts a story in music. The culmination of this trend in music is the "total art work" (*Gesamtkunstwerk*) cultivated by Richard Wagner in his mature operas, in which he attempted to merge music, words, scenery, and action in an all-encompassing unity.

Love of Far-Away Times and Places

Still another aspect of Romantic boundlessness was a love for exotic themes and far-away times and places. Artists and art lovers of the period had a special fondness for the Middle Ages, which gave rise to a neo-Gothic revival in architecture, the "Gothic" romance, and countless novels, plays, and poems set in the medieval past (e.g., Scott's *Ivanhoe*, Tennyson's *Idylls of the King*, and Wagner's *Ring* cycle). Oriental and African themes were also popular.

Love of the Strange, Mysterious, and Supernatural

Romantic artists also probed the darker and the more fantastic realms of the imagination. Horror stories (e.g., *Frankenstein*), nightmarish paintings (e.g., Fuseli's *The Nightmare*), and mysteries abounded, as did fairy tales, legends, and folk myths.

An Affinity with Nature

Nature also exercised a strong influence on Romantic art. Romantic artists felt a deep affinity with "wild," untamed nature, which they saw as an overpowering, mysterious, primordial force. Nature represented, too, an ideal state unspoiled by civilization and an escape from industrialized urban life. References to nature abound in Romantic art; in fact, nature is often one of the artist's most potent means for conveying atmosphere and mood.

Nationalism

An awakening of interest on the part of ethnic groups and nations to their individual histories led to an increase in national pride and attempts to rediscover ethnic roots and folk cultures. To establish particular national themes, Romantic artists based numerous works of art on national heroes, historic events, folk legends, myths, folk songs, dances, and the like. In music, this movement toward nationalism was particularly strong in the late nineteenth century (see chapter 24).

ROMANTICISM IN MUSIC

General Characteristics

As noted in the introduction to this chapter, the Romantic style in music was a natural outgrowth of tendencies toward dramatic expression already present during the Classical period. Moreover, Romantic composers continued to use Classical forms, although sometimes in a freer manner, and they continued to employ major-minor tonality in essentially the same manner as the Classicists, at least for the first half of the nineteenth century. To these established practices, however, they brought distinctive approaches that reflect the general characteristics of Romanticism described earlier.

Several general traits of Romantic music may be noted: (1) Composers exploited all the musical elements for personal expression and developed more individualistic, personal styles than in earlier periods. (2) The favorite mediums were those that offered the greatest opportunities for personal expression either on an intimate scale (e.g., the art song and the character piece for piano) or on a grand one (e.g., symphonic music and opera). Abstract genres, such as the sonata and chamber music, and more impersonal media, such as choral music, were not cultivated as extensively. (3) Composers felt an extremely close affinity with poetry and other types of literature and with the graphic arts. This manifested itself in countless ways in their music. (4) The Romantic sense of boundlessness and yearning for the unattainable had a great effect on the development of the musical language of the nineteenth century, especially in the areas of melody, harmony, tonality, and form. (5) Composers generally wrote either for a small group of friends or knowledgeable music lovers who could understand the subtleties of their art or for the broader, less sophisticated concert-going public. Composers adapted their music to their audience. (6) As in the Classical period, amateur music making in the home continued to be popular. Nearly every middle class family owned a piano; thus, easily playable music for solo piano, songs, duos for piano and another instrument, and arrangements of operas and orchestral music for piano were in great demand. (7) Compositions of the period vary greatly in length, from miniatures (e.g., solo songs and piano character pieces) to works of gargantuan proportions (e.g., Wagner's operas and Mahler's symphonies). (8) Technical virtuosity reached new heights, and virtuoso composer-performers such as Liszt and Paganini were much admired by audiences. This reflects in part the nature and level of sophistication of the audience itself. (9) Romantic nationalism found expression in music in an important late-nineteenth-century movement (see chapter 24).

Specific *Characteristics*	The exploitation of musical elements for personal expression led, in turn, to specific stylistic traits in Romantic music.

MELODY

Melody in Romantic music often serves to express the feeling of unfulfilled yearning. As a result, melodic style is more overtly emotional and more effusive than in the past; phrases are often longer, more irregular, and build slowly to more sustained climaxes; and the pitch range of melodies is greatly expanded (particularly in orchestral and piano music). Romantic composers generally preferred warm, songlike melodies to the motivic melodies found, for example, in Haydn and Beethoven. Whereas in the Classical period a theme often seems to be only the starting point for development, Romantic themes are more often beautiful, memorable tunes in their own right (perhaps partly because of the need to appeal to a broader, less sophisticated concert-going public). Folk songs and folklike melodies appear as well, particularly in the music of nationalist composers. Romantic composers sometimes also use the same thematic material in two or more movements of a multimovement composition, in which case the composition is said to be *cyclic*. Especially after 1850, melodies can be quite chromatic.

HARMONY AND TONALITY

Some of the most radical and far-reaching achievements of the Romantic period are in the area of harmony and tonality. Although major-minor tonality was still the basis of harmony, composers began to conceive of tonality not only as a means of logical structure but also as a way of achieving highly personal and moving emotional effects. Modulations became more frequent and more wide-ranging until, in some of the music of Wagner and his successors, a state of almost continual modulation exists, which expresses perfectly the endless striving of the Romantic. In the process, though, the sense of a key center is weakened.

To this increased tonal "flux" the Romantic composer also brought a heightened interest in new and unusual chord progressions, more colorful (i.e., more chromatic) and unstable chords, and more extensive uses of dissonance. By the end of the nineteenth century, this greater use of chromaticism and dissonance had seemingly exhausted the possibilities of the major-minor system. Many composers began to look for alternative approaches, thus opening the door to even more radical developments in the early twentieth century (see chapter 25).

RHYTHM

Romantic composers exploited rhythm, too, for expressive purposes, employing a greater variety of rhythmic patterns and more frequent changes of meter and tempo within movements. A new technique introduced was *tempo rubato*, an elastic, flexible tempo that made much use of slight accelerandos and ritardandos as the expression of the music demanded.

DYNAMICS

In their exploitation of dynamics for personal expression, Romantic composers employed a wider range of dynamics than did Classical composers (a range of *pppp* to *ffff* as opposed to the earlier range of *pp* to *ff*), more precise indications of crescendo and diminuendo, and, in general, more dramatic uses of dynamic contrasts.

TEXTURE

Homophony was still the prevailing type of texture during the Romantic period; counterpoint played a subsidiary though important role. Romantic texture is also characterized by an increased richness of sound as composers came to prefer thick, warm voicings, "lush" orchestrations, and denser, more complex harmonies to the sparse, transparent textures of Classical music.

FORM

Romantic composers continued to use forms inherited from the Classical period but often did so in a freer manner, blurring the edges between sections and movements and otherwise altering the outer form to fit a more subjective approach to inner content. Following the practice of Beethoven, composers also explored thematic interrelationships within and between movements to a greater extent than before, using cyclic writing (see earlier) and other more subtle ways of achieving unity (see chapter 22).

TONE COLOR

Romantic composers were the first to consider tone color, or timbre, equal in importance to melody and harmony. They used it to obtain a wide variety of moods and effects. Among the many new instruments introduced into general use during the period were the piccolo, the English horn, the contrabassoon, the clarinet and saxophone families, the trombone, the tuba, the cornet, the modern chromatic harp, the celesta, and a host of percussion instruments. Many other instruments were improved. The addition of valves to the trumpet and horn, for example, at last made them fully chromatic. The piano became larger and stronger (with metal braces and a cast-iron frame), its range was extended to more than seven octaves, and, through a number of mechanical improvements, its tone became more singing and it became capable of producing the subtlest nuances of tonal shadings.

The tremendous growth of the orchestra to an ensemble containing sometimes over a hundred performers and to one that has essentially its present composition (see chapter 10), is another illustration of the widespread interest in tone color during this period. The woodwind and brass sections were expanded into complete families that now, because of improvements in construction, could assume roles equal in importance to those of the strings. Favorite instrumental colors were the clarinet, bass clarinet, French and English horns, and harp. Composers developed the art of orchestration to unprecedented heights, treating the orchestra like a vast palette from which to draw rich and infinitely varied combinations of tone colors. In the hands of such virtuoso orchestrators as Berlioz, Wagner, Mahler, Strauss, Tchaikovsky, and Debussy, the orchestra became an instrument of immense subtlety and power.

In addition, bands enjoyed a surge in popularity, partly because of the improvements in woodwind and brass instruments. Choral societies were organized throughout Europe and the United States.

The Romantic movement that swept through Europe in the nineteenth century changed music as it did the other arts, bringing a return, as in the Baroque period, to a greater emphasis on subjective, emotional qualities. It did not bring, however, a return to the Baroque style itself. In the first place, the composer's goals had changed. Whereas the Baroque composer sought to depict rather rigid, conventional affections, the Romantic composer's intent was personal expression in all its ever-changing and infinitely varied manifestations. Even more important, musical forms and the musical language had evolved tremendously since the Baroque period. Thus, the stylistic pendulum did not return to exactly the same place, because Romantic composers, like all artists of all eras, were challenged to respond in ways that were appropriate to their own specific time and circumstances.

Although Romantic composers still worked within the major-minor tonal system and, for the most part, continued to use forms inherited from the Classical period, they transformed these in the cause of personal expression, creating in the process a distinctive new style in its own right. By the end of the nineteenth century, emotionalism, inherited forms, and even the major-minor system itself had all reached a breaking point, forcing still another reevaluation of goals and means. Before this point was reached, however, Romantic composers produced some of the most poetic, touching, and emotionally rich music ever written— music that still constitutes the bulk of the concert repertoire.

For Additional Study

GENERAL:

Abraham, Gerald. *A Hundred Years of Music*. 4th ed. London: Duckworth. 1974.

Blume, Friedrich. *Classic and Romantic Music: A Comprehensive Survey*. Translated by M. D. Herter Norton. New York: Norton. 1970.

The EAV Art and Music Series. "Romanticism in Art and Music." Distributed by Educational Audio Visual, Inc. (Pleasantville, NY). Videocassette.

The EAV History of Music. Part 5: "Early Romanticism"; Part 6: "Later Romanticism." Distributed by Educational Audio Visual, Inc. (Pleasantville, NY). Videocassettes.

Einstein, Alfred. *Music in the Romantic Era*. New York: Norton. 1947.

Longyear, Rey M. *Nineteenth-Century Romanticism in Music*. 3d ed. Englewood Cliffs, NJ: Prentice-Hall. 1988.

Music & Man Series. "Schubert: The Young Romantic"; "The Waltz City"; "The Turn of the Century." Distributed by Films for the Humanities & Sciences (Princeton, NJ). Videocassettes.

Plantinga, Leon. *Romantic Music*. New York: Norton. 1984.

BIOGRAPHIES:

Barzun, Jacques. *Berlioz and His Century*. Boston: Little, Brown & Co. 1969.

Brown, David, et al. *The New Grove Russian Masters I*. New York: Norton. 1986.

Brown, Maurice J. E., with Eric Sams. *The New Grove Schubert*. New York: Norton. 1983.

Chissell, Joan. *Schumann*. New York: Collier Books, 1962; rev. ed. London: Dent, 1977.

Cooke, Deryck. *Gustav Mahler: An Introduction to His Music*. 2d ed. Cambridge, Eng.: Cambridge University Press. 1988.

___, et al. *The New Grove Late Romantic Masters*. New York: Norton. 1985.

Del Mar, Norman. *Richard Strauss: A Critical Commentary on His Life and Work*. 3 vols. Philadelphia: Chilton Books, 1969–1973; reprint with corrections,1978.

Lockspeiser, Edward. *Debussy*. Rev. 5th ed. London: Dent. 1980.

MacDonald, Malcolm. *Brahms*. New York: Schirmer. 1990.

Newman, Ernest. *Life of Richard Wagner*. 4 vols. London: Cassell, 1933–1947; reprint, 1976.

Radcliffe, Philip. *Mendelssohn*. London: J. M. Dent; New York: Farrar, Strauss, & Giroux, 1967; rev. ed., 1976.

Temperly, Nicholas, Gerald Abraham, and Humphrey Searle. *The New Grove Early Romantic Masters I*. New York: Norton. 1985.

Walker, Alan, comp. *Franz Liszt: The Man and His Music*. 2d ed. London: Barrie & Jenkins. 1976.

Walker, Frank. *The Man Verdi*. New York: Knopf. 1962.

Warrack, John. *Tchaikovsky*. New York: Scribner; London: Hamish Hamilton. 1973.

___, Hugh MacDonald, and Karl-Heinz Köhler. *The New Grove Early Romantic Masters II*. New York: Norton. 1985.

Zamoyski, Adam. *Chopin: A New Biography*. Garden City, NY: Doubleday. 1980.

22

Instrumental Music in the Romantic Period

1812 Beethoven, *Symphony No. 8*

1813–1822 Schubert, Symphonies 1–8

1823 Beethoven, *Symphony No. 9*

1825 Chopin's Op. 1 (*Rondo* in C minor)

1826 Mendelssohn, Overture to *A Midsummer Night's Dream*

1827 Death of Beethoven; Schubert, 8 *Impromptus* (D. 899, 935)

1828 Schubert's last compositions (e.g., *Symphony No. 9*, last three piano sonatas) and death (age 31)

1830 Berlioz, *Symphonie fantastique*

1831 Schumann's Op. 1 published

1833 Mendelssohn, *Symphony No. 4* ("Italian")

1835 Schumann, *Carnaval*

1839 Chopin, *Preludes*, Op. 28; Liszt publishes his *12 Transcendental Études* (rev. 1851); Liszt, *Piano Concerto No. 2 in A Major*

1841 Schumann, *Symphony No. 1*

1842 Chopin, *Polonaise in A-flat Major*, Op. 53; Mendelssohn, *Symphony No. 3* ("Scottish") and Incidental Music to *A Midsummer Night's Dream*

1844 Mendelssohn, *Violin Concerto in E Minor*

1847 Death of Mendelssohn (age 38)

1848 Liszt, *Les Préludes*

1849 Death of Chopin (age 39)

1851 Schumann, *Symphony No. 4*

1853   Liszt, *Sonata in B Minor*

1856   Death of Schumann (age 46)

1857   Liszt completes his *Faust Symphony*

1866   Anton Bruckner, *Symphony No. 1*

1875   Tchaikovsky, *Piano Concerto No. 1*

1876   Brahms, *Symphony No. 1*

1880   Smetana, *Má vlast* completed

1885   Brahms, *Symphony No. 4*

1886   Death of Liszt (age 75)

1887   Bruckner, *Symphony No. 8*

1888   Franck, *Symphony in D Minor*; Rimsky-Korsakov, *Scheherazade*; Mahler, *Symphony No. 1*

1889   Richard Strauss, *Don Juan*

1891   Brahms, *Clarinet Quintet*, Op. 115

1892–1893   Brahms publishes character pieces for piano (Opp. 116, 117, 118, 119)

1893   Tchaikovsky, *Symphony No. 6*; Dvořák, *Symphony No. 9* ("From the New World")

1894   Brahms, *Clarinet Sonatas*, Op. 120; Debussy, *Prelude to "The Afternoon of a Faun"*

1896   Richard Strauss, *Also sprach Zarathustra*; Death of Bruckner; Mahler, *Symphony No. 3*

1897   Death of Brahms

Because of its unique ability to touch the listener's deepest feelings without the specific connotations of words or physical images, instrumental music was an ideal Romantic art form. Romantic composers cultivated instrumental music extensively, finding in it a medium perfectly suited to the expression of every possible emotional nuance.

For their large multimovement works, Romantic composers, for the most part, still preferred the sonata-cycle genres established during the Classical period, such as the sonata, symphony, and concerto. They also continued to rely largely on Classical forms for individual movements (binary, ternary, rondo, sonata form, and so on). Yet they did contribute several characteristic new instrumental genres, most notably the character piece for piano and the symphonic poem (or tone poem) for orchestra.

This chapter explores the main developments in instrumental music during the period, with an emphasis on the works of Franz Schubert (1797–1828), Felix Mendelssohn-Bartholdy (1809–1847), Frédéric Chopin (1810–1849), Hector Berlioz (1803–1869), Robert Schumann (1810–1856), Franz Liszt (1811–1886), and Johannes Brahms (1833–1897). The contri-

butions of nationalist, late Romantic, and Impressionist composers at the end of the nineteenth century are discussed separately in chapter 24.

NEW PIANO GENRES

During the first half of the nineteenth century, the piano evolved from the delicate instrument of Mozart's time into essentially the concert grand that we know today. In addition to being a fixture in middle class homes throughout Europe and America, the piano became the instrument par excellence for a new class of virtuoso performers who came into prominence with the rise of public concerts. The piano recital grew in popularity until, by the early twentieth century, it occupied a central position on the concert scene.

The principal new piano genre to emerge was the *character piece*, in which all the main aspects of the period, such as nationalism, literary associations, fantasy, and exoticism, found expression.

The Character Piece

The term *character piece* denotes a type of nineteenth-century composition, most often written for piano, that is aimed at conveying a particular mood, character, style or extramusical idea.

TYPES

The most common titles used to designate character pieces are: *album leaf, arabesque, bagatelle* ("trifle"), *ballade, barcarolle, berceuse, caprice, fantasy* (or *fantasia, fantasie* or *fancy*), *impromptu, intermezzo* ("interlude"), *moment musical, nocturne* ("night piece"), *novelette* ("short story"), *prelude, rhapsody, romance* (or *romanza*), *scherzo*, and *song without words*. Dance pieces and *études* (see below) are sometimes also included under this heading, as are pieces with descriptive titles, such as "Soaring," "The Poet Speaks," and the like. Composers sometimes grouped several character pieces into sets, or cycles; Robert Schumann was particularly notable in this respect.

CHARACTERISTICS

Character pieces range in size from extremely short fragments, through miniatures of a page or two, to large works in rondo or sonata form. Shorter examples may consist of no more than a period, while moderate-sized examples may have a binary, ternary, or rondo form or a freer design. They range in difficulty from virtuoso showpieces to simple compositions playable by beginning students.

Étude

A special type of free form cultivated primarily during the nineteenth century is the *étude*, or *study*, which is aimed at developing some technical aspect of performance. The étude began as a mere finger exercise used for lessons. However, in the hands of Romantic masters such as Chopin, Schumann, and Liszt it became a composition of artistic worth suitable for concert performance.

Stylized Dances

A number of new dance types gained prominence in the nineteenth century and were well represented in the piano music of the time. Several of these originated as folk or ethnic dances, and their use often reflects nationalistic tendencies on the part of the composer. Among the most common dances were the following:

Quadrille French square dance, alternating 2/4 and 6/8 meters
Polka Bohemian, fast, duple meter
Mazurka Polish, slow, medium or fast tempo, triple meter
Waltz Austrian origin, moderate or fast, 3/4 meter
Ländler Bavarian-Austrian, lively, 3/4 meter
Polonaise Polish, moderate tempo, triple meter (continued
    from the eighteenth century)
Tarantella Italian, fast, 6/8 meter
Galop Possibly of German origin, fast, duple meter

Dances appeared as individual pieces, as part of a set of similar dances (e.g., a set of waltzes) or as movements in a sonata cycle, replacing the scherzo.

Representative Composers

All the focal composers of this chapter made important contributions to the piano literature with the exception of Berlioz. A summary of their works for piano follows, not including sonatas and concertos, which are discussed later.

SCHUBERT

Schubert's many piano works include several sets of character pieces: six *Moments musicaux* (D. 780; pub. 1828); eight *Impromptus* (D. 899, D. 935; composed 1827); and three *Klavierstücke* (Piano Pieces, D. 946; composed 1828). These became the model for later composers of character pieces. An important larger work is the *Wandererfantasie* (Wanderer Fantasy) in C major, D. 760 (1822).

CHOPIN

Chopin is often referred to as the "poet of the piano" because of his finely wrought, singing melodies, rich chromatic harmonies, subtle use of tempo rubato, and warmly expressive legato style. In his many exquisite piano works the Romantic style comes into full bloom. He is noted particularly for his character pieces, which include twenty-seven études, four fiery scherzos, four ballades, twenty-six preludes, four impromptus, and numerous nocturnes, waltzes, mazurkas, and polonaises.

Chopin's mazurkas, based on a Slavic dance in triple meter, range in mood from melancholy to exuberant. With their use of Polish rhythms, harmonies, and melodic traits, they are early examples of Romantic nationalism. His polonaises also evoke the majestic spirit of his native land; a popular favorite is the heroic *Polonaise in A-flat Major*, Op. 53. The more intimate side of Chopin's nature finds expression in his nocturnes, preludes, waltzes, and impromptus. Graceful, sensitive, and expressive, these works are among the most beautiful piano works in the literature.

MENDELSSOHN

A Romantic composer with a Classical sense of proportion and decorum, Mendelssohn wrote piano music of elegance and sensitivity rather than bravura display. Among his most important piano works are the forty-eight *Songs without Words*, published in six books; the *Andante and Rondo Capriccioso*, Op. 14 (c. 1824); the *Variations sérieuses* in D minor, Op. 54 (1841); the *Fantasia* in F-sharp minor, Op. 28 (1833); and the *Six Preludes and Fugues*, Op. 35 (1836).

SCHUMANN

Character pieces grouped in sets or cycles make up the bulk of Schumann's piano music. Among his collections of character pieces are *Papillons* (Butterflies, Op. 2; 1829–1831); *Carnaval* (Op. 9; 1835); *Fantasiestücke* (Fantasy Pieces, Op. 12; 1837); *Kinderszenen* (Scenes from Childhood, Op. 15; 1838); *Davidsbündlertänze* (Dances of the League of David, Op. 6; 1837); and *Album für die Jugend* (Album for the Young, Op. 68; pub. 1848). An important large work is the collection of *Symphonische Etüden* (Symphonic Études, Op. 13, C-sharp minor; 1834).

Schumann's piano music, much of which is programmatic, exemplifies the impetuous, even contradictory, aspects of musical Romanticism. Schumann even personified the different sides of his personality as the characters Florestan (the passionate extrovert), Eusebius (the dreamer), and Raro (the wise master), who appear in several of his literary writings and compositions, along with other members of the imaginary League of David invented by Schumann, who struggled against the Philistines of music.

LISZT

Liszt, who played his first piano concert at age eleven, gained fame as a performer, conductor, and composer. Influenced by the phenomenal technique of the violinist Niccolò Paganini (1782–1840), he extended the technique of the piano to its extreme limits. Nearly all Liszt's music is programmatic. In addition to numerous transcriptions, arrangements, and separately published compositions, Liszt left twenty Hungarian rhapsodies, twelve extremely difficult *Études d' exécution transcendante* (Transcendental Études; 1826, rev. 1839, 1851); several collections of character pieces, such as the three books of *Années de Pèlerinage* (Years of Pilgrimage); and the *Totentanz* (Dance of Death; 1849, rev. 1853, 1859) for piano and orchestra, based on the plainsong *Dies irae*. A perennial favorite is the *Hungarian Rhapsody No. 2* (1847), a dazzling virtuoso showpiece that strongly evokes the gypsy spirit of Liszt's homeland.

BRAHMS

Brahms was the Romantic composer in whose music Classical form and craftsmanship blended most perfectly with Romantic expressiveness. His musical style is characterized by an introspective seriousness; rich, full textures; rather somber harmonies; frequent doubling of melodic lines in octaves, thirds, and sixths; and the use of duple meter against triple meter and other types of cross rhythms. His smaller works for piano include ballades, rhapsodies, fantasias, capriccios, intermezzos, waltzes, and Hungarian dances. Important larger works include the *Variations and Fugue on a Theme by Handel*, Op. 24 (1861) and the *Variations on a Theme by Paganini*, Op. 35 (1863).

OTHER COMPOSERS

Other representative Romantic composers of piano music are discussed in chapter 24.

PROGRAM MUSIC

General Aspects

DEFINITION

The term program music denotes instrumental music with certain extramusical associations, such as a story, poem, scene from nature or other literary or pictorial subject. Such extramusical aspects are normally indicated by the title of the composition or by explanatory comments (a "program") provided by the composer. Program music is distinguished from absolute music, or pure music, which stands entirely on its own merits and has no intrinsic association with extramusical ideas.

CHARACTERISTICS

Program music draws primarily upon music's power to evoke moods, emotions, and atmospheres. To a lesser extent it may draw also upon music's capacity to imitate certain sound effects such as bird calls, the bleating of sheep or the rumble of thunder. Although knowledge of the title and program may enhance the pleasure of listening to an example of program music, it is also possible to appreciate the music simply as music, without the extramusical associations.

RISE

Although scattered examples of program music appear in earlier Western music (e.g., Vivaldi's *The Four Seasons* and Haydn's *The Creation*), program music first emerged as an important genre in the piano and orchestral music of the nineteenth century, beginning with Beethoven's Sixth (*Pastoral*) Symphony of 1808. As noted earlier, the nineteenth century was a time of very close relationships among the arts, and many Romantic composers were themselves accomplished writers; thus it is not surprising that they should explore literary and pictorial associations in their music.

Types of Program Music

The main types of program music include descriptive pieces for piano and, for orchestra, the program symphony, concert overture, symphonic poem, and incidental music.

DESCRIPTIVE PIECES FOR PIANO

As noted earlier, character pieces for piano sometimes contain descriptive titles that have extramusical associations. These constitute a type of program music.

PROGRAM SYMPHONY

As its name implies, a program symphony is a symphony with programmatic aspects. Beethoven's Sixth (*Pastoral*) Symphony set an early precedent for this type of symphony, with movements entitled "Awakening of Pleasant Feelings on Arriving in the Country," "Scene by the Brook," "Happy Gathering of Country Folk," "Thunderstorm," and "Shepherd's Song: Happy and Thankful Feelings after the Storm." Although this symphony includes some musical imitations of nature, such as the depiction of a storm and bird calls, Beethoven intended that the music be an "expression of feelings rather than depiction." Most later composers of program music followed this general aim as well. Among the most well-known later program symphonies are Berlioz's *Symphonie fantastique* (1830) and *Harold in Italy* (1834) and Liszt's *Faust Symphony* (1854–1857).

CONCERT OVERTURE

A concert overture is a one-movement composition, usually in sonata form, that has programmatic associations. It grew out of and was modeled after the opera overture, which often suggests the moods and ideas of the opera that follows. Unlike the opera overture, however, the concert overture is not intended as a prelude to a stage work; it is an independent composition for concert performance. Representative examples include Mendelssohn's

The Hebrides (or *Fingal's Cave*; 1830) and *Calm Sea and Prosperous Voyage* (1828–1832), Brahms's *Academic Festival Overture* (1880) and *Tragic Overture* (1880), and Tchaikovsky's (1840–1893) *Romeo and Juliet* (overture-fantasy; 1869) and *1812 Overture* (1880).

SYMPHONIC POEM

A symphonic poem (or tone poem), like the concert overture, is a one-movement programmatic work for orchestra. Unlike the concert overture, which normally uses sonata form, the symphonic poem has greater flexibility, incorporating traditional designs such as sonata form; rondo; theme and variation; and freer, irregular forms.

The symphonic poem was the nineteenth century's most original contribution to the large instrumental forms. Created by Franz Liszt in the late 1840s and 1850s, it became the most widely cultivated type of orchestral program music in the second half of the century. Among the most famous of the many symphonic poems of the period are Liszt's *Les Préludes* (1848); Richard Strauss's (1864–1949) *Don Juan* (1889), *Death and Transfiguration* (1889), *Till Eulenspiegel's Merry Pranks* (1895), *Also sprach Zarathustra* (1896), *Don Quixote* (1897), and *Ein Heldenleben* (A Hero's Life; 1898); Jean Sibelius's (1865–1957) *Finlandia* (1899); and Paul Dukas's *The Sorcerer's Apprentice* (1897).

Symphonic poems, particularly those of Richard Strauss, provide examples of some of the most colorful orchestral writing of the Romantic period, and most make use of the technique of thematic transformation pioneered by Liszt. Programmatic elements range from the evocation of general moods or ideas to the depiction of details as specific as the bleating of sheep. In Strauss's tone poems especially, a wide variety of formal structures are used, ranging from sonata forms (e.g., *Don Juan* and *Death and Transfiguration*), theme and variations (*Don Quixote*), and rondos (*Till Eulenspiegel's Merry Pranks*) to free sectional structures (e.g., *Also sprach Zarathustra*).

INCIDENTAL MUSIC

Incidental music, written to be performed before and during a play, includes such forms as overtures, interludes, background music, marches, and dances. Its purpose is to set the mood for certain scenes. (Film music is a present-day manifestation of this type of music.) Representative Romantic examples include Mendelssohn's music for *A Midsummer Night's Dream* (1842), Georges Bizet's (1838–1875) for *L'Arlésienne* (1872), and Edvard Grieg's (1843–1907) for *Peer Gynt* (1875; reorchestrated 1886). Composers sometimes arranged their incidental music for a given drama into an orchestral suite for independent concert performance.

WORKS BASED ON THE SONATA CYCLE

Developments in the Sonata Cycle

Romantic composers continued to write symphonies, concertos, sonatas, and chamber music based on the sonata cycle. The starting point for the Romantic sonata cycle was Beethoven, in whose works most nineteenth-century developments found precedence.

NUMBER OF MOVEMENTS

Romantic composers continued Beethoven's trend of varying the number of movements in the sonata cycle from as few as two movements to as many as six. They also continued his tendency to eliminate pauses between the movements, leading ultimately to a fusing of the various movements into a single large movement (e.g., Liszt's *Piano Sonata in B Minor* and *Piano Concerto No. 2 in A Major*). On the whole, however, the four-movement cycle for the symphony and sonata and the three-movement cycle for the concerto still remained the most common schemes.

THEMATIC INTERRELATIONSHIPS

To bring unity to the sonata cycle as a whole, classical composers, particularly Beethoven, had explored various means of interrelating the themes of the various movements of the cycle. These ranged from making subtle motivic connections between the themes to overtly using a theme in more than one movement. Romantic composers seized upon the idea of thematic interrelationships among movements as a virtual "law" of musical unity, leading to such techniques as Liszt's "thematic transformation," the use of one or more themes or thematic fragments in several movements of a large work, modified (or transformed) as necessary to fit the changing moods and musical situations. Similar techniques for interrelating the themes of the various movements underlie Berlioz's "idée fixe," Brahms's "developing variations," Mahler's "constant variation," Franck's "cyclical treatment," and Sibelius's "organic evolution of a germ idea."

THE FIRST MOVEMENT

As before, the first movement is almost invariably a fast movement in sonata form. Slow introductions are frequent, often beginning in a nontonic key and occasionally being reduced to a mere gesture of a few measures. Romantic composers sometimes treated sonata form with great freedom. More often, however, they tended to approach it in an almost "textbook" fashion, hardening the flexible approaches of the Classical period into a virtual mold.

The second key area of the exposition was still most often the dominant (in major-key movements) or the relative major (in minor-key movements), though composers frequently used other keys as well; in such cases, keys related to the tonic by the interval of a third were most common.

The development section was the most problematical area for Romantic composers because they tended to think in full-fledged tunes, which do not lend themselves as well as the motivic themes of Classical composers to contrapuntal treatment and melodic fragmentation for developmental purposes. Recapitulations generally adhere to Classical practice. Large codas, as in Beethoven, are common, and they often serve as the climax to the movement.

The gradual increase in modulations and overall tonal instability in music of the period led to a corresponding weakening of the sonata-form structure, which had been based originally on the clear juxtaposition of keys.

THE SLOW MOVEMENT

Slow movements typically exhibit an A B A form, rondo form or sonatina form and are often related tonally to the key of the first movement by the interval of a third. In these movements Romantic composers were able to give full expression to their lyrical, expressive tendencies, and they produced many truly beautiful and poetic examples.

THE THIRD MOVEMENT

By 1800 the scherzo had replaced the minuet as the preferred third movement design, and it remained in general use throughout the nineteenth century. Also used were various dance forms (e.g., the waltz, Ländler or, for nostalgic purposes, even the minuet) and music of an intermezzo or marchlike character. Sometimes this movement is in the tonic key, as in the past; just as often, though, it might be in a different key. As in the Classical period, this movement and the slow movement are sometimes inverted in order; they may also be merged, creating the sense of a three-movement cycle.

THE FINALE

As in the Classical period, the finale is usually a fast movement in the tonic key (often in the tonic major when the first movement is in minor, to end on a positive note), and it typically exhibits a rondo, sonata or sonata-rondo form or, less commonly, a fugal, variation or free-sectional design. To many Romantic composers, the role of the finale was to bring the cycle to a triumphant close, which led sometimes to overcomplicated, overblown forms. The writing of a successful finale was a problem that challenged even the best composers.

The Symphony

Two main trends are apparent in the Romantic symphony, both of which originated in the symphonies of Beethoven: (1) toward absolute music and continued reliance on Classical forms and (2) toward program music and freer, more experimental approaches.

SCHUBERT

Schubert's nine symphonies, none of which are programmatic, represent a transitional stage between the Classical and Romantic styles. His early symphonies are Classical in approach, influenced primarily by Haydn and

Mozart. However, his last two rank as the first truly Romantic symphonies because of their singing melodies, adventuresome harmony, and sensitive treatment of orchestral tone color, though both still retain Classical forms. Of the first of these, the *Symphony No. 8 in B Minor*, D. 759 ("Unfinished"; 1822), Schubert completed only the first two movements plus the beginning of the third; nevertheless, it has remained his most popular symphony. In his *Symphony No. 9 in C Major*, D. 944 ("The Great"; c. 1825–1828), Schubert expanded the size to "heavenly lengths" (to quote Schumann). At times the music has difficulty sustaining this length.

MENDELSSOHN

Mendelssohn left five symphonies and thirteen smaller *sinfonie* (discovered in 1960). Although several have descriptive titles, none are programmatic. Mendelssohn used the standard Classical four-movement scheme for his symphonies, yet the spirit of the music is Romantic. The two most popular symphonies have geographical titles: *Symphony No. 3 in A Minor*, Op. 56 ("Scottish"; 1842) and *Symphony No. 4 in A Major*, Op. 90 ("Italian"; 1833). In the *Scottish* symphony, the four movements are played without a break, paralleling a trend found also in several of Mendelssohn's concertos. The *Italian* symphony, with its vivacious first movement and dashing Saltarello finale, is a particularly happy example of Mendelssohn's genius.

SCHUMANN

Schumann composed four symphonies, in B-flat major ("Spring," Op. 38; 1841), C major (Op. 61; 1846), E-flat major ("Rhenish," Op. 97; 1850), and D minor (Op. 120; composed 1841, published 1851). His symphonies are warmly expressive Romantic works with sometimes unorthodox internal structures. In the *Symphony No. 4 in D Minor*, for example, the four movements are joined without a break, through harmonic means and, before the finale, a transitional passage. Moreover, there are thematic interrelationships among the movements—the slow introduction to the first movement provides motives for thematic material of all four movements. Schumann's symphonies are essentially non-programmatic, although the *Rhenish Symphony* is somewhat programmatic.

BERLIOZ

Berlioz was the first of several composers, including Liszt and Wagner, who introduced some of the most radical developments in Romantic music. The most famous of his orchestral works, all of which are programmatic, is the *Symphonie fantastique* (Fantastic Symphony; 1830). Based upon a typical four-movement cycle with an added march movement, the symphony depicts five opium-influenced visions experienced by its lovesick hero. Each movement features a recurring theme, the *idée fixe* ("fixed idea"), which represents the hero's beloved; the theme is modified depending on the programmatic situation. This technique was to have a strong influence on the later development of cyclic symphonic forms. Berlioz's

Symphonie fantastique is notable also for its vivid programmatic depictions and its extremely original and colorful orchestration. Berlioz was one of the first of the great Romantic orchestrators as well as the founder of modern conducting.

LISZT

Liszt's two symphonies, like those of Berlioz, are both programmatic. In the *Faust Symphony* (1854–1857), his masterpiece, Liszt used interrelated themes among the movements and thematic transformations in an inspired blending of literary and musical elements. His *Dante Symphony* (1855–1856) is a lesser work.

BRAHMS

Brahms, more oriented toward Classical ideals, rejected program music and many other current trends of his day in favor of absolute music and a return to Classical approaches. Weighed down by the daunting example of Beethoven's symphonies, he did not complete his first symphony until age forty-three. It was worth the wait: his four symphonies—in C minor (Op. 68; 1876), D major (Op. 73; 1877), F major (Op. 90; 1883), and E minor (Op. 98; 1885)—are all masterworks that combine the best of Classical form and developmental craft with a rich, Romantic musical language and full, well-blended orchestral colors.

OTHER COMPOSERS

Important later Romantic composers of symphonies include Anton Bruckner (1824–1896), Pyotr Tchaikovsky (1840–1893), Antonin Dvořák (1841–1904), Jean Sibelius (1865–1957), and Gustav Mahler (1860–1911). Their works are discussed in chapter 24.

The Concerto

In the nineteenth-century concerto, the symbol of the soloist as the heroic individual struggling against the masses (the orchestra) was developed to a higher degree than ever before, spurred on by a new class of superstar soloists, such as Paganini and Liszt, who turned the concerto into a dramatic showcase for their phenomenal talents. From a technical standpoint, Romantic composers brought to culmination two major trends begun by Beethoven: (1) the elimination of the double exposition in the first movement and (2) the gradual merging of the various movements into a single movement. Of the focal composers in this chapter, Mendelssohn, Schumann, Liszt, and Brahms made the most significant contributions to the genre.

MENDELSSOHN

Mendelssohn's concertos include three for one piano, two for two pianos, and two for violin. Mendelssohn was the first to abandon the double exposition of the first movement in favor of a single exposition with the soloist participating from the beginning. He also took steps toward merging the various movements by inserting transitional passages between one or more movements in several of his concertos. Both of these innovations appear in his *Violin Concerto in E Minor*, Op. 64 (1844), which is one of the finest in the literature. In the first movement of this concerto, Mendelssohn also placed the cadenza, not close to the end as was traditional, but as the *retransition* from the development to the recapitulation, a stroke of genius that transformed the cadenza from a mere display passage added to the form into a functional part of the music.

SCHUMANN

Schumann's concertos include the *Piano Concerto in A Minor*, Op. 54 (1845), the *Cello Concerto in A Minor*, Op. 129 (1850), and the *Violin Concerto in D Minor* (1853). The piano and cello concertos are lyrical works, devoid of virtuosic display, that follow Mendelssohn's structural innovations. The violin concerto, on the other hand, is an uneven work that harks back to the earlier Classical double-exposition format.

LISZT

Liszt composed two major concertos for piano, in E-flat major (1849; revised 1853, 1856) and A major (1839; revised 1849, 1853, 1857, 1861). The A major concerto is, at last, a true one-movement concerto, in essence a nonprogrammatic symphonic poem for piano and orchestra that dispenses altogether with the tutti-solo alternation of the Classical concerto.

BRAHMS

Brahms contributed two concertos for piano, one for violin, and one double concerto (violin and cello), all of which exhibit the strong Classical influences found in his sonatas and symphonies. Rejecting the progressive developments of Liszt, Brahms restored the boundaries between the movements and returned to the Classical conception of concerto form.

OTHER COMPOSERS

Other important Romantic composers of concertos include Tchaikovsky (*Piano Concerto No. 1 in B-flat Minor* [1875] and *Violin Concerto in D Major* [1878]), Grieg (*Piano Concerto in A Minor* [1868, revised 1906–1907]), and Dvořák (*Cello Concerto in B Minor* [1895]).

The Sonata

The Romantic sonata developed similarly to the symphony and concerto, with the main trends being the interrelation of themes between movements and the interlocking or merging of movements. As in the symphony, Beethoven's influence was all-pervasive throughout the period.

SCHUBERT

Schubert's sonatas include some twenty-three for piano (including incomplete works) and ten ensemble sonatas. Perhaps the finest are the last three piano sonatas: D. 958, C minor; D. 959, A major; and, above all, D. 960, B-flat major (all composed in 1828). The last of these is noteworthy in particular for its expansive form and beautiful, lyric melodies.

WEBER

Carl Maria von Weber (1786–1826), noted for his operas, was also a significant pioneer of the Romantic sonata. He left at least fourteen sonatas.

MENDELSSOHN

Mendelssohn's sonatas include six for piano, six or seven for piano and one other instrument, and six for organ. About half, including all the piano sonatas, were written by his eighteenth year. Of these, the two earliest piano sonatas, written when he was twelve, are among the most remarkable examples of musical precocity in Western musical history. The cello sonata, Op. 58, ranks with Mendelssohn's best chamber music, and the six organ sonatas, Op. 65, are among the most popular works in that genre.

SCHUMANN

Schumann's most important sonatas are his three full-scale sonatas for piano (Op. 11, F-sharp minor; Op. 14, F minor; and Op. 22, G minor) and two sonatas for violin and piano (Op. 105, A minor; Op. 121, D minor).

BRAHMS

After Beethoven, Brahms ranks first in importance in the history of the sonata. His sonatas include three early works for piano (Op. 1, C major; Op. 2, F-sharp minor; and Op. 5, F minor); three for violin and piano (Op. 78, G minor, 1879; Op. 100, A major, 1886; Op. 108, D minor, 1888); two for cello and piano (Op. 38, E minor, 1865; Op. 99, F major, 1886); and two for clarinet and piano (Op. 120, F minor, E-flat major; 1894). The Op. 5 sonata is a particular favorite among pianists; the D minor violin sonata is an excellent example of writing on a symphonic scale; and the clarinet sonatas are among the finest masterworks of Brahms's late style.

LISZT

Liszt's most important sonata is the *Sonata in B Minor* (1852–53). Its form is innovative, combining the separate sonata movements into one large (769-measure) sonata-form movement, with extensive thematic interrelationships and thematic transformation present throughout. This sonata thus represents the final step in the trend toward the merging of movements and increased thematic interrelationships, making it comparable to Liszt's solution in the *Piano Concerto No. 2 in A Major*.

Chamber Music

Because of its abstract nature, chamber music was cultivated primarily by those composers who retained the closest ties to Classical tradition: Schubert and Brahms above all, and Mendelssohn and Schumann to a lesser degree.

SCHUBERT

Schubert's mature chamber works include an Allegro in C minor for string quartet (D. 703; 1820); three complete string quartets (D. 804, A minor, 1824; D. 810, D minor, 1824–1826; D. 887, G major, 1826); an octet in F major (D. 803; 1824); two piano trios (D. 898, B-flat major, c. 1827; D. 929, E-flat major, 1827); and his chamber masterpiece, the *String Quintet in C Major* (D. 956, 1828). Also popular is his early *Piano Quintet in A Major* (D. 667, "Trout," 1819).

The *String Quartet in A Minor* is memorable for its poignantly sad first movement and minuet and its cheerful finale in Hungarian style. The *String Quartet in D Minor*, also serious in tone, is noteworthy for its second-movement set of variations on Schubert's song "Death and the Maiden" and for the fiery energy of its Presto finale. The *Octet in F Major*, a delightfully bright work, is a late example of the Classical-style divertimento. Most sublime of all is the *String Quintet in C Major*. Schubert's use of a second cello as the fifth instrument in this work, rather than the customary second viola, imbues it with a warm, rich timbre. In addition, its beautifully singing melodic lines, rich harmonics, and subtle instrumental interplay make it one of the loveliest examples of chamber music in the first half of the Romantic period.

MENDELSSOHN

Mendelssohn's chamber music includes piano trios, piano quartets, string quartets, two string quintets, a sextet for piano and strings, and an octet. Among the best of these are the *Octet in E-flat Major*, Op. 20 (1825); the *String Quartet in F Minor*, Op. 80 (1847); and the piano trios in D minor (Op. 49; 1839) and C minor (Op. 66; 1845).

SCHUMANN

Schumann's most important chamber works, all composed in 1842, include three string quartets, a piano quintet, a piano quartet, and *Phantasiestücke* (Fantasy Pieces) for piano trio (Op. 88). Of these, the *String Quartet in A Major*, Op. 41, and the *Piano Quintet*, Op. 44, are beautiful examples of his mature style.

BRAHMS

Brahms ranks first among nineteenth-century composers of chamber music and sonatas. Among his twenty-four chamber works are two string sextets, three string quartets, two string quintets, a clarinet quintet, three piano trios, a clarinet trio, a horn trio, three piano quartets, a piano quintet, and seven duo sonatas (discussed earlier), many of which are masterpieces of the highest order. Particularly to be recommended are the piano quartets in G minor (Op. 25; late 1850s) and C minor (Op. 60; 1874); the *Piano Quintet in F Minor* (Op. 34a; 1864); the late piano trios in C major (Op. 87; 1882) and C minor (Op. 101; 1886); the *String Quintet in G Major* (Op. 111;

1890); and, above all, the *Clarinet Quintet in B Minor* (Op. 115; 1891). In these works, as in his symphonies and sonatas, Brahms's mastery of the structural complexities of the Classical sonata cycle, expressed in a richly colored Romantic musical language, reveal him to be the true heir to the tradition of Haydn, Mozart, and Beethoven.

Romantic composers left a rich legacy of instrumental music both in traditional genres such as the symphony, concerto, and sonata and in newer genres such as the character piece for piano and the symphonic poem. These works comprise the bulk of today's concert repertoire. As in all periods, some composers retained closer ties to past tradition (e.g., Schubert, Mendelssohn, Brahms, and, to some extent, Schumann) while others were more progressive (e.g., Berlioz and Liszt).

For Additional Study

Cuyler, Louise. *The Symphony*. New York: Harcourt Brace Jovanovich. 1973.

Dickinson, Alan E. F. *The Music of Berlioz*. London: Faber. 1972.

Frisch, Walter, ed. *Schubert: Critical and Analytical Studies*. Lincoln: University of Nebraska Press. 1981.

Layton, Robert, ed. *A Companion to the Concerto*. New York: Schirmer Books. 1989.

Musgrave, Michael. *The Music of Brahms*. Boston: Routledge & Kegan Paul. 1985.

Newman, William S. *The Sonata Since Beethoven*. Chapel Hill, NC: University of North Carolina Press, 1970; 3d ed., New York: Norton, 1983.

Samson, Jim, ed. *Chopin Studies*. Cambridge, Eng.: Cambridge University Press. 1988.

Searle, Humphrey. *The Music of Liszt*. 2d rev. ed. New York: Dover. 1966.

Todd, R. Larry, ed. *Nineteenth-Century Piano Music*. New York: Schirmer Books. 1990.

The University of Delaware Videodisc Music Series. Disc 2: Hector Berlioz, *Symphonie fantastique*, Fifth Movement; Disc 4: Frédéric Chopin: *Polonaise*, Op. 53. Distributed by the University of Delaware (Newark, DE). Interactive videodisc.

Veinus, Abraham. *The Concerto*. New York: Dover. 1964.

Walker, A., ed. *Robert Schumann: The Man and His Music*. London: Barrie & Jenkins, 1972; 2d ed., 1976.

Recommended Listening

(Works by nationalist, late Romantic, and Impressionist composers appear in chapter 24.)

MUSIC FOR PIANO:

Brahms, Johannes. *Intermezzo in A Major*, Op. 118, No. 2

Chopin, Frédéric. *Ballade No.1 in G Minor*, Op. 23

___. *Études*: E major, Op. 10, No. 3; C minor ("Revolutionary"), Op. 10. No. 12

___. *Mazurkas*: B-flat major, Op. 7, No. 1; A minor, Op. 17, No. 4

___. Nocturnes: E-flat major, Op. 9, No. 2; B major, Op. 9, No. 3; F minor, Op. 55, No. 1

___. *Polonaise in A-flat Major*, Op. 53

___. *Preludes*: C major, Op. 28, No. 1; E minor, Op. 28, No. 4

___. *Waltzes*: D-flat major ("Minute Waltz"), Op. 64, No. 1; C-sharp minor, Op. 64, No. 2

Liszt, Franz. *Hungarian Rhapsody No. 2*

Mendelssohn, Felix. *Lieder ohne Worte* (Songs without Words): "Venetian Boat-Song No. 3" in A minor, Op. 62, No. 5; "Spinning Song" in C major, Op. 67. No. 4; "The Shepherd's Complaint" in B minor, Op. 67, No. 5

Schubert, Franz. *Four Impromptus*, D. 935

___. *Piano Sonata in B-flat Major*, D. 960.

Schumann, Robert. *Carnaval*, Op. 9

CHAMBER MUSIC:

Brahms, Johannes. *Clarinet Quintet in B Minor*, Op. 115

___. *Piano Quartet in G Minor*, Op. 25

___. *Piano Quintet in F Minor*, Op. 34a

___. *Sonatas for Clarinet and Piano*, Op. 120 (F minor, E-flat major)

Mendelssohn, Felix. *Piano Trios*: D minor, Op. 49; C minor, Op. 66

Schubert, Franz. *String Quartet in A Minor*, D. 804

___. *String Quintet in C Major*, D. 956

Schumann, Robert. *Piano Quintet in E-flat Major*, Op. 44

CONCERTO:

Brahms, Johannes. *Violin Concerto in D Major*, Op. 77

Liszt, Franz. *Piano Concerto No. 2 in A Major*

Mendelssohn, Felix. *Violin Concerto in E Minor*, Op. 64

Schumann, Robert. *Piano Concerto in A Minor*, Op. 54

SYMPHONY AND PROGRAM MUSIC:

Berlioz, Hector. *Symphonie fantastique*

Brahms, Johannes. Four Symphonies: No. 1 in C minor, Op. 68; No. 2 in D major, Op. 73; No. 3 in F major, Op. 90; No. 4 in E minor, Op. 98

Liszt, Franz. *A Faust Symphony*

___. *Les Préludes*

Mendelssohn, Felix. Incidental Music to *A Midsummer Night's Dream*

___. *Symphony No. 4 in A Major* ("Italian"), Op. 90

Schubert, Franz. *Symphony No. 8 in B Minor* ("Unfinished"), D. 759; *Symphony No. 9 in C Major* ("Great"), D. 944

Schumann, Robert. *Symphony No. 4 in D Minor*. Op. 120

23

Vocal Music in the Romantic Period

1813 Rossini wins his first international acclaim with *Tancredi* and *L'italiana in Algeri*

1814 Schubert, "Gretchen am Spinnrade," his first masterpiece

1816 Rossini, *Il barbiere di Siviglia*, his operatic masterpiece

1821 Weber, *Der Freischütz*, establishes German Romantic opera

1828 Schubert, *Mass in E-flat Major* (D. 950) and his death

1829 Rossini, *Guillaume Tell*, his last opera

1830 D. F. E. Auber, *Fra Diavolo*; Donizetti's first major operatic success (*Anna Bolena*)

1831 Meyerbeer, *Robert le diable*, establishes French grand opera; Bellini, *La sonnambula* and *Norma*

1832 Wagner's first opera (*Die Hochzeit*)

1835 Halévy, *La Juive*; Donizetti, *Lucia di Lammermoor*; Bellini, *I Puritani*

1836 Meyerbeer, *Les Huguenots*; Mendelssohn, *St. Paul*

1837 Berlioz, *Requiem*

1840 Schumann's "Year of Song": over 100 Lieder, including the cycles *Frauenliebe und Leben* and *Dichterliebe*

1842 Wagner's *Rienzi* performed, his first operatic triumph; Verdi, *Nabucco*, his first great operatic success

1843 Donizetti, *Don Pasquale*, his comic masterpiece

1845 Wagner, *Tannhäuser*

1846 Mendelssohn, *Elijah*

1848 Wagner, *Lohengrin* (first performed 1850)

1853 Verdi, *Il trovatore* and *La traviata*, the culmination of his first period

1855 Offenbach, *Orphée aux enfers*

1859 Gounod, *Faust*; Wagner, *Tristan und Isolde*

1863 First performance of Part 2 of Berlioz's *Les Troyens*

1867 Wagner, *Die Meistersinger*

1869 Brahms, *Alto Rhapsody*; first performance of *Ein deutsches Requiem* establishes Brahms as a composer

1871 Verdi, *Aïda*, the culmination of his middle period

1874 First performance of Musorgsky's *Boris Godunov*; Johann Strauss II, *Die Fledermaus*; Verdi, *Requiem*

1875 First performance of Bizet's *Carmen*

1876 Wagner's Bayreuth Theater opens and the *Ring* cycle is performed in its entirety

1881 Mahler, *Das klagende Lied*, his first important work

1882 Wagner, *Parsifal*

1883 Death of Wagner

1887 Verdi, *Otello*, his greatest serious opera

1888 Wolf, *Gedichte von Mörike*

1890 First performance of Part 1 of Berlioz's *Les Troyens*; first performance of Mascagni's *Cavalleria rusticana*

1892 Leoncavallo, *I Pagliacci*

1893 Verdi, *Falstaff*, his last opera; success of Puccini's *Manon Lescaut* establishes his fame outside of Italy

1894 Fauré, *La bonne chanson*

1897 Death of Brahms

1899 Mahler, *Des Knaben Wunderhorn*

1900 Puccini, *Tosca*

1901 Death of Verdi

*V*ocal *music continued to flourish during the Romantic period, particularly opera and a new genre, the art song. While choral music was of secondary importance, composers made notable contributions in this area as well.*

ART SONG

The term *art song* denotes a category of solo vocal song, normally with piano accompaniment. Unlike the folk song, the art song is the creation of a single composer rather than "the people." Unlike both the folk song and the popular song, it is a work of serious artistic intent. Finally, unlike the operatic aria, it is often a single independent piece rather than part of a larger structure, although composers have sometimes chosen to group several songs into a set, called a *song cycle* (see below).

Despite the importance of song throughout the history of Western music, the art song as a genre was a product of the Romantic period. It arose from (1) an outpouring of lyric poetry, especially in Germany, at a time when composers felt a deep affinity for literature and a desire to unite music and poetry, and (2) the perfection of the piano as an ideal accompanying instrument, capable of the most subtle expressive nuances.

In its ability to convey lyric and intimate expression in a concise form, the art song is the counterpart of the character piece for piano. German art song comprises the most important body of literature in this category, followed by French and Russian.

Characteristics of Art Song

COMPONENTS

The chief components of the art song are the text, vocal melody, and accompaniment.

Text. Art song composers of the Romantic era drew particularly on the poems of the nineteenth-century German authors Johann Wolfgang von Goethe, Friedrich Schiller, Heinrich Heine, Wilhelm Müller, Eduard Mörike, Friedrich Rückert, and Joseph von Eichendorff; the Englishman George Gordon, Lord Byron; and the French poets Paul Verlaine, Stéphane Mallarmé, and Charles Baudelaire. The favorite subjects were love and unrequited love, nature, and the fleeting quality of life and happiness. Art song texts deeply affected the shape and character of the music, while the music, in turn, enhanced the emotion and meaning of the text.

Vocal Melody. Composers carefully constructed the vocal melody of the art song to reflect the general mood of the poetry and sometimes even to depict specific words, in the manner of earlier word painting. Melodies were more often lyric in quality than dramatic.

Accompaniment. Although the art song is normally composed for piano accompaniment, occasionally composers have used orchestral accompaniment for more elaborate settings (e.g., many of the songs of Gustav Mahler). The accompaniment supports the vocal melody, and it often provides a brief introduction, interludes, and a postlude.

Composers give considerable attention to the accompaniment, which, like the melody, aids the effective musical expression of the text. Often the accompaniment is of equal importance to the vocal melody. An example of the effective use of accompaniment is Schubert's "Gretchen am Spinnrade" (Gretchen at the Spinning Wheel), which uses a fast repetitive figure to represent both the whirring of the spinning wheel and Gretchen's restlessness as she sings of her lover. The accompaniment pauses momentarily on the word *kiss* while Gretchen reflects, then haltingly begins again as the song resumes.

FORM

The musical form of an art song is partly determined by its poetic structure, although composers exhibit some freedom in establishing the setting of the text. Poetry is usually written in units of several lines; these are known as *stanzas* or *strophes*. Strophes, subdivided into phrases or periods (see chapter 8), constitute the main structural units of a song. The total length of a song is determined by the length and number of strophes.

There are four main form types used in art song: (1) strophic, (2) through-composed, (3) modified strophic, and (4) *scena*.

Strophic Form. In strophic settings, each stanza of the poem has the same music. Schubert's "Heidenröslein " (Little Heath Rose) and "An Sylvia" (Who Is Sylvia?) exemplify this form.

Through-composed Form. The term *through-composed* comes from the German word *durchkomponiert*. A through-composed song is composed from beginning to end without repetitions of whole sections, enabling it to follow the changing moods or ideas of the text and to mirror every shade of meaning in the words. Schubert's "Erlkönig" (Erlking) is an example of this form type.

Modified Strophic Form. In this type of form, some of the strophes are set to identical music, while others or parts of others are set to different music. Some examples of this are Schubert's "Die Forelle" (The Trout) and "Du bist die Ruh' " (You Are Rest).

Scena. A *scena*, comparable to an operatic scene, has a free sectional structure, with different episodes in varying tempos and moods. An example is Schubert's "Die Erwartung" (Expectation).

SONG CYCLE

A group of art songs based on a common theme or on an actual story line connecting the various poems is known as a *song cycle*. The individual songs can be performed both separately and in sequence in the cycle itself. Beethoven's *An die ferne Geliebte* (To the Distant Beloved, Op. 98; 1816) was the first song cycle of the nineteenth century. Many later nineteenth-century composers contributed to this genre (discussed below), as have a number of composers in the twentieth century.

German Art Song

During the nineteenth century, examples of the German art song (*Lied*; plural, *Lieder*) far outnumbered those from other countries, partly because of the special character of the German Romantic movement, with its tremendous wealth of lyric poetry and the intense literary interests of German composers. The principal Lieder composers were Schubert, Schumann, Brahms, Wolf, and Mahler.

SCHUBERT

Schubert was the first major proponent of the Lied. Although he suffered from poverty, ill health, and lack of public recognition, he was an unusually prolific composer, sometimes writing six or seven Lieder in a single morning. In addition to his many instrumental and larger vocal works, he left over 600 Lieder, despite his death at the young age of thirty-one. His incredible gift for writing beautiful melodies, his sensitivity to harmonic color, his wonderfully varied and apt piano accompaniments, his settings that reflect every nuance of his texts, and his unique blend of Classical formality and Romantic tenderness set the standard for the future high quality of the German Lied. In addition to his many independent songs, Schubert wrote two excellent song cycles, *Die schöne Müllerin* (The Fair Maid of the Mill, D. 795; 1823) and *Die Winterreise* (Winter Journey, D. 911; 1827), both based on poems of Wilhelm Müller. (*Schwanengesang*, a collection published after his death, was not intended as a cycle.)

SCHUMANN

With Schumann, who so suffered from emotional turmoil that he spent his last years in an asylum, we encounter a fully-blown Romantic style, characterized by warmly lyric melodies, colorful harmonies, and a wide range of emotional expression. Schumann's songs are particularly notable for their beautiful wedding of words and music and for the equal partnership between the voice and piano.

Nearly 150 of Schumann's more than 300 Lieder were written in his "year of song," 1840, the year of his marriage to Clara Wieck, the daughter of his music teacher and herself the first woman to have an international career as a pianist. Among his works are several song cycles, the best known of which are two written in 1840: *Dichterliebe* (A Poet's Love) and *Frauenliebe und Leben* (A Woman's Love and Life).

BRAHMS

Influenced by the Lieder of Schubert and Schumann, Brahms wrote over 250 songs, plus folk song arrangements and two masterful cycles: *Romanzen aus L. Tiecks Magdelone* (Romances from L. Tieck's *Magdelone*, Op. 33; published between 1868 and 1869) and his masterpieces in the genre, *Vier ernste Gesänge* (Four Serious Songs, Op. 121; 1896), based on biblical texts.

In general, Brahms's songs have a serious, restrained quality, although he did write some humorous Lieder. Particularly poignant are his settings of poems that reflect on death, such as "Feldeinsamkeit," Op. 86, No. 2; "Immer leiser wird mein Schlummer," Op. 105, No. 2; and "Auf dem Kirchhofe," Op. 105, No. 4. The Vier ernste Gesänge also deal with the subject of death, progressing from a pessimistic outlook in the first two songs, to acceptance of death in the third, to praise of love (charity) as the greatest of Christian virtues in the fourth.

WOLF

Hugo Wolf (1860–1903) composed 250 highly expressive Lieder in a late Romantic style influenced by Richard Wagner and characterized by flexible phrases, sensitive text settings, frequently chromatic harmony, balanced treatment of vocal line and accompaniment, and a preference for modified strophic and through-composed form. Though he wrote no song cycles, he published several collections of songs based on poems by a single author (Mörike, Eichendorff, Goethe, Michelangelo) and on translations of Spanish poems (two *Spanisches Liederbucher*) and Italian poems (two *Italienisches Liederbucher*). Like Schumann, he spent his last years in an asylum.

MAHLER

The Bohemian-born composer Gustav Mahler (1860–1911), a major composer of Lieder and symphonies at the end of the Romantic period, left three volumes of *Lieder und Gesänge* (Lieder and Songs) for voice and piano and several collections of Lieder for one or more solo voices and orchestra. Among the latter are such works as *Lieder eines fahrenden Gesellen* (Songs of a Wayfarer; 1883–1885); *Des Knaben Wunderhorn* (The Boy's Magic Horn; 1892–1899); *Kindertotenlieder* (Songs about the Deaths of Children; 1901–1904); and *Das Lied von der Erde* (The Song of the Earth; 1908–1909).

Mahler's music has a uniquely personal, bittersweet, turn-of-the-century *Weltschmerz* (world-weariness) that is summarized perfectly by a recurring phrase that appears in the first song of *Das Lied von der Erde*: "Dark is life, is death." Equally pessimistic about the prospects of life and of death, Mahler captured exquisitely the ambivalence that reigned at the turn of the century as the Austrian empire faded, old traditions crumbled, and the world headed for war.

OTHER COMPOSERS

Among the many other composers who wrote Lieder were Carl Loewe (1796–1869), Mendelssohn, Peter Cornelius (1824–1874), and Richard Strauss.

French Art Song

A small but excellent body of French art song, known as *mélodie*, was cultivated in the second half of the nineteenth century and the early twentieth century by such composers as Berlioz, Gabriel Fauré (1845–1924), Ernest

Chausson (1855–1899), Henri Duparc (1848–1933), and Claude Debussy (1862–1918). Fauré is noted for several song cycles, among them *La bonne chanson* (The Good Song; 1892–1894) and *L'horizon chimérique* (The Chimerical Horizon; 1921). Debussy's most important songs are the two sets of *Fêtes galantes* (Gallant Festivals; 1891, 1904); *Chansons de Bilitis* (1898); and *Trois ballades de Villon* (Three Ballades of Villon; 1910).

Russian Art Song

The most important Russian composers of art songs were Tchaikovsky, Sergey Rachmaninoff (1873–1943), Alexander Gretchaninov (1864–1956), Reinhold Glière (1875–1956), and Modest Musorgsky (1839–1881). Musorgsky's songs, among the best of the nineteenth century, include three song cycles: *Detskaya* (The Nursery; 1872), *Bez solntsa* (Sunless; 1874), and *Pesni i plyaski smerti* (Songs and Dances of Death; 1874).

CHORAL MUSIC

Following the precedent of Beethoven in his *Ninth Symphony*, Romantic composers (e.g., Berlioz, Liszt, and Mahler) sometimes included vocal soloists and chorus in their symphonies and other large orchestral works. In such works, they often treated the chorus as simply another orchestral "color." In addition, they also continued to write oratorios, Masses, and other works in which the chorus was of primary interest.

Oratorio

The Romantic oratorio flourished primarily in England and Germany. Oratorios were modeled after those of Handel and the Classical masters, adapted to the new Romantic musical language and expanded orchestral resources.

Among the principal oratorios of the period are Mendelssohn's *Paulus* (St. Paul; 1836) and *Elias* (Elijah; 1846); Berlioz's *L'Enfance du Christ* (The Infancy of Christ; 1854); Liszt's *Die Legende von der heiligen Elisabeth* (The Legend of St. Elizabeth; 1862) and *Christus* (1867); Brahms's *Ein deutsches Requiem* (A German Requiem, Op. 45; 1868), set to passages from the German Bible rather than the traditional liturgical text; César Franck's (1822–1890) *Les béatitudes* (The Beatitudes; 1879); and Sir Edward Elgar's (1857–1934) *The Dream of Gerontius* (1900).

Masses and Other Sacred Choral Music

Notable works in this category include Schubert's six Masses, particularly the last two (A-flat major, D. 678; E-flat major, D. 950); Gioacchino Rossini's (1792–1868) *Stabat Mater* (1832, 1841); Mendelssohn's Psalm settings; Brahms's motets for female chorus (Opp. 29, 74, and 110); Berlioz's monumental *Requiem* (1837) and *Te Deum* (1849); Liszt's Festival Mass for the consecration of the cathedral at Gran, Hungary (1855), and his *Hungarian Coronation Mass* (1867); Verdi's superb *Requiem* (1874); Charles Gounod's (1818–1893) *St. Cecilia Mass* (1885); Fauré's lovely *Requiem* (1887); and Anton Bruckner's (1824–1896) many sacred works.

One of the most popular of all large Romantic choral works is Verdi's *Requiem*, a monumental work (a little over ninety minutes in length) for four vocal soloists, chorus, and large orchestra. Although it is a setting of the traditional text of the Requiem Mass, it has the drama and general musical style of a Verdi opera. Among its many immortal musical moments, a few that may be mentioned include the hushed opening chorus (*Requiem aeternam*); the *Kyrie* for the four soloists and chorus; the mighty *Dies irae*, with its thunderous opening, off-stage trumpets in the *Tuba miram* section, lovely *Recordare* and *Ingemisco*, and plaintive *Lacrymosa*; the *Sanctus*, with its jubilant contrapuntal choral writing; and the closing *Libera me*.

Cantata

In reference to compositions of the Romantic period, the term *cantata* refers loosely to a concert work for chorus, perhaps one or more vocal soloists, and orchestra that is smaller in scale than an oratorio, usually less dramatic, and often based on a secular subject. Among the leading compositions in this genre are Mendelssohn's six secular cantatas, particularly *Die erste Walpurgisnacht* (Op. 60; 1832); Berlioz's *La damnation de Faust* (The Damnation of Faust; 1846); Schumann's *Das Paradies und die Peri* (Paradise and the Peri; 1843); and, above all, several of Brahms's masterful works: the *Alt-Rhapsodie* (Alto Rhapsody, Op. 53; 1869), the *Schicksalslied* (Song of Destiny, Op. 54; 1871), *Nänie* (Op. 82; 1881), and the *Gesang der Parzen* (Song of the Fates, Op. 89; 1882).

Brahms's *Alto Rhapsody*, for contralto solo, male chorus, and orchestra, is an outstanding example of this genre. Much shorter than an oratorio—less than fifteen minutes in length—it presents in concise form and with profound emotional depth the vision of a lost soul filled with hate and a prayer to God to renew his spirit.

OPERA

The Romantic period was a glorious age of opera, an age of such giants as Rossini, Donizetti, Bellini, Verdi, Wagner, and Puccini. Indeed, the great majority of the operas in today's repertory date from this century, when composers wore their hearts on their sleeves and aimed unabashedly at sweeping up the audience in the passions and conflicts of the characters on the stage. The main centers of operatic activity were in France, Italy, and Germany.

France

In Paris, the operatic capital of Europe during the first half of the nineteenth century, three types of opera flourished: grand opera and opéra comique in the first half of the century and lyric opera in the second half.

GRAND OPERA

Influenced by the French tradition of operatic spectacle dating back to Lully, by the rise of large-scale "heroic" operas during the late eighteenth and early nineteenth centuries (e.g., G. Spontini's *La Vestale* of 1807), and by the post-Revolutionary French bourgeois taste for the big and spectacular, a new type of opera arose during the second quarter of the nineteenth century. Known as *grand opera*, this new type of production is characterized by (1) serious plots dealing with historical topics or current events; (2) huge choruses, crowd scenes, elaborate ballet entertainments (*divertissements*), and ornate costumes and scenery; (3) an emphasis on action over lyric song, with a resulting predominance of narrative singing over arias; (4) prominent use of ensembles of all sizes, ranging from duets to full chorus; and (5) expanded orchestral resources.

The leading composer of grand opera was Giacomo Meyerbeer (1791–1864), whose principal works include *Robert le diable* (Robert the Devil, 1831), the opera that established the genre; *Les Huguenots* (1836); *Le Prophète* (The Prophet, 1849); and *L'Africaine* (The African, produced posthumously, 1865). Others include D. F. E. Auber's (1782–1871) *La muette de Portici* (The Deaf Girl of Portici, 1828); Rossini's *Guillaume Tell* (William Tell, 1829); and Jacques Halévy's (1799–1862) *La Juive* (The Jewess, 1835). Grand opera also influenced works by Bellini (*I Puritani*), Verdi (*Les vêpres siciliennes* and *Aïda*), and Wagner (*Rienzi*).

OPÉRA COMIQUE

Opéra comique continued to flourish, using smaller performing forces than grand opera, a simpler musical style, and spoken dialogue rather than recitative. Plots ranged from broad comedy to more serious drama. Representative works include *La Dame blanche* (The White Lady, 1825) by Adrien Boieldieu (1775–1834); *Zampa* (1831) and *Le pré aux clercs* (The Field of

Honor, 1832) by Ferdinand Hérold (1791–1833); and *Fra Diavolo* (Brother Devil, 1830) by Auber. George Bizet's (1838–1875) *Carmen* (1875), one of the finest, and today one of the most popular, operas of the century, was also first classified as an opéra comique because of its use of spoken dialogue, despite its tragic plot and gritty realism. (Recitatives were added after Bizet's death.)

After 1850 a new type of comic opera emerged—*opéra bouffe*, which was lighter in style and placed more emphasis on wit and satire. Its chief exponent was Jacques Offenbach (1819–80), whose major works are *Orphée aux enfers* (Orpheus in the Underworld, 1855) and *La belle Hélène* (Beautiful Helen, 1864). Offenbach's works influenced the development of *operetta*, another form of comic opera, which is light and sentimental in character and contains spoken dialogue and dancing. The leading operetta composers were Gilbert and Sullivan in England (*H.M.S. Pinafore*, *The Mikado*, and others) and Johann Strauss II in Vienna (e.g., *Die Fledermaus* [The Bat], 1874).

LYRIC OPERA

Lyric opera, a type of all-sung opera midway between opéra comique and grand opera, emerged after 1850. Charles Gounod's *Faust* (1859) is the most famous example of lyric opera. Other examples include *Mignon* (1866) by Ambroise Thomas (1811–1896) and Bizet's *Les pêcheurs de perles* (The Pearl Fishers, 1863).

OTHER OPERAS

Among other important French operas of the period are Berlioz's *Benvenuto Cellini* (1838) and the Romantic consummation of the French heroic tradition, *Les Troyens* (The Trojans; 1856–1858); *Lakmé* (1883) by Léo Delibes (1836–1891); *Samson et Dalila* (Samson and Delilah, 1877) by Camille Saint-Saëns (1835–1921); and *Manon* (1884) and *Thaïs* (1894) by Jules Massenet (1842–1912).

Italy

Because of its well-established operatic tradition, Italian opera was less affected by the experimentation that swept other countries during the Romantic period and remained generally more conservative. Italian composers retained the distinction between opera seria and opera buffa, for example, until opera buffa gradually faded in importance as composers turned more exclusively to serious subjects. But, above all, Romantic Italian opera remained a "singer's opera." Even in the works of such composers as Verdi and Puccini, who explored orchestral colors fully and expertly, the orchestra never predominated as it did in German opera. Rather, the focus remained on the expression of human emotions through beautiful singing, resulting in some of the most memorable vocal writing ever produced.

The leading Italian opera composers of the nineteenth century are among the most popular opera composers of all time: Rossini, Gaetano Donizetti (1797–1848), and Vincenzo Bellini (1801–1835) of the first half of the century; Giuseppe Verdi (1813–1901) of the second half of the century; and, at the very end of the century, Giacomo Puccini (1858–1924).

ROSSINI, DONIZETTI, AND BELLINI

Rossini. Rossini was the leading Italian opera composer of the early nineteenth century, internationally renowned for both his serious and his comic operas. In their clarity of form and lightness of texture, his operas mark the transition from Classical to Romantic styles. In addition, their catchy melodies, lively rhythms, imaginative orchestration, witty character- izations, and memorable stage effects make them as fresh and engaging today as they were in Rossini's day.

Although he wrote many fine serious operas—e.g., *Tancredi* (1813), *Otello* (1816), *La donna del lago* (The Lady of the Lake, 1819), and the grand opera *Guillaume Tell* (1829)—Rossini is most remembered today for his comic operas. Among these are *L'italiana in Algeri* (The Italian Woman in Algiers; 1813); *La Cenerentola* (Cinderella; 1817); *La gazza ladra* (The Thieving Magpie; 1817); and his masterpiece, *Il barbiere di Siviglia* (The Barber of Seville; 1816), which ranks with Mozart's *Figaro* and Verdi's *Falstaff* among the finest Italian comic operas.

Donizetti. Donizetti dominated Italian bel canto opera after Rossini's retirement in 1830. In his approximately seventy operas, both serious and comic, the often highly ornate vocal line clearly dominates the orchestra. A favorite aria form of Donizetti, as of other Italian composers of the time, is the *cavatina*, an expressive slow movement, followed by a *cabaletta*, a virtuosic allegro section with usually an exciting climactic ending. Among Donizetti's most-performed operas today are the serious opera *Lucia di Lammermoor* (1835), with its famous Sextet and "Mad Scene"; the comic operas *L'elisir d'amore* (The Elixir of Love; 1832) and *Don Pasquale* (1843), his comic masterpiece; and the opéra comique, *La fille du régiment* (The Daughter of the Regiment; 1840).

Bellini. The operas of Bellini, who died at age thirty-four, are more refined than Donizetti's, with subtler harmonies, exquisitely shaped melo- dies reminiscent of Chopin's, and an approach that blends bel canto lyricism and dramatic tension. Chief among his operas, all serious, are *I Capuleti e i Montecchi* (The Capulets and the Montagues; 1830); *La sonnambula* (The Sleepwalker; 1831); *Norma* (1831); and *I Puritani* (The Puritans; 1835).

VERDI

The dominant figure in Italian opera during the second half of the nineteenth century, Verdi was a popular hero whose strong nationalistic feelings led him to resist foreign influences in his operas and to develop national operatic tendencies to their highest perfection. Blessed with an unerring sense of theater and an unsurpassed melodic gift, Verdi brought to Italian opera a virile, even brutal, dramatic passion and directness of expression.

Characteristics. Beginning in a Donizetti-influenced style, Verdi's operas—nearly all of which are on serious subjects—show a steady growth toward more refinement and depth of characterization, closer interrelationships between plot and music, more varied and prominent use of the orchestra, more venturesome harmonies, and a more seamless flow of musical and dramatic action. Though his last two operas came to resemble Wagner's in their greater use of the orchestra and almost continuous music (as opposed to separate independent numbers), they do not represent a departure from Italian tradition but instead are the logical culmination of its tendencies. Moreover, Verdi never embraced the German preference for mythological and supernatural themes or the concept of the character as symbol. He remained instead unswervingly true to the Italian conception of opera as the expression of *human* emotions through *vocal* melody.

Operas. Verdi's best first-period operas show considerable growth, from the raw emotion of such early successes as *Nabucco* (1842) and *Attila* (1846) to the powerful characterizations of *Rigoletto* (1851) and *Il trovatore* (The Troubadour; 1853) and the more refined style of *La traviata* (The Fallen Woman; 1853). His middle-period operas show continued growth in character delineation, orchestration, harmonic inventiveness, and flexibility of form. The principal works of this period are *Un ballo in maschera* (A Masked Ball; 1859); *La forza del destino* (The Force of Destiny; 1862, revised 1869); and the culminating work, *Aïda* (1871), which sums up all of Verdi's developments to date and represents a fusion of Italian "human" opera and French "heroic" grand opera.

Sixteen years later, Verdi—then nearing the age of eighty—came out of retirement to produce his last two operas, *Otello* (1887) and *Falstaff* (1893), both set to dramas by Shakespeare. Incorporating all of the advances noted earlier, these two sublime masterworks represent the apex of 300 years of Italian operatic tradition: *Otello*, the culmination of serious opera; *Falstaff*, the culmination of comic opera.

PUCCINI AND OTHER VERISMO COMPOSERS

At the end of the nineteenth century a new type of realistic opera arose, called *verismo opera.* Influenced by the literary works of Flaubert, Zola, and others, verismo opera emphasized everyday events of the lives of common people. Pietro Mascagni's (1863–1954) *Cavalleria rusticana* (Rustic Chivalry; 1890) and Ruggiero Leoncavallo's (1858–1919) *I pagliacci* (The Clowns; 1892) exemplify this style. So do the operas of Giacomo Puccini (1858–1924), which rival Verdi's in popularity with today's audiences and often surpass them in lushness of orchestration, richness of harmony, and

Romantic sentimentality. Among Puccini's best-known operas are *La bohème* (The Bohemian Girl; 1896); *Tosca* (1900); *Madama Butterfly* (1904); and *Turandot* (unfinished at his death).

Germany

German opera, of minor importance during the eighteenth century, enjoyed a golden age during the nineteenth, beginning with the Romantic opera of the first half of the century and culminating in the music dramas of Richard Wagner (1813–1883) in the second half. In Wagner's operas especially the Romantic tendencies toward nationalism, medievalism, magic, and experimentation in harmony and form found their fullest expression.

ROMANTIC OPERA

During the first quarter of the nineteenth century, the Singspiel evolved into full-fledged German Romantic opera. This new genre was characterized by (1) a preference for subjects drawn from medieval legends, folklore, and fairy tales; (2) an interest in supernatural elements and in wild, mysterious nature; (3) an emphasis on mood, atmosphere, and setting over characterization and human conflicts, with the result that vocal melody plays a less prominent role than it does in Italian opera; (4) frequent use of folk songs or folklike melodies in addition to conventional arias; (5) much use of harmonic and orchestral colors for dramatic expression; and (6) a tendency to treat characters not simply as individuals but as symbols (e.g., of good or evil). The leading composer of German Romantic opera was Carl Maria von Weber, whose chief works were *Der Freischütz* (1821), which established the genre, *Euryanthe* (1823), and *Oberon* (1826).

WAGNER AND THE MUSIC DRAMA

No other late Romantic composer exerted a greater influence on the future course of music than did Richard Wagner, the charismatic genius who dominated German opera during the second half of the nineteenth century. In addition to bringing German Romantic opera to its culmination and forging a new type of opera, the *music drama*, his masterful orchestrations, his manner of developing motives, and his innovations in musical form influenced later composers of orchestral music and operas alike. Moreover, the extreme chromaticism and wide-ranging modulations of several of his late operas brought major-minor tonality to its breaking point, opening the door to the radical developments of the early twentieth century.

Early Operas. Wagner's early operas were in established traditions. *Rienzi* (1840, performed 1842), his first success, was a grand opera, and his next operas—*Der fliegende Holländer* (The Flying Dutchman; 1841, performed 1843), *Tannhäuser* (1845), and *Lohengrin* (1848, performed 1850)— brought German Romantic opera to its peak. Yet already in these, the characteristics that were to mark his later operas began to emerge: the use of myths, legends, and German history as his sole subject matter; the countering of supernatural forces by the idea of redemption; and the expansion of the role of the orchestra (all beginning in *The Flying Dutchman*); the increased use of chromaticism (beginning in *Tannhäuser*); and the use of recurring themes, together with a gradual abandonment of clear distinctions between recitative and aria in favor of a more flexible arioso style (beginning in *Lohengrin*).

Exile. In 1849 Wagner fled to Switzerland to avoid imprisonment for his participation in the May 1849 uprising. While in exile he formulated theories concerning the integration of music and drama. Among these was his theory about the *Gesamtkunstwerk* (unified art work), that is, a dramatic work that successfully fuses poetry, scenic design, staging, action, and music into an all-encompassing unity. He concluded that the orchestra should be the focal point of the drama. He also formulated the idea of the *Leitmotif* (leading motive), a musical theme or motive associated with a person, thing or idea in an opera, that sounds (usually in the orchestra) at each appearance or mention of the subject, to lead the listener through the opera. A Leitmotif may be varied or combined with other motives as the dramatic situation demands. The recurrence of Leitmotifs also contribute to the unity of the opera.

Wagner's Music Dramas. Wagner put his theories into practice in his later operas, which he called *music dramas*. In these he also did away with the traditional division of the music into separate numbers (arias, ensembles, ballets, and the like) in favor of a more seamless flow of music and a flexible arioso style known as *endless melody*.

Wagner's music dramas, for which he wrote his own librettos, include *Tristan und Isolde* (1859), epoch-making in its chromaticism; *Die Meistersinger von Nürnberg* (The Mastersingers of Nuremberg; 1861–1867), a comic opera that ranks with Verdi's *Falstaff*; *Parsifal* (1882), his last opera; and his most ambitious project, *Der Ring des Nibelungen* (The Ring of the Nibelung; 1848–1874), a cycle consisting of the four operas *Das Rheingold* (The Rhine Gold), *Die Walküre* (The Valkyrie), *Siegfried*, and *Die Götterdämmerung* (The Twilight of the Gods).

Composed over a period of a quarter century, the *Ring* cycle ranks as one of the greatest achievements of Western music. Its scope is huge: the four operas are respectively two-and-a-half hours, five hours, five hours, and six hours in length, and they deal with epic themes on a monumental scale with remarkable unity and coherence. Wagner's librettos for the cycle, drawn from Nordic myths and from legends taken from the medieval German epic, the *Nibelungenlied*, are filled with gods, demigods, heroes, giants, dwarfs, and magic. The drama—a tale of greed and the lust for power—revolves around the struggle of its characters to possess a ring made from Rhine gold which gives its owner unlimited power (although it also has a curse attached to it), a struggle that is resolved only when the ring is returned to the Rhine at the end of the cycle. In the *Ring* cycle, Wagner's use of a seamless flow of music (as opposed to separate numbers), endless melody, leitmotives, and the orchestra as a major "character" in the drama is at an extremely high level. The *Ring* cycle had its premiere at Bayreuth (in Bavaria) in 1876 in a theater especially designed by Wagner for his music dramas.

*F*rom the intimate scale of the art song to the monumental scale of Wagner's "Ring" cycle, vocal music of the nineteenth century reflects the Romantic spirit in infinitely varied ways. Romantic vocal music ranks with the finest vocal music of other periods and remains at the very heart of today's concert and operatic repertory.

For Additional Study

Ashbrook, William. *The Operas of Puccini.* New York: Oxford University Press. 1968.

Brown, Maurice J. E. *Schubert Songs.* Seattle: University of Washington Press. 1967.

Budden, Julian. *The Operas of Verdi.* 3 vols. New York: Praeger. 1973–82.

Crosten, William L. *French Grand Opera: An Art and a Business.* New York: King's Crown Press, 1948; reprint, New York: Da Capo Press, 1972.

Dahlhaus, Carl. *Richard Wagner's Music Dramas.* Translated by Mary Whittall. Cambridge, Eng., and New York: Cambridge University Press. 1979.

Dean, Winton. *Georges Bizet: His Life and His Work.* 3d ed. London: Dent. 1975.

Dent, Edward J. *The Rise of Romantic Opera.* Edited by Winton Dean. Cambridge, Eng.: Cambridge University Press. 1976.

Gossett, P., et al. *The New Grove Masters of Italian Opera.* New York: Norton. 1983.

Grout, Donald J. *A Short History of Opera.* 2d ed. New York: Columbia University Press. 1965.

Harrison, Max. *The Lieder of Brahms.* New York: Praeger. 1972.

Sams, Eric. *The Songs of Hugo Wolf.* London: Methuen, 1961; 2d ed., 1981.

———. *The Songs of Robert Schumann.* 2d ed. London: Methuen. 1975.

The University of Delaware Videodisc Music Series. Disc 3: Karl Loewe, Johann F. Reichardt, Franz Schubert, *Erlkönig*; Johannes Brahms, *Schaffe in Mir, Gott*; Giacomo Puccini, *La bohème* (selected scenes). Distributed by the University of Delaware (Newark, DE). Interactive videodisc.

Recommended Listening

ART SONG AND SONG CYCLE:

Brahms, Johannes. *Romanzen aus L. Tiecks Magdelone*, Op. 33 (song cycle); "Die Mainacht," Op. 43, No. 2; "Wiegenlied," Op. 49, No. 4 (the famous "Brahms Lullaby"); "Feldeinsamkeit," Op. 86, No. 2; "Immer leiser wird mein Schlummer," Op. 105, No. 2; "Auf dem Kirchhofe," Op. 105, No. 4; *Vier ernste Gesänge*, Op. 121 (song cycle)

Debussy, Claude. *Chansons de Bilitis*

Fauré, Gabriel. "Lydia"; "Après un rêve"; *La bonne chanson* (song cycle)

Mahler, Gustav. *Des Knaben Wunderhorn* (10 songs with orchestra); *Das Lied von der Erde* (song cycle, or symphony, for tenor, contralto or baritone, and orchestra)

Musorgsky, Modest. *Pesni i plyaski smerti* (Songs and Dances of Death; song cycle)

Schubert, Franz. "Gretchen am Spinnrade," D. 118; "Heidenröslein," D. 257; "Erlkönig," D. 328; "Der Wanderer," D. 489; "Du bist die Ruh'," D. 776; *Die schöne Müllerin*, D. 795 (song cycle); "An Sylvia," D. 891; *Die Winterreise*, D. 911 (song cycle); "Der Doppelgänger," (from *Schwanengesang*, D. 957)

Schumann, Robert. "Die beiden Grenadiere"; *Frauenliebe und Leben*, Op. 42 (song cycle); *Dichterliebe*, Op. 48 (song cycle)

Wolf, Hugo. *Gedichte von Mörike*: "Das verlassene Mägdlein," "In der Frühe"; *Spanisches Liederbuch*: "In dem Schatten meiner Locken"

CHORAL MUSIC:

Berlioz, Hector. *L'Enfance du Christ*; *Grande messe des morts* (Requiem)

Brahms, Johannes. *Ein deutsches Requiem* (A German Requiem), Op. 45; *Alt-Rhapsodie* (Alto Rhapsody), Op. 53; *Schicksalslied* (Song of Destiny), Op. 54

Mendelssohn, Felix. *Elias* (Elijah; oratorio)

Schubert, Franz. Masses in A-flat major (D. 678) and E-flat major (D. 950)

Verdi, Giuseppe. *Requiem*

OPERA:

Bellini, Vincenzo. *Norma*: "Casta diva"

Berlioz, Hector. *Les Troyens*: "Lament of Cassandra" (Act 1); Chorus, "Gloire, gloire à Didon" (Act 3); "Hunt Scene" (Act 3); Septet and Chorus, "Tout n'est que paix et charme," and Duet, "Nuit d'ivresse et d'extase infinie!" (Act 4); "Dido's Immolation" (Act 5)

Bizet, Georges. *Carmen*: "Habanera"; "Séguidille" ("Près des remparts"); "Toréador en garde" ("Toreador Song"); "Je dis que rien"; Quintet, "Nous avons en tête une affaire"

Donizetti, Gaetano. *L'elisir d'amore*: "Una furtiva lagrima"

___. *Lucia di Lammermoor*: "Sextet"; "Mad Scene"

Gounod, Charles. *Faust*: "Avant de quitter ces lieux"; "Ah! Je ris" ("Jewel Song"); "Vous qui faites l'endormie" ("Mephisto's Serenade"); "Le Veau d'Or"

Leoncavallo, Ruggiero. *I pagliacci*: "Vesti la giubba"

Meyerbeer, Giacomo. *Les Hugenots*: Duet, "Tu m'aimes?" (Act 4); Act 5, Scena and Trio

Puccini, Giacomo. *La bohème*: "Che gelida manina"; "Mi chiamano Mimi"; Duet, "O soave fanciulla"; "Quando m'en vo' " (Musetta's waltz)

___. *Madama Butterfly*: "Un bel dì vedremo"; "Flower Duet"

___. *Tosca*: "Vissi d'arte"; "Se la giurata fede"; "E lucevan le stelle"

___. *Turandot*: "Non piangere, Liù"; "Nessun dorma"; "Tu, che di gel sei cinta"

Rossini, Gioacchino. *Il barbiere di Siviglia*: "Largo al factotum"; "Una voce poco fa"; "La calunnia"

Verdi, Giuseppe. *Aïda*: "Celeste Aïda"; "Ritorna vincitor"; Act 2 Finale; "O patria mia"; Duet, "O terra, addio"

___. *Otello*: Iago's "Credo"; "Ora e per sempre addio!"; Act 3, Finale; Act 4 (complete)

___. *Rigoletto*: Ballata, "Questa o quella"; Aria, "Caro nome"; Scena, "Pari siamo!" and Duet, "Deh non parlare al misero"; Scena, "La rà, la rà, la la, la rà" and Aria, "Cortigiani, vil razza dannata"; Canzone, "La donna è mobile"; "Quartet" (Act 3)

___. *La traviata*: Violetta's scene from Act 1 ("Ah, fors' è lui," "Sempre libera"); "Di provenza"; Quintet, "Prendi, quest' é l'immagine"; Octet, "Di sprezzo degno si stesso rende"

___. *Il trovatore*: "Anvil Chorus"; "Stride la vampa!"; "Mal reggendo"; "Di quella pira"; Duet, "Ai nostri monti"

Wagner, Richard. *Die Götterdämmerung*: "Siegfried's Rhine Journey"; "Siegfried's Funeral March"; "Brünnhilde's Immolation"

___. *Lohengrin*: Prelude to Act 1; "Elsa's Dream"; "Bridal Chorus" (Act 3); "In fernem Land"

___. *Tannhäuser*: Overture; "Dich, teure Halle"; "Pilgrim's Chorus"; "Song to the Evening Star" ("O du mein holder Abendstern")

___. *Tristan und Isolde*: Prelude to Act 1; "Love Duet"; "Liebestod" ("Love Death");

___. *Die Walküre*: Beginning of Act 3 ("The Ride of the Valkyries"); Act 3, scene 3

Weber, Carl Maria von. *Der Freischütz*: Overture; Aria, "Durch die Wälder, durch die Auen"; Aria, "Leise, leise, fromme Weise"; Act 2 Finale: Wolf's Glen Scene

24

Nationalism, Late Romanticism, and Impressionism

1848 Revolutions in European capitals; Marx and Engels, *The Communist Manifesto*

1851 Melville, *Moby Dick*

1855 Whitman, *Leaves of Grass*

1857 Dred Scott decision

1859 Darwin, *Origin of Species;* John Brown raids Harpers Ferry

1861 American Civil War begins; serfs emancipated in Russia; unification of Italy

1863 *Emancipation Proclamation*

1865 Civil War ends; Lincoln assassinated

1866 First transatlantic cable; American Federation of Labor established

1867 Alaska purchased from Russia

1869 First transcontinental railway in United States; Suez Canal opens

1870 Franco-Prussian War; Schliemann excavates Troy

1871 Paris Commune; Unification of Germany; Bismark German chancellor

1872 Nietzsche, *Birth of Tragedy;* Monet, *Impression: Sunrise*

1874 First "Impressionist" group exhibition in Paris

1875 Tolstoy, *Anna Karinina*

1876 Bell invents telephone; Wagner opens theatre at Bayreuth; Mallarmé, *Afternoon of a Faun*

1877 Edison invents phonograph

1879 Sir George Grove, *Dictionary of Music and Musicians*

1880 Irish insurrection; Pavlov's experiments on conditioned reflexes; Dostoevsky, *The Brothers Karamazov*

1881 Tsar Alexander II killed; President Garfield shot; Panama Canal begun; Boston Symphony Orchestra founded; Renoir, *Boating Party Luncheon;* Henry James, *Portrait of a Lady*

1882 Koch discovers tuberculosis germ; Berlin Philharmonic founded; Manet, *Bar at the Folies Bergères*

1883 Daimler patents automobile engine; Metropolitan Opera House opens; Concertgebouw founded; Nietzsche, *Also sprach Zarathustra;* Stevenson, *Treasure Island*

1884 Pasteur develops inoculation against rabies; Twain, *Huckleberry Finn;* Seurat, *Sunday Afternoon on the Island of La Grande Jatte;* Rodin, *Burghers of Calais*

1885 First electric street car in United States; Brooklyn Bridge completed

1886 Rousseau, *Un Soir de carnaval*

1888 Van Gogh, *The Sunflowers*

1889 Paris International Exhibition; Eiffel Tower opens

1891 Doyle, *Adventures of Sherlock Holmes*

1892 First American automobile; Toulouse-Lautrec, *At the Moulin Rouge*

1895 X-rays discovered; Crane, *The Red Badge of Courage;* Homer, *Northeaster*

1896 Queen Victoria, Diamond Jubilee; first modern Olympic Games; radioactivity of uranium discovered; Gaugin, *Maternity*; Marconi invents wireless telegraph

1898 Spanish-American war; Radium discovered

1899 Boer War

1900 Chinese Boxer rebellion; Philadelphia Orchestra founded; Freud, *Interpretation of Dreams;* first dirigible; Conrad, *Lord Jim*

1901 Queen Victoria dies; Edward VII becomes King of England; Planck develops Quantum Theory

1903 Wright brothers' first successful flight; Shaw, *Man and Superman*

1904 Russo-Japanese war; Chekhov, *The Cherry Orchard;* Rolland, *Jean Christophe*

1905 Einstein, *Special Theory of Relativity;* first Russian Revolution

1906 San Francisco earthquake and fire; New Music Society of America formed to promote music of American composers

1907 First music broadcast on radio; Picasso, *Les Demoiselles d' Avignon*

1908 First Model T

1909 Peary reaches North Pole; Frank Lloyd Wright completes Robie House

1910 First subatomic particles discovered; Russell and Whitehead, *Principia Mathematica;* John Philip Sousa's band tours the world

1911 Amundsen reaches South Pole; Wharton, *Ethan Frome;* de Chirico, *La nostalgie de l'infini*

1912 *Titanic* sinks; Balkan wars; Duchamp, *Nude Descending a Staircase;* Kandinsky, *Improvisation*

1913 New York Armory Show; Mann, *Death in Venice;* John Sloane, *Sunday Women Drying their Hair;* Braque, *Musical Forms;* Proust, *Remembrance of Things Past;*

1914 Victor Herbert forms American Society of Composers, Authors, and Publishers (ASCAP); World War I begins; Panama Canal opens; Griffith, *Birth of a Nation;* Frost, *North of Boston*

*T*wo *great forces shaped Western music in the last quarter of the nineteenth century, Nationalism and Late-Romanticism. Nationalist composers sought, through the use of folk or traditional musical materials, a national style or ethnic identity. Late-Romantic composers sought, through the musical innovations of Richard Wagner, to transcend mundane experience altogether.*

NATIONALISM

Romantic nationalism sprang from two sources: the political awakening of ethnic groups and nationalities caused by the great revolutions (American, 1776; French, 1789) of the eighteenth century; and the sense of individual alienation created by the new industrial society. Each source led Romantic composers to their ethnic roots and to the folk cultures of their native lands.

Musical nationalism is most evident in those areas that had not previously developed a strong tradition of art music: Russia, Eastern and Northern Europe, and the United States. Although the nationalistic movement represented a reaction to mainstream Romanticism, it does not represent a break from it: a variety of dialects may be added to a language without changing its essentials. However, by the first decades of the twentieth century, these dialects began to threaten the Romantic language itself.

National or Ethnic Programs

Titles, extramusical programs or texts that reflect ethnic traditions or nationalist political aims were often sufficient to excite Nationalist sympathies. Patriotic works became common in the nineteenth century and composers gradually began to incorporate native materials into the language as a way of unambiguously establishing a particular national character.

Musical Characteristics of Nationalism

The folk and traditional music of Russia, Europe, and North America was distinct from Western art music; as a result, the presence of melodies, harmonies or rhythms associated with those traditions was clearly recognizable as a national or ethnic attribute. These materials greatly augmented the Romantic musical language, adding exotic new colors to the Nationalist composer's palette.

MELODY

The traditional musics of Russia, Eastern Europe, and North America are largely modal rather than tonal. Those of Russia and of Eastern and Northern Europe quite often contain elements that reflect the influence of other, non-Western musical traditions such as those of Islam and India. The use of such folk tunes or traditional melodies within a work of otherwise Romantic language would tend both to call attention to their origin and exaggerate their peculiar character.

HARMONY

The modal character of much folk music makes it difficult to set within the traditional harmonic language of Western art music. As a result, a composer's effort to set a modal traditional melody might easily lead either to harmonic peculiarities—progressions not normally found in art music—or to a deemphasis of harmony altogether.

RHYTHM

The metrical structure of Western art music is tied to its complex harmonic structure. Traditional music tends not to be structured around harmonic progressions, but rather around simultaneous improvisations upon a single tune. Thus, its texture is more fluid and often more complex rhythmically than Western art music. The music of Nationalist composers often reflects this fluidity and complexity.

Russia

Though greatly influenced by German Romanticism, Imperial Russia had closer ties to France and its less ponderous, more colorful dialect of Romanticism. Early Nationalists, like Mikhail Glinka (1804–1857), colored this French Romantic style with uniquely Russian subjects and musical idioms, creating one of the most striking Nationalist schools of the nineteenth century.

THE FIVE

Of the generation of Russian composers that followed Glinka, one group, known as "The Five," remains the most significant.

Modest Musorgsky (1839–1881). Now seen as one of the most influential of the group, Musorgsky, in his own day, was considered an amateur. (Much of his music was even "corrected" after his death.) It is now clear that his music, in its original form, reveals a remarkably original musical imagination—one born of a profound understanding of Slavic traditional music rather than poor craftsmanship. His music fueled the Nationalistic tendencies of a later, more radical generation (the young Debussy in particular [see below]). He composed operas, symphonic and piano works, and songs. The opera *Boris Godunov* and *Pictures at an Exhibition* —originally a piano work, though known popularly in a later orchestral transcription by Ravel (see below)—are his best-known works.

Nikolay Rimsky-Korsakov (1844–1908). Though largely self-taught, he was the most famous and successful of "The Five." He produced many colorful and evocative symphonic works and operas. Exotic orchestral and harmonic colors distinguish his style and greatly influenced his pupil Igor Stravinsky (see chapter 25). The symphonic suite *Scheherazade* is his best-known work.

Other Composers in "The Five." Aleksandr Borodin (1833–1887) is the best-known of the remaining composers of the group. He wrote symphonies, chamber music, songs and operas. The opera *Prince* Igor and the symphonic poem *In the Steppes of Central Asia* are his best-known works. César Cui (1835–1918) and Mily Balakirev (1837–1910), the remaining members of the group, are seldom heard today.

PYOTR ILICH TCHAIKOVSKY

The best-known of Russian composers, Tchaikovsky (1840–1893) wrote six symphonies, popular concertos and operas, as well as songs and chamber music. Though thoroughly grounded in the Austro-German symphonic school, he occasionally found inspiration for his musical material in Slavic traditional and ethnic music. Though his symphonies are "absolute" music, they are permeated with the sounds of the Russian countryside and thus, to Russians, are "Nationalistic." His ballets take for their subject Russian fairy tales (*The Nutcracker*) and Slavic myths (*Swan Lake*). His most famous works are symphonic: the overture-fantasy *Romeo and Juliet,* the ballet suites *The Nutcracker* and *Swan Lake,* and his *Symphony* No. 4, No. 5, and *No. 6.*

Europe

Those countries on the periphery of the Western art music tradition produced some of the most vital Nationalistic music.

CZECHOSLOVAKIA

Bedřich Smetana (1824–1884). Smetana is known primarily for his set of six interrelated symphonic poems entitled *Má vlast* (My Homeland), but his *String Quartet* in E Minor ("From My Life") and the opera *The Bartered* Bride, are also well known.

Antonín Dvořák (1841–1904). Dvořák was a friend and admirer of Brahms and a prolific composer of symphonic, chamber and piano works. Many of his minor works have overtly Nationalistic programs. A visit to the United States in the closing years of the century inspired his most famous work—the *Symphony No. 9* ("From the New World").

SCANDINAVIA

Edvard Grieg (Norway, 1843–1907). His incidental music to Ibsen's *Peer Gynt* and the *Piano Concerto in A Minor* are his best-known works.

Jean Sibelius (Finland, 1865–1957). Though Sibelius lived well into the twentieth century, his major works are thoroughly Romantic in style and tone. He composed seven symphonies and numerous other orchestral works. The *Second Symphony* and the tone poem *Finlandia* are his best-known works.

SPAIN

The piano suite *Iberia* by Isaac Albéniz (1860–1890) is typical of nineteenth-century Spanish Nationalism, as are the piano and symphonic works of Enrique Granados (1867–1916).

United States

On the periphery of Western art music, art music composers in the United States found in vernacular music a source for their National style.

Louis Marie Gottschalk (1829–1869). The majority of Gottschalk's works are for piano or piano and orchestra. He was one of the first composers to introduce African-American idioms into concert works.

George Chadwick (1854–1931). Chadwick wrote symphonic music and songs. Although German trained, he gradually shed the conservatory style in favor of one that made frequent use of American vernacular melodies and rhythms. His *Second Symphony* and *Symphonic* Sketches are representative.

Edward Macdowell (1861–1908). Macdowell was the first of a long line of German-trained concert composers in the United States to develop a thoroughly individual style. He sought to create a music that used American subjects while still remaining firmly based upon German models. His works often carry picturesque or nostalgic titles. His *Indian Suite* and *Woodland Sketches* are characteristic of his Nationalist style.

LATE ROMANTICISM

"Late Romantic" refers specifically to a group of Austrian and German composers who saw themselves as the musical and spiritual heirs of Richard Wagner. In general, however, any Romantic composer at the end of the nineteenth century who did not have an overtly Nationalistic style might be called Late Romantic.

The Late Romantics

The early Romantics sought transcendence, escape from the banality and ugliness of life in the newly industrialized cities. Romantic art—in particular, Romantic music—became their refuge. By the end of the nineteenth century, the sentimental and nostalgic aspect of Romanticism had become a part of Middle Class sensibilities. The vast scale and emotional impact of Wagner's music drama seemed to transport this new "romantic" middle class into a world of myth, romance, and heroic purpose. But the Wagnerian effects began to pale with time, and those Late Romantic composers who followed him faced an increasingly jaded public, one that required of them ever more powerful effects, and ever more potent programs.

GENERAL CHARACTERISTICS OF LATE ROMANTICISM

Scope. Late Romantic composers share with late Beethoven and Wagner an interest in large-scale structures. Their works tend to be vast both in terms of time and the musical forces required for performance. As a result, Late Romantic works often present a public, or monumental aspect.

Complexity. The musical language of Late Romanticism arises from the formal, melodic, and harmonic innovations of Wagner, and its attendant desire to impress or to provoke a response. As a result, the Late Romantic style often falls prey to sentimentality (overindulgence in nostalgic or melodramatic emotions) or even decadence (overindulgence in effect or the effort to shock, provoke, or titillate).

MUSICAL CHARACTERISTICS OF LATE ROMANTICISM

The source of most Late Romantic music is Wagner and late Beethoven. The melodic, harmonic, and formal innovations of these two form the bedrock of Late Romantic style.

Melody. In Late Romantic works, melodies tend to be long and dramatic. Wagner's "endless melody" is the model.

Harmony. The impact of Wagner's music comes mainly from his harmonic language. The fundamental relationship of major-minor tonality is that of dominant to tonic, or that of tension or unrest to release or rest. Using chromaticism (that is, notes and harmonies not in the main key or scale), Wagner was able to extend states of tension and delay points of rest until the appropriate moment in the drama. Though dramatically effective, chromaticism of this order challenged the very basis of major-minor tonality: the scale. As harmonic progressions relied more on chromatic alterations and less upon the fundamental scale degrees, tonality itself became more and more unstable. The drama inherent in this instability is in large part responsible for the overpowering effect of Late Romantic music.

Genre. Late Romantics favored the larger orchestral genres, in particular the symphony and the tone poem. Opera, though prominent in the output of one of the most important composers of the period, played a less important role in general. Wagner, it was felt, had exhausted that genre. Of the smaller genre, only the art song is favored; yet often, even the art song is transformed into something monumental, as in the orchestral songs (for voice and orchestra) of Mahler and Strauss.

ANTON BRUCKNER

A devout Catholic, and an organist and professor of counterpoint in Vienna (he taught Mahler and Wolf), Bruckner (1824–1896) produced nine gigantic symphonies, three movements of a tenth, and several religious choral works. Though an avowed Wagnerian, he had little interest in opera. Bruckner's symphonies are vast, several times as long as a Beethoven symphony, and usually require orchestras augmented by auxiliary brass and woodwinds. Their texture ranges from great brass chorales and learned contrapuntal sequences to vast, portentous themes supported by atmospheric string harmonies. To many, the symphonies suggest not only Bruckner's background as an organist, but the timelessness and spiritual depth of religious ritual itself. Bruckner's *Symphony* No. 4, "The Romantic," is the most frequently performed; his *Symphony No. 9,* left incomplete at his death, is the most admired.

GUSTAV MAHLER

One of the great conductors of the nineteenth century, and the first modern superstar conductor, Mahler (1860–1911) nevertheless found time to write nine complete symphonies, several song cycles for voice and orchestra, and many individual songs. Almost all the symphonies come down to us with programs. Four of the symphonies require voice or voices and chorus. All require augmented orchestras, and all except the first and fourth require virtually an entire evening to perform. The literary programs are Romantic, tending to focus on the idealization of nature and on dreams of redemption. Bruckner's great influence on Mahler can be seen primarily in the scale, texture, and specific musical ideas of the latter's symphonies.

Mahler's works are at times disarmingly simple, at other times grandiose and bombastic. These great contrasts frequently create a sense of irony or even satire. His many songs for voice and piano as well as for voice and orchestra achieve the best balance between irony and sentimentality. His symphonies *No. 1* and *No. 4* are the most frequently performed, his symphonies *No. 6, No. 7* and *No. 9* the most admired.

RICHARD STRAUSS

The works of Strauss (1864–1949) fall into three clearly defined stages. The works of his first period are reminiscent of Brahms (1880s). The tone poems (1890s) and several operas (1890s–World War I) of his second period are written in a luscious Late Romantic style. The works of his third period, those written during and after World War I, are more circumspect and conservative in style.

The tone poems of the second period, like the symphonies of Bruckner and Mahler, require large orchestras and great expanses of time. Their programs are typically romantic: *Tod und Verklärung* (Death and Transfiguration), *Till Eulenspiegels lustige Streiche* (Till Eulenspiegel's Merry Pranks), *Also sprach Zarathustra* (after Nietzsche, the great Romantic philosopher), and *Ein Heldenleben* (A Hero's Life). The music is grand, intense, and seldom anything less than extravagant. In operas like *Salome* (1905) and *Elektra* (1909), the chromatic material that underlies certain moments of high dramatic tension can no longer be understood in terms of major-minor tonality, but takes on a musical life of its own. (See chapter 25, below.)

Other Late Romantics

Though not overtly influenced by Wagner, other composers developed individual and provocative Late Romantic styles.

ALEKSANDR SKRYABIN

A composer of symphonic and piano works, Skryabin (1872–1915) created a chromatic, somewhat Impressionist and entirely idiosyncratic style. The tone and subject matter of his works often reflect his mystical inclinations. His *Sonata No. 7* ("White Mass") for piano and *Prometheus* for orchestra are among his best-known works.

SERGEY RACHMANINOFF

Rachmaninoff (1873–1953) composed mainly symphonic and piano works, all in a brooding late-romantic style. Though living well into the twentieth century, his best-known works—among them the *Second Piano Concerto*—were written before middle age.

GABRIEL FAURÉ

A composer primarily of songs and chamber music, Fauré (France, 1845–1924) steered a crooked stylistic course, but one that always places him somewhere between Brahms (the chamber music) and Debussy (the songs and orchestral works).

SIR EDWARD ELGAR

A Romantic composer whose early works reveal an admiration for Brahms, and his later ones a modest interest in Strauss, Elgar (England, 1857–1934) wrote primarily symphonic and choral works. His orchestral work, *Enigma Variations,* is characteristic.

IMPRESSIONISM

The style popularly termed Impressionism arose in France in the 1890s. Though its origin is inevitably associated with the development of the young Claude Debussy (see below), several generations of nineteenth century French composers laid the foundation for the Impressionist style. In the last half of the nineteenth century, while most European Romantics were still rushing to the Wagnerian camp, many French Romantics drew away from the heavy, Austro-German idiom. Instead, they created a uniquely French dialect that was lighter in style and relied more on instrumental and ethnic colors than on chromaticism and structural complexity. The style became known as *Impressionism,* by analogy with the French Impressionist painters, whose paintings were similarly colorful, atmospheric, and characteristically French.

Musical Characteristics

In large part, the musical style of Impressionism can best be understood by contrast with the Late Romantic style of Austro-German composers. Whereas the Late Romantics relied heavily on chromaticism, Impressionists went back to medieval and ancient modes; while the Late Romantics were interested in the extremes of tension and release, the Impressionists concerned themselves with relatively flat, decorative, and atmospheric moods free of Romantic melodrama.

MELODY

Impressionist melodic material is often modal. It frequently derives from ancient church modes or from exotic, non-Western traditions. Often melodic and harmonic material derives from certain synthetic modes, such as the whole-tone (formed by a succession of six whole steps) or the octatonic (formed by four whole-step/half-step alternations).

HARMONY

Impressionist harmony is essentially triadic, but less directed than nineteenth-century tonality. Triads are often colored by added sevenths and ninths. The standard, directed harmonic progressions of major-minor tonality are replaced by nonstandard, undirected successions of triads.

RHYTHM

As the harmonic language became less directed, the rhythm of Impressionist music became less tied to meter and pulse. As a result, Impressionist works often seem unmetered, floating and with no clear sense of pulse.

INSTRUMENTAL COLOR AND FORM

With Impressionist music instrumental color becomes as important in musical design as harmonic or thematic formalisms. Impressionist compositions often combine lush colors with the simpler traditional forms; in more sophisticated work in the style, the colors help generate unique forms that rely more on shifting colors, textures, and harmonies than on traditional thematic repetition and harmonic completion.

Claude Debussy

Arguably the first "modern" composer, Debussy (France, 1862–1918) sought to create a purely French music free of Wagnerian influence, and in so doing paved the way for many of the innovations of the twentieth century. The first work in his mature style, *Prélude à l'après midi d' un faun* (Prelude to "The Afternoon of a Faun"), is based upon a poem by the enigmatic Symbolist poet Stéphane Mallarmé. (Because of Debussy's early association with the poets and painters of the Symbolist school, some scholars suggest that "Symbolist," rather than "Impressionist," would be a better label for his style.) His single completed opera, *Pellé as et Mélisande,* is decidedly un-Wagnerian and understated. Almost overnight, this one work established Debussy's new style as a national style. It is now considered characteristically French, and Debussy a "Nationalist" to his countrymen and -women.

Maurice Ravel

Ravel (France, 1875–1937), an extraordinary orchestrator and pianistic innovator, was one of the first to adopt Debussy's new style. Though his style has many similarities to that of Debussy, it is at once both more colorful and decorative and more conservative, being more nearly tied to nineteenth-century tonality. His most famous work is the ballet, *Bolero;* less famous but more characteristic are his *Rhapsodie espagnole,* and *Daphnis et Chloé.* He wrote several stage works of which the opera-ballet, *L'Enfant et les sortilèges (The Child and the Spells)* is the best known. In the 1920s, his Impressionist style began to pick up characteristics of Neoclassicism (see chapter 25, below) and even elements of jazz.

Other Impressionist Composers

The American Charles Tomlinson Griffes (1884–1920) developed an Impressionist style not completely divorced from Romanticism. His best-known works, such as *The Pleasure Dome of Kubla-Khan,* were originally for piano, though Griffes arranged several of them for orchestra later.

Frederick Delius (1862–1934), an Englishman who spent many years in France, developed his own form of Romantic Impressionism. His was colored with New World ethnic material derived from a time spent in tropical Florida. He wrote orchestral works and opera.

The Romantic Nationalists and Late Romantics expanded the range of musical subjects and the nature of musical material. The Impressionists took this new palette and used it to defy traditional Western art music conventions. Each group, in its own way, brought the language of Bach and Beethoven to crisis, each paved the way for a new generation, a new century, and a new music.

For Additional Study

Brown, David, et al. *The New Grove Russian Masters 1.* New York: Norton. 1986.

Cooke, Deryck, et al. *The New Grove Late Romantic Masters.* New York: Norton. 1985

Dahlhaus, Carl. *Between Romanticism and Modernism.* Berkeley: University of California. 1980.

___. *Nineteenth-Century Music.* Trans., J. Bradford Robinson. Berkeley: University of California. 1989

Longyear, Rey M. *Nineteenth-Century Romanticism in Music.* 3d Edition. Englewood Cliffs, NJ: Prentice-Hall. 1988.

Platinga, Leon. *Romantic Music.* New York: Norton. 1984.

Strunk, Oliver. *Source Readings in Music History: The* Romantic Era. New York: Norton. 1950.

Tyrrell, John, et al. *The New Grove Turn-of-the-Century Masters.* New York: Norton. 1985.

Recommended Listening

Bruckner, Anton. *Symphony No. 9*

Chadwick, George. *Second Symphony*

Debussy, Claude. *Prélude à l'après midi d'un faun* (Prelude to "The Afternoon of a Faun")

Dvořák, Antonín. *Symphony No. 9* ("From the New World")

Elgar, Edward. *Enigma Variations*

Grieg, Edvard. *Peer Gynt*

Macdowell, Edward. *Woodland Sketches*

Mahler, Gustav. *Symphony No. 4.*

Musorgsky, Modest. *Pictures at an Exhibition* for piano

Rachmaninoff, Sergey. *Second Piano Concerto*

Ravel, Maurice. *Rhapsodie espagnole*

Rimsky-Korsakov, Nikolay. *Scheherazade*

Skryabin, Aleksandr. *Sonata No. 7*

Sibelius, Jean. *Second Symphony*

Smetana, Bedřich. *The Moldau*

Strauss, Richard. *Till Eulenspiegel lustige Streiche* (Till Eulenspiegel's Merry Pranks)

Tchaikovsky, Pyotr Ilich. *Romeo and Juliet*

25

The Modern Period to World War II

1900 Chinese Boxer rebellion; Philadelphia Orchestra founded; Freud, *Interpretation of Dreams;* first dirigible; Conrad, *Lord Jim*

1901 Queen Victoria dies; Edward VII becomes King of England; Planck develops Quantum Theory

1903 Wright brothers' first successful flight; Shaw, *Man and Superman*

1904 Russo-Japanese war; Chekhov, *The Cherry Orchard;* Rolland, *Jean Christophe*

1905 Einstein, *Special Theory of Relativity;* first Russian Revolution

1906 San Francisco earthquake and fire; New Music Society of America formed to promote music of American composers

1907 First music broadcast on radio; Picasso, *Les Demoiselles d'Avignon*

1908 First Model T

1909 Peary reaches North Pole; Frank Lloyd Wright completes Robie House

1910 First subatomic particles discovered; Russell and Whitehead, *Principia Mathematica;* John Philip Sousa's band tours the world

1911 Amundsen reaches South Pole; Wharton, *Ethan Frome;* de Chirico, *La nostalgie de l' infini*

1912 *Titanic* sinks; Balkan wars; Duchamp, *Nude Descending a Staircase;* Kandinsky, *Improvisation*

1913 New York Armory Show; Mann, *Death in Venice;* John Sloane, *Sunday Women Drying their Hair;* Braque, *Musical Forms;* Proust, *Remembrance of Things Past;*

1914 Victor Herbert forms American Society of Composers, Authors, and Publishers (ASCAP); World War I begins; Panama Canal opens; Griffith, *Birth of a Nation;* Frost, *North of Boston*

1915 Maugham, *Of Human Bondage;* Morgan, *Mechanism of Mendelian Heredity*

1916 Einstein, *General Theory of Relativity;* Wright completes Imperial Hotel in Tokyo

1917 United States enters war; Bolshevik revolution in Russia; first jazz recording; first printed use of word *jazz;* Yeats, *Wild Swans at Coole*

1918 World War I ends; Cather, *My Antonia;* Spengler, *Decline of the West*

1919 Treaty of Versailles; League of Nations formed; Mussolini founds Italian Fascist party

1920 Women's suffrage granted by Nineteenth Amendment; first commercial radio broadcast

1921 Varèse organizes International Guild of Composers for the promotion of twentieth-century music; Wittgenstein, *Tractatus;* Mondriaan, *Painting No. 1;* Chaplin's *The Kid* released

1922 International Society for Contemporary Music formed in Salzburg; Insulin discovered; Eliot, *The Wasteland;* Joyce, *Ulysses;* Rilke, *Sonnets to Orpheus;* Fitzgerald, *The Great Gatsby*

1923 Soviet Union established; Klee, *At the Mountain of the Bull*

1924 Lenin dies; Stalin comes to power; Kafka, *The Trial*

1926 Hemingway, *The Sun Also Rises;* first TV transmission

1927 Lindbergh flies the Atlantic solo; Heisenberg propounds his uncertainty principle; Woolf, *To the Lighthouse;* O'Neill, *Strange Interlude*; first important "talking" picture: *The Jazz Singer*

1928 Penicillin developed; first all-sound film; Lawrence, *Lady Chatterley's Lover;* Benét, *John Brown's Body*

1929 Great Depression begins; Faulkner, *The Sound and the Fury;* Ortega y Gasset, *Revolt of the Masses*

1930 Pluto discovered; Hopper, *Early Sunday Morning;* Wood, *American Gothic;* Crane, *The Bridge*

1931 Empire State Building opens; Japan invades Manchuria

1933 Roosevelt inaugurated; Hitler becomes German Chancellor

1935 Italy invades Ethiopia; Orozco, *Man in Four Aspects*

1936 Spanish Civil War; Dos Passos, *U.S.A.* trilogy

1937 Japan invades China; Hill discovers chloroplast reaction in plants; Picasso, Guernica

1938 First-ever Carnegie Hall jazz concert (Benny Goodman's band); Nuclear fission demonstrated; Dufy, *Regatta*

1939 World War II begins; Broadcast Music Inc. (BMI) established in competition with ASCAP; Joyce, *Finnegans Wake;* Steinbeck, *The Grapes of Wrath; Citizen Kane, The Wizard of Oz* and *Gone With the Wind* released

1940 Roosevelt elected to third term; Churchill becomes British prime minister; first microwave radar and electron microscope developed

1941 Pearl Harbor; United States enters World War II; Atlantic Charter

1943 Italy surrenders; Chagall, *Crucifixion*

1944 Allied invasion of France, then Germany

1945 Germany surrenders; atom bombs destroy Hiroshima and Nagasaki; radio astronomy; first jet-propelled planes and rockets

The first two-and-a-half decades of the twentieth century revolutionized Western civilization. Einstein's special theory of relativity changed forever our understanding of the universe and our place in it. The invention of the airplane and automobile and the wide-spread use of electric power, radio, telephones, and streetcars transformed everyday life. The United States' rise to global significance along with the success of the Russian Revolution transformed the political power structure of the world, offering both the hope of democratic rule and social justice as well as the terrifying prospect of global destruction.

That Western art should mirror—even predict—this Babel of innovation and transformation should not surprise us; that the images, sounds and words that resulted should be as startling and disturbing as Einstein's theories or Wittgenstein's philosophy is no wonder. Modern artists not only changed the nature of Western art; they shook its very foundations.

CHARACTERISTICS OF MUSICAL MODERNISM

Not all twentieth-century music is "modern." Many composers continued in the Romantic manner well into the twentieth century. The terms *twentieth-century music* or *modern music* refer generally, however, to the music of those composers who directly confronted the aesthetic and philosophical problems of the Modern Age. Those problems were complex. Not surprisingly, the art that arose from them was complex as well. Still, we can trace the complexity of Modern Art in general, and Modern music in particular, to a few central issues. By understanding the issues we begin to understand the music.

General Characteristics of Modernism — Musicians, artists, writers, philosophers, scientists, and politicians convey their vision to others through language. Each language is unique to its particular field. What the language communicates, whether abstract or concrete, is its meaning. A musical language, for example, is comprised of tones, rhythms, harmonies, textures, instrumental colors, and the systematic organization of all of these. On the other hand, a scientific language is comprised of logical and mathematical symbols combined systematically to establish axioms and prove theorems.

What happens when a scientist—Einstein for example—suspects that physical reality is structured in some novel way? The available scientific languages may not provide means to express a new reality nor the means to communicate the new meaning that such a reality might imply. In Einstein's case, the old language of physics gave way to a new, expanded language, one that enabled him to share this new vision of reality with fellow scientists and this new meaning with the world.

At the turn of the twentieth century, composers found themselves similarly constrained by the language of nineteenth-century Romanticism. In order to express their vision of contemporary reality, Modern composers required new and expanded languages.

THE LIMITATIONS OF LANGUAGE

Artists strive to express their meaning in a language intelligible to their audience. If their attempt fails, they have two options: either change the meaning to fit the language or change the language to convey the meaning. When the world changed, as it did radically in the latter nineteenth and early twentieth centuries, artists—in this case, composers—changed with it. More conservative composers strove to express their contemporary experience with a nineteenth-century language; more radical composers chose instead to create a new language, one that corresponded to Modern reality.

Transcendence. By the end of the nineteenth century, the impressive successes of science seemed to have settled (in science's favor) the debate between science and religion. Many nineteenth-century political theories suggested that the motivation for human activity was material rather than moral. Turn-of-the-century Freudian psychology suggested that our pasts shaped our presents and imprisoned us within ourselves. The Romantics sought to transcend this mundane materialism, they desired some more ideal state of being and awareness. By the turn of the century, this desire seemed impossible to fulfill, yet at the same time it became all the more desirable.

Fragmentation. In the first two decades of the twentieth century, Western civilization seemed on the verge of disintegration. Traditional religion, political alliances, and social organization served no longer to bind but to separate. Nineteenth-century Romantics sought through art—in particular, music—a wholeness and idealized experience denied to them by an increasingly materialistic and fragmented society. The giants of the era—Schoenberg and Stravinsky in music, Eliot and Joyce in literature, Picasso and Kandinsky in art—arranged these fragments into new languages that enabled Modern artists to communicate their visions to the contemporary world.

THE LIMITATIONS OF MEANING

At the turn of the century, Modern experience seemed not only fragmented, but also meaningless. Some artists sought to find new meanings in the old languages; others sought to create new languages and new meanings. Still other artists rejected the idea of meaning altogether, embracing instead those very aspects of modern experience that many sought to escape.

The Nonrational. Freudian psychology changed attitudes about the source of meaning; now it was the unconscious, rather than the conscious being, that shaped the individual. Modern science hypothesized a world in which occurrences could be predicted only statistically; chance, rather than mechanics, ruled the cosmos. Many Modern artists—among them, composers—sought to reflect this world of random occurrence not only in their work but in their methods of creation as well. The creative act was to reflect nature in its manner of operation; it was to be random, unintentional and impersonal.

Loss of Self. Romantic artists were egoists; they integrated themselves into their works, and their works reflected their own, individual personalities. Many Modern artists sought rather to remove themselves *from* their work; they sought to create works as arbitrary, random, and impersonal as the works of Nature itself. As a result, their relationship to their work became more complex; rather than being the creator of the work, they were the conduit for it.

TRADITION UNDERMINED

Thus the entire tradition of Western art began to crumble. In music, some composers retained traditional Romantic attitudes and meanings while creating new languages to revitalize their ability to convey these meanings (for example, Expressionism and Serialism). Other composers tried to retain the traditional language while conveying new attitudes and meanings (for example, Neoclassicism and *Gebrauchsmusik*). Still others threw out the traditions of both language and meaning, starting anew.

Musical Characteristics

Not surprisingly, the materials of Modern music are more fragmented and complex than those of Romantic music. The musical language shared by the West throughout most of its history was replaced in the twentieth century by a multitude of other languages. No single language was shared by more than a few composers at a time. We can isolate certain techniques and tendencies that are characteristically "Modern"; but these are general characteristics only, and no single work is likely to exhibit all or even most of them.

TONALITY

Turn-of-the-century Nationalist composers found that traditional tonality could not contain the modal and nonharmonic aspect of their ethnic or national musics. In their works, major-minor tonality began to disintegrate as conventional harmonic progressions were abandoned in order to accommodate ancient, non-Western modes. At the same time, Late-Romantic composers continued and expanded the radical chromaticism of Wagner, further weakening traditional harmonic progressions.

METER AND RHYTHM

Traditional meter and rhythm are tied to the harmonic structure of major-minor tonality. Music created outside that traditional tonality need not remain tied to traditional metrical and rhythmic structure. The extremes of Modern music are represented on the one hand by music that relies upon simple, often primitive, rhythmic regularity (for example, Primitivism), and, on the other, by music that is so rhythmically complex as to suggest no regular rhythmic structure at all (for example, Expressionism). Other Modern styles use traditional metrical regularity to make palatable a more adventuresome pitch structure (for example, Neoclassicism). In general then, the rhythmic structure of Modern music is more varied, complex, and irregular than that of nineteenth-century music.

TEXTURE

Modern music ranges from monolithic textures fabricated from regularly repeated and irregularly accented blocks of sounds (for example, "The Augurs of Spring" from Stravinsky's *The Rite of Spring* or the fourth of Webern's *Six Pieces, Op. 6*), to thick textures in which many seemingly unrelated melodic fragments are combined to form a complex polyphony (for example, "Introduction" from *The Rite of Spring* or the first of the *Six Pieces, Op. 6*). Such extremes are often found within individual works, sometimes within successive sections of a work.

FORM

Traditional tonality relied on harmonic progression and formal thematic development. Modernist composers, free of these traditional harmonic constraints, found it necessary to jettison traditional formal constraints as well. The new music required a broader, more diverse set of techniques. And in these new works, form arose from the musical material itself, not historical precedent. Works created their own unique forms.

SOUND AND TIMBRE

In the effort to find new modes of organization and expression, composers looked beyond even pitch and rhythm to the very nature of sound. In some works, the repetition and transformation of orchestral colors largely replaced traditional motivic development (for example, Debussy's *Prelude to "The Afternoon of a Faun"* or Ravel's *Bolero*). In other works, the development of instrumental color replaced thematic organization itself (for example, "Colors" from Schoenberg's *Five Orchestral Pieces, Op. 16* or Varèse's *Hyperprism*). With this renewed interest in instrumental colors came an increased interest in unpitched percussion instruments. Noise, pure sound became an essential ingredient of many Modern works—and virtually the only ingredient in some (for example, Varèse's *Ionisation* or Antheil's *Ballet mécanique*).

FUNCTION

Many modern composers retained the Romantic view that music could and should transform life. Many rejected Romanticism in favor of an older and more practical role for music and the composer: the artisan decorating civilization. Many denied the aesthetic component altogether; they viewed music as political or philosophical activism. Some rejected art itself, creating a kind of antiart, self-conscious and absurd; they made fun of the music establishment that they deplored, at the same time that they used it. The modern artist felt the need to redefine art and its relation to society and Everyday life.

MAJOR TRENDS AND COMPOSERS

Each composer solved the problems of musical modernism in a unique way; each solution, therefore, was personal. As a result, most of the twentieth-century composers discussed below are as difficult to categorize as the century itself. We can only attempt in the following to trace general tendencies or major trends.

Expressionism and Serialism

Expressionism represents a radical extension of German Romanticism. Through distortion, allegory, exaggeration, and eventually abstraction, Expressionists sought to provoke the viewer or audience to social action or interior transformation. In music the term is usually applied to music composed between 1909 and 1922 by the composers of the Second Viennese School (the "first" Viennese school being that of Mozart, Beethoven, and Schubert). The Second Viennese school centered around the Austrian composer, Arnold Schoenberg (see below).

Serialism is a technique of composition, not a style. The term refers to a music fabricated from a basic ordering of musical elements, usually pitch. The fundamental ordering is called a "set," a "tone row," or simply a "row." Other orders may be obtained by manipulating the set with traditional, contrapuntal techniques. The initial set is called the "original" or "prime" ordering ("P" in figure 25.1). One may reverse or retrograde the original order ("R"), invert and produce a mirror-image of it ("I"), or both retrograde *and* invert it ("RI").

The Four Transformations of a Set of Three Tones

Fig 25.1

Schoenberg's method of twelve-tone composition is an example of Serialism and arose directly from the musical concerns of his Expressionist period. In twelve-tone composition, a fundamental ordering of the twelve tones of the chromatic "scale" is used to generate all the material for a work. (See figure 25.2.)

The Four Transformations of a Twelve-Tone Set

Fig 25.2

Serialism is the term that refers to any such concern with order; thus, the twelve-tone method is a special type of Serialism. There are many others. And though many composers who used serial or twelve-tone techniques in the first half of the twentieth-century share similar styles, the technique itself does not preclude any style.

MUSICAL CHARACTERISTICS

Tonality. Though often highly organized, Expressionistic music is organized quite differently from that of the eighteenth and nineteenth centuries; thus, musicians call Expressionist music *atonal* or "without tonality"— meaning without major-minor tonality. With the invention of the twelve-tone method, the style became markedly more organized and the term *atonal* became less appropriate. Works that use this method are generally called *twelve-tone* rather than *atonal*.

Melody. Romantic melodies tend to be smooth and fluid. Expressionist melodies tend to be angular and fragmented. Yet they retain enough of the Romantic character to seem distortions or exaggerations of Romantic style. As composers turned increasingly to serial techniques, their melodies showed less resemblance to "expressive," Romantic themes and became, thus, less "Expressionist."

Harmony. The atonal harmony of Expressionist works is complex by comparison with nineteenth-century tonal harmony. Atonal harmony is seldom triadic and often contains intervals (such as seconds and sevenths) that are considered dissonant in traditional tonality. In Expressionist and serial music, harmony and melody often flow from the same source: a melodic motive might be expressed as a chord, or a tune might become a harmony. In such works, a distinction between "harmony" and "melody" is difficult to establish.

Color and Texture. Textures in Expressionist music became more and more chamber-like. The massed orchestral sonorities of Late Romantics like Strauss gave way to thinner, more open textures in which the instruments of the orchestra were treated as soloists joined together into a gigantic chamber ensemble.

From this novel concept of the orchestra arose several influential new textures. *Klangfarbenmelodie* (tone-color melody, introduced by Schoenberg in the third of his *Five Orchestral Pieces, Op. 16,* creates textures in which instrumental colors change with each note. From the Klangfarbenmelodie concept arose *pointillism,* in which tones or small sets of tones, each played by different instruments, are dispersed throughout a texture. (Webern's *Concerto, Op. 24* is the classic example.) The ear assembles the tiny units of a pointillistic texture into a whole in much the same way as the eye assembles a mosaic of small colored tiles into an image. (The term *pointillism* is borrowed from the visual arts where it is used to describe the works of Georges Seurat [1859–1891], who painted with dots of colors rather than brush strokes.)

Form. The most favored Expressionist form is *continuous variation.* In continuous variation one idea is immediately transformed into another, and that new idea into yet another. (The continuous variation technique arises from the motivic music of Beethoven and, especially, Brahms.) We seldom find closed forms in Expressionist music. However, as composers adopt serial techniques, they tend to return to closed forms and large-scale structures.

Scale. Expressionist compositions tend to be short. They stand in sharp contrast to the gargantuan works of Late Romantics such as Bruckner, Mahler, and Strauss. Despite their relative brevity, Expressionist works are often packed with violent changes of mood, texture, and instrumental color. Audiences tend to experience them as "intense" rather than "brief." With the return to closed forms, compositions became longer and more uniform in texture and mood.

THE SECOND VIENNESE SCHOOL

Arnold Schoenberg (Austria, 1874–1951). Self-taught, Schoenberg attracted attention at the turn of the century with two startling works in an advanced, Late Romantic style: the string quintet *Verklärte Nacht* (Transfigured Night, 1899) and the dramatic oratorio *Gurre-lieder* (Songs of Gurre, 1901–1911). An intense association with Expressionist painters and intellectuals combined with personal and aesthetic struggles brought on a crisis in 1909. In a startling series of dramatic symphonic, and chamber works culminating in *Pierrot lunaire* (Moonstruck Pierrot, 1912), Schoenberg abandoned major-minor tonality for a style that relied entirely on motivic variation for both melodic and harmonic content. The new style was dubbed *atonal* by its detractors, and the name stuck.

By the 1920s Schoenberg had imposed a new order on this style with a method known as the twelve-tone method, or technique. Schoenberg's twelve-tone works, although retaining the angular melodies and dissonant harmonies of his atonal style, rely more upon traditional forms and phrase structure.

Schoenberg's best-known Expressionist works are *Pierrot lunaire* and the *Five Orchestral Pieces, Op. 16* (1909). The *Piano Suite, Op. 25* (1923), *Violin Concerto, Op. 36* (1934), and the opera *Moses and Aaron* (1931–1932) are the best-known works from his twelve-tone period.

Anton Webern (Austria, 1883–1945). A pupil of Schoenberg, Webern evolved a distinct, aphoristic style characterized by brevity and economy of material, *Klangfarbenmelodie,* and pointillistic textures. His music is overtly the most abstract and enigmatic of the Second Viennese school. Yet, after World War II, Webern's music exerted by far the greatest influence on other composers. Webern's earlier works are clearly Expressionist. In mid-life, however, he adopted Schoenberg's twelve-tone method. In his late twelve-tone works, Webern applied serial techniques to rhythm and instrumentation as well as to pitch. These late works inspired a generation of younger postwar composers. (See *Integral Serialism,* chapter 26.)

Webern's *Five Movements for String Quartet, Op. 5* (1909), and *Six Pieces for Orchestra, Op. 6* (1909) are his most Expressionist works. The *Concerto, Op. 24* (1934) and *Variations for Orchestra, Op. 30* (1940) are his best-known serial works.

Alban Berg (Austria, 1885–1935). Also a pupil of Schoenberg and close friend of Webern, Berg created a style more overtly lyrical, dramatic, and Romantic than that of either. His first opera, *Wozzeck* (1914–1921), is Expressionist in both style and subject matter. Berg ties each scene of *Wozzeck* to a closed musical form, using the musical drama inherent in such forms to support the drama on stage. The technique revolutionized opera in the twentieth century. Berg's later twelve-tone works retain both his characteristic lyricism and fascination with extramusical programs. Though not a prolific composer, Berg composed works in most of the standard genre. Still, his fame rests on his two operas, the atonal *Wozzeck* and twelve-tone *Lulu* (1935).

OTHER EXPRESSIONIST AND SERIAL COMPOSERS

Ruth Crawford Seeger (United States, 1901–1953). Seeger's work is angular, rhythmically charged, and dissonant. Her technique is serial. The *String Quartet* (1931) exemplifies her vigorous style.

Ernst Křenek (Austria, b. 1900). After composing a number of successful works using jazz and vernacular idioms, Křenek embraced Schoenberg's twelve-tone method. Among his best-known works are two operas: the Weill-like *Jonny spielt auf* (Johnny Strikes Up the Band, 1927), and the twelve-tone *Karl V* (1930–1933).

Carl Ruggles (United States, 1876–1971). Ruggles's serial techniques create works stylistically Expressionist. His *Men and Mountains* and *Suntreader* (1926–1931), both bold and dramatic symphonic works, are his best known.

Primitivism

Primitivism is less a movement than an attitude prevalent in Europe in the decade before World War I. Artists who had rediscovered the primitive power of folk and non-Western art sought to reproduce this primal quality in their own work. New movements such as Cubism (Picasso, Braque) in France and the Blue Rider group (Kandinsky, Marc) in Germany were inspired in large part by the stylized, abstract quality of much "primitive" art. Their works of this prewar period reflect the direct and often violent quality of such art. In music, Primitivism is synonymous with a single work of one composer, Igor Stravinsky's *Le sacre du printemps* (The Rite of Spring).

IGOR STRAVINSKY

Along with Schoenberg, Stravinsky (Russia, 1882–1971) is one of the two most influential composers of the early part of the century. He rose to fame with three ballets written in quick succession, culminating in 1913 with *The Rite of Spring*. Though full of Slavic folk material and melodies, *The Rite of Spring* was organized into blocks of seemingly unrelated material juxtaposed without apparent transition and held together by incessant, brutal rhythmic patterns. At its first performance, this radical organization, combined with a provocative choreography, precipitated a riot. The work was nevertheless immensely successful.

During World War I, Stravinsky toned down the violent style of *The Rite of Spring* in a series of works that still, however, relied upon Slavic folk materials. The works of this period, sometimes referred to as his Russian period, culminated in *Les Noces* (The Wedding, 1917–1921), a stylized rendering of a rustic village wedding. In the 1920s, Stravinsky abandoned both his Primitivist and Russian style. The style that he created to replace it became one of the most imitated styles of the century. (See Neoclassicism, below.)

OTHER COMPOSERS INFLUENCED BY PRIMITIVISM

Béla Bartók (Hungary, 1881–1945). Though considered a nationalist (see below), Bartók composed several early works overtly influenced by Primitivism. His ballet *The Miraculous Mandarin* (1919) combines many of the most violent rhythmic characteristics of *The Rite of Spring* with the exotic tonalities of Slavic folk culture.

Carl Orff (Germany, 1895–1982).   Orff's brand of Primitivism is considerably milder than that of either Stravinsky or Bartók. Still, Orff's *Carmina Burana* (1936) retains much of the rough, earthy character of the medieval poems that it sets.

Futurism

An artistic and literary movement that arose in Italy at the end of World War I, Futurism sought to reflect modern, mechanized society in art. Futurist attitudes and subjects are anti-Romantic and self-consciously "scientific." Futurist composers saw noise as the characteristic sound of the Modern Age and sought by various means to introduce it into their music. Sometimes called *bruitisme* in France (from *bruit*=noise), the movement exerted considerable influence in the years between the world wars.

LUIGI RUSSOLO

Russolo (Italy, 1885–1947) invented what he called "the art of noise" and instruments to make it. All that survives of his work is a seventy-eight rpm recording and some prose.

EDGARD VARÈSE

Though born in France, Varèse (French-American, 1885–1965) composed most of his mature works in the United States in the 1920s and 1930s, during which time he allied himself with several of the most important literary and artistic Futurists. His style owes much to Stravinsky's *The Rite of Spring*. His works rely on the unorthodox use of woodwinds, brass, and expanded percussion sections.

Varèse's concept of sound as a physical object to be shaped and molded led him to an interest in new, electronic instruments. Late in life he realized his dream of a music of pure sound in the tape piece (see chapter 26), *Poème électronique* (1958). His best-known works are *Hyperprism* (1924) and *Ionisation* (1931). The pseudoscientific titles reflect his Futurist orientation.

OTHER "FUTURIST" COMPOSERS

George Antheil (United States, 1900–1959). Antheil's later work, much of it for Hollywood, is in a relatively conservative Neoclassical style; however, his reputation rests mainly upon his Futurist sound track to the art film *Ballet mécanique* (Machine Ballet, 1924), scored for percussion, airplane engines, and various other noisemakers.

Henry Cowell (United States, 1897–1965). By any account, Cowell was an eclectic composer. His reputation, however, rests most securely on a series of early piano works that use tone-clusters ("chords" formed by adjacent, chromatic tones) and the inside of the piano (where the performer plays directly upon the piano strings). Though Cowell is not usually associated with Futurists proper, his concern with sound itself—in particular, with noise—places him in this camp. His piano works from the 1920s—such as *The Aeolian Harp, The Tiger,* and *The Banshee*—are his best known.

Dada

Coming together during World War I, the Dadaists (the word *Dada* has no intended meaning) saw the war as corrupt and Western culture as bankrupt. They expressed a clear antiart aesthetic; however, their *Dada Abends* (Dada Evenings), though satirical by intent, ended up promoting and developing many important Modernist artists, genres and techniques. Not all the composers listed below were directly associated with the Dada movement itself, but all reflect some important aspect of it.

ERIK SATIE

The early piano works of Satie (French, 1866–1925) greatly influenced the young Debussy. However, his later Dadaist works jettison not only the sentimental and sensuous aspects of nineteenth-century Romanticism but virtually all pretensions to cultural significance as well. Satie invented what he called *Musique d'ameublement* (Musical Furnishings), a music that was not to be listened to anymore than wall-paper was to be looked at. (Muzak, the restaurant and department store music named after the corporation that markets it, is a successful commercial implementation of the idea.) Satie's titles are funny, ironic, and often satirical: *Three Pieces in the Form of a Pear, Truly Flabby Preludes (for a Dog), Disagreeable Impressions*. The music is equally ironic. It might either lurch from humor to satire or to inanity within a single work, or it might present a flat, enigmatic and earnest aspect that suggests, for no apparent reason, a put-on. Inconsequential vernacular material and numbing repetitions are characteristic. The ballets *Parade* (1917) and *Rélâche* (1924) best exemplify this later style. On the other hand, his early piano works *Sarabandes* and *Gymnopédies* (1887) are decidedly Impressionist and greatly influenced the young Debussy. Satie wrote a brief, comic autobiography entitled *Memoirs of an Amnesiac*.

OTHER COMPOSERS INFLUENCED BY DADA

Sir William Walton (England, 1902–1983). Though of a staid, conservative bent in later life, Walton began his long career in 1922 with a work entitled *Façade*. *Façade* is a romp, drawing from the music hall, jazz and Stravinsky. Its combination of satire, put-on, and overt humor is Dada-like.

Darius Milhaud (France, 1892–1974). A disciple of Satie and one of the most prolific of composers, Milhaud's early works, especially the Dada-like *Le Boeuf sur le toit* (The Ox on the Roof, 1920) and the jazzy *La Création du monde* (The Creation of the World, 1923) are his best known.

Virgil Thomson (United States, 1896–1989). Thomson's opera, *Four Saints in Three Acts* (1934), mixes vernacular materials with Satie-like simplicity. The result is Dada.

Neoclassicism

Neoclassicism is a movement that sought to return to closed forms and the imitative counterpoint of the eighteenth century while retaining the more varied harmonic and rhythmic palette of the twentieth. The style arose in the 1920s, and it was not until Stravinsky abandoned the style in the 1950s that it began to pale. Though only a handful of composers were thorough Neoclassicists, virtually every active composer between the world wars was affected in some way by this movement.

STRAVINSKY

Stravinsky initiated Neoclassicism with his ballet score, *Pulcinella* (1919). He went on to develop and practice the style until the early 1950s. Of all his Neoclassical works, the *Symphony of Psalms* (1930) is most frequently performed. Stravinsky turned, in the last two decades of his life, to Serialism, a technique latent in all of his earlier styles. In works like *Movements* (1959) and *Requiem Canticles* (1966), Stravinsky wed his Neoclassical preference for closed forms and historical models to an aphoristic manner reminiscent of late Webern.

OTHER COMPOSERS INFLUENCED BY NEOCLASSICISM

Sergey Prokofiev (Russia, 1891–1953). Prokofiev developed a colorful style that shares many similarities with Stravinsky's Neoclassicism. His best-known work is *Peter and the Wolf* (1936), though the *Classical Symphony* (1916–1917) or the *Third Piano Concerto (1921)* are more characteristic of his early Neoclassical style.

Kurt Weill (Germany, 1900–1950). To Weill, music was a vehicle for social change. He adopted a Neoclassical style mixed with jazz and other vernacular materials. *Dreigroschenoper* (Threepenny Opera, 1928), his best-known work, was written in collaboration with the activist playwright Bertolt Brecht.

Francis Poulenc (France, 1899–1963). A disciple of Satie when young and a devout Neoclassicist in later years, Poulenc is best known today for his songs and religious works. The a cappella cantata *Figure humaine* (1943) and *Mass* (1937) are among his best works.

Arthur Honegger (French, 1892–1955). Honegger's early Futurist orientation is evident in the railroad tone poem *Pacific 231* (1923). A modest Neoclassical style tinged with Romanticism characterizes his later work, such as the *Symphony No. 5 (1951).*

Benjamin Britten (England, 1913–1976). Britten developed an eclectic style and is placed with the Neoclassicists mainly because of his preference for closed forms and his relatively conservative, sometimes Romantic, language. He worked in all media. *A Ceremony of Carols* (1942), the opera *Peter Grimes* (1945), and the *War Requiem* (1962) are his best-known works.

Dmitry Shostakovich (Russia, 1906–1975). Although his style is indebted to Neoclassicism, Shostakovich owes as great a debt to the Romantic and Late Romantic symphonists. In particular, his style resembles that of Mahler in its formal designs, spare textures, and ironic tone. Though known in the West primarily for his eleven symphonies, Shostakovich composed opera, ballets, and chamber and piano works as well. His *Symphony No. 5* (1937) is by far his best-known work, but the symphonies *No. 7* (1941) and *No. 8* (1943) are the most admired.

Carl Nielsen (Denmark, 1865–1931). Nielsen wrote symphonic works in a dissonantly expressive Romantic style. However, his later works tend toward Neoclassicism. His *Fifth Symphony* (1922) is his best-known work.

Samuel Barber (United States, 1910–1981). Like Britten, Barber was a musical conservative. Perhaps better called a Neoromantic than a Neoclassicist, his best-known works are the *Adagio for Strings* (1936), and the orchestral song *Knoxville: Summer 1915* (1947).

Roy Harris (United States, 1898–1979). Harris wrote chamber and symphonic works in a style derivative of Neoclassicism but exhibiting many of the characteristics of American Nationalism (see "Nationalism in the United States," below) as well. The *Third Symphony* (1938) is his best-known work.

Gebrauchsmusik

Gebrauchsmusik ("music for use") is associated primarily with composer Paul Hindemith.

PAUL HINDEMITH

(Germany, 1895–1963) was a prolific composer who wrote in several different styles. However, after the experiments of his early music, he developed his own conservative dialect of the Neoclassical idiom. Greatly concerned with music education, Hindemith developed a style simple and direct enough for use in training the young. He called this style *Gebrauchsmusik* and proceeded to outline it in a series of pedagogical texts as well as to write works in it for almost all the standard Western instruments. His orchestral works are direct, occasionally colorful, and sometimes dramatic. As a whole his style avoids Romantic expression, relying instead on what he considered responsible craftsmanship. His many sonatas for woodwinds and brass are well known to young instrumentalists. His symphony *Mathis der Mahler* (Matthias the Painter, 1934) and *Symphonic Metamorphoses* on themes of Weber (1943) are frequently performed.

Nationalism

Nationalism remained a force in music well into the twentieth century. As the tonal language of the eighteenth and nineteenth centuries dissolved, composers looked for a source of renewal. Nationalists found it in the vernacular and traditional music of their people.

BÉLA BARTÓK

Beginning his career in a Late Romantic style reminiscent of Strauss, Bartók (Hungary, 1881–1945) quickly saw the possibilities of Stravinsky's Primitivism (see above). In a series of works written during World War I, he wed that bold new style to Slavic folk material, creating in the process one of the most individual styles of the century. Throughout the 1920s and 1930s Bartók adopted many Neoclassical techniques while still retaining the ethnic flavor of his native land. His most famous works are the *Concerto for Orchestra* (1943), the string quartets *No. 4* and *No. 5* (1928, 1934), and the *Music for Strings, Percussion, and Celesta* (1936).

NATIONALISTS IN THE UNITED STATES

Nationalism in the United States took two forms in the twentieth century: (1) an atmospheric, almost mystical representation of the American past, usually with reference to an idealized frontier spirit; and (2) a glorification of the vital, progressive American present, usually with reference to modern popular culture (jazz) or technology. The first type draws inspiration from folk and patriotic music; the second type shares many stylistic and programmatic characteristics with European Futurism. Though both styles are seldom present in a single work, most of the composers listed below created works of both types.

Charles E. Ives (1874–1954). Ives worked as an insurance man and composed on weekends. He sought to create a truly American music that reflected not only the place but also its spirit. He stayed clear of the musical profession and published his works at his own expense. Few of them were publicly performed in his lifetime. Most of his works were written between the turn of the century and the end of World War I. Ives favored dense, dissonant textures colored with melodic fragments drawn from popular, patriotic or religious tunes. With such a style Ives sought to express experience directly, without the intercession of traditional musical technique and untroubled by the stylistic anachronisms that resulted. Ives wrote symphonic, chamber, piano, and choral works, as well as over 100 songs. *Three Places in New England,* (1908-1914) and *The Unanswered Question* (1906) are his best-known works; the *Concord Sonata* and *Fourth Symphony* (1909-1916) are his most admired.

John Alden Carpenter (1876–1951). Carpenter was a railroad shipping magnate who, like Ives, was a weekend composer. He created many songs, ballets and instrumental works that depict American urban life, all written in a distinctive Modernist style. His jazzy ballet *Skyscrapers* (1928) remains his best-known work.

George Gershwin (1898–1937). Gershwin was not only a successful composer of popular songs (see chapter 28), but he was also one of the first American composers to gain an international reputation in the concert realm. His *Rhapsody in Blue* (1924) and *American in Paris* (1928) wed an Impressionist palette to the rhythms and melodies of American jazz. Gershwin's *Porgy and Bess* (1935) is a landmark of American musical theater.

Aaron Copland (1900–1990). Copland composed in many styles, but his most popular and distinctive works come from the years before and during World War II. His lean, seemingly simple and overtly optimistic style has become associated in the American popular mind with the American frontier and perhaps even with the American character. Copland's style has influenced several generations of American composers. He wrote an opera, songs, and many symphonic, chamber, and piano works. His ballets *Appalachian Spring* (1934) and *Billy the Kid* (1938) are his best known.

OTHER NATIONALIST COMPOSERS

Zoltán Kodály (Hungary, 1882–1967). Kodály's work resembles that of Bartók, though its harmonic language is more traditional. Kodály wrote symphonic and chamber works, of which the symphonic suite *Háry János* (1926) is the best-known.

Leoš Janáček (Czechoslovakia, 1854–1928). Janáček's style is less homogeneous than that of either Bartók or Kodály, the Slavic Nationalism giving way on occasion to Romantic lyricism. Janáček is unusual among artists in that most of his works were written in relative old age. Of these, the best known are the opera *Makropulos Affair* (1925) and the orchestral work *Sinfonietta* (1926), both written in his early seventies.

Manuel de Falla (Spain, 1876–1946). De Falla's style exhibits the characteristics of both Impressionism and Neoclassicism. The orchestral suites from the two ballets, *El amor brujo* (Love, the Magician; 1915) and *El Sombrero de tres picos* (The Three-cornered Hat, 1919) are his best-known works.

Ottorino Respighi (Italy, 1879–1936). Respighi, like Stravinsky, was a student of Rimsky-Korsakov. He was a romantic Impressionist who turned toward Neoclassicism in his later years. He is best known for his symphonic works, the most famous of which are *Fontane di Roma* (Fountains of Rome, 1917) and *Pini di Roma* (Pines of Rome, 1924).

Ralph Vaughan Williams (England, 1872–1958). Vaughan Williams studied with Ravel, but added to the French Impressionist style a sturdy, consonant English sound derived from English folk songs. He wrote symphonies, operas, songs and choral works. His *Sea Symphony* (1910) is one of his best-known works.

Heitor Villa-Lobos (Brazil, 1887–1959). Villa-Lobos sought to fuse Brazilian idioms with traditional Western forms and techniques. There resulted a style rhythmically charged yet couched in Neoclassical counterpoint. The several numbered works entitled *Chôrus* and *Bachianas Brasileiras* are his best known.

Microtonality and Non-Western Influences

Throughout the century, composers have found inspiration in non-Western musics. The interest arises in large part from the Modern composer's search for new tonal materials. Non-Western musics offer to Modern composers not only exotic new scales and instruments, but also new tuning systems. These exotic tuning systems often involve tones that fall between the twelve chromatic tones of the traditional Western tuning system (called *Equal Temperament*). Tuning systems that create tones not present in equal temperament are called *microtonal*.

HARRY PARTCH

Partch (United States, 1901–1976) not only developed his own tuning system, but he invented and built the special instruments necessary to perform in those tuning systems. He drew inspiration from Japanese noh and kabuki drama for such works as *Delusion of the Furies* (1969) and *The Dreamer That Remains* (1972).

OTHER MICROTONAL COMPOSERS

Composers such as Alois Hába (Czechoslovakia, 1893–1973) and Julian Carillo (Mexico, 1875–1965) dealt extensively with such "microtonal" tuning systems. Composers Henry Cowell (United States, 1897–1965) and Colin McPhee (United States, 1901–1964) exhibited notable non-Western characteristics in their music as well. More recently, Ben Johnston (United States, b. 1925), a protégé of Partch, has composed numerous works using alternative tuning systems, such as the *Sonata for Microtonal Piano* (1965).

In the first half of the twentieth-century composers sought both a new role in society and a source for new musical materials. New styles sprang up from the ashes of the old. Older styles were resuscitated and radically transformed. And finally, the centuries old musical language of the West gave way to a Babel of new languages and competing idioms. Western music became as fragmented and complex as Modern society itself.

For Additional Study

Abraham, Gerald, et al. *The New Grove Russian Masters 2*. New York: Norton. 1989.

Austin, William, et al. *The New Grove Twentieth-Century American Masters*. New York: Norton. 1988.

Cowell, Henry. *American Composers on American Music*. New York: Ungar. 1962.

Griffiths, Paul. *A Concise History of Avant-Garde Music from Debussy to Boulez.* New York: Oxford U. Press. 1978.

McVeagh, Diana, et al. *The New Grove Twentieth-Century English Masters.* New York: Norton. 1986.

Morgan, Robert. *Twentieth-Century Music.* New York: Norton. 1990.

Nectoux, Jean-Michel, *et al. The New Grove Twentieth Century French Masters.* New York: Norton. 1990.

Neighbor, Oliver, *et al. The New Grove Second Viennese School.* New York: Norton. 1983.

Salzman, Eric. *Twentieth-Century Music: An Introduction.* 3d ed. Englewood Cliffs, NJ: Prentice-Hall. 1988.

Schorske, Carl. *Fin-de-Siècle Vienna.* New York: Knopf. 1980.

Shattuck, Roger. *The Banquet Years.* New York: Vintage Books. 1955.

Slonimsky, Nicolas. *Music since 1900.* 4th ed. New York: Scribner. 1971.

Watkins, Glenn. *Soundings: Music in the Twentieth Century.* New York: Schirmer. 1988.

Recommended Listening

Antheil, George. *Ballet mécanique*

Bartók, Béla. *String Quartet No. 5*

—. *Concerto for Orchestra*

Berg, Alban. *Wozzeck*

Britten, Benjamin. *War Requiem*

Copland, Aaron. *Appalachian Spring*

Cowell, Henry. *The Banshee*

Falla, Manuel de. *El amor brujo* (Love, the Magician).

Hindemith, Paul. *Symphonic Metamorphosis*

Ives, Charles. *Three Places in New England*

—. *Concord Sonata*

Janáček, Leoš. *Sinfonietta*

Milhaud, Darius. *La création du monde* (The Creation of the World).

Orff, Carl. *Carmina Burana*

Partch, Harry. *The Dreamer That Remains*

Poulenc, Francis. *Mass*

Prokofiev, Sergey. *Classical Symphony*

—. *Third Piano Concerto*

Satie, Erik. *Parade*

Schoenberg, Arnold. *Pierrot lunaire* (Moonstruck Pierrot)

—. *Suite for piano, Op. 25*

Shostakovich, Dmitry. *Symphony No. 5*

Stravinsky, Igor. *Le sacre du printemps* (The Rite of Spring)

—. *A Symphony of Psalms*

Varèse, Edgard. *Hyperprism*

—. *Poème électronique* (Electronic poem)

Walton, Sir William. *Façade*

Webern, Anton. *Six Pieces for Orchestra, Op. 6*

—. *Concerto, Op. 24*

Weill, Kurt. *Threepenny Opera*

26

The Modern Period since World War II

1945   Germany surrenders; atom bombs destroy Hiroshima and Nagasaki; radio astronomy; first jet-propelled planes and rockets

1946   First United Nations assembly; Nuremberg trials

1947   India becomes Independent; Williams, *A Streetcar Named Desire*

1948   Berlin airlift; Gandhi assassinated; first long-playing records (LPs)

1949   Communist Mao Tse-Tung deposes Chinese Nationalists; Soviet Union explodes atomic bomb; Cold War begins; Orwell, *1984;* Miller, *Death of a Salesman*

1950   Korean War begins; hydrogen "superbomb" exploded

1951   Salinger, *The Catcher in the Rye*

1952   Eisenhower elected president; Elizabeth II becomes queen of England

1953   Korean War ends; Rosenbergs executed for treason; Malenkov succeeds Stalin; Watson and Crick model DNA; Beckett, *Waiting for Godot*

1954   McCarthy hearings televised; Supreme Court outlaws school segregation; first atomic submarine; war in Indochina; e.e. cummings, *Poems*

1955   Warsaw Pact signed; serum for infantile paralysis developed

1956   Suez Crisis; Hungarian Revolt; First "Warsaw Autumn" International Festival of Contemporary Music; Elvis Presley's first TV appearance

1957   First civil rights bill; Kerouac, *On the Road;* first national broadcast of "American Bandstand"; Soviet Union launches *Sputnik*

1959   Alaska and Hawaii become states; Castro takes power in Cuba

1960   Kennedy elected President; "the pill" introduced; first successful laser

1961   Soviets put first man in space; Shepherd makes first American sub-orbital flight; Bay of Pigs invasion; the "twist" introduced

1962 Cuban missile crisis; Glenn first American to orbit earth; *Mariner 2* encounters Venus; Albee, *Who's Afraid of Virginia Woolf?*; Lincoln Center for the Performing Arts opens in New York; Carson, *Silent Spring*

1963 Kennedy assassinated; Beatles tour United States; Friedan, *The Feminine Mystique*; Supreme Court outlaws school prayer

1964 Dr. Martin Luther King, Jr., wins Nobel Peace Prize

1965 First space walk; American "involvement" in Vietnam increases dramatically; *Autobiography of Malcolm X*; King marches in Alabama

1966 France withdraws from NATO

1967 Israeli-Arab "Six-Day War"; heart transplant; Lilly, *The Mind of the Dolphin*

1968 King and Robert Kennedy assassinated; Nixon elected president; Soviets invade Czechoslovakia; student uprisings in France and United States; National Guard fires on students at Kent State; police fire on students at Jackson State

1969 Americans land on moon; Woodstock; De Gaulle resigns French presidency; Beatles break up

1970 United States invades Cambodia; first Earth Day; Toffler, *Future Shock*

1971 Indo-Pakistan War; *Pentagon Papers* published; *John F. Kennedy Center for the Performing Arts* opens in Washington, D.C.

1972 Nixon reelected; Wallace shot; Black September terrorists murder Israeli athletes at Munich Olympics

1973 Vietnam War ends; first energy crisis; "Watergate" begins; Agnew resigns under indictment; Solzhenitsyn, *The Gulag Archipelago*; Supreme Court decides *Rowe vs. Wade*

1974 Nixon resigns in wake of Watergate

1975 Spanish dictator Franco dies; International Women's Year

1976 *Viking II* lands on Mars; Mao Tse-Tung dies; Carter elected president; United States Bicentennial Celebrations

1977 New York blackout; massacres by Amin in Uganda; TV production of Haley's *Roots*; *Star Wars* released

1978 Camp David accord between Israel and Egypt; first test-tube baby born; Pei's East Wing of the National Gallery opens; Pluto's moon Charon discovered

1979 Shah of Iran deposed; Americans taken hostage in Iran

1980 Reagan elected President; John Lennon murdered

1981 Egyptian President Sadat assassinated; American hostages in Iran freed; *Columbia* first space shuttle in orbit

1982 Equal Rights Amendment defeated; wars in Lebanon and the Falkland Islands; first heart transplant

1984 AIDS virus identified; MTV inaugurated; Reagan reelected

1985   Gorbachev becomes First Secretary of the Soviet Union; compact disks (CDs) gain wide acceptance; Live Aid concerts

1986   Space shuttle *Challenger* explodes; Iran-Contra scandal; Soviet nuclear disaster at Chernobyl

1988   Bush elected President

1989   Pro-democracy demonstrations crushed in China; Berlin Wall falls; *Voyager 2* encounters Neptune

1990   Reunification of Germany; Cold War ends; Iraq invades Kuwait

1991   Gulf War

In the decade that followed World War II it seemed that a common Western musical style was possible, one forged from the radical Serialism of Anton Webern. But simultaneously, a renewed interest in the ideas of Dadaist and Futurists artists gave rise to the concept of indeterminacy and to a music created from random processes called aleatoric music.

By the 1970s both Serialism and Indeterminacy had paled before the eclectic style of a younger generation. Not until the 1980s, with the success of Minimalism, did a single stylistic school again exert a pervasive influence. Minimalism's ability to draw popular music audiences has once again raised the hope, seemingly abandoned since the 1920s, that an art music might be both "serious" and "popular." From this Post-Modern world has arisen many diverse styles.

FROM WORLD WAR II TO THE 1960s

Two disparate aesthetics emerge in the postwar years. One sought to control every aspect of music through serial techniques, the other sought to free even the composer from control through the use of random processes.

Integral or Total Serialism

The term *Integral Serialism* (sometimes referred to as *Total Serialism*) describes a method that controls every aspect of a work—pitch, rhythm, instrumentation, and so forth—through serial techniques. Such works are rigidly structured and determinate, leaving little to chance.

MUSICAL CHARACTERISTICS

In general, all the characteristics of prewar Serialism are present and intensified in Integral Serialism.

Melody. The melodies of Integral Serialism are angular, with large leaps and dissonant intervals.

Harmony. As in prewar Serialism, the distinction between "melody" and "harmony" is ambiguous since both arise from the same serial source. Harmony is varied, complex, and dissonant.

Rhythm. Because of the application of serial techniques to rhythm, durations become even more varied and seemingly erratic. Traditional pulse and metrical organization remain only in the conventions of notation.

Texture. Textures are polyphonic. *Klangfarbenmelodie* and uniformly pointillistic textures are common.

Form. Since form is often serially fabricated, it tends—like rhythm—to be nonperiodic and complex. However, as the major serial composers become influenced by nondeterminate processes (see "Chance," below), the notion of form changes. Even while still serializing pitch and rhythm some composers begin using so-called "open forms." An open form is one in which the parts of a work may be rigidly determinate but the order in which those parts are performed is not. For example, a work in open form might consist of many serially organized and thoroughly notated phrases the order of which is chosen by the performer. Such works as Brown's *Available Forms*, Boulez's *Third Piano Sonata* or Stockhausen's *Klavierstück XI* are examples of open forms.

MAJOR COMPOSERS

Olivier Messiaen (France, b. 1908). Messiaen's interest in medieval Christian and traditional Indian music led to a unique language based on pitch and rhythmic modes that by the late 1940s reflected the preoccupations of Integral Serialism. His devotion to Catholicism, his infatuation with bird songs and the East combined to create a colorful and exotic style. Messiaen's works make no effort at Romantic expression, but rather take on the formal, stylized, and ceremonial aspect of a religious service; for this reason, they are often described as *ritualistic*. He has written many orchestral, piano, and chamber works as well as choral works and solo songs. Messiaen has produced numerous works for the organ (his instrument) all with evocative Christian titles. Other important works include his *Quatuor pour la fin du temps* (Quartet for the End of Time, 1941), *Trois petites liturgies pour la Présence Divine* (Three Short Liturgies for the Divine Presence, 1944), and the symphony *Turangalîla* (1948).

Milton Babbitt (United States, b. 1916). Babbitt extended Schoenberg's twelve-tone method, creating a closed system that rivals traditional tonality in its depth and complexity. He was the first to apply serial techniques to rhythm (*Three Compositions for Piano,* 1947) and to integrate orchestration, dynamics, and articulation into the twelve-tone system. His work with the RCA synthesizer (see below) has produced a number of important works for live performer and pre-recorded tape. Babbitt's style is pointillistic, complex and uncompromising; it is one of the most individual styles of the century. He has written piano, chamber, symphonic, and vocal works. Among his most performed works are the *Composition for Four Instruments* (1948), *Partitions* (1957), and *Phonemena* (1970). Babbitt's *Philomel* (1964) for live voice and pre-recorded tape is a classic of electronic music (see below).

Pierre Boulez (France, b. 1925). A student of Messiaen and one the earliest theorists of Integral Serialism, Boulez is not only a composer, but a conductor, critic, and promoter of new music. Boulez's works retain some of the Eastern inflections and ritualistic character of Messiaen. Several of his works from the 1950s—such as *Third Piano Sonata* (1956–57) and the orchestral song cycle *Pli selon pli* (Fold upon Fold, 1957–1962)—were written in open form. His best-known and most influential work is *Le marteau sans maître* (The Hammer without a Master, 1954).

Karlheinz Stockhausen (Germany, b. 1928). Another student of Messiaen and, in the early 1950s, a colleague of Boulez, Stockhausen evolved a more ambitious form of Integral Serialism, one more rigorous and uncompromising than that of either. In *Gruppen* (Groups, 1955–1957), a work for three orchestras, he extends the serial idea even to the spatial distribution of sound. His contact with Cage (see below) in the early 1950s turned him, however, in less determinate directions. His best-known works are *Klavierstück XI* (Piano Piece XI, 1956; a serial piece with an "open" form), and *Gruppen*.

Luciano Berio (Italy, b. 1925). Although Berio's brand of serialism was warmer, more lyric, and more approachable than either that of Boulez or Stockhausen, his application of serial technique was as least as thorough. His *Circles* (1960) for voice and percussion controls not only all aspects of the sound, but the movement of the performers on the stage as well. By the mid 1960s his work took on a more eclectic character, however. His *Sinfonia* (1968) retains many of the techniques of Integral Serialism, but combines them with elements of open form and pastiche (see below).

Elliott Carter (United States, b. 1908). In the early 1950s Carter developed a compositional method only tangentially related to Schoenberg's twelve-tone technique, but one that relied upon complete serial control over all the pitch and rhythmic material of a work. The surface of Carter's music is complex, dissonant, and rhythmically charged. Like Babbitt, his style is thoroughly individual. The *String Quartet No. 1* (1950-51) is the first in his mature style. Carter's best-known work is the *Double Concerto* (1961), which Stravinsky deemed "a masterpiece."

Aleatoric Music

A music is referred to as *aleatoric* (from *alea,* Latin for "dice") when some aspect of it has been determined by some random process. In the late 1940s, John Cage single-handedly introduced the idea to the musical world and proceeded to provide it with a philosophical and aesthetic grounding. Aleatoric music arose in response to the increasingly determinate techniques of Integral Serialism. Many composers, opposed to such rigid control, began to look instead for compositional methods that might bypass the conscious mind and tap the unconscious, or even ones that might bypass the composer's psyche altogether. Eastern philosophies whose aim is to suppress the ego (such as philosophical Taoism or Zen Buddhism) and certain ideas advanced by prewar Dadaists (especially the painter Marcel Duchamp, 1887–1968) served as the starting point for the movement.

CHANCE MUSIC

Chance music is one in which *all* the compositional decisions (Which pitch? Which duration? Which instrument? and so on) are made by some random process, such as tossing a coin or consulting a random number table.

Musical Characteristics. Since the materials of chance music are generated at random, there is no clearly definable style that can be associated with it. The only control exercised by the composer is in the selection of the random process and in its interpretation (that is, in its translation into musical notation).

John Cage (United States, b. 1912). In the late 1940s, Cage proposed the idea of aleatoric music in general and Chance music in particular. In his Chance work *Music of Changes* (1951) for example, Cage determined every detail of the score through random processes suggested by the *I Ching* (Book of Changes), an ancient Chinese divination text. Cage's aesthetic arose in large part from his association with the Abstract Expressionist and Action Painters in New York (Rothko, Kline, Pollock), as well as from his interest in Zen Buddhism and the Dadaist philosophy of Duchamp.

Cage seeks to eliminate the composer from the "composition" and to blur the distinction between music, noise, and silence. He does this in order that the determinate, ordered world of art might merge with the unordered, "accidental" world of everyday life. Cage's *4' 33"* (Four Minutes and Thirty-three Seconds, 1952) in which "nothing" happens is the classic expression of this aesthetic attitude.

The works of Cage that precede his interest in Chance methods are equally remarkable. He invented what he called the *prepared piano*, a piano whose strings have been "prepared" with various foreign objects in order to alter the sound. His *Sonatas and Interludes* (1946–1948) was composed for such an instrument.

Cage has written a great deal of prose, much of it created through random processes. His first book, *Silence* (1961), is the clearest statement of his aesthetic.

INDETERMINACY AND IMPROVISATION

A music is "indeterminate" (that is, nondeterminate) if the composer leaves some, but not *all*, the compositional decisions up to chance, random processes or the performer. In the 1950s Cage used the term for any music that relied on some sort of random process, but the term has since taken on a more restricted meaning.

One result of the interest in nondeterminate processes was a renewed interest in improvisation. When the composer requires the performer to create significant musical material, the work is considered *improvisational;* when the performer chooses only between one course and another the music is considered *indeterminate.*

Musical Characteristics. In indeterminate music, the composer's imagination still governs the style even though some details of the work are left "indeterminate." For example, notation might be indeterminate when the composer specifies the instrument, the dynamics, and the general range but not the specific pitches. Form might be indeterminate when the composer creates a number of fully notated fragments but leaves their order up to the performer, creating a so-called *open form.*

In thoroughly improvisational works, in which the performer creates the musical material on the spot, it will be the performer's musical personality that defines that work's character.

Morton Feldman (United States, 1926-1987). Feldman's early scores, dating from his association with Cage, are "indeterminate" works, using unconventional graphic notations that specified pitch and rhythm only approximately. His *King of Denmark* is characteristic of this early style.

Earle Brown (United States, b. 1926). Brown incorporates rhythmic, pitch and formal indeterminacy into his works, using graphic and generalized notation. The *Available Forms* series composed in the early 1960s is representative of his style.

Lukas Foss (United States, b. 1922). In the late 1950s, Foss formed the Improvisational Chamber Ensemble, probably the first non-jazz improvisational group in the West. In works like *Time Cycle* (1960), he incorporated improvisation, indeterminacy, and serial techniques.

Other composers. In the 1980s and 1990s several other composers, such as J. K. Randall (United States, b. 1929), Ben Boretz (United States, b. 1934), and Pauline Oliveros (United States, b. 1932), have concerned themselves with improvisation. In the process, they have reinterpreted both the social and musical role of composer and performer.

PROBABILITY

In probabilistic music, random processes are controlled by a probability function. A purely random process produces values evenly distributed between some upper and lower limit; a so-called "controlled random process", one limited by a probability function (the familiar bell-shaped curve, for instance), might instead produce values that cluster around some specified median value. In mathematics, a controlled random process is referred to as a *stochastic* process. Music that uses such processes is often referred to as *Stochastic music*.

Yannis Xenakis (b. 1922). Rumanian-born of Greek parents and a long time resident of Paris, Xenakis trained as an architect as well as a musician. He pioneered a technique that has come to be known as *algorithmic composition*. Using mathematical formulas drawn from probability theory and statistical analysis to generate the details of his compositions, he produced a series of striking and influential works. That mathematics and music are in some way wed is an ancient notion and one that Xenakis has sought to manifest. The massive, physical quality of much of his music owes a debt to Varèse. His *Pithoprakta* (1956) and *Stratégy* (1962) are his best-known works.

Other composers. Probabilistic or Stochastic composition thrives today under a variety of different names, but most involve digital computers. (See "Computer Music," below.)

ELECTRONIC MUSIC

The development of electronic media transformed contemporary music. Various electronic instruments, such as the Hammond organ and *ondes martenot* ("Martenot's waves"), were available before World War II; but it was only with the development of the magnetic tape recorder during the war that the storage, retrieval and editing of sound became possible. Soon after the war, composers used these new tools to create works directly on magnetic tape. Both the Futurists' dream of an art of pure sound and the Integral Serialist dream of absolute control seemed within reach.

Tape Music

The term *Tape music* refers to works produced, complete, on magnetic tape. Several studios in Europe and the United States were dedicated to this medium. In the early 1950s, composers Otto Luening (United States, b. 1900) and Vladimir Ussachevsky (United States, b. 1911) of Columbia University founded one of the first studios dedicated to the production of Tape music. At the same time in Cologne, Germany, Herbert Eimert (Germany, 1897–1972) founded one of the first important European studios.

TECHNIQUES OF TAPE MUSIC

Classic Studio. Studios such as those at Columbia and in Cologne are referred to as *classic studios*. The Classic studio is comprised of a bank of oscillators (electronic tone generators), filters, mixers, and tape recorders. Sounds are recorded or generated electronically; they are then filtered and mixed and recorded (or re-recorded) on magnetic tape. The tape is spliced, remixed and rerecorded as necessary. Composers such as Mario Davidovsky (United States, b. 1934), Bülent Arel (Turkey, b. 1918), Kenneth Gaburo (United States, b. 1926), and Stockhausen (see above) pioneered the technique. Stockhausen's *Gesang der Jünglinge* (Song of the Youths, 1956) and Varèse's *Poème électronique* (1958; see chapter 25) are considered classics of Tape Music.

Analog Synthesizers. A synthesizer is an electronic instrument that integrates all the elements of the Classic studio (oscillators, filters, and so on) into a single unit. An *analog* synthesizer is one that does not use digital (computer) technology.

The RCA Mark II synthesizer, unveiled in 1955, was the first analog music synthesizer. The RCA synthesizer was a large, vacuum tube machine housed at the Columbia studio (now called the Columbia-Princeton Electronic Music Center). With this synthesizer, composers were able to control pitch and rhythm precisely without the laborious tape splicing and re-recording necessary in the classic studio. The RCA synthesizer was used principally by composers Milton Babbitt (see above) and Charles Wuorinen (United States, b. 1938). Babbitt's *Ensembles for Synthesizer,* 1962–1964) and Wuorinen's *Time's Encomium,* (1969) were produced on this machine.

Using integrated circuits rather than tubes, engineers were soon able to compress the RCA-type synthesizer into one integrated portable unit. The best-known of these mass-marketed analog synthesizers are the Moog, Buchla, and Arp. The Moog can be heard in the popular album *Switched on Bach* created by Walter (Windy) Carlos (United States, b. 1949). Morton Subotnik (United States, b. 1933) created his *Silver Apples of the Moon* (1967) on the Buchla.

Digital Synthesizers. Digital synthesizers are small computers dedicated to the production of sound. In the same way that Compact Discs (CD's) are able to reproduce sound with greater ease and higher fidelity than conventional (analog) methods, digital synthesizers are able to *create and manipulate* sounds more easily and efficiently than is possible on the analog synthesizer. The Syn-Clavier is one of the first and most complex of the digital synthesizers; the various Yamaha DX-7 types are simpler and more common.

TYPES OF TAPE MUSIC

There are two distinct types of Tape Music, *musique concrète* and *pure electronic.* However, many tape works (Stockhausen's *Gesang der Jünglinge* and Varèse's *Poème électronique*, see above) combine the two types.

Musique Concrète. *Musique concrète* ("solid" or "substantial" music) is a Tape Music created from recorded natural sounds. It was first produced in classic studios by composers Pierre Schaeffer (b. 1910) and Pierre Henry (France, b. 1927) at French National Radio in the late 1940's. Henry's *Apocalypse de Jean* (Apocalypse of John) is a classic of the genre.

Pure Electronic. *Pure electronic* tape music has as its source sounds created by electronic instruments and written directly onto tape. The synthesizer works of Babbitt and Subotnik as well as the classic studio works of Davidovsky (such as the *Study No. II, 1966*) are all pure electronic works.

Computer Music

In conventional (analog) recording, sound registers on magnetic tape as a fluctuating electric field. In order to manipulate this recorded sound, the composer must reproduce it and then re-record it. The process degrades the quality of the original recording as each generation of successive re-recording adds noise and hiss to the final product. In Computer Music, however, sound is stored as a string of numbers. Numerical files are easily copied, manipulated and mixed without any degradation. The computer's numerical files are converted to electronic voltages that can drive a loud speaker by a digital-to-analog converter—or *DAC* for short.

The production of sound by computer is referred to as *computer synthesis.* A Chance or stochastic method that uses the computer is referred to as *computer-aided* composition.

COMPUTER SYNTHESIS

Computer synthesis involves producing finished compositions and performances (on digital or analog tape) by computer rather than Classic Studio technique.

Significant Composers. Composers such as John Chowning (United States, b. 1934), Barry Vercoe (United States, b. 1938), James Dashow (United States, b. 1944), Paul Lansky (United States, b. 1944), Charles Dodge (United States, b. 1944) have produced a large body of work that is generated and performed by computers.

Computer Music Centers. The leading centers of creation and research in computer music have, in the United States, been at universities. Stanford University, the Massachusetts Institute of Technology, the University of Illinois, the University of California at San Diego, and Princeton University have all helped pioneer the field. The major European center is Institut de Recherche et Coordination Acoustique/Musique (Institute for Coordination and Research in Acoustics and Music) known as *IRCAM* established by Boulez in 1977.

COMPUTER-AIDED COMPOSITION

The computer is ideal for Stochastic or Probabilistic composition. The computational efficiency of the computer has led several composers, such as Lejarin Hiller (United States, b. 1924) and James Tenney (United States, b. 1934), to create works the details of which are calculated by computers using random number generators and probability functions. A compositional method that uses such stochastic techniques is referred to as *algorithmic composition*.

Live Electronics

Electronic sound can be combined with live performance in three ways. A performer may be asked to perform along with a prerecorded tape; or a performer might perform an electronic instrument (such as a synthesizer) live; or electronic instruments might be used to alter and expand the sound produced by a conventional instrument performed live.

Varèse's *Déserts* (Deserts, 1954) is one of the first works to combine live instrumentalists with pre-recorded tape music. Mario Davidovsky's *Synchronism* series (1960-70s) for solo instruments and pre-recorded tape is the best-known of the genre, followed closely by Milton Babbitt's several important works for live vocalist and tape (especially *Philomel,* 1964).

Stockhausen (*Mikrophonie I*, 1965) and many other composers frequently use instruments from the Classic Studio to manipulate sounds performed live. Interactive computer technology now makes such manipulation easier and greatly expands the possibilities of the medium. Composers Morton Subotnik (United States, b. 1933), Roger Reynolds (United States, b. 1934), and Daniel Gutwein (United States, b. 1951) frequently use live digital technology in their works.

OTHER MOVEMENTS AND TRENDS

The movements and trends outlined below only partially complete an end-of-the-century catalogue.

Pure Sound

The concerns of composers of electronic Music with pure sound is reflected as well by many composers who work with conventional instruments.

NEW POLISH SCHOOL

In the late 1950s a group of Polish composers, sometimes known as the *New Polish School,* created a music that relied purely on changing colors and sound density. The movement arose during the "Warsaw Autumn" festivals of contemporary music, partially in reaction to conservative Soviet domination. The style relies heavily on toneclusters (chords comprised of many adjacent chromatic notes), massed instrumental timbres, and unconventional instrumental techniques.

Krzysztof Penderecki (Poland, b. 1933). Penderecki is the best-known member of the school. His *Threnody to the Victims of Hiroshima* (1961) and *St.Luke's Passion* (1963) are classics of the style.

Witold Lutosławski (Poland, b. 1913). Lutosławski's early work is Neoclassical with a Nationalistic character derived from Bartók. In the 1950s, however, he adapted the style of his younger colleagues to his own purpose. The result is an individual style that allies characteristics of the New Polish school with his own individual formal and harmonic concerns. His *Symphony No. 3* (1983) is characteristic of his unique style.

György Ligeti (Hungary, b. 1923). Ligeti's *Atmosphères* (1961) is a thorough expressions of the New Polish aesthetic. His *Double Concerto* (1972) and subsequent works are, however, more eclectic in character and might just as easily be classified as Minimalist (see below).

TEXT-SOUND COMPOSITIONS

Text-Sound works derive from what is called *concrete poetry.* The sound of a Text-Sound piece is made up entirely of phonemes, words or phrases. These vocal sounds are treated as sonic objects rather than as intelligible speech. Therefore, the "text" of a Text-Sound work does not necessarily, or even usually, make linguistic sense. Early dadaists Hugo Ball and Kurt Schwitters pioneered the technique. Modern Text-Sound works are often created on tape as *musique concrète.* Cage and Gaburo have written several Text-Sound works. Charles Amirkhanian (United States, b. 1945) works exclusively within this genre.

Eclecticism

More than in any other period of Western musical history, composers of the last half of the twentieth century have crossed and joined styles and idioms. Some of these mixed styles are described below.

THE THIRD STREAM

Music of the *third stream* is created as the other two streams (jazz and art music) join. Mixed idioms are so common today that the term has only historical significance.

Gunther Schuller (United States, b. 1925). Schuller coined the term and created a series of works that joined modern, "cool" jazz (see chapter 28) with a pointillistic serial technique reminiscent of early Webern. His *Studies on Themes of Paul Klee* (1959) is a Third Stream classic.

John Lewis (United States, b. 1920). Lewis formed the Modern Jazz Quartet. His *Sketch* is characteristic of his Third Stream style.

PASTICHE

Pastiche refers not only to the mixing of styles but also to their super-imposition. Music of this type achieves its special character from the resulting stylistic anachronisms. The second movement of Berio's *Sinfonia* (1968), in which an entire movement of a Mahler symphony is performed while serial and text-sound material is layered on top, is an extreme example of the technique.

Jacob Druckman (United States, b. 1928). Many of his works from the 1970s intersperse colorful, pointillistic material with quotations from seventeenth-century opera or other anachronistic styles. He has written symphonic and chamber works. His *Lamia* for voice and orchestra is a colorful example of this idiom.

George Crumb (United States, b. 1929). Crumb's concern for sound, his use of unconventional instrumental techniques, and his poetic programs place him in a unique position in the period. His style is delicate and subtle. Often Crumb relies on pastiche for dramatic or programmatic effect. In "V. Music of the Starry Night" from *Music for a Summer Evening* (1974), a fugue from Bach's *Well-Tempered Clavier* continuously interrupts the otherwise thick and dissonant texture. Crumb's notation is often indeterminate. His *Ancient Voices of Children* (1970) is his best-known work.

Peter Maxwell Davies (England, b. 1934). Davies's early work relied heavily on historical pastiche. (He has recently developed a staid, more conservative style.) Davies has written operas, as well as symphonic, chamber, and multi-media works (see below). His *Eight Songs for a Mad King* (1969) is one of his best-known work.

David Del Tredici (United States, b. 1937). Del Tredici's mature works rely to a large extent on stylistic pastiche. Within a single work he can easily range stylistically from Strauss, to Schoenberg, to Gilbert and Sullivan with everything from polkas to fugues in between. His campy *Final Alice* (1976) is typical.

William Bolcolm (United States, b. 1938). Bolcolm's orchestral song cycle *Songs of Innocence and Experience* (1983–1984) combines historical *and* vernacular styles.

Joseph Schwantner (United States, b. 1943). Schwantner's style is reminiscent of Crumb's (see above), but his harmonic palette incorporates more tonal materials. His *Sparrows* (1979) ranges from New Age-like euphony (see below) to avant-garde angularity, with medieval-style dances in between.

George Rochberg (United States, b. 1918). Although a devout and thorough Serialist in his early years, Rochberg has since composed many works, such as the *Violin Concerto* (1975), which take on the stylistic character of earlier centuries.

Performance Art

The 1960s produced a kind of theatrical event referred to as a *happenings*. In a happening, performers project films and slides, they dance and make music—all simultaneously. The audience was meant to move throughout the performance space as all this went on. The happening was largely ruled by chance, and had more the aspect of carnival than concert. From the impetus supplied by the happening, more formalized multimedia works followed, in which music, film, and dance were combined and mixed to some more controlled end. In the 1980s a multimedia genre called *Performance Art* took shape. Works in this genre focus upon a single artist who is responsible both for the music, the staging, and the performance. Laurie Anderson (United States, b. 1947) is the best-known name in the field. Her multi-media performance work *United States* (1983) is an important example of the genre.

Other Significant Composers of Various Modernist Schools

UNITED STATES

Roger Sessions (1896–1985). Sessions developed his own complex brand of Neoclassicism in the 1920s, but in the late 1940s he turned toward serial techniques. The thick, dissonant, and lyrical textures of his Eighth Symphony (1968) are characteristic of this later style.

Stefan Wolpe (1902–1972). Like Varèse, Wolpe was European born and trained; but, also like Varèse, it was in the United States that he wrote his greatest works and exercised the greatest influence. Both Feldman (see above) and Shapey (see below) were his students in New York in the 1950s. Wolpe's unique and uncompromising serial idiom can be heard in his *Enactments* for Three Pianos (1950–1953). His later works, such as *Piece for Two Instrumental Units* (1962–1963), are outwardly more simple.

Ralph Shapey (b. 1921). Shapey refers to himself as a "radical traditionalist." His brash, dissonant idiom resembles in many respect the style of Wolpe, his teacher; yet, in its scale and ritualistic character, it is unique. His *Rituals* (1959) for orchestra and jazz combo is a startling combination of hard-edged postwar Serialism and atonal Bop (see chapter 28).

Donald Martino (b. 1931). Martino has created an uncompromisingly complex serial idiom that manages to combine the rigorous musical logic of Babbitt with the lyric suppleness of Dallapiccola (see below). The *Triple Concerto* (1978) for three clarinets and chamber orchestra is one of his best-known works.

Charles Wuorinen (b. 1938). Wuorinen's Serialism is thorough and complex. In recent works, he has used probabilistic techniques. His orchestral work *A Reliquary for Igor Stravinsky* (1978) is characteristic of his austere, often ritualistic style.

Salvatore Martirano (b. 1927). Martirano has used both serial and probabilistic techniques. Most recently he has designed a live Electronics performance environment called the *Sal-Mar Construction.*

Christian Wolff (b. 1936). Politically motivated and using techniques derived from Cage's notion of indeterminacy, Wolff has written mostly chamber and piano works.

Ellen Taafe Zwilich (b. 1939). Zwilich utilizes serial techniques in a moderate, lyric style, writing symphonic and chamber works.

Younger Americans. Composers Joel Eric Suben (b. 1946), Maurice Wright (b. 1949), Tobias Picker (b. 1954), and Steven Mackey (b. 1954) are typical of the younger more eclectic generation of American composers whose styles are as varied as their methods of composition.

EUROPE

Postwar Serialists. Bruno Maderna (Italy, 1920-1973), Luigi Nono (Italy, 1924-1990), and Henri Posseur (Belgium, b. 1929) each achieved considerable international success in the 1950s and 1960s with eclectic, serial styles.

Luigi Dallapiccola (Italy, 1904-1975). Dallapiccola's early Neoclassical style evolved after World War II into an Italianate gloss of Webern's austere Serialism. His *Sicut Umbra* (1970) is one of his best-known works.

Hans Werner Henze (Germany, b. 1926). Henze's work has explored most contemporary idioms and techniques. He has written operas, symphonic and chamber works. His *Tristan* for piano, orchestra, and tape is typical of his later eclectic style.

Harrison Birtwistle (England, b. 1934). Birtwistle's technique is as much probabilistic as serial. He has written works in all genre. Birtwistle's orchestral work *The Triumph of Time* (1972) is one of his best-known

Oliver Knussen (England, b. 1952). Knussen is an eclectic composer of opera, symphonic and chamber works. His opera *Where the Wild Things Are* (1979–1983), based upon Maurice Sendak's popular children's book, is representative of his style.

Thea Musgrave (b. 1929). Musgrave works in a modest, lyrical idiom, writing operas, symphonic and chamber works. Her opera *Mary, Queen of Scots* is her best-known work.

SOUTH AMERICA AND ASIA

Alberto Ginastera (Argentina, 1916-1983). Both a nationalist and eclectic, Ginastera wrote operas, symphonic, chamber and piano works. His *Piano Sonata* (1952) is his most-performed work.

Toru Takemitsu (Japan, b. 1930). Takemitsu uses serial techniques in the service of an eclectic yet nationalistic style that weds contemporary Western idioms to traditional Japanese aesthetic values. He has written symphonic and chamber works, and movie scores. His orchestral work *November Steps* (1967) is one of his best known.

"POST-MODERNISM" AND POST-MODERN MUSIC

Tradition and historical process appear increasingly irrelevant to present-day musicians. This is reflected in both the self-conscious and self-referential style of the Modernist avant-garde; as well as in those more current styles that seem to regard even Modernism itself as irrelevant.

Minimalism

The term *Minimalism* is generally used to refer to a style that originated in the 1960s, but did not begin to garner notice until the late 1970s. In the 1980s it achieved a degree of public success unparalleled by any other movement in the century.

Minimalism is characterized by a repetitive use of simple materials: regular pulse and meters, and rudimentary major-minor tonality.

THE MINIMALISTS

La Monte Young (United States, b. 1935). Young's simple, trance-like textures, each built from traditionally consonant musical materials, are often referred to as *trance music*. Young's style set the stage for Minimalism proper. His *Composition 1960* is representative.

Terry Riley (United States, b. 1935). Riley's *In C* (1964) is perhaps the first, certifiably Minimalist work.

Steve Reich (United States, b. 1936). Reich is the most sophisticated composer of the American group. Like Pärt (see below), he shows the influence of Neoclassical Stravinsky. Reich's *Music for 18 Musicians* (1975) is typical.

Philip Glass (United States, b. 1937). Glass is the best-known and most stereotypically "Minimalist" of the American group. His opera *Einstein on the Beach* (1976) was an unprecedented international success.

John Adams (United States, b. 1947). Adams is the youngest and most conservative of the American group. He has achieved considerable success writing for more traditional media and in a more eclectic style than others of the Minimalist group. His orchestral work *Short Ride in a Fast Machine* and the opera *Nixon in China* are his best-known.

Arvo Pärt (Estonia, 1935). Neither so repetitive nor pulsed as that of the American Minimalists, Pärt's music has achieved an immense success in the late 1980s, his recordings occasionally "crossing over" into the New Age (see below) market. His harmonic palette is derived from the Neoclassical Stravinsky. In this way, and in others, his style resembles that of Reich. Pärt's *Tabula rasa* (Blank Slate) and *Passio* (Passion) are among his best-known works.

OTHER "MINIMAL" STYLES

Several other composers who are not Minimalists exhibit characteristics that are decidedly "minimal." Some are overtly influenced by the Minimalists; others have arrived at the style from other directions.

Musical Characteristics. The music of these composers is simple in texture and generally atonal. It tends to be direct, fastidious and abstract, calling to mind the prose of Samuel Beckett, an author set by both the composers listed below.

Morton Feldman. Feldman developed an extremely quiet and ethereal style. With as much silence as sound, his later works remain flat-surfaced and abstract. *Rothko Chapel* (1971) is frequently performed.

Earl Kim (United States, 1920). Kim's music is more theatrical than Feldman's, but as fastidious and spare. His *Earthlight* (1975) is among his best-known works.

New Age

New Age is an idiom that straddles boundaries. Combining elements of Minimalism, non-Western music, and the flat euphony of Muzak, New Age has discovered a group of consumers apparently dissatisfied with both the art and commercial music available to them. New Age is a "popular" music; but it is one that replaces love lyrics with moods, and songs in closed forms with flat-surfaced, atmospheric improvisations. The recordings of pianist George Winston (United States, b. 1949; *Winter into Spring,* 1980) and Andreas Vollenweider (Switzerland, b. 1953; *Down to the Moon,* 1986) are typical of the idiom.

Since World War II, Western art music has been driven alternatively by the desire for greater control over the materials of music, and the desire to relinquish that control. The subsequent styles have been alternatively complex, dissonant, and forbidding, and relatively simple, euphonious and approachable. Any attempt to outline such a recent past can only be provisional. Still, it is clear that postwar art music is as diffuse and fragmented as was its prewar forebears; it is less clear what the future holds.

For Additional Study

Austin, William, et al. *The New Grove Twentieth-Century American Masters.* New York: Norton. 1988.

Bowers, Jane and Judith Tick, eds. *Women Making Music: The Western Art Tradition. 1150-1950.* Urbana: University of Illinois. 1986.

Cage, John. *Silence*. Middletown, CN: Wesleyan University Press. 1961.

Cowell, Henry. *American Composers on American Music*. New York: Ungar. 1962.

Griffiths, Paul. *Modern Music: The Avant-Garde Since 1945*. London: Dent. 1981.

Lipman, Samuel. *Music After Modernism*. New York: Basic Books. 1979.

McVeagh, Diana, et al. *The New Grove Twentieth-Century English Masters*. New York: Norton. 1986.

Morgan, Robert. *Twentieth-Century Music*. New York: Norton. 1990.

Nectoux, Jean-Michel, et al. *The New Grove Twentieth-Century French Masters*. New York: Norton. 1990.

Rockwell, John. *All-American Music: Composition in the Late Twentieth-Century*. New York: Vintage. 1984.

Salzman, Eric. *Twentieth-Century Music: An Introduction*. 3d ed. Englewood Cliffs, NJ: Prentice-Hall. 1988.

Slonimsky, Nicolas. *Music Since 1900*. 4th ed. New York: Scribner. 1971. Supplement, 1986.

Straus, Joseph Nathan. *Remaking the Past: Musical Modernism and the Influence of the Tonal Tradition*. Cambridge: Harvard University Press. 1990.

Watkins, Glenn. *Soundings: Music in the Twentieth-Century*. New York: Schirmer. 1988.

Recommended Listening

Adams, John. *Short Ride in a Fast Machine*

Babbitt, Milton. *Philomel*

Berio, Luciano. *Sinfonia*

Boulez, Pierre. *Le marteau sans maître* (The Hammer without a Master).

Cage, John. *Sonatas and Interludes*

Carter, Elliott. *String Quartet No. 1*

Crumb, George. *Ancient Voices of Children*

Dashow, James. *Sequence Symbols*

Davidovsky, Mario. *Synchronism No. 7*

Feldman, Morton. *Rothko Chapel*

Glass, Philip. *Einstein on the Beach*

Foss, Lukas. *Echoi*

Kim, Earl. *Earthlight*

Lansky, Paul. *Idle Chatter*

Lutoslawski, Witold. *Symphony No. 3*

Martino, Donald. *Triple Concerto*

Messiaen, Olivier. *Turangalîla*

Pärt, Arvo. *Tabula Rasa* (Blank Slate)

Penderecki, Krzysztof. *Threnody to the Victims of Hiroshima*

Reich, Steve. *Music for 18 Musicians*

Reynolds, Roger. *The Emperor of Ice Cream*

Schuller, Gunther. *Studies on Themes by Paul Klee*

Sessions, Roger. *Eighth Symphony*

Stockhausen, Karlheinz. *Gesang der Jünglinge* (Song of the Youths)

Varèse, Edgard. *Déserts* (Deserts)

——. *Poème électronique*

Xenakis, Yannis. *Pithoprakta*

Part Three

American Popular Music

27

American Popular Music to 1900

1848 Revolutions in European capitals; Marx and Engels, *The Communist Manifesto*

1851 Melville, *Moby Dick*

1855 Whitman, *Leaves of Grass*

1857 Dred Scott decision

1859 Darwin, *Origin of Species;* John Brown raids Harpers Ferry

1861 American Civil War begins; serfs emancipated in Russia; unification of Italy

1863 *Emancipation Proclamation*

1865 Civil War ends; Lincoln assassinated

1866 First transatlantic cable; American Federation of Labor established

1867 Alaska purchased from Russia

1869 First transcontinental railway in United States; Suez Canal opens

1870 Franco-Prussian War; Schliemann excavates Troy

1871 Paris Commune; Unification of Germany; Bismark German chancellor

1872 Nietzsche, *Birth of Tragedy;* Monet, *Impression: Sunrise*

1874 First "Impressionist" group exhibition in Paris

1875 Tolstoy, *Anna Karinina*

1876 Bell invents telephone; Wagner opens theatre at Bayreuth; Mallarmé, *Afternoon of a Faun*

1877 Edison invents phonograph

1879 Sir George Grove, *Dictionary of Music and Musicians*

1880 Irish insurrection; Pavlov's experiments on conditioned reflexes; Dostoyevski, *The Brothers Karamazov*

1881 Tsar Alexander II killed; President Garfield shot; Panama Canal begun; Boston Symphony Orchestra founded; Renoir, *Boating Party Luncheon;* Henry James, *Portrait of a Lady*

1882 Koch discovers tuberculosis germ; Berlin Philharmonic founded; Manet, *Bar at the Folies Bergères*

1883 Daimler patents automobile engine; Metropolitan Opera House opens; Concertgebouw founded; Nietzsche, *Also Sprach Zarathustra;* Stevenson, *Treasure Island*

1884 Pasteur develops inoculation against rabies; Twain, *Huckleberry Finn;* Seurat, *Sunday Afternoon on the Island of La Grande Jatte;* Rodin, *Burghers of Calais*

1885 First electric street car in United States; Brooklyn Bridge completed

1886 Rousseau, *Un Soir de carnaval*

1888 Van Gogh, *The Sunflowers*

1889 Paris International Exhibition; Eiffel Tower opens

1891 Doyle, *Adventures of Sherlock Holmes*

1892 First American automobile; Toulouse-Lautrec, *At the Moulin Rouge*

1895 X-rays discovered; Crane, *The Red Badge of Courage;* Homer, *Northeaster*

1896 Queen Victoria, Diamond Jubilee; first modern Olympic Games; radioactivity of uranium discovered; Gaugin, *Maternity*; Marconi invents wireless telegraph

1898 Spanish-American War; Radium discovered

1899 Boer War

1900 Chinese Boxer rebellion; Philadelphia Orchestra founded; Freud, *Interpretation of Dreams;* first dirigible; Conrad, *Lord Jim*

1901 Queen Victoria dies; Edward VII becomes King of England; Planck develops Quantum Theory

T wo folk traditions joined to form American popular music: (1) that of the British Isles, brought to the New World by its first settlers; and (2) that of central Africa, brought to the New World by African slaves.

ANGLO-AMERICAN MUSIC

Early Sacred Music

The Puritan Pilgrims, belonging to a strict Protestant sect, disapproved of the fine arts. The Bible itself sanctioned psalms and hymns of praise, however. The English psalm-singing styles that the Puritans brought to the New World were not the complex polyphonic styles of Catholic church music but the rather simpler vernacular styles of everyday life.

PSALM BOOKS

In England, Protestant sects produced many psalm books—metrical translations of the psalms often set to lively, vernacular dance tunes. The *Ainsworth Psalter* (1612), brought over with the Plymouth settlers, was such a volume. Indeed, the first book published in the colonies was *The Bay Psalm Book* (1640), although psalms and the tunes associated with them were so familiar that the publication did not even contain musical notation.

SINGING SCHOOLS

The "proper" method of singing became, by the early eighteenth century, a necessary social grace. Singing masters traveled from town to town, holding several meetings a week, teaching hymn tunes, psalms, anthems and *fuguing tunes* (anthems that included brief sections of imitative counterpoint). Singing schools and singing teachers flourished, and by the Revolution had become a major social institution in the Colonies.

THE "YANKEE TUNESMITHS"

America's first composers of notated music (generally choral, usually sacred) arose from this institution of social singing. These composers maintained the cheerful liveliness of vernacular song and dance as well as the sturdy earnestness of the Puritan hymn. Historians have dubbed this group of Colonial composers "the Yankee Tunesmiths."

Musical Characteristics. The melodies grew from the catchy tunes of the vernacular; they were easily learned and easily remembered. Their strong, spirited rhythms were drawn from dance. Their harmony is sturdy and plain, uncomplicated by the studied dissonances and complex polyphony of the learned European style. As a result, the music was colorful and popular and presented an idealized image of the people who made and performed it.

Justin Morgan (1747–1798). A school master and tavern keeper by trade and breeder of the Morgan horse (for which he is best known), Morgan was in addition an avid musician and composer. Among his several works the fuguing time "Montgomery" was the most popular.

Jeremiah Ingalls (1764–1838). Like Morgan a man of many trades (farmer, tavern keeper, cooper), he delighted in music and published not only volumes of learned sacred music but also, in his *Christian Harmony,* versions of traditional New England folk hymns and psalmody. His *Northfield* is typical.

William Billings (1746–1800). The most famous of the Colonial composers, Billings was self-taught. A familiar of Paul Revere and Sam Adams, he published many volumes of *songbooks,* collections of music for sacred and patriotic occasions. Many of his marches served the Revolutionary militia. His publications were so successful that Billings became perhaps the first composer in the United States to make a living from his music. His *Washington* typifies his patriotic mode.

SHAPE-NOTE NOTATION

After the Revolution, the young country became more "sophisticated" in its tastes. The sturdy, rough-hewn quality of the Yankee Tunesmiths now seemed primitive and crude, a relic from a frontier past. Billings, for example, outlived his popularity, dying in poverty as European "learned" styles became the rage.

The Yankee singing tradition shunned by the urbanized North found root in the rural South. Preserved in singing books and incorporating regional inflections and styles, this rural choral style exerted an influence on most of the important vernacular styles of the nineteenth and early twentieth centuries. In the nineteenth century the music spread through the rural South and West in a notation called shape-note. Derived from an eighteenth century English notation called *Fasola* (*fa-so-la*: the fourth, fifth, and sixth scale-degrees of traditional solfège), the shaped notes showed the relative pitch of the tunes by relating shapes to scale-degrees. (See figure 27.1.) This allowed singers otherwise unable to read musical notation to sing tunes on sight.

F Major Scale in Shape-Note Notation

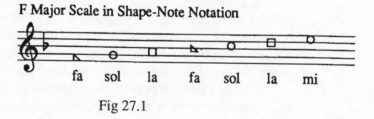

Fig 27.1

The first southern shape-note tune book was *Kentucky Harmony* (1816), but the most influential was the *Sacred Harp*. It was published in 1844 and survives today in several later editions. In fact, the shape-note style is often referred to as *Sacred Harp singing*. "Amazing Grace" is perhaps the most familiar tune preserved by this tradition.

Folk Music

The folk or traditional music of rural, white America derives from that of the British Isles. We can trace some, though not all, of the differences between rural American folk music and its Anglo-Irish prototype to the influence of African-American idioms.

MUSICAL CHARACTERISTICS

Anglo-American folk music is predominantly a solo vocal music. The melodies are often modal, the meter variable, and the text narrative. The fiddle, guitar, banjo, mandolin, dulcimer, and harmonica (or mouth organ) are favored instruments.

BALLADS

The traditional or folk cultures of the British Isles are, in large part, transmitted through song, the ballad especially. Strophic, with a repeated refrain, the ballad carried a narrative text, often sentimental or dramatic, frequently tragic. It was generally sung without accompaniment; but the accompaniment, when present, was simple and supportive. English, Irish and Scotch immigrants brought these songs to the United States, where they survive today principally in New England and Appalachia. Such familiar tunes as "The Cherry Song" ("I gave my love a cherry . . .") and "Wayfaring Stranger" are typical.

OCCUPATIONAL SONGS

Other songs relating the humor and perils of the workplace —songs of mining, railroading, and cowherding—arose in the New World from similar Old World models. "Blow the Man Down," a sea chantey (sea song), is a well-known example of the type, as are the familiar "John Henry" (railroading) and "Home On the Range" (cowpunching).

INSTRUMENTAL MUSIC

Purely instrumental music of the early United States is associated with dancing or marching and is generally simple and monophonic.

Marches. Following a venerable Old World tradition, fife and drum corps from the eighteenth and early nineteenth centuries marched to traditional tunes performed in unison or simple parallel harmonies. Billings and other Yankee Tunesmiths wrote and published such marching tunes.

Dance. Dance tunes were performed on a single fiddle or guitar, occasionally accompanied by simple chords. The American square dance and its associated music developed from the eighteenth- and nineteenth-century English *quadrilles*. The "caller," however, is uniquely American and adds a characteristically American spontaneity to the otherwise rigidly formalized quadrille. The American *round dance* is similar, but for couples.

OTHER FOLK TYPES

The musical folk traditions of many other countries and cultures found fertile ground in the United States. Russian and Eastern European types thrive in many American cities, and Scandinavian types in the northern Great Plains. Certain German ("O Tannenbaum") and French ("Frère Jacques") traditional tunes have even entered the American mainstream tradition.

Composed Vernacular Music

In the nineteenth century, every middle class home had its upright piano; it formed the center of domestic entertainment. The ability to make music on demand was a highly valued social attribute. The music on these occasions was light and generally sentimental or patriotic.

THE PARLOR SONG

Some of these songs were traditional, others were composed. The composed songs are of the sort often called *parlor songs*. The majority modeled themselves on arias from early nineteenth-century English light-operas.

Stephen Foster (1826–1864). Foster began by writing patriotic and sentimental tunes or marches in the familiar British manner, but it was not until he adopted what he called his "Ethiopian" style that his music became widely popular. Though a caucasian from Pittsburgh, and writing for a middle class of predominantly Western-European ancestry, his spiritual-like songs (see "Spiritual," below) appealed to this largely conservative, Protestant public. He expressed not just the pious sentimentality of stereotypical slaves, but also their underlying grief and sorrow as well. The plaintive tone of such popular Foster songs as "Old Folks at Home" and "Old Black Joe" did much to fuel popular abolitionist sentiment. Other Foster songs, like "Jeanie with the Light Brown Hair," are characteristic of his sentimental British manner.

The Parlor Song at the Turn of the Century. By the 1890s the parlor song had left the parlor and become the staple of public musical entertainments called *vaudevilles* (see chapter 28). It attained a new level of musical sophistication in such tunes as "The Good Old Summertime," "The Man on the Flying Trapeze," and "The Band Played On," while still retaining its homely sentimental tone. Such tunes are the forerunners of the American musical comedy song (see Chapter 28, below).

THE PATRIOTIC SONG

The United States already had a long tradition of patriotic songs, extending from those of the Yankee Tunesmiths to the political ballads of the early nineteenth century. The parlor song tradition generated its share of patriotic lyrics as well. The sentiments aroused by the Civil War in particular were profound, finding their way into such immensely popular tunes as "John Brown's Body," "The Battle Hymn of the Republic," "When Johnny Comes Marching Home," and "Dixie."

THE MARCH

The march had always been a favored American vernacular idiom, reflecting the young nation's patriotic sentiments. From the fife and drum groups of the eighteenth century, to the African-American marching bands of New Orleans, to the famous bands and band leaders of the turn of the century, much of the first 150 years of American history was played out against the march.

John Philip Sousa (1854–1932). Of Hispanic ancestry, he became and remains one of America's most famous composers. Although a composer of symphonic music and operettas, he is best known for his marches. Sousa led a professional band that toured the world performing marches and other American vernacular idioms. His marches all follow a similar form in which, after a brief introduction, there is a verse in several repeated sections; the "trio" follows, in which a lyric tune is followed by a more active middle section (the "dogfight") and then returns dramatically. Sousa's march "Star and Stripes Forever" has achieved the status of a national icon.

AFRICAN MUSIC IN AMERICA

African musical idioms came to America with the slaves. The musical elements most highly developed in those idioms—rhythm, call-and-response texture, improvisation—remained. Those elements absent or less developed—tonality, closed-forms—were replaced by more European techniques.

African Music

African music is varied. Here we can only address those general characteristics that are reflected in African-American music.

MUSICAL CHARACTERISTICS

Rhythm. African music is organized around rhythm. In one sense, African rhythm is similar to European: it is pulsed and metrical. Unlike most European music, however, African music often presents several meters simultaneously in a texture known as *rhythmic polyphony*. Such complexity is characteristic of western and central Africa, the homeland of most American slaves.

Melody. In the Bantu language—one of the dominant languages of western and central Africa—a word spoken on a high pitch has a different meaning from that of the "same" word spoken on a low one. Song (in the European sense) is difficult, and a melody that sets such a language is directly shaped by the words being set. As a result, African melodies are often constructed around short, repeated and varied melodic phrases.

Texture. Rhythmic polyphony is common, as are responsorial or antiphonal textures, where a leader alternates with a group, or where two groups alternate between themselves, often in imitation of each other. Such a texture is called *call-and-response* style.

Harmony. Though simple by comparison, African harmonies show some similarities to those of Western Europe. Melodies are often sung in parallel harmonies, and—as in the Mbira ("thumb-piano") music of the Shona peoples—are often triadic, sometimes suggesting European dominant/tonic progressions.

Function. Music was a part of the African's daily life; work, religion, play, and war all had their musics. In the New World, African slaves maintained this sense of music's everyday importance.

The Music of Slavery

During the period of slavery, African music was transformed by contact with the vernacular European tradition. In the process, characteristic Black idioms arose.

WORK SONGS

Slaves' lives were harsh, consisting almost entirely of hard physical labor. Not surprisingly, their music found expression in their work.

The Field Holler. A patterned work song, very close to pure African idioms, the Field Holler was generally "sung" by a lone worker in the field, on the river boat, or in the kitchen. As much speech as song, it began with a high cry that swooped down to a softer, lower murmuring. Its modulated and bent pitches, its glides and its keening tone were later absorbed into the blues (see below).

Group Work Songs. Group work songs were related to the field holler but were more regularly pulsed. They were used to pace periodic work. Often performed in a call-and-response style, they gradually took on a definite European harmonic character, circulating regularly through rudimentary harmonic progressions—a technique not entirely foreign to pure African music (see "Harmony," above).

RELIGIOUS MUSIC

African religion is inseparable from its music. Although masters forced African slaves to adopt their European-style religion, slaves retained many familiar African musical practices in their services.

Ring Shout. A Ring Shout was a circle dance performed with rhythmic clapping and shouting. It suggests various pure African styles of singing dance. Often a ring shout was built around a Bible story told in call-and-response style.

Song Sermons. Black religious services took on the form of the European Christian service, but the substance retained its own African flavor. The sermon, in particular, was often chanted in the rhythmic, shouted style familiar from the fields and accompanied by rhythmic responses and exclamations from the congregation.

Lining Out. Since most rural congregations were unable to read, hymns were not sung from hymnals but lined out—that is, the preacher would sing one line, and the congregation would then repeat it. This technique (called "deaconing" in England) was ideal for the African call-and-response style of performance already familiar to blacks, and it quickly became a characteristic feature of their worship services.

Spirituals. After the Civil War, black singing groups (such as the Fisk University Jubilee Singers) popularized a Europeanized sacred song known as a *spiritual*. Though the tunes were traditional, and retained many characteristically "African" rhythmic, tonal, and textural features, they were set to European-style harmonic progressions and within European closed-forms. In performance, however, much of the European flavor found in the published versions was hidden beneath more typically black inflections and call-and-response textures. Such tunes as "Sometimes I Feel Like a Motherless Child," "Michael Row the Boat Ashore," and "Joshua Fought the Battle of Jericho" are typical.

THE BLUES

The blues arose gradually from the traditional field or folk holler. In the blues, however, the complaint became increasingly secular: themes of betrayal and unrequited love are common. The genre left the workplace, free hands now accompanying the voice on guitar. However, it remained solitary, plaintive, and characteristically speechlike. The scooped notes and dipped tones of the style, now pitted against conventionalized European-style harmonies, became known as *blue notes,* giving the style its name. As the idiom became more popular and more public, it picked up its familiar twelve-bar form. (See figure 27.2.)

Blues Progression

Measure: 1 2 3 4 5 6 7 8 9 10 11 12
Harmony: I —————————— IV — I —— V-(IV) I ——

Fig 27.2

Black "Vernacular" Music

Characteristically black traits greatly influenced nineteenth-century commercial music, a music primarily of the white middle class. White composers found that the public responded enthusiastically to this synthetic style. This early influence helped pave the way for the even more powerful influence of African-American idioms in the twentieth century.

THE MINSTREL SHOWS

Minstrel shows were a sort of musical revue in which white performers, their faces blackened by burnt cork, performed skits and songs inspired by what they understood to be "negro" humor and music. The style inspired many white composers, such as Stephen Foster, to compose sentimental, spiritual-like secular songs for predominantly white musical consumers. After the Civil War, blacks themselves began to take part in the minstrel show circuit, transforming it into a truer expression of their cultural idioms.

Buck-and-wing. A quick, syncopated dance, the buck-and-wing was the forerunner of tap dancing. It was popularized by minstrel shows in the last quarter of the nineteenth century.

Cakewalk. A syncopated dance that parroted Southern gentility, the cakewalk was often performed as a satirical grand finale to a Minstrel show.

RAGTIME

Ragtime is, essentially, an African-American version of the popular march style of turn-of-the-century America. An instrumental style—usually for piano, sometimes for bands—it was sold in sheet music. Its syncopations—or "ragged" rhythms (figure 27.3)—were derived, in part, from the cakewalk.

"Ragged" Cakewalk Rhythms

Fig 27.3

Scott Joplin (1868–1917). Born in the South, he moved to the North to pursue his musical career. His rags follow standard closed forms very much like the traditional march. The angular syncopations suggest improvisation but are carefully composed. The harmonic language is more mannered than that of the blues. Because of this European-style sophistication, it was one of the first truly African-American idioms made palatable to a largely white audience.

*A*merican vernacular music flourished in the nineteenth century. From its varied sources came, in the twentieth century, a popular music that would spread beyond the United States to Europe and, eventually, to the rest of the world.

For Additional Study

Ammer, Christine. *Unsung: A History of Women in American Music.* Westport, CT: Greenwood. 1980.

Chase, Gilbert. *America's Music, from the Pilgrims to the Present.* 2d rev. ed. Westport, CT: Greenwood. 1981.

Hamm, Charles. *Yesterdays: Popular Song in America.* New York: Norton. 1979.

Hamm, Charles. *Music in the New World.* New York: Norton. 1983.

Hitchcock, H. Wiley. *Music in the United States: A Historical Introduction.* Englewood Cliffs, NJ: Prentice-Hall. 1974.

Mellers, Wilfred. *Music in a New Found Land.* New York: Oxford. 1987.

Merriam, Alan P. *African Music in Perspective.* New York: Garland. 1982.

Nettl, Bruno. *Folk and Traditional Music of the Western Continents.* Englewood Cliffs, NJ: Prentice-Hall. 1973.

Nketia, J. H. Kwabena. *The Music of Africa.* New York: Norton. 1974.

Oliver, Paul, et al. *The New Grove Ragtime, Blues and Jazz.* New York: Norton. 1986.

Roach, Hildred. *Black American Music, Past and Present.* Boston: Crescendo Publications. 1973.

Southern, Eileen. *The Music of Black Americans.* 2d ed. New York: Norton. 1983.

Tirro, Frank. *Jazz: A History.* New York: Norton. 1977.

Tischler, Barbara. *An American Music: The Search for an American Musical Identity.* New York: Oxford. 1986.

Recommended Listening

Historical recordings of vernacular music are difficult to come by. The reader might look to the *New World* recording series held by most listening libraries. They are listed below by number and topic.

Folk/Black traditional: NW226, 236, 239, 245, 264, 278, 283
Nineteenth-century vernacular styles: NW202, 220, 265, 293
Brass band: NW266, 280
Ragtime: NW 235, 259, 269
Traditional blues: NW 252

28

American Popular Music and Jazz after 1900

1900 Chinese Boxer rebellion; Philadelphia Orchestra founded; Freud, *Interpretation of Dreams;* first dirigible; Conrad, *Lord Jim*

1901 Queen Victoria dies; Edward VII becomes King of England; Planck develops Quantum Theory

1903 Wright brothers' first successful flight; Shaw, *Man and Superman*

1904 Russo-Japanese war; Chekhov, *The Cherry Orchard;* Rolland, *Jean Christophe*

1905 Einstein, *Special Theory of Relativity;* first Russian Revolution

1906 San Francisco earthquake and fire; New Music Society of America formed to promote music of American composers

1907 First music broadcast on radio; Picasso, *Les Demoiselles d'Avignon*

1908 First Model T

1909 Peary reaches North Pole; Frank Lloyd Wright completes Robie House

1910 First subatomic particles discovered; Russell and Whitehead, *Principia Mathematica;* John Philip Sousa's band tours the world

1911 Amundsen reaches South Pole; Wharton, *Ethan Frome;* de Chirico, *La nostalgie de l'infini*

1912 *Titanic* sinks; Balkan wars; Duchamp, *Nude Descending a Staircase;* Kandinsky, *Improvisation*

1913 New York Armory Show; Mann, *Death in Venice;* John Sloane, *Sunday Women Drying their Hair;* Braque, *Musical Forms;* Proust, *Remembrance of Things Past;*

1914 Victor Herbert forms American Society of Composers, Authors, and Publishers (ASCAP); World War I begins; Panama Canal opens; Griffith, *Birth of a Nation;* Frost, *North of Boston*

1915 Maugham, *Of Human Bondage;* Morgan, *Mechanism of Mendelian Heredity*

1916 Einstein, *General Theory of Relativity;* Wright completes Imperial Hotel in Tokyo

1917 United States enters war; Bolshevik revolution in Russia; first jazz recording; first printed use of word *jazz;* Yeats, *Wild Swans at Coole*

1918 World War I ends; Cather, *My Antonia;* Spengler, *Decline of the West*

1919 Treaty of Versailles; League of Nations formed; Mussolini founds Italian Fascist party

1920 Women's suffrage granted by Nineteenth Amendment; first commercial radio broadcast

1921 Varèse organizes International Guild of Composers for the promotion of twentieth-century music; Wittgenstein, *Tractatus;* Mondriaan, *Painting No. 1;* Chaplin's *The Kid* released

1922 International Society for Contemporary Music formed in Salzburg; Insulin discovered; Eliot, *The Wasteland;* Joyce, *Ulysses;* Rilke, *Sonnets to Orpheus;* Fitzgerald, *The Great Gatsby*

1923 Soviet Union established; Klee, *At the Mountain of the Bull*

1924 Lenin dies; Stalin comes to power; Kafka, *The Trial*

1926 Hemingway, *The Sun Also Rises;* first TV transmission

1927 Lindbergh flies the Atlantic solo; Heisenberg propounds his uncertainty principle; Woolf, *To the Lighthouse;* O'Neill, *Strange Interlude*; first important "talking" picture: *The Jazz Singer*

1928 Penicillin developed; first all-sound film; Lawrence, *Lady Chatterley's Lover;* Benét, *John Brown's Body*

1929 Great Depression begins; Faulkner, *The Sound and the Fury;* Ortega y Gasset, *Revolt of the Masses*

1930 Pluto discovered; Hopper, *Early Sunday Morning;* Wood, *American Gothic;* Crane, *The Bridge*

1931 Empire State Building opens; Japan invades Manchuria

1933 Roosevelt inaugurated; Hitler becomes German Chancellor

1935 Italy invades Ethiopia; Orozco, *Man in Four Aspects*

1936 Spanish Civil War; Dos Passos, *U.S.A.* trilogy

1937 Japan invades China; Hill discovers chloroplast reaction in plants; Picasso, *Guernica*

1938 First-ever Carnegie Hall jazz concert (Benny Goodman's band); Nuclear fission demonstrated; Dufy, *Regatta*

1939 World War II begins; Broadcast Music Inc. (BMI) begun in competition with ASCAP; Joyce, *Finnegans Wake;* Steinbeck, *Grapes of Wrath; Citizen Kane, The Wizard of Oz* and *Gone With the Wind* movies released

1940   Roosevelt elected to third term; Churchill becomes British prime minister; first microwave radar and electron microscope developed

1941   Pearl Harbor; United States enters World War II; Atlantic Charter

1943   Italy surrenders; Chagall, *Crucifixion*

1944   Allied invasion of France, then Germany

1945   Germany surrenders; atom bombs destroy Hiroshima and Nagasaki; radio astronomy; first jet-propelled planes and rockets

1946   First United Nations assembly; Nuremberg trials

1947   India becomes Independent; Williams, *A Streetcar Named Desire*

1948   Berlin airlift; Gandhi assassinated; first long-playing records (LPs)

1949   Communist Mao Tse-Tung deposes Chinese Nationalists; Soviet Union explodes atomic bomb; Cold War begins; Orwell, *1984;* Miller, *Death of a Salesman*

1950   Korean War begins; hydrogen "superbomb" exploded

1951   Salinger, *The Catcher in the Rye*

1952   Eisenhower elected president; Elizabeth II becomes queen of England

1953   Korean War ends; Rosenbergs executed for treason; Malenkov succeeds Stalin; Watson and Crick model DNA; Beckett, *Waiting for Godot*

1954   McCarthy hearings televised; Supreme Court outlaws school segregation; first atomic submarine; war in Indochina; e.e. cummings, *Poems*

1955   Warsaw Pact signed; serum for infantile paralysis developed

1956   Suez Crisis; Hungarian Revolt; First "Warsaw Autumn" International Festival of Contemporary Music; Elvis Presley's first TV appearance

1957   First civil rights bill; Kerouac, *On the Road;* first national broadcast of "American Bandstand;" Soviet Union launches *Sputnik*

1959   Alaska and Hawaii become states; Castro takes power in Cuba

1960   Kennedy elected President; "the pill" introduced; first successful laser

1961   Soviets put first man in space; Shepherd makes first American sub-orbital flight; Bay of Pigs invasion; the "twist" introduced

1962   Cuban missile crisis; Glenn first American to orbit earth; *Mariner 2* encounters Venus; Albee, *Who's Afraid of Virginia Woolf?;* Lincoln Center for the Performing Arts opens in New York; Carson, *Silent Spring*

1963   President John F. Kennedy assassinated; Beatles tour United States; Friedan, *The Feminine Mystique*; Supreme Court outlaws school prayer

1964   Dr. Martin Luther King, Jr., wins Nobel Peace Prize

1965   First space walk; American "involvement" in Vietnam increases dramatically; *Autobiography of Malcolm X*; King marches in Alabama

1966 France withdraws from NATO

1967 Israeli-Arab "Six-Day War;" heart transplant; Lilly, *The Mind of the Dolphin*

1968 Dr. Martin Luther King and Robert Kennedy assassinated; Nixon elected president; Soviets invade Czechoslovakia; student uprisings in France and United States; National Guard fires on students at Kent State; police fire on students at Jackson State

1969 Americans land on moon; Woodstock; De Gaulle resigns French presidency; Beatles break up

1970 United States invades Cambodia; first Earth Day; Toffler, *Future Shock*

1971 Indo-Pakistan War; *Pentagon Papers* published; *John F. Kennedy Center for the Performing Arts* opens in Washington, D.C.

1972 Nixon reelected; Wallace shot; Black September terrorists murder Israeli athletes at Munich Olympics

1973 Vietnam War ends; first energy crisis; "Watergate" begins; Agnew resigns under indictment; Solzhenitsyn, *The Gulag Archipelago*; Supreme Court decides *Rowe vs. Wade*

1974 Nixon resigns in wake of Watergate

1975 Spanish dictator Franco dies; International Women's Year

1976 *Viking II* lands on Mars; Mao Tse-Tung dies; Carter elected president; United States Bicentennial Celebrations

1977 New York blackout; massacres by Amin in Uganda; TV production of Haley's *Roots*; *Star Wars* movie released

1978 Camp David accord between Israel and Egypt; first test-tube baby born; Pei's East Wing of the National Gallery opens; Pluto's moon Charon discovered

1979 Shah of Iran deposed; Americans taken hostage in Iran

1980 Reagan elected President; John Lennon murdered

1981 Egyptian President Sadat assassinated; American hostages in Iran freed; *Columbia* first space shuttle in orbit

1982 Equal Rights Amendment defeated; wars in Lebanon and the Falkland Islands; first heart transplant

1984 AIDS virus identified; MTV inaugurated; Reagan reelected

1985 Gorbachev becomes First Secretary of the Soviet Union; compact disks (CDs) gain wide acceptance; Live Aid concerts

1986 Space shuttle *Challenger* explodes; Iran-Contra scandal; Soviet nuclear disaster at Chernobyl

1988 Bush elected President

1989 Pro-democracy demonstrations crushed in China; Berlin Wall falls; *Voyager 2* encounters Neptune

1990   Reunification of Germany; Cold War ends; Iraq invades Kuwait

1991   Gulf War

*P*rior to World War I, pseudo-African idioms—the nineteenth-century "Ethiopian" parlor songs and Minstrel shows of white composers, and the cakewalks and rags of early twentieth-century African-American composers—became immensely popular with the white middle class. Black idioms were Westernized in order to meet the commercial demands of the fledgling music industry and in order to render black idioms accessible to a consumer of predominantly Western European origin.

American composers and musicians quickly realized, however, that these new idioms—idioms built upon Western European functional harmony, but ones that retained the unique rhythmic and tonal inflections of the African-American tradition—provided not only fertile ground for their imaginations, but a popular music ideally suited for a society disillusioned by war and distrustful of its own past. To this day, many scholars refer to the first decades of the twentieth century as The Jazz Age.

JAZZ

Jazz arose in the South in the early years of the twentieth century, the word itself was first used in print in 1917. The syncopated rhythms and improvisational character of jazz are characteristically African-American, the instrumentation and harmonic structure European.

Jazz before World War II

African-American ragtime and blues were brought together with more Western European harmonic elements in vital, urban environments like turn-of-the-century New Orleans. The style was initially called *playing hot*, but eventually became known as *jazz*.

ORIGINS

Two New Orleans genre seem to have combined, early in this century, to form jazz.

Marching Bands. Marches and marching bands were as popular in New Orleans at the turn of the century as in the rest of the United States. African-American bands played almost constantly—for parades, picnics, and even funerals. Marches were generally "ragged" in performance—that is, performed in the syncopated and ragged rhythms familiar to us from ragtime (see chapter 27). Since the musicians were self-taught, they played by ear, improvising variants at will.

Storyville. In old New Orleans the red-light district was called Storyville. Here black, white, and mixed races (creoles) intermingled relatively freely. The various saloons, gambling joints, and bordellos each featured a lone pianist or, possibly, a small band. These musicians "ragged," improvised renditions of marches and ragtime tunes appear to have been the first pure jazz. When Storyville was closed down at the end of World War I, jazz moved up the Mississippi to Kansas City, Chicago, and then New York.

EARLY JAZZ STYLES

The New Orleans Style. New Orleans-style jazz, essentially an instrumental style, is built around a pre-composed melody performed freely by the "lead" cornet; the clarinet and trombone improvise a harmonic counterpoint around it. The rhythm is syncopated in the manner of ragtime, and the improvisations are inflected with scoops and bent tones—"blue notes"—derived from the blues. Perhaps the most characteristic feature of New Orleans-style jazz and, eventually, all jazz styles is its "swung" rhythms; thus, a rhythm such as that shown in figure 28.1 would be performed as in figure 28.2—that is, "swung."

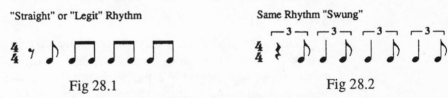

"Straight" or "Legit" Rhythm   Same Rhythm "Swung"

Fig 28.1   Fig 28.2

The Chicago ("Dixieland") Style. The New Orleans style was, for the most part, the province of blacks and creoles. As it gradually spread up the Mississippi to Chicago and a predominantly white, middle-class audience, it took on a more Europeanized aspect. The resultant "Chicago style" was initially a province of white bands and was especially popular with white college students. Ironically, this Chicago style is more often referred to today as *Dixieland*. Many of the most famous practitioners of the Chicago style were, however, African-American, having adopted the style by economic necessity and adding to it the characteristic "hot" (frenzied, blues-inflected) flavor of the New Orleans style. The first commercial jazz recordings (c. 1917) were in this Chicago style. The style has a quick-step beat emphasizing the second and third beat of four, in contrast to the even four-beat of New Orleans-style jazz.

W. C. Handy (1873–1958). Handy's blues reflect the marchlike structure of ragtime. Many of his compositions, such as "Basin Street Blues" and "Saint Louis Blues" became early jazz standards.

Ferdinand "Jelly Roll" Morton (1885–1841). Morton was an influential New Orleans pianist and band leader. His carefully composed arrangements, performed in a "hot," driving style, set the format for the "swing" era arrangement (see below). He is perhaps the first pure jazz composer. Morton claimed to have invented jazz in 1902 by playing rags and stamping out the New Orleans four-beat underneath with his feet. Recordings made with his band, the Red Hot Peppers, are typical.

Joe "King" Oliver (1885–1938). Leader of a well-known Chicago-style band, King Oliver's Creole Jazz Band, his "hot" cornet improvisations laced with blue notes influenced his young second trumpet player, Louis Armstrong. Oliver's "Dippermouth Blues" and the Oliver-Armstrong duet in "Snake Rag" (both recorded in 1923) are classics.

Louis "Satchmo" Armstrong (c. 1898–1971). One of the most influential musicians of early jazz, Armstrong developed a virtuosic style of trumpet improvisation built upon earlier piano styles. In "Heebie Jeebie" (1926) he introduced "scat" singing—a vocal improvisation using nonsense syllables. His recordings with his Hot Five and Hot Seven combos are typical.

Bix Beiderbecke (1903–1931). A Chicago-style trumpeter, Beiderbecke made several successful recordings before his early death and has maintained a dedicated following.

SWING STYLE

A mellower, more romantic style gradually arose in the 1930s. The style was built around large bands (*big bands*) that performed composed arrangements of popular songs, their middle sections spiced—in the Chicago manner—with improvised solos. The period of the swing style is often called the *big band era*.

Duke Ellington (1899–1974). Though a successful pianist and band leader, Ellington is best known as a composer and arranger. Adopting the format of Jelly Roll Morton's arrangements, Ellington composed or arranged virtually everything his band performed. He quickly developed a unique style. His harmonic palette is varied and chromatic, his orchestrations colorful and innovative. Combined they lend his compositions a characteristic elegance. Often moody and frequently melancholy in tone, they contrast sharply with the predominantly up-beat tone of the other big bands. His "Black and Tan Fantasy" (1927) and "Mood Indigo" (1930) are classics.

Benny Goodman (1909–1986). His band was perhaps the first to exhibit a true, uncompromising jazz style. Known as "The King of Swing," Goodman was a consummate soloist, his clarinet style a model of discipline and sophistication. His big band at the time of the famous Carnegie Hall concert (1938), boasted some of the biggest names in swing (Gene Kruppa, drums; Harry James, trumpet; Lionel Hampton, vibes). The recording of that concert, culminating in a hair-raising rendition of "Sing, Sing, Sing," is a classic of the era.

Other Composers and Band Leaders. Paul Whiteman (1890–1967), Fletcher Henderson (1898–1952), Glenn Miller (1904–1944), and Count Basie (1904–1984) all led important and successful big bands.

VOCAL STYLES

The popular song flourished with the new recording technology. Though early jazz was in large part instrumental, the jazz audience still demanded songs.

Blues. The commercial blues of the twentieth century is only a distant cousin of the original blues. The harmonies had become standardized and Westernized, the music composed.

Bessie Smith (1894–1937). Probably the most famous of the early blues singers, known as "the Empress of the Blues," Smith's life seemed to mirror her lyrics and perhaps helped fuel her emotional, riveting style. Her "Lost Your Head Blues " and "Nobody Knows You When You're Down and Out" are typical.

Cabaret Singers. Every club, hotel, and radio station had its jazz band and along with it a singer who could deliver up the latest popular favorite. These "cabaret singers" took on many of the characteristic inflections of jazz, even improvising ("scat singing") on occasion. This jazz-oriented song style can be heard in the recordings of Billie Holiday, Ella Fitzgerald, and Sarah Vaughan. Mel Tormé and Tony Bennett, in very different ways, continue this jazz-oriented style today.

Pop Singers. By recording with popular big bands during the swing era, some cabaret singers reached the status of popular idols. Bing Crosby (1904–1977) was the first and sold the most records. Frank Sinatra (b. 1915), beginning as a side man for various big bands, became one of the most popular singer of the century; it was not until the great popular success of Rock-and-Roll that any other entertainers ever rivaled his popularity. Both Crosby and Sinatra, as well as female pop stars such as Lena Horne and Judy Garland, provided a middle-of-the-road product to musical consumers, one drawn as much from musical comedy and Tin Pan Alley (see below) as from jazz. The career of each expanded into films and ultimately survived the demise of the big band style. Contemporary performers such as Barbra Streisand (b. 1942) come out of this tradition.

Jazz after World War II

The immense success of the swing style left many musicians frustrated. The essentially commercial, composed format of swing was a far cry from the improvisatory freedom and convention-thwarting abandon of early jazz. In the 1940s, instrumentalists began to gather in small groups, or "combos," to improvise together or "jam." Some of these players left the swing circuit and began to perform only in this smaller, freer format.

BEBOP

In Kansas City and New York, musicians began to develop a harder driving, more abstract and complex instrumental style known as *Bebop* or *Bop*. A self-conscious, intellectual style, its early proponents were out to make jazz serious and new.

Musical Characteristics. Generally, bebop was performed by a small combo of soloists. Its rhythm was more varied and unpredictable than in earlier jazz styles; the drummer-and-bassist were no longer a mere "rhythm section." Improvisations were virtuosic, emphasizing long strings of fast notes with alternating accents. Harmonically, the style was complex and analytical. The flatted fifth, one of the more distant "blues notes" of earlier jazz styles, became bop's emblem.

Charlie Parker (alto sax; 1920–1955). He was one of the greatest of jazz's many great improvisors. His sound was rough by comparison with the lush saxophone sound of the swing band, and his technique more dazzling and extroverted. It was his style, more than any other, that shaped bebop. His "Koko" (1945) and "Cherokee" (1942–1943) are characteristic.

Other talented musicians—such as Dizzy Gillespie (trumpet, b. 1917), Max Roach (drums, b. 1924), Thelonius Monk (pianist/composer, 1917–1982), and Art Tatum (piano, 1904–1956) all left their imprint on the bop style.

"COOL" JAZZ

The angular, rapid-fire style of bop gave way in the 1950s to a mellower, less driving style. It retained, however, the intellectual rigor of bop as well as its abstract and personal character. As a result, the new style was considered "cool"—by comparison with the "hot," or more rhythmically charged style of bop.

Miles Davis (b. 1926). His "Boblicity" (1949) is one of the finest and earliest examples of the "cool" style. His hi-tech, low-temperature trumpet improvisations have become legend.

"Cool" Combos. The Modern Jazz Quartet and the Dave Brubeck Quartet (featuring the virtually arctic alto sax of Paul Desmond) were popular exponents of the style. "Take Five" by the Brubeck group even achieved a sort of Top Forty success. Lester Young (tenor sax; 1909–1959), Stan Getz (tenor sax; b. 1927), and Lennie Tristano (piano; 1919–1978) helped shape the cool style.

"FREE" JAZZ

In the 1960s, cool styles gave way to free-form improvisation. "Free" improvisations took on characteristics both of certain non-Western styles (African, Indian or Far Eastern) and of the Western avant-garde (see chapter 26). The style is often ecstatic and frenzied, frequently modal, and occasionally atonal.

Ornette Coleman (alto sax; b. 1930). His 1960 recording, *Free Jazz,* launched the style. His improvisations were not constrained by harmonic changes or, in some cases, even by tonality.

John Coltrane (sax; 1926–1967). A technical wizard of the bebop style, his compositions and improvisations became progressively more individualistic. On the one hand he began composing around modes reminiscent of the Near East, adding drones and other characteristically "Eastern" devices. On the other, he became interested in pure sound, his improvisations so ecstatic as to be reduced to expressionistic shrieks and wails. Before his early death, he had influenced the style of many of his contemporaries. Like Charlie Parker, Coltrane has become one of the legends of modern jazz.

FUSION OR "JAZZ ROCK"

A style contemporaneous with free jazz, fusion combined cool jazz with some of the rhythmic and orchestrational characteristics of rock and Latin American idioms. Miles Davis' *In a Silent Way* (1969) is a sophisticated example of the style. Chick Corea, Herbie Hancock, Wayne Shorter, and Joe Zawinul also contributed to the style. Groups like Weather Report forged a fusion style that relied less on individual improvisation than on ensemble sound; their "Birdland" (1977) is typical.

AMERICAN MUSICAL THEATRE

The Broadway Musical is perhaps the United States' unique contribution to world theatre. Its development follows that of the American popular music industry.

Early Years

In the nineteenth century, American urban popular music was primarily European in origin. However, in New York at the turn of the century, a generation of immigrants, better able than natives to see the popular potential of American idioms, began to fashion a unique American popular song style.

TIN PAN ALLEY

New York was the center for commercial music publishing at the turn of the century. This fledgling industry was known as *Tin Pan Alley,* from the continuous sound of song writers hawking their tunes on the publisher's out-of-tune—or "tinny"-sounding—pianos. In general, a "Tin Pan Alley" composer writes songs—in contrast, to the "Broadway composer" who writes musicals. Most composers of the period did both.

Irving Berlin (1888–1990). Russian by birth, he arrived in New York as an infant and grew up on the Lower East Side, the Bowery. Self-taught, he produced hundreds of songs over a long career, making of the Tin Pan Alley style a mode of expression not only popular but sincere. Such tunes as "Top Hat" and "Cheek to Cheek" are classics of the genre. But Berlin is perhaps best known for the three immensely popular songs "Alexander's Ragtime Band," "God Bless America," and "White Christmas."

Vaudeville. Vaudeville is a musical revue consisting of songs, dances, and skits; it is descended from the nineteenth-century Minstrel show. Many well-known songwriters, comedians, and popular entertainers—like Al Jolson (1886–1950) and Eddie Cantor (1892–1964)— began in vaudeville.

OPERETTA

The comic operas, or operettas, of Johann Strauss (Austria, 1825–1899) and Jacques Offenbach (France, 1819–1880) were popular in the turn-of-the-century United States. Examples of the genre, which required lavish costumes and sets, as well as trained singers, were most often produced in urban centers, especially New York.

Victor Herbert (United States, 1850–1924). He adapted the European operetta to the New York stage in such works as *Babes in Toyland* and *Naughty Marietta*. He was one of America's first super-star popular artists.

The Movies. Interest in operetta renewed briefly in the late 1930s with the film vehicles for Jeannette MacDonald (1901–1965) and Nelson Eddy (1901–1967). Their film version of Herbert's *Naughty Marietta* (1935) is typical.

EARLY MUSICALS

George M. Cohan (1878–1942). An Irish-American theatrical entrepreneur, he introduced "musical comedies"—comic plays with songs—to New York audiences in the early 1900s. Unlike minstrel and Vaudeville shows, Cohan's musical comedies were tied to a plot; unlike operetta, the tunes were lighter and closer to the vernacular, being thus better suited to his American middle class audiences. His *Yankee Doodle Dandy* and *Give My Regards to Broadway* are typical.

Sigmund Romberg (1887–1951). In works like *The Student Prince* he developed the characteristic format of the Broadway Musical: spoken dialogue interspersed with dramatically motivated songs.

Jerome Kern (1885–1945). Trained as a serious composer in Europe, he returned to New York to write musicals, his first in 1912. With his *Showboat* (1927) he made both his fortune and, arguably, the first true Broadway musical, integrating romance, drama, comedy, song and dance.

The Broadway Musical

The "Broadway musical" or "musical comedy" or, simply, the "musical" came of age in New York in the 1920s. Though essentially a commercial theatre, many musicals have proven of more lasting significance.

GENERAL CHARACTERISTICS

Plot. The plots are romantic, often involving picturesque settings and characters, and are almost always administered with a strong dose of comedy. Although the plots are often merely a skeleton to be fleshed out with song and dance, they are sometimes more, as in Kern's *Showboat* and Bernstein's *West Side Story.*

Format. Spoken dialogue is interspersed with usually relevant songs, dances, and choruses.

SIGNIFICANT COMPOSERS

Cole Porter (1891–1964). Porter was born into a wealthy American family, and his Tin Pan Alley songs and Broadway-style musicals express the wit and irony of the urban sophisticate. His musical *Anything Goes,* and the title song in particular, are characteristic.

George Gershwin (1898–1937). Writing for Broadway and Tin Pan Alley, Gershwin was one of the few to publicly transcend the genre, gaining legitimacy in the art music world as well. His musical *Porgy and Bess,* often produced as an opera today, is a sincere and moving attempt to set Dobose Heywood's novel of black life in New Orleans to an idiom rooted in African-American vernacular music. "Summertime" is perhaps its best known song. Gershwin's Tin Pan Alley tunes, like "Fascinatin' Rhythm," are standards.

Richard Rodgers (1902–1979) **and Oscar Hammerstein II** (1895–1960). Composer and lyricist respectively, Rodgers and Hammerstein were responsible for some of the most popular and longest-lived works of the genre. In their works dialogue and music work together to advance the plot, the songs playing a dramatic rather than a merely decorative role. Their first collaboration, *Oklahoma,* was the first modern musical to use dance to develop character and to advance the plot. Their other collaborations include *South Pacific, Carousel, The King and I* and *The Sound of Music.*

Leonard Bernstein (1918–1990). Though a world-renowned conductor and composer of many "serious" compositions, Bernstein's lasting fame will come from his musical theatre works. His *West Side Story* (1957) became the model for a new generation of serious musical theatre composers. The work demonstrated that neither a serious plot nor challenging music need affect a musical's popular success if each enhances the other.

Stephen Sondheim (b. 1930). Beginning as a lyricist (for Bernstein's *West Side Story,* among other musicals) and later becoming a lyricist-composer, Sondheim brought a new level of dramatic and musical sophistication to the genre. Unlike those of his European contemporaries (see below), his works rely for their effect on dramatic and literary wit combined with an eclectic musical imagination. His *Company* (1970) and *Sweeney Todd* (1979) are typical.

THE MUSICAL IN FILMS

Between the mid-1930s and mid-1960s, the movies were a vital source of popular music. From the two 1933 hits, Busby Berkeley's *42d Street* and the first Fred Astaire/Ginger Rogers vehicle, *Flying Down to Rio,* to the Barbara Streisand hits of the 1960s, *Hello Dolly* and *Funny Girl,* the movie musical helped shape popular musical tastes.

THE MUSICAL ABROAD

Long popular in the rest of the world, the American musical has mainly been the provenance of American composers. Recently, however, a number of European composers have been successful in the genre. The European examples seem to rely more on scenic effect and general spectacle than do their American counterparts.

Andrew Lloyd Webber (England, b. 1948). Webber's *Jesus Christ Superstar* (1971) was the first of a long line of lavish and theatrically dazzling hit musicals that he composed in the 1970s, such as *Evita,* and *Cats.*

Claude-Michel Schönberg (France, b. 1944). Schönberg's *Les Misérables* (1987) and *Miss Saigon* — achieved considerable success despite their formidable lengths and extravagant theatrical demands.

COUNTRY AND WESTERN

A direct if adulterated descendent of the Anglo-American folk culture of the Southeast and West, country and western music is now an established part of the commercial music industry. In its Nashville incarnation it clearly combines these Anglo-American folk roots with the blues and other African-American idioms.

Early Style

Country and western music was primarily a local, rural entertainment until the 1920s. By then radio stations had begun to proliferate throughout the South and Southwest, giving previously isolated rural communities a greater sense of community and shared traditions.

THE GRAND OLE OPRY

In 1925, WSM in Nashville, Tennessee, began broadcasting a regular radio show devoted to country music. *The Grand Ole Opry*, as it was called, brought country musicians into the regional and national spotlight, providing them with a sense of legitimacy denied them by Tin Pan Alley, which saw "hillbillies" and their culture as little more than the butt of jokes. Devoted to all aspects of rural musical culture, the Opry promoted not only traditional singing groups like the Carter Family and singing cowboys like Jimmie Rodgers but also dancers, comedians, and instrumental styles like "bluegrass."

BLUEGRASS

The Grand Ole Opry seems responsible for the popularity of a string band style of music called *bluegrass*. Southern string bands—comprised of traditional string instruments like fiddle, banjo, mandolin, and guitar—performed in a style thoroughly diatonic and harmonically simple but rhythmically complex and extraordinarily virtuosic. They performed traditional folk materials—sometimes songs, sometimes dance tunes. Groups like the Skillet Lickers (1920–30s), the Monroe Brothers (1940s) and Lester Flatt (1914–1979) and Earl Scruggs (b. 1924), whose Foggy Mountain Boys remained together from 1948 to 1969, are bluegrass legends.

Western Styles

In the 1920s and 1930s many Southern rural families migrated to Texas, Oklahoma, and California, having been wiped out by the Great Depression. They took their music with them, picking up regional styles along the way. In Texas, Hispanic rural idioms fused with local cowboy styles and southern "country" to produce a hybrid made popular by a long line of Hollywood singing cowboys such as Gene Autry, Tex Ritter, and the Roy Rogers/Dale Evans duo. The early form of the idiom was called "western swing style," and then simply "western."

The style was such a success that Nashville country singers began adopting Western dress as well as aspects of western performance style. "Western" became firmly tied to "country."

Country Blues

In the late 1940s country and western styles began to fuse with other rural styles—in particular rural blues (see "Rhythm and Blues," below). This "country blues" style was made immensely popular by Hank Williams (1923–1953), whose simple tunes and sentimental lyrics ("Hey Good Lookin'," 1951), now laced with blues-like pathos, became the prototype for the early rock-and-roll song.

Recent Trends

In the last twenty years, country and western music has become a mainstream idiom. Many country and western performers now cross over regularly onto pop or rock charts.

POP-COUNTRY

Beginning in the 1950s, many country and western performers began producing a more commercially sophisticated, market-oriented product. Patsy Cline 1932–1963) pioneered the cross-over with her 1961 hit "I Fall to Pieces." Entertainers like Glen Campbell, Chet Atkins, Roger Miller,

Loretta Lynn, Johnny Cash, and Dolly Parton produced mainstream hits and helped to remove the hillbilly stigma that attached in the popular suburban and urban mind to "country" music. This slick and sophisticated country and western sound now is synonymous with the "Nashville sound."

TEXAS HONKY-TONK

Partly in response to the commercialization of the Nashville sound, several performers have gained a considerable following by returning to their musical roots. Willie Nelson and George Jones, though having quite different styles, have both returned to a spare, often raw and uncompromising, western style associated with East Texas. At the same time, Nelson's mellow, sentimental recordings of mainstream standards hark back to the western swing style. The recordings of Marty Robbins and Roy Orbison exhibit certain characteristics of this East Texas style as well.

CAJUN MUSIC

The Louisiana delta has produced its own country style associated with the descendants of the rural French-speaking population known as Cajuns. The style has recently achieved a place of its own in the country and western idiom. Hank Williams Jr.'s cajun-influenced style is characteristic of the blend.

ROCK-AND-ROLL

Rural African-American blues idioms, honky-tonk piano styles, and white hillbilly-style country fused in the early 1950s. The new music became known as *rock-and-roll* and then, in the 1960s, simply as *rock*.

Early Rock-and-Roll

The roots of rock-and-roll, like those of any vernacular idiom, are difficult to trace, primarily because they are so diffuse and eclectic. The following outlines a few of the significant sources and proponents of the style.

CONTRIBUTING IDIOMS

Gospel Hymns. Nineteenth-century Protestant revivals gave birth to a new style of composed hymn. Though the composers were mostly white, by the end of World War I the tunes had become popular in African-American churches. Wedded to the commercial blues performance style and performed as solos with choir or in small vocal ensembles, the new style was called *gospel*.

Rhythm and Blues ("R and B"). An African-American dance idiom that arose in the 1940s, R and B follows a simple commercial blues format, joining blues and gospel styles to secular lyrics and dance rhythms. Typically, repeated note values are not "swung" as in the jazz styles but performed "legit," or in equal values. This "legit" or "straight" rhythmic style becomes characteristic of much rock-and-roll, distinguishing it clearly from most jazz styles.

Boogie-woogie. This is a piano style that combines a complex walking bass and simple blues progressions to a driving, energetic rhythm. Sometimes called "honky-tonk" style, thus showing its origin in the barrelhouse piano style of early jazz, it seems to have thrived in rural clubs and road-houses known as honky-tonks. There it assimilated some of the characteristics of rhythm and blues. A modified version of this style of piano playing is often used as well to accompany gospel performances.

Rock-a-Billy. A rural country and western style that emerged in the early 1950s, it joined a country format to hard-driving R and B materials. Hank Williams's country blues exerted a significant influence on the style.

Performers. Little Richard, Fats Domino, Chuck Berry, and Bo Diddley all helped to transform traditional R and B into rock-and-roll. Jerry Lee Lewis took the boogie-woogie piano style, rock-a-billy, and R-and-B rhythms and forged yet another version of rock-and-roll. Lewis's two 1957 hits "Whole Lotta Shakin' Goin' On" and "Great Balls of Fire" are classics.

THE EMERGENCE OF ROCK-AND-ROLL

It was not until the mid-1950s that rock-and-roll attracted a popular following. Its raucous, multiracial, and generally noisy format became associated with rebellious youth; many adults in positions of authority saw it as a positive danger to "national morals." However, its commercial success quickly won out over such criticism.

Bill Haley (1925–1981) **and His Comets.** His "Rock Around the Clock" (1955) set the tone and style for rock-and-roll's popular success.

Elvis Presley (1935–1977). His first big hit, "Heartbreak Hotel" (1956), set the stage for a popular success rivaled since only by the Beatles (see below) and before only by Bing Crosby and Frank Sinatra. He retained stylistic ties to rock-a-billy and gospel idioms throughout his career. In performance, his overt sexuality and extravagant mannerisms were proof, to his critics, of what they feared most in the new style, and, to Presley's young fans, of the liberating power of the new idiom.

Buddy Holly (1938–1959). Starting out in Texas with various country and western groups and inspired by Presley's rock-a-billy style, Holly made a splash with two 1957 hits, "That'll Be the Day" and "Peggy Sue." Heartfelt lyrics and an idiosyncratic performance style combined with gawky, ordinary looks established him in the minds of his fans as a popular Everyman, providing a sharp contrast to Presley's glamorous good looks and theatrical performance style.

Teen Rock. In the late 1950s record companies targeted middle class, white teenagers with a heavily promoted and sanitized version of rock-and-roll known today as "teen" rock. The music was bland and up-beat by comparison with the style already mentioned. Lyrics provided chaste and sentimental tales of young love, the trials of high school life , and, on occasion, "tragic" stock-car love-deaths—all as imagined by middle-aged record producers. It is the first truly "suburban" style of popular music. The style produced any number of instantaneous "teen idols" such as Pat Boone, Frankie Avalon, Connie Francis, Rick Nelson, and Leslie Gore.

Soul. In the 1960s, a number of African-American musicians deeply rooted in gospel and R and B created a rock style know as *soul*. James Brown ("Please, please, please," 1956), Ray Charles ("Right Time," 1959), and Aretha Franklin ("I Never Loved a Man the Way I Love You," 1967) were the pioneers and major exponents of the style. In recent years many white singers have adopted the style with success. Hall and Oates and Michael Bottom are characteristic proponents of this "blue-eyed" soul style.

Motown. Motown ("motor town") Records in Detroit began marketing a glitzy style of commercialized soul known since as *motown*. Such entertainers as Little Stevie Wonder ("Fingertips," 1963), the Supremes ("Where Did Our Love Go," 1964) the Temptations ("My Girl," 1965), and the Supremes' Diana Ross ("Ain't No Mountain High Enough," 1970) became immensely successful.

"Rock"

Rock-and-roll underwent a kind of renaissance in the 1960s, rebounding from its former commercialization and finding, once again, its roots. Ironically, the impetus for this revival came from abroad. Henceforth, rock-and-roll tended to be known simply as "rock."

THE ENGLISH INVASION

In the early 1960s several English groups, still listening to the "pure" rock-and-roll, R and B, and rock-a-billy styles of 1950s United States, remade rock-and-roll, supplanting the "teen" rock styles that dominated the American popular scene with a fresh, more sophisticated version of 1950s rock-and-roll. This British style is sometimes referred to as the *British beat*.

The Beatles. Their models were the Chuck Berry R-and-B style as well as Elvis Presley's rock-a-billy vocals. By their 1964 American tour they had become virtual icons of a new youth-oriented popular culture. They incorporated into their style non-Western and historical Western idioms as well as an older, more sophisticated attitude toward songwriting that had its roots in Tin Pan Alley. They pioneered the "concept" album with their *Sergeant Pepper's Lonely Hearts Club Band* (1967).

Rolling Stones. The "bad boys" of the English invasion, the Rolling Stones stuck to the R-and-B roots while the Beatles explored more eclectic styles. Sexually charged and always rebellious, the "Stones," along with the Beatles, dominated the 1960s rock scene. The Stones' style of rock is sometimes called *British R and B*.

AFRICAN-AMERICAN DANCE MUSIC

Disco. In the early 1970s a sub-culture dance style called disco— (from *discotheque,* a kind of mid-1960s rock dance club) arose in large cities. Essentially a silky, "sophisticated" take on soul, disco achieved a broader success with Donna Summers' "Love to Love You Baby" (1975) and peaked in 1978 with the Bee Gees' soundtrack to *Saturday Night Fever*. Though the style has, for the most part, been absorbed into Funk, remnants remain in the recordings of Paula Abdul and similar performers.

Funk. The clipped, mechanical rhythmic tracks of Disco gradually combined with soul into a dance music called Funk. In Funk, complex polyrhythmic improvisations fused with simple harmonic vamps into a style evident as early as 1969 in James Brown's "Papa's Got a Brand New Bag." In the 1970s groups like Kool and the Gang ("Funky Stuff") and War ("The Cisco Kid") brought the style a broader audience.

Rap. Rap is a kind of improvised rhyme performed over a Funk-like rhythmic vamp developed by urban blacks in the mid-1970s. Deriving from an African-American tradition of improvised rhyme—Mohammed Ali's comic doggerel is a contemporary example—or the rhymed "toasting" of Jamaican disc jockeys, it began to reach a broader audience with recordings like "Rapper's Delight" (1979) by the Sugar Hill Gang. Grandmaster Flash's 1981 hit "The Message" made clear rap's politically charged origins. An athletic and often mimetic dance style called *break-dancing* is frequently associated with rap performances.

OTHER ROCK DIALECTS

With the rock renaissance and the Beatles' eclectic style, came a proliferation of other styles.

Beach Music. Associated primarily with one group, the Beach Boys, the style not only expanded the harmonic vocabulary of rock but helped create the California surfer stereotype of contemporary popular culture. Arriving on the scene in the mid-1960s, the style quickly achieved a devoted following which it maintains to this day.

Folk-Protest. The revival of folk music in the late 1950s combined with the generally rebellious tone of the 1960s to form "folk" rock. Retaining the musical simplicity of folk music, as well as its narrative song style, performers like Joan Baez; Bob Dylan; Peter, Paul and Mary; and Joni Mitchell often combined it with rock instrumentations or rhythms. Their lyrics alternated between political protest and expressions of personal alienation.

Acid or Psychedelic Rock. The San Francisco counter-culture of the 1960s produced a kind of alternative rock that reflected, on the one hand, the desire for transcendence—by natural or chemical means—and, on the other, the romantic, blue-collar directness of old time rock-and-roll. The spacey, trance-like atmospheres of Grace Slick and the Jefferson Airplane are characteristic of the former; the country-blues of the Grateful Dead is characteristic of the latter. The blues guitar of Jimi Hendrix and his Jimi Hendrix Experience was probably the most innovative and extreme of the group, followed closely by Janis Joplin, whose reckless, no-holds-barred performance style bordered on the suicidal.

Rock Opera. In the late 1960s and early 1970s, a short spurt of musical theatre works built around rock scores began to appear. Galt MacDermot's *Hair* was one of the first musical theatre works of this sort. Though a full-fledged Broadway musical, *Hair* ushered in a broader genre known as *rock opera*. The Who's *Tommy* was perhaps the first work in the new genre, and Andrew Lloyd Webber's rock-inspired *Jesus Christ Superstar* was the greatest popular success.

Punk Rock. Punk rock evolved in England in the mid-1970s. An expression of working class frustration and antiestablishment hostility, its violent and aggressive style quickly burnt itself out, but not before stimulating a wave of stylistic innovations. The style is simple, harsh, and overtly political. The Sex Pistols characterize the style in name as well as in sound.

New Wave. A number of groups adopted the simple, almost mechanical musical style of the punk bands, while investing them with a decidedly more sophisticated, eclectic and postmodern sensibility. Groups like the Clash and the Talking Heads and the singer Elvis Costello have created a bare, sometimes robotic, sometimes manic style that still retains the satirical and political edge of punk.

Heavy Metal. The 1970s produced as well a hard, frenzied, concrete style known as *heavy metal* that arouse from the high volume, high intensity style of some British R and B groups. Led Zepplin, Cream, and the Jimi Hendrix Experience helped formulate the style in partial response to the increasingly over-produced, concept rock of the day. Groups like Black Sabbath, Iron Butterfly, and Def Leppard are typical.

Other Trends

Rock continues to be a vital and changing popular idiom. It encompasses more and more disparate styles and musical dialects on the one hand and, on the other, continues to return, periodically, to its roots.

Traditional Rock. In the late 1970s performers like Bruce Springsteen spearheaded a return to fundamental rock-and-roll. As part of the same movement, older groups like the Rolling Stones and the Grateful Dead have found a new generation eager for their now-traditional styles.

Salsa. An offshoot of Latin American popular styles, Salsa arouse in the Puerto Rican and Cuban communities of New York in the 1950s and 1960s. Celia Cruz ("The Queen of Salsa"), Tito Puente, and—more recently—Reuben Blades have each helped shape the idiom.

Reggae. The mid-1970s introduced the United States to reggae, an idiom that fused motown soul to Caribbean rhythms and political sensibilities. Many mainstream rock musicians have adopted aspects of the style. The songs and recordings of Bob Marley (Jamaica, 1945–1981) brought the idiom into the international spotlight.

Eclectic. Many rock composers and musicians are unclassifiable, either having, like Michelle Shocked and Kate Bush such eclectic and versatile styles, or like Randy Newman and Tom Waits, such idiosyncratic ones, that they fall into no ready-made category.

At the turn of a new century, it is clear that popular music, the music of the "populace," has supplanted almost all other Western musical idioms; but it is less clear whether the "populace" or commerce dictates that music. And whether or not the commercial music industry drives Western culture itself, as it sometimes seems, it is certain that the next century will be driven by "popular" culture.

For Additional Study

Brown, Charles T. *The Art of Rock-and-Roll*. Englewood Cliffs, NJ: Prentice-Hall. 1983.

Charters, Samuel B. *The Country Blues*. New York: Rinehart. 1959.

Collier, James Lincoln. *The Making of Jazz*. Boston: Houghton Mifflin. 1978.

Coker, Jerry. *Listening to Jazz*. Englewood Cliffs, NJ: Prentice-Hall. 1978.

Ellington, Duke. *Music is My Mistress*. New York: Doubleday. 1973.

Green, Stanley. *The World of Musical Comedy*. New York: Ziff-Davis. 1960.

Hamm, Charles. *Yesterdays: Popular Song in America*. New York: Norton. 1979.

Jablonski, Edward, and Lawrence Stewart. *The Gershwin Years*. New York: Doubleday. 1973.

Litweiler, John. *The Freedom Principle: Jazz After 1958*. New York: Da Capo Press. 1984.

Megill, Donald D., and Richard S. Demory. *Introduction to Jazz History*. Englewood CLiffs, NJ: Prentice-Hall. 1984.

Miller, Jim, ed. *The Rolling Stone Illustrated History of Rock-and-Roll*. Rev. version. New York: Random House. 1980.

Oliver, Paul, *et al. The New Grove Ragtime, Blues and Jazz*. New York: Norton. 1986.

Schuller, Gunther. *Early Jazz: Its Roots and Musical Development*. New York: Oxford. 1968.

—. *The Swing Era: The Development of Jazz, 1930-1945*. New York: Oxford. 1989.

Tanner, Paul O., and Maurice Gerow. *A Study of Jazz*. 4th ed. Dubuque, IA: Wm. C. Brown. 1981.

Tirro, Frank. *Jazz: A History*. New York: Norton. 1977.

Recommended Listening

Historical recordings of popular music and jazz are sometimes difficult to come by. The best sources are two important collections, each held by most listening libraries.

For historic jazz: *The Smithsonian Classic Jazz Collection.* Washington, D.C.: Smithsonian Recordings. 1977.

For other American popular and traditional idioms refer to the *New World* recording series, listed below by number and subject.

Gospel: NW294.
Tin Pan Alley: NW215, 233, 238, 248, 229.
Musical comedy: NW221, 240.
Country and western music: NW207, 225, 287, 290.
Early blues, ragtime, and early jazz: NW 235, 252, 256, 259, 269.
Swing era: NW217, 250, 274, 284, 295, 298.
Post-swing jazz: NW242, 271, 275.
Historic rock-and-roll styles: NW249, 261.

Index

B

Z